Strategic Sisterhood

REBECCA TUURI

Strategic Sisterhood

The National Council of Negro Women
in the Black Freedom Struggle

The University of North Carolina Press *Chapel Hill*

This book was published with the assistance of the Authors Fund
of the University of North Carolina Press.

The University of North Carolina Press has been a member of the
Green Press Initiative since 2003.

Library of Congress Cataloging-in-Publication Data
Names: Tuuri, Rebecca, author.
Title: Strategic sisterhood : the National Council of Negro Women in the
    black freedom struggle / Rebecca Tuuri.
Description: Chapel Hill : University of North Carolina Press, [2018] |
    Includes bibliographical references and index.
Identifiers: LCCN 2017044667| ISBN 9781469638898 (cloth : alk. paper) |
    ISBN 9781469638904 (pbk : alk. paper) | ISBN 9781469638911 (ebook)
Subjects: LCSH: National Council of Negro Women—History—20th century. |
    African American women—Societies and clubs—History—20th century. |
    African American women—Civil rights—History—20th century. |
    Black power—United States—History—20th century.
Classification: LCC E185.86 .T89 2018 | DDC 305.48/896073—dc23
LC record available at https://lccn.loc.gov/2017044667

Cover illustration: NCNW leadership laying a wreath at the Mary McLeod Bethune
statue in Lincoln Park (unidentified photographer, courtesy of the Mary McLeod Bethune
Council House National Historic Site, National Archives for Black Women's History,
NCNW Records, series 14, #0484).

Portions of this book were previously published in a different form and are used here with
permission. Chapters 2 and 3 include material from " 'This Was the Most Meaningful Thing
That I've Ever Done': The Personal Civil Rights Approach of Wednesdays in Mississippi,"
Journal of Women's History 28, no. 4 (2016): 89–112 (copyright © 2016 Journal of Women's
History, Inc.). Chapters 5 and 7 include material from " 'By Any Means Necessary': The
Flexible Loyalties of the National Council of Negro Women in the Black Freedom Struggle,"
in *U.S. Women's History: Untangling the Threads of Sisterhood*, ed. Leslie Brown, Jacqueline
Castledine, and Anne Valk, 32–48 (New Brunswick: Rutgers University Press, 2017)
(copyright © 2017 Rutgers, The State University).

To the women of the National Council of Negro Women

Contents

Abbreviations in the Text xi

Introduction 1

CHAPTER ONE
Maneuvering for the Movement: The World of Broker Politics
in the NCNW, 1935–1963 12

CHAPTER TWO
Creating a Ministry of Presence: Setting Up an Interracial Civil Rights
Organization, 1963–1964 37

CHAPTER THREE
High Heels on the Ground: The Power of Personal Witness, 1964 56

CHAPTER FOUR
We Have, Happily, Gone beyond the Chitchat over Tea Cups Stage:
Moving beyond Dialogue, 1965–1966 80

CHAPTER FIVE
You Know about What It's Like to Need a Good House:
The Changing Face of the Expert, 1966–1970 103

CHAPTER SIX
But If You Have a Pig in Your Backyard . . . Nobody Can Push You Around:
Black Self-Help and Community Survival, 1967–1975 128

CHAPTER SEVEN
The Power of Four Million Women: Growing the Council,
1967–1980 149

CHAPTER EIGHT
Mississippi, Who Has Been the Taillight, Can Now Be the Headlight:
The Council's International Work, 1975–1985 177

Conclusion 203

Acknowledgments 211

Appendix 1. 1964 Wednesdays in Mississippi Participants 215

Appendix 2. 1965 Wednesdays in Mississippi Participants 219

Appendix 3. Project Womanpower Staff 223

Appendix 4. NCNW International Seminar 225

Notes 227

Bibliography 277

Index 301

A photograph gallery appears after p. 102.

Graph and Map

GRAPH

Local growth of Mississippi National Council of Negro Women
   in the 1960s and 1970s   163

MAP

Project Womanpower Community Service Institutes, 1967–68   118

Abbreviations in the Text

AAUW	American Association of University Women
ANLCA	American Negro Leadership Conference on Africa
CAA	Council on African Affairs
CAW	Congress of American Women
CCC	Commission on Community Cooperation
CDGM	Child Development Group of Mississippi
COFO	Council of Federated Organizations
CORE	Congress of Racial Equality
CRC	Civil Rights Congress
CSW	Commission on the Status of Women
CUCRL	Council for United Civil Rights Leadership
CWU	Church Women United
HUD	Department of Housing and Urban Development
IWY	International Women's Year
LEAA	Law Enforcement Assistance Administration
LWV	League of Women Voters
MFDP	Mississippi Freedom Democratic Party
MPE	Mississippians for Public Education
NAACP	National Association for the Advancement of Colored People
NACW	National Association of Colored Women
NCCW	National Council of Catholic Women
NCJW	National Council of Jewish Women
NCNW	National Council of Negro Women
NWCCR	National Women's Committee on Civil Rights
NWRO	National Welfare Rights Organization
OEO	Office of Economic Opportunity

PCSW   President's Commission on the Status of Women

SCLC   Southern Christian Leadership Conference

SDEDD   South Delta Economic Development District

SDS   Students for a Democratic Society

SNCC   Student Nonviolent Coordinating Committee

TWWA   Third World Women's Alliance

USAID   United States Agency for International Development

WC   Woman's Convention

WICS   Women in Community Service

WIMS   Wednesdays in Mississippi; later Workshops in Mississippi

WU   Womanpower Unlimited

YWCA   Young Women's Christian Association

Strategic Sisterhood

Introduction

When Gulfport civil rights activist Sammie Lee Gray-Wiseman finally had the chance to meet Dr. Dorothy Height, the president of the National Council of Negro Women (NCNW, or council), she was excited. It was 1967, and Gray-Wiseman had been working on a new council project to institute a low-income home ownership program in North Gulfport, Mississippi. In order to establish the program, NCNW required that a local section be established in the area first. Once Gray-Wiseman had gathered the necessary signatures and membership dues, NCNW representatives Unita Blackwell—a black grassroots leader from Mayersville, Mississippi—and Dorothy Duke—a white housing expert from Lorain, Ohio—began to search for the site for the new subdivision. Height came down shortly thereafter.

Although Height stayed for less than twenty-four hours, she made a tremendous impact on Gray-Wiseman. Being around her was "just like you being in the company of a queen. . . . She spoke very nicely, and she was funny, and [despite being] a lady of her caliber or standards . . . she was as sweet as she could be."[1] In a 2008 interview, Owen Brooks, head of the grassroots poverty organization the Delta Ministry in the late 1960s, agreed that Height was impressive: "She is one of the black women in this country that I really have a great admiration for." Student Nonviolent Coordinating Committee (SNCC) and Mississippi Freedom Democratic Party (MFDP) activist Charles McLaurin also recalls his esteem for Height. She was "the person who was at the top . . . who brought the money or who brought the resources. . . . They're high in your eye."[2] Brooks's and McLaurin's own Mississippi-based activism challenged white supremacy more directly than did the council's personal, behind-the-scenes work, yet both admired Height. Brooks recognized that Height was willing to make the political compromises necessary for black community survival and progress, yet she "could handle bureaucrats in the fashion that she needed to handle them, in order to win the day for the cause. And she would win the day."[3]

In many recent and influential histories of the postwar black freedom struggle, black middle-class women, such as those who belonged to the NCNW, have been largely overlooked in favor of more visible, outspoken, and radical activists, who took to the streets during the civil rights and Black Power movements. Other important studies have considered only working-class women's activism.[4] Many activists and scholars take for granted the idea that council women shrunk from real activism in hopes of preserving their respectability and status both nationally and locally. Yet from their positions of power, moderates often fought for and aided more radical causes. Mary McLeod Bethune formed the council in 1935 to unite black women's sororities, professional organizations, and auxiliaries to act as a clearinghouse to augment the political and professional power of black women. As an umbrella organization speaking on behalf of many different black women's organizations, the NCNW was able to insert the concerns of black women and the black community more generally into national political debates.[5] While the council was committed to public moderation through interracial, nonviolent, and mainstream civil rights work, it also helped fund and support the more radical and grassroots activists, who advocated black separatism, black nationalism, anti-imperialism, and a willingness to use force if necessary. The council's mid-twentieth-century activism thus challenges clear divisions between radical and moderate black activism in this period.[6] The full story of the civil rights movement and the subsequent Black Power movement can only be told by exploring a wide variety of organizations, institutions, and strategies, and recognizing the roles played by middle-class, nationally connected moderates as well as youthful and community-based radicals.

In addition, while recent histories have stressed the importance of local women in fueling and providing the backbone of the civil rights movement, many council women were not only its foot soldiers but also its torchbearers.[7] Charles Payne has argued that male-centered narratives, and even male historians, have created a "conceptual equipment" of the civil rights movement that has overlooked or misunderstood women-led efforts as less significant because they were led by women.[8] Indeed, the council has been a victim of this very oversight.[9] From the time of its founding through the present, the NCNW's leadership has included some of the most prominent national black leaders in the country: Mary McLeod Bethune, Anna Arnold Hedgeman, Sadie Alexander, Daisy Lampkin, Mabel Keaton Staupers, Edith Sampson, Arenia Mallory, Patricia Harris, Dorothy Height, Maida Springer Kemp, Marjorie Lawson, Jeanne Noble, Lena Horne, Fannie Lou Hamer, and Unita Blackwell.[10] While most formal leadership in the civil rights movement came from black men's organizations, the council also provided such formal leadership, as its members served as consultants to presidents, business leaders, and leaders of voluntary organizations.[11] NCNW women were often the only women at civil rights leadership gatherings or the only black members of women-only groups. Therefore, women in the civil rights movement were not only the backbone of the movement but, at least within the council, its leadership as well.

Despite working through a voluntary women's organization, NCNW women had the political, social, and economic cachet to bring resources to black communities in the mid-twentieth century. Longtime president Dorothy Height served as a leader within important women's organizations, such as Delta Sigma Theta and the Young Women's Christian Association (YWCA) before and during her NCNW presidency. In addition, she served on a variety of important postwar advisory committees, including President Kennedy's 1961 Commission on the Status of Women; the Department of Defense's Advisory Committee on Women in the Services; and the White House's National Commission for the Protection of Human Subjects of Biomedical and Behavioral Research.[12] Both liberal and conservative presidents admired this organization. At the same time, radicals working daily to improve the conditions of life on the ground, such as Brooks and McLaurin in Mississippi, also respected the council.

Many excellent histories of the civil rights movement at the local level have shown how the grassroots participation of black men and women within local communities was what provided the purpose, energy, and viability to the larger national movement.[13] The council recognized this during the mid-1960s, when it also developed a local approach to its national civil rights work, drawing on grassroots leadership and expertise, while also tapping into its cross-country network of well-respected local and national women.[14] Classic studies of black women's activism have shown that black women have had a long tradition of acting as "centerwomen," "bridge leaders," and "diplomats," providing a communication link between national civil rights activists and the local community.[15] In addition to serving as leaders, the women of the council also called themselves "bridge-builders," "communicators," and "catalysts," as they facilitated "authentic" conversations not just between national and local people but also between rich and poor, black and white, and conservative and liberal women.[16] The council's ability to bring women together was augmented by its powerful national network, which linked women in local communities around the country to provide a unified voice. Members of the Jackson-based civil rights women's organization Womanpower Unlimited (WU) recognized the power of this black women's network when they voted to disband their local organization and become part of the council in 1966. Formed as a local organization to bring resources to civil rights activists imprisoned first during the Freedom Rides and later during voter registration and direct-action campaigns, the members of this group joined the council after deciding that their local work could be better realized with the help of a national platform.[17]

Relying on a long local tradition of black self-help and racial uplift, the council also utilized the national connections with prominent politicians and businessmen made possible by its leaders' respectable reputations.[18] With the money that it received, thanks in large part to the perception of NCNW leadership as moderate and welcoming to (especially white) liberals, the council was able to gain support and funding from the federal government as well as from private philanthropic organizations and corporations for projects that would later aid a broad spectrum of black women. The council was firmly committed to American liberalism, including President Johnson's War on Poverty, and it took advantage of what Kent Germany has identified as "soft state" funding for Johnson's Great Society, which came from grants, private groups, and nonprofit organizations concerned with improving the "soft spaces of the human mind."[19] As Johnson's Great Society programs sought to better understand the psyche and dynamics of poor black communities, the council highlighted its role as an organization of women of African descent while downplaying its elitist reputation, and it positioned itself as an ideal agency to work with the federal government to bring resources directly to these same communities.

To tell this complex story, this book traces the important work of the council from the time of its founding through the present, with an emphasis on its work in the 1960s and 1970s. Chapter 1 explores the early history of the council's activism, which sought to place black women in positions of power within American society, while also lobbying for racial change. Although the council tried to recruit lower-income women to its ranks, its most prominent organizations were college-based sororities, and it emphasized networking and professionalization, which were often unattainable for poor women.[20] The college-educated background of its constituency as well as its emphasis on black women's entry into mainstream America contributed to its elitist reputation among black Americans and its moderate reputation among whites. While much of the council's moderate public strategy was chosen, part of it was born of necessity. More often than not, black middle-class women in the twentieth century had to employ pragmatic methods in order to have their voices heard. While they did have to compromise some elements of their struggle for equality by joining mainstream liberal organizations, they were able to insert their concerns into the conversation in these same spaces.[21]

Beginning in the early 1960s, the council shifted its focus under the new leadership of Dorothy Height, who had become president of the council in 1957, to become more directly involved in the civil rights movement and the later War on Poverty. As a black women's organization with an extensive reach, the council also wanted to highlight and support women's interests in the larger civil rights movement. Women were often excluded from leadership positions in the civil rights movement, but Height continued to stress the concerns of women in the movement. Although Height was the president of the NCNW, she was not included on the organizing committee of the March on Washington, nor was she asked to speak during the event.[22] In order to ensure that women's concerns were still heard, Height defied a request by the march's leadership to not hold subsequent gatherings and organized a meeting for the next day. She hoped to bring women's groups together to brainstorm how the civil rights movement could incorporate more activities oriented toward education, childcare, and housing.[23] Delegates to the August 29 meeting listened to the stories of young women who had been imprisoned for their activism and mistreated in jail. For Height, the post-march meeting "gave a kind of validity to the things that the National Council of Negro Women was organized to deal with, but which somehow got subdued as you were thinking purely of getting a Voting Rights Act."[24] Scholars have long examined the importance of "activist mothering" and "othermothering" in the Black Freedom Movement, but it is usually focused on the local efforts of women to help student activists and youth.[25] Instead, the council provided a national platform and agenda for the principles of activist mothering and othermothering.

Chapters 2, 3, and 4 explore the council's shift to more direct civil rights activism after the March on Washington. While becoming more involved in the movement, however, the council maintained its elitism and promoted itself as an organization to provide professional and lobbying assistance to other civil rights groups. Despite individual members' activism, which often insisted on structural change to combat racism, the major civil rights projects that the council implemented in the early to mid-1960s continued to rely on a liberal strategy of eliminating racism through personal moral suasion of whites.[26] Height and an interracial delegation of women who were present at the post–March on Washington meeting traveled to Selma in October 1963 to personally witness and investigate the horrible treatment of young protesters who had been jailed. The council's Selma trip later provided the model for Wednesdays in Mississippi (WIMS), the NCNW's first major national civil rights project. WIMS formed in 1964 to help with the Freedom Summer voter registration efforts in Mississippi. WIMS was two-thirds white and one-third black and included upper middle-class northern Protestant, Catholic, and Jewish women. These elite women hoped to "build bridges of understanding" between northern and southern and white and black women, as well as lend their influential support to civil rights initiatives, including the Council of Federated Organizations (COFO) and the Mississippi Freedom Democratic Party (MFDP). The women returned in 1965 to work as teachers for Head Start, focusing on their status as experts in childhood development and education.

Through its sponsorship of the interracial WIMS, the council was able to build up a network of influential black and white supporters. Some of the women of WIMS were personally transformed through their participation in this group and began organizing civil rights projects in their own northern backyards after their return from Mississippi. Some participants, such as Ruth Batson and Flo Kennedy, became even more directly involved in supporting grassroots women in Mississippi. Other WIMS participants began to fund-raise for the council, using their impressive social connections (see appendixes 1 and 2). WIMS women included Jean Benjamin, wife of the chairperson of United Artists Corporation; Laya Wiesner, wife of the dean of sciences (and later president) of MIT; and Etta Moten Barnett, Broadway star and wife of Claude Barnett, founder of the Associated Negro Press. The chairperson of WIMS was Polly Cowan, heir of the Spiegel mail-order-catalog business and wife of the former president of CBS. Height used these connections when she appointed prominent Connecticut WIMS woman Hadassah national board member Gladys Zales to codirect the council's main membership drive with Lena Horne in 1966. The two worked to secure five hundred life memberships, for a potential gain of $50,000. Together they convinced Mary Lindsay, wife of the mayor of New York, to host a fund-raising banquet for the campaign. Prominent women such as Horne, Zales, and the other women of WIMS helped the NCNW both raise money and remain visible and relevant among white liberals, who continued to wield the majority of political, economic, and social power in the 1960s.[27]

Perhaps most important to the long-term growth of the NCNW, Wednesdays in Mississippi also connected the council more firmly to a cast of inspirational, intelligent, and highly motivated women activists in Mississippi. Through WIMS, the council worked with local Mississippi heroines, including Fannie Lou Hamer and Annie Devine, prominent leaders in SNCC and MFDP. The Jackson black women's civil rights organization, Womanpower Unlimited, was also impressed by the council's sponsorship of Wednesdays in Mississippi.

Historian Tiyi Morris argues that by organizing and sponsoring WIMS, the council "had established the effectiveness of a national organization in addressing the problems WU focused on and demonstrated the council's dedication to the region."[28] The council gave WU women the opportunity to continue their local volunteerism on a national scale, and in return, the council gained new members.

Chapters 5 and 6 explore the beginnings of the council's shift in the late 1960s to more grassroots poverty work, first in Mississippi and then across the country. A watershed moment for the council was its winning of 501(c)(3) tax-exempt status in May 1966, retroactively to December 1965. This freed the NCNW from relying solely on member fees for its activist work; now it could apply for external grants, at which it was quite successful. The Ford Foundation, Rockefeller Brothers Fund, and other private foundations donated money to the council in the 1960s and 1970s. Governmental organizations—including the departments of Labor, Housing and Urban Development, and Justice; the Agency for International Development; and the Office of Economic Opportunity—awarded grants to the NCNW. The council also secured money from private corporations, including IBM, AT&T, and Chase Bank. The council used this newfound grant money to hire staff. In 1963, the NCNW had only three full-time staff members, but by 1975, it had sixty regular employees and forty-one additional staff members doing poverty work around the country.[29] The council used these staff positions as a way to infuse its organization with new members and fresh ideas.[30] In 1975, one-quarter of these staff members were from Mississippi.[31]

In its early years, the council had been composed predominantly of elite women, who were themselves teachers, social workers, administrators, or other white-collar professionals (or married to prominent men); by the mid-1960s, the council began to attract more women who did not embody the previous model of respectable womanhood.[32] Height and the council's executive leadership embraced this change, despite the organizational growing pains it brought, as some members resisted the new recruits.[33] In 1966, the council received a two-year, $300,000 grant from the Ford Foundation for its next major initiative, Project Womanpower, envisioned as an avenue not only to bring aid to a broad base of black women but also to recruit those same women to join the council.[34] Throughout its two-year existence, Project Womanpower sought to bring together black women from all walks of life to help them learn how to network successfully and be more effective at identifying sources of governmental and private funding during the War on Poverty for their volunteer work. Far from co-opting the movement, the moderate council gave new pathways for young and grassroots activists to continue their activism.[35] The council hired young women from SNCC, the Congress of Racial Equality (CORE), the Southern Christian Leadership Conference (SCLC), and Students for a Democratic Society (SDS)—including Frances Beal, Merble Reagon, Prathia Hall, Janet Douglass, Doris Dozier, and Gwendolyn R. Simmons—as staff for this new initiative. Reagon recalls that the young staff felt that within Project Womanpower "we were doing what we needed to do" in working on civil rights and poverty projects around the country, "and because of people's perception about black women's clubs, . . . we could get a lot done under the radar."[36] After the end of Project Womanpower, Beal stayed on as the editor of the council newspaper, the *Black Woman's Voice*, until 1975. During her nine years as a paid staff member with the NCNW, Beal continued to pursue her activism on the side, writing her foundational "Double Jeopardy: To Be Black and Female"; founding the important feminist, antiracist, and anti-imperialist organization the Third World Women's Alliance; and publishing the newspaper *Triple Jeopardy*.[37]

Yet these changes were not always easy for the council. For one thing, the council struggled with how to address black power. In December 1966, Dorothy Height believed it a misguided approach and called for its elimination, claiming, "It is unfortunate that the phrase 'black power' was ever conceived."[38] Height was especially worried about driving away white support from the movement.[39] But in a few short years, the council began to advocate bolder positions in line with the self-determination of black power. A July 1969 national affiliate meeting advocated a position that was much more radical. A statement from the meeting read, "Now we understand what our black youth have been saying to us. . . . The government by its actions seems to be informing us that it will not protect the rights of the Black community nor the lives of our children." The council went on to state that it would defend the rights of black Americans "by any means necessary."[40] NCNW's use of this phrase, taken from Malcolm X's own words at the founding of the Organization of Afro-American Unity, was clearly a far cry from Height's earlier public statement against adopting the slogan of black power. The council was undoubtedly reacting to the rollback of school integration efforts and social welfare policies under Nixon, but women like Beal, Reagon, and Hall also influenced the council's shift.[41] As Height later recalled, "We had been treating symptoms rather than causes," and though she believed in quiet tactics and dialogue, she also came to appreciate the need for a more direct approach in attempting to change power relationships.[42]

In addition to the young staff assembled for Project Womanpower, new members recruited after 1966 pushed the traditional leaders of the council in new directions, not only ideologically but also programmatically. Fannie Lou Hamer first worked with the council through Wednesdays in Mississippi and later worked with the council to address poverty in Mississippi. The council purchased fifty sows and five boars for Hamer's cooperative Freedom Farm in Sunflower County, Mississippi. By 1973, the pig bank was producing over three thousand pigs. Hamer and other local Mississippi women also worked with the council to staff three day-care centers for low-income women in the state. One of these centers began as a project to house unwed teenage mothers, but its purpose was changed after resistance from local congressman Thomas Abernethy, who claimed that the Okolona home would harbor prostitutes. Feeling that it had no viable alternative to fight against his racist and sexist accusation, the NCNW altered its strategy and instead created a day-care center, staffed by the young mothers, on the property. While the council caved to white resistance in this case, it still helped local women by both employing them in and admitting their children to the day-care center. The council also helped create the low-income home ownership program Turnkey III, which Sammie Lee Gray-Wiseman had first worked on in Gulfport, and implemented it around the country.[43]

Chapter 7 explores how in the late 1960s and 1970s the council took on a new identity, not as an organization of elite black women but as a major national organization speaking on behalf of all black women. It pushed, promoted, and challenged itself as it tried to bring women around the country into its ranks through targeted programming, policy changes, and publicity. One slide show from 1970—"There's Something in It for You"—talked about the great potential of a council-sponsored project that was helping black men and women own their own homes. Another, "The Power in Four Million Women"—created a few years later and narrated by Ruby Dee—was used as a promotional tool for recruitment. The council came to see its mission as providing a conduit between a growing constituency of grassroots black women and high-level contacts at the state and federal levels.

Chapter 8 explores the shift in the mid-1970s as the NCNW tried to take its self-help abroad. Its efforts drew on a presumed solidarity with other women of African descent from around the world, but unlike so many other black internationalist activists and organizations in the 1960s and 1970s, the council did not disavow American liberalism. In 1975, the council received the first of its grants from the United States Agency for International Development (USAID) to aid in its efforts at development for women. Ultimately, the council received over $1.7 million from USAID by 1985. The first project funded was a month-long seminar for women of African descent concurrent with the UN's International Women's Year (IWY) conference in Mexico City. Conference participants then traveled to Mississippi to view NCNW's projects and meet renowned civil rights leaders and then NCNW leaders Hamer, Blackwell, Devine, and Amzie Moore, among other local Mississippi activists. The council then received another grant from USAID to create an international division, which created a skills bank registry and worked to create new self-help development projects for women in Botswana, Lesotho, and Swaziland by early 1976. The NCNW targeted these three countries—which were land-locked by and economically dependent on South Africa—in hopes that it could bring aid directly to rural women whose husbands worked in South African mines for months at a time. The council believed that it had much to offer because of its rural poverty work in Mississippi. Unfortunately, the council's small staff abroad; limited familiarity with the political, economic, and social structures in these countries; resistance from USAID; and infighting between local organizations meant that by the early 1980s, the council's only long-standing self-help project was a pig farm in Swaziland. While the council tried to establish rural cooperatives, livestock banks, and childcare centers in these countries, it ultimately reverted to its most familiar and established strategy—helping to better train women and increase their professional networks.

The council's efforts were also sometimes limited by its need to uphold public respectability. For instance, Height backed down when confronted with Congressman Abernethy's bogus charge of the council supporting prostitution in the Okolona project, and the council never publicly condemned the slanderous attacks of Senator Russell Long, who called the women of the National Welfare Rights Organization (NWRO), another organization composed mainly of black women, "brood mares" in 1967. Height did not openly advocate the positions of the NWRO, such as its insistence that women receiving welfare should not be forced to endure invasions into their intimate lives to secure aid.[44] However, the council did provide other means for supporting welfare mothers. Within its series of poverty workshops in the late 1960s, the council provided a platform for women receiving welfare to speak out about their experiences. NCNW also encouraged its local sections to organize marches and activities during the Poor People's Campaign and to speak out against welfare cuts that were damaging to black mothers and children.[45]

Height also included NWRO leaders as panelists at council-supported conferences.[46]

Though fraught with tension and at times limited in its success, the council was a major player in the mid-twentieth-century Black Freedom Movement. The group displayed flexibility and creativity as it adapted to shifting political terrains—from the postwar efforts to support human rights, to the civil rights movement's efforts to sustain an interracial beloved community, to the Black Power movement's embrace of black self-determination, and finally to the international push both against apartheid and for women in development. The NCNW made crucial decisions not only to help black Americans gain social, political, and economic equality, but also to support initiatives that helped strengthen its organizational presence at home and abroad. Its pragmatic use of public moderation, as well as its vast network of affiliate organizations and local sections, helped it not only gain financial support and bring crucial resources to black women throughout the twentieth century but also survive as the largest black clubwomen's organization in America today.[47]

CHAPTER ONE

Maneuvering for the Movement
The World of Broker Politics in the NCNW, 1935–1963

In February 1960, the nation was riveted as students across the South protested Jim Crow through a series of defiant sit-ins at local restaurants. Two months later, Ella Baker called these same students to a conference at Shaw University, where they formed SNCC—one of the most effective civil rights organizations of the 1960s. Half a year later, another conference drew together black youth, but this one was quite different. In November 1960, the National Council of Negro Women celebrated its silver anniversary. To mark the momentous occasion, the council returned to New York, the city of its founding. While students in Greensboro, North Carolina, had shown their support for the movement by putting their bodies on the line, the council had taken a different approach. Among other activities, the council hosted a High Tea for Youth, sponsored by Personal Products, Inc., the makers of Modess pantiliners. The council also hosted a gala, which featured a "Fall-Winter Fashions" show, sponsored by Miss Louise Gardner, program director of the International Ladies' Garment Workers' Union, and Miss Melba Linda Page, a fashion consultant.[1]

The council's interest in social events seemed out of touch with the dangerous, direct-action projects of groups like CORE and SNCC; and the reflections of Dorothy C. Quinn, the 1960 convention coordinator, reveal the stark contrast between the seeming selflessness of direct-action civil rights workers and the selfishness of NCNW coordinators. Quinn lamented that the New York convention "revealed a picture of New York at its worst." Low attendance and high costs made organizers who requested money for their efforts "[appear] like 'irresponsible vultures' upon prey."[2] Convention planning in the spring of 1960 focused too little time on the annual convention and too much time on the NCNW International Debutante Ball, which was held in New York a little over a month before the convention. Other council leaders were consumed with planning the Washington Debutante Cotillion, taking place just eleven days after the convention.[3] The very fact that these elite social events disrupted its annual convention suggests the NCNW's distance from the innovative civil rights demonstrations unfolding across the South.

Although council members were sipping tea rather than protesting at lunch counters, they were not indifferent to the direct-action protests around the country; however, they saw their roles within the council as observers, financial supporters, and lobbyists, not as people engaged in direct action. The NCNW invited such speakers as the Reverend L. Francis Griffin, president of the Prince Edward County Christian Association, and Jean Fairfax of the American Friends Service Committee to talk about their efforts to reopen the public schools in Prince Edward County, Virginia, since the county had closed them in May 1959.[4] Also speaking at the convention were Thurgood Marshall, legal counsel for the National Association for the Advancement of Colored People (NAACP); Alexander J. Allen, associate director of the National Urban League; and Andrew Young, associate director of the National Council of Churches' Department of Youth Work.[5] NCNW members didn't want to lead the direct-action charge for civil rights, but they wanted to work in support of such groups. In addition, council women studied the legislation being passed at all levels of government and sought out "representation on all strategic Boards of the Community engaged in Civil Action."[6] They were not indifferent, but they sought to create change from the inside of the boardroom, conference, or private meeting. In its first twenty-five years, the council was a volunteer organization with limited finances but large social and political influence. While individual council members certainly put their bodies and lives on the line for civil rights in other organizations, within the NCNW they fought more for the political and economic opportunities for black women. Using their prominent positions, they also tried to influence national policy as well as work in a more supportive role for other civil rights campaigns.

To Deliver "a Mighty Blow"

On December 5, 1935, twenty years to the day before the start of the Montgomery bus boycott, Mary McLeod Bethune called leaders of twenty-nine black women's organizations to the 137th Street Branch of the Manhattan YWCA in Harlem to create a new organization of organizations.[7] She hoped that together, under the "umbrella" of a new national council, black women could raise a mighty voice through which to fight for change for themselves and their communities.[8] Black women participated in male- and white-dominated organizations, such as the NAACP and the YWCA, but they also had a long tradition of activism in black sororities, such as Alpha Kappa Alpha and Delta Sigma Theta, as well as in black women's religious, professional, and political organizations. Still, the activism of these black women's clubs was isolated and often local. Bethune envisioned that her organization would harness the power of black women's groups to speak as the definitive national lobbying voice of black women. As Bethune said, "If I should tap you with one finger, you may not even know that you have been touched. If I use two fingers, you may know that you were tapped. But if I bring together all the fingers of my hand into a fist, I can give a mighty blow."[9] Historian Deborah Gray White notes that unlike previous black women's feminist organizations that had insisted on defending black womanhood, the council was more concerned with "the practical world of broker politics."[10] The council was composed of the members of its affiliated women's organizations, but it also gave individual women the opportunity to join the national council directly as life members. Finding this initial set up inadequate after a year, the council later expanded to include local councils, initially known as metropolitan councils, in which there were five or more subordinate branches of affiliates. Other local councils were set up in rural areas, as were junior councils. In the 1940s, the NCNW implemented regional areas to help with creation, programming, and coordination of local councils around the country. During Dorothy Height's presidency, local councils became known as sections, and the regional organization changed to a state organization.[11] In order to be most effective, the council, in its first three decades of existence, took a moderate position—through its willingness to work within established American governmental and economic systems, promote the professional interests of black women, and work interracially if it might serve the needs of the black community.

Bethune had the personal and professional experience necessary to create such an organization. Born to formerly-enslaved parents in Mayesville, South Carolina, on July 10, 1875, she was the fifteenth of seventeen children. As a child, Bethune studied not only how to read and write but also how to maneuver in the worlds of white benevolence and paternalism in white-funded missionary schools. Her educational experiences included working with white as well as black teachers. First she met black teacher and mentor Emma J. Wilson at Trinity Mission School. Then she attended Scotia Seminary, a school to train black teachers and social workers, with a scholarship funded by white Quaker missionary Mary Crissman. Later she attended the Moody Bible Institute, where she was the only black person among dozens of white students and teachers.[12] Bethune would use these experiences of dealing with white philanthropy and paternalism to her advantage in her later endeavors.

Though interracial, her education had also prepared her to be a "race woman," epitomizing the late nineteenth-century ideology promoted by the black community—including black feminist organizations such as the National Association of Colored Women (NACW)—that educated black women had a responsibility to "lift as we climb."[13] In 1904, Bethune implemented her own institution of racial uplift when she opened the Daytona Educational and Industrial Training School for Negro Girls with only $1.50 and five students.[14] To stabilize the school, she enlisted an impressive group of trustees, including James N. Gamble, co-owner of Procter and Gamble. She used the connections of Booker T. Washington to enlist support from wealthy philanthropists like Thomas White, founder and head of the major White Sewing Machine Company, and John D. Rockefeller.[15] The school continued to grow under Bethune's leadership, changed its name a few times, and in 1923 merged with the Cookman Institute—a coed college run by the Methodist Church. Bethune was president from 1923 to 1942, briefly taking the presidency back in 1946. Although women were founding schools at this time, it was rare for them to be college presidents; this was another one of Bethune's remarkable accomplishments.[16] Meanwhile, Bethune's race work and careful strategizing also manifested within black women's clubs. She was the president of the Florida Federation of Colored Women's Clubs from 1917 to 1924, and president of the NACW from 1924 to 1928, defeating Ida B. Wells for the position.[17] Bethune's activism within black feminist organizations strengthened bonds between black women while also helping them lobby for civil rights.

Bethune had worked within the mainstream American political system as well. Bethune was appointed by President Calvin Coolidge to the White House Conference on Child Welfare, by president Herbert Hoover to the American Child Health Association, and by Franklin D. Roosevelt to the Federal Office of Education of Negroes.[18] In 1927, after attending a National Council of Women meeting sponsored by Eleanor Roosevelt, Bethune began a friendship with Franklin D. Roosevelt's mother when, unlike the rest of the white guests, Sara Delano Roosevelt invited Bethune to sit beside her. This friendship with Sara eventually extended to Eleanor as well. The Roosevelt women's friendship helped Bethune bolster her power in Franklin D. Roosevelt's administration and secure her most notable political appointment as director of the Division of Negro Affairs of the National Youth Administration from 1936 to 1942. Her political appointments in both Republican and Democratic administrations gave her an insider's perspective on the workings of government, especially the importance of interracial alliances, which opened doors for African Americans who had traditionally been excluded from the political scene.[19]

In her relationship with Eleanor and Franklin Roosevelt, and other politicians, Bethune emphasized practicality, and she was willing to make deals as necessary. Historian Bettye Collier-Thomas has called Bethune a "shrewd politician and a power broker with few equals."[20] Deborah G. White has labeled her a "chameleon," maneuvering through the world by employing the necessary approach to achieve her desired end. White writes, "She was the consummate politician, always tailoring her remarks to please her audience."[21] Her tactics were varied and could not be encompassed in a single ideology. As Audrey Thomas McCluskey argues, Bethune and her generation of leaders "required a multiple consciousness that envisioned the empowerment of their disinherited sex and race."[22] As an appointee of FDR, Bethune was careful not to alienate him, while also pushing for more opportunities for black women during the New Deal and World War II.[23]

Bethune's networking had an important impact on the council's visibility as an organization. In 1943, she wanted to raise enough money to buy a permanent home for the NCNW in Washington, D.C. Having been rebuffed from purchasing a space on Dupont Circle by a racist seller, Bethune set her sights on a lovely Victorian home at 1318 Vermont Avenue, near Logan Circle. After getting approval from the council, despite its dire financial situation at the time, Bethune worked hard to raise the $15,500 to purchase the home. Eleanor Roosevelt helped Bethune secure $10,000 from department store founder Marshall Field for the purchase.[24] Pittsburgh NCNW member Daisy Lampkin, a longtime leader in both the NACW and the NAACP, chaired the national committee to raise the remaining $5,500.[25] Not only was the council house the headquarters of the organization, as well as Bethune's home, it also served as a place to house both domestic and foreign dignitaries who were often discriminated against when visiting Washington, D.C.[26] For instance, in 1945 Maida Springer was selected as a black delegate to represent labor interests on a trip abroad, sponsored by the U.S. Office of War Information. When no Washington, D.C., hotel would accommodate her as she waited to embark, she stayed at the council house.[27] In the 1950s, dignitaries from Ghana, Nigeria, Guinea, Liberia, and South Africa—including Kwame Nkrumah and Madame Sékou Touré—visited the NCNW house.[28] In another example of its political connectedness, the council's 1951 souvenir yearbook, produced in honor of its "sweet sixteen" birthday, included well wishes from President Harry Truman, New York congressman Jacob Javits, Missouri senator James P. Kem, Massachusetts senator Henry Cabot Lodge, and many other prominent politicians and businesspeople.[29]

Bethune held great power within black activist communities as well. She held office in the National Urban League and the NAACP. From 1936 to 1952, she was the president of the Association for the Study of Negro Life and History (ASNLH). She published work in the *Journal of Negro History* (ASNLH's corresponding journal) and had columns in both the *Pittsburgh Courier* and the *Chicago Defender*. Her speeches were reproduced in *Opportunity*, the *Crisis*, and *Ebony*. She worked for both racial uplift and self-help, and this endeared her to many in the black community. As Audrey Thomas McCluskey and Elaine M. Smith claim, "She appealed to blacks as a role model and leader, and to white progressives as a voice of reason and conciliation on racial matters."[30] She sought to be a bridge between worlds.

Bethune also used respectability politics to attempt to "subvert the *effects* of sexism and white racism" toward black women.[31] Bethune's Daytona Institute emphasized professional skills, but it also insisted on training women to be more feminine in order to combat white racism that assumed the black woman's inherent immorality. At the same time, her emphasis on teaching domestic arts indicates her belief that African American women "must be recognized and accepted first *as women* in order to promote social change."[32] The council not only sought to open up the workplace to black women but also insisted that black women had a "responsibility to maintain a professional attitude and appearance," best illustrated by a "Hold Your Job" campaign under Bethune.[33] Bethune and the clubwomen of the council insisted that while the job market must open to black women, they, in turn, must adhere to ideals of respectability in dress, speech, and behavior.

In emphasizing the black woman's respectability, Bethune continued to use an activist tactic of late nineteenth-century women's clubs, promoting the idea that the black woman must be beyond moral reproach by being more proper than white women. The clubs hoped that these efforts would combat the stereotypes of black women as lascivious and impure, and ultimately make segregation unsustainable. For example, as Evelyn Brooks Higginbotham pointed out in her classic work *Righteous Discontent*, the black women involved in the development of the National Baptist Convention at the end of the nineteenth century used the idea of respectability to make political gains for their race. Having been excluded from positions of authority within the traditional church governance, black Baptist women developed the Woman's Convention (WC). Instead of challenging dominant gender roles that called for the submission of women to men, the WC directed its energy to fighting racism through feminine espousal of virtue, cleanliness, and respectability. In 1915, the executive board of the WC wrote, "Fight segregation through the courts as an unlawful act? Yes. But fight it with soap and water, hoes, spades, shovels and paint, to remove any reasonable excuse for it, is the fight that we will win."[34] Their mission was not only to advocate the legal overhaul of segregation but also to call for quiet examples of virtuous feminine ability to slowly chip away at it. Although they did not directly challenge stereotypes that labeled black women as dirty, lazy, or domineering, African American clubwomen found agency in their methods.[35] The NCNW certainly challenged segregation, but it continued to adhere to the idea that black women must behave and dress in a feminine, respectable way in order to be most effective at challenging segregation and discrimination.[36]

Yet at the same time that the NCNW emphasized respectability, it also employed a more modern concept of networking to place black women, as career- and civic-minded persons, in as many government positions and volunteer organizations as possible. Council women hoped that this strategy would result not only in legislation promoting black women's economic interests but also in the hiring of black women in private businesses as well as in the state, local, and national agencies created by the New Deal. Unlike the earlier activism of the NACW and other black women's organizations, the NCNW focused on obtaining jobs and other practical gains for black women rather than speaking out as defenders of their femininity.[37]

The NCNW also fought for black women's career opportunities both before and during World War II. In a prepared statement to the House of Representatives, which was delivered by Congressman Louis Ludlow in June 1940, Bethune highlighted the council's "united patriotism" and insisted that the Roosevelt administration train black women for military service. NCNW also strongly condemned segregation in the military, especially after the passage of a recent War Department policy to enforce segregation and limit black power in the army.[38] Bethune pushed for admission of black women into the military and became a special assistant to the Secretary of War to select the first black officers to the Women's Army Auxiliary Corps. When training facilities were segregated in Des Moines, Iowa, the NCNW launched a campaign to push for their desegregation.[39] The NCNW also pushed for black women to be included in defense industry jobs. Using her personal connections to Franklin and Eleanor Roosevelt, Bethune helped push FDR to pass Executive Order 8802, eliminating discrimination in defense industry jobs, and to create a Fair Employment Practices Commission. After A. Philip Randolph threatened to bring 100,000 African Americans to a march on Washington scheduled for July 1, 1941, Bethune called for a meeting of the NCNW to be held in Washington, D.C., on June 30. This threat of bringing thousands of additional black women to Washington on the eve of the march put further pressure on FDR to push forward with the executive order in late June. He ultimately signed the executive order into law on June 25.[40]

In addition to Bethune, other leaders within the council pushed for the opening up of the American workplace to black women. NCNW parliamentarian and executive committee member Sadie Alexander was one of the first black women to earn a PhD in economics and a law degree from the University of Pennsylvania. She was also the first black woman to practice law in Pennsylvania. She bitterly resented the racism and sexism she faced as an economist, and pursued a law degree when all serious economics jobs were closed to her. She insisted that more African American women be included in industrial jobs in the 1930s and that black women's labor had significant value and should help them gain greater citizenship rights.[41] NCNW founder and executive committee member Mabel Staupers also worked tirelessly to open up more job opportunities for black women in the federal government. In 1934, she became the first paid executive secretary of the National Association of Colored Graduate Nurses, which had been founded in 1908, after the two leading national nurses' associations (the American Nurses' Association and the National League for Nursing Education) refused to accept black nurses as individual members of their organizations. Staupers successfully led the fight for the integration of black nurses into the U.S. Army and Navy during World War II and into the American Nurses Association in 1948.[42] While working to build a powerful base to pressure the federal government to desegregate the military nursing corps, Staupers drew on the larger network of the council.[43] While NCNW members Alexander and Staupers may have been fighting for employment opportunities for black women, their success also helped fuel the black freedom struggle in the 1930s and 1940s. As Darlene Clark Hine has argued, black professionals in the World War II era, while sometimes motivated by personal concerns, were best positioned because of their "education, respectability, and expertise and the authority that they enjoyed in the black community" to "open the crack in the edifice of white supremacy" that would flood open in the next two decades.[44] The NCNW brought together such professionals and sought to boost their power. The council's insistence that black women deserved to be full citizens in American political and economic spheres was a bold position for the time.

While the NCNW pushed to open up economic opportunities, it also supported other civil rights efforts. From its inception, the NCNW also concentrated on pushing black women and men to register to vote. It instituted a citizenship training program that reached 63,000 women in twenty-six states by 1940.[45] Following the release of President Truman's Committee on Civil Rights' report *To Secure These Rights*, the NCNW pushed for adoption of a Ten Point Program in November 1947. The council fought to pass legislation against lynching; poll taxes; and discriminatory housing, education, hiring, and pay. It also called for reforms to Social Security to include farm workers and domestic servants; endorsement of the UN; federal aid for health services; and support for programs to combat hunger and juvenile delinquency. When Truman adopted his civil rights platform for the 1948 presidential election, the NCNW—though nonpartisan—helped mobilize voter registration, which likely contributed to Truman's surprise victory. Then in the early 1950s the NCNW worked to support civil rights programs sponsored by the NAACP and the National Emergency Civil Rights Mobilization, comprised of sixty organizations, to push for the passage of civil rights legislation.[46]

Challenges

Despite their efforts at fighting for better jobs and work conditions for black women, the NCNW had difficulty recruiting working-class women to the organization. Although Bethune was the daughter of farmworkers and helped establish a school for rural black women in Daytona, the council's reputation remained solidly middle class. One of the main causes for this was the struc-ture of the council. Bethune wanted the council to speak on behalf of black women through affiliated institutions, such as black sororities, women's pro-fessional organizations, lodges, and women's auxiliary organizations. The most influential groups in the council were the sororities, and even though these groups were heavily involved in social justice and service, they could not break from their elitist image.[47] In 1944, after two years of consideration as to whether or not to join the council, the Ladies' Auxiliary of the Brother-hood of Sleeping Car Porters—a working-class black women's group—finally joined. However, it quickly found that the larger council ignored poorer women's concerns, and the group left the council one year later.[48]

Subsequent NCNW presidents were also unable to change this elitist im-age and boost the membership of the council. After working for fourteen years as council president, Bethune stepped down in 1949 at the age of seventy-four. Dorothy B. Ferebee, head of medical services at Howard Uni-versity, took over the presidency for four years. Ferebee heralded from a prestigious lineage of clubwomen. Her great aunt was Josephine St. Pierre Ruffin, one of the founders of the Boston New Era Club as well as the later NACW.[49] Of all the young women whom Bethune had groomed to be her potential successor, Ferebee was her favorite.[50] However, Ferebee had a dif-ficult time following Bethune, who was beloved by both the council and broader public.[51] She also suffered a major tragedy only months after being elected president, when her eighteen-year-old daughter died. Although Ferebee claimed that her daughter had contracted pneumonia, scholar Diane Kiesel has convincingly shown that the daughter likely died after securing an illegal abortion. On top of all that, Ferebee divorced only four months after her daughter's death. Ferebee's ex-husband blamed Dorothy for their daughter's death, believing that the daughter must have worried that she would embarrass Ferebee in her new post at the council if she had a child out of wedlock. Ferebee's adherence to the explanation of pneumonia as the cause of her daughter's death suggests her deep concern with maintaining her family's and the NCNW's respectable reputations.[52]

Ferebee struggled as council president. From the time of its founding, the council had been short on money, relying on the membership fees of its affiliate organizations and local councils. In 1943, Bethune nearly bankrupted the council as she pushed through the purchase of the headquarters at Vermont Avenue. Although the council remained stable for a few years, by 1946 their expenses were drastically greater than the money coming in. By February 1949, only a few short months before Ferebee would take over, Bethune was so desperate to add money to the council's treasury that she wrote wealthier members of the council requesting that they give loans. She wrote to Chicago lawyer Edith Sampson, requesting $1,000 to keep the council from collapsing. Sampson had to fight tooth and nail to be repaid by the council.[53]

Ferebee not only had to deal with this financial crisis but also had the misfortune of taking over NCNW leadership at the height of the Red Scare. Despite the council's long-standing proclamations of patriotism, it still fell under suspicion. Bethune was investigated in 1943 by the Dies Committee for her connections to the National Negro Congress and other left-leaning organizations.[54] Then, while Ferebee was visiting Germany to observe war conditions in 1951, a House Un-American Activities Committee report named Ada Jackson, head of the Brooklyn council, and Vivian Mason, vice president of the national NCNW, as signers of a peace petition with suspected communist ties. Instead of standing firmly against such red-baiting, the council quickly informed both that they must prove the allegations false within fifteen days. Mason complied, but Jackson refused and caused further headaches for the council. Two years later, Ferebee would be investigated as well. The council also suffered financially in this period because donors were too frightened to donate to organizations deemed subversive simply by their commitment to interracial activism or to international affairs.[55] With all these pressures, Ferebee struggled to establish her authority as the head of the council. Bethune remained in the wings of the organization until Ferebee left office in

November 1953. Although Ferebee had wanted Dorothy Height to succeed her, Bethune wanted Vivian Mason. Ultimately, Bethune got her way, suggesting the pull Bethune still had over the organization.[56]

Vivian Mason's presidency overlapped with major events of the early civil rights movement. She promoted programs that stressed the council's know-how in promoting interracialism. One month after the *Brown v. Board of Education* decision, the heads of the council's affiliate organizations met to affirm their commitment to helping with school desegregation.[57] They argued that as women, they were the ones closest to the school community through their PTA participation, conferences with teachers, and transportation of their children to and from school. In 1955, Mason launched a major council initiative to help with integration of schools, but the program's goals remained vague. Overall, the council wanted to "organize opportunities for discussion in interracial groups to help promote understanding of the significance of the decision," try to influence public opinion through the media, and urge family members to support integration. In addition, the council sought to be "an effective clearing house of vital information on local experiences," providing information about local school boards and state and local governments.[58] One year later the council hosted an Interracial Conference of Women to discuss how women of all races and religions could fight for civil and human rights as a major feature of its annual convention, and it also sponsored programming in support of Rosa Parks and Autherine Lucy, the first African American to integrate the University of Alabama.[59]

Although she tried to boost programming to promote interracial education in the wake of the *Brown* decision, Mason, like her predecessors, was also hindered by the council's dire financial situation. She attempted to raise funds from within by beginning a life membership campaign in 1954, but this still did not alleviate the financial crisis.[60] She also sought outside money for this project, but she ran into roadblocks. Nelson A. Rockefeller gave the council $7,500 to help remove it from debt and then help with some of its programming. The philanthropic fund declined further requests for support for programs in 1956 and 1957, citing in an internal memo, "It is clear that the Council continues to lack leadership and organization of the sort needed to launch an effective program."[61] That leadership would soon arrive.

Reaching a New Height

Much like Bethune had done, Dorothy Irene Height—the fourth NCNW president, elected November 1957—skillfully maneuvered through the white-dominated world of government and private foundations as well as black organizations. As a black employee of the YWCA, Height had one foot in the white clubwomen's world and another in the black clubwomen's movement. The NCNW relied largely on white funding while it pursued social justice for black women, a position that often forced Height to take a more moderate approach. The council was often the first choice of white women's organizations looking for black participation to achieve integrated groups.

Although Height had long worked in interracial groups, she did not escape discrimination as a black woman. She was born in Richmond, Virginia, on March 24, 1912, but moved with her family at age four to Rankin, Pennsylvania, a small mining town on the outskirts of Pittsburgh. Her parents were both committed members of the local Baptist church. Her father was a building contractor and her mother was a nurse, so Height grew up in an upwardly mobile family. Despite her training as a nurse, Height's mother could not get a job in a hospital and instead worked for a private family. Thus, young Dorothy grew up with a keen sense of the professional limitations and personal constraints that black women in America faced. Reflecting on her mother's work for the private family and her feelings toward the family's daughter in particular, Height recalled, "I learned both to like and to hate [her] because it almost seemed to me that at every important event in my life, my mother had to be at her house, and so on. I liked her because she had a long narrow foot and I thought, beautiful new shoes, nice clothes."[62] Even as a child, Height grew frustrated with the racial system that forced her mother into private nursing and took her away for extended periods. Yet she also envied and even admired the affluence of the white girl that her mother looked after. Height sought to transcend her frustration as best she could by excelling academically.

Height was a very bright student and often honored for her intelligence, hard work, and commitment to school and religious work, but racism dimmed her rising star. She was accepted to Barnard in 1929, but she was not admitted because the college's quota of two black women had already been filled. Height was devastated, but she decided to apply that same day to NYU. Once NYU dean Ruth Schaeffer saw Height's letter from Barnard officials explaining Height's acceptance (and rejection) as well as her transcript and entrance exam scores, Schaeffer admitted her on sight. "A girl who makes these kinds of grades doesn't need an application to enroll at NYU," the dean stated.[63] Height went on to excel at NYU, receiving her baccalaureate degree in three years and using the fourth year of her college scholarship, funded by the Elks club, to get a master's degree in educational psychology in 1933.[64]

Even as a student at the predominantly white NYU, Height carved out a space for black companionship, organizing a black student group called the Ramses Club. Among other activities, the group sponsored a lecture series named for W. E. B. Du Bois and a discussion group named for Paul Robeson. Hulan Jack and Constance Baker Motley, who later became prominent civil rights activists, were also members of the group.[65] While in school, Height also took on a volunteer position as assistant to the director at a community center in Brownsville, a neighborhood in Brooklyn. After graduating from NYU, she went to work for the New York Department of Welfare, which placed her back in Brownsville, where she was asked to "handle all of the . . . protest groups."[66] From this position, she eventually became a personnel supervisor over five district welfare offices. The job sometimes required her to work on behalf of the local government, even when she thought that petitioners were being treated unfairly. She had worked in unions and with activists outside her professional career, and felt troubled when representing management against the unions: "I had to speak on behalf of management against people that I often thought were being mistreated." And so when she was offered a job with the Greater New York Council of Churches to become director of youth services, she resigned from the welfare department. A short while later, the Harlem YWCA recruited her as well.[67] Although she did not enjoy her time at the welfare department from 1933 to 1937, she gained great insight into how a local government organization functioned, and she would later use this knowledge as head of the NCNW.

While in New York, Height became heavily involved in the vibrant activist and intellectual spaces of 1930s Harlem. She lived in Harlem with her sister while a student at NYU and after graduation. In this exciting setting, she became active in a variety of groups and initiatives affiliated with the Popular Front, a leftist coalition that brought together leaders from the Communist Party and more liberal organizations, many of whom were civil rights workers.[68] Height was the chairperson of the Harlem Christian Youth Council, which helped organize eighty-eight youth groups in the area—including the Young Communist League—and was heavily involved in youth conferences and protests. Height even worked with Adam Clayton Powell's "Don't Buy Where You Can't Work" campaign.[69] Through her activities in Harlem, Height met other activists and intellectuals, such as James Farmer, Kenneth Clark, James Robinson (who created Operation Crossroads Africa), Henry Winston, Juanita Mitchell (of the NAACP), and Ethel James Williams.[70] She was impressed with the fact that despite their personal beliefs, these radicals held fast to their ideals. In contrast, she said, members of Christian activist groups were less likely to fight for systemic racial change, instead offering excuses about how difficult it would be for whites to adjust if changes were made. Though at times she disagreed ideologically with the more militant activists, she maintained a respect for them and their tactics. This helped her later work with the more militant members during the height of the Black Power movement. "I have to see militancy as my way of using my approach to mak[e] a direct head-on attack on problems, rather than just vaguely discussing them," she claimed in 1974.[71]

Though willing to work with radicals, including those who embraced black nationalism or communism, Height was more committed to a moderate approach, grounded in ecumenical, interracial, Christian activism. As a girl in Pennsylvania, she had helped integrate the Sunday school classes of her local Baptist church by teaching Bible classes to white children.[72] She joined the interracial National Christian Youth movement in 1934 and a year later became the vice chairperson for North America of the United Christian Youth Movement, while working for the department of welfare. As she recalls, "It was not a Sunday school type of thing. For instance, my chief interest was in economic order, so I was going to the Labor Temple and learning about economics, and the relation between the economy and life and work, that sort of thing." She was interested in the "relation between faith and action."[73] In 1937, she attended a World Conference of Churches in England, which left a deep impression on her. While there, she came to appreciate that "to be ecumenical means to be what you are, but open. In other words, I don't have to be what you are, and you don't have to be what I am, for us to work together. And I think that has been my understanding."[74] Her pragmatic ecumenism also extended to her social activism.

Height's work with the YWCA incorporated her spirituality and interest in social justice.[75] In 1937 she was hired as assistant director of the 137th Street branch, working with powerful black leaders Cecilia Cabaniss Saunders and Anna Arnold Hedgeman.[76] One year later, she became director of the Emma Ransom House, a YWCA-run lodging house for up to 165 black working women and travelers passing through New York.[77] In 1939, she moved to Washington, D.C., to become the executive of the Phyllis [sic] Wheatley YWCA. In 1944, Height moved back to New York to become the secretary for interracial education for the YWCA, a position that planted her on the national staff for over three decades. Thanks largely to Height's work on the national staff, the YWCA established its Interracial Charter in 1946, proclaiming that the national organization move from segregated to integrated clubs. In 1949, Height became director for training; and in 1965, head of the

Department of Racial Justice.[78] While gaining paid employment at the YWCA, Height also served as president of Delta Sigma Theta sorority from 1947 to 1958 and of the NCNW from 1957 to 1977, when she stopped working for the YWCA (though she stayed on as president of the NCNW until 1998).

The YWCA was unique in its early commitment to nationwide integration within its ranks.[79] According to historian Abigail Lewis, "The Y was distinctive in that it fostered both an interracial and ecumenical community."[80] Lewis points out that contrary to scholarly claims that black women, when forced to choose between gender- or race-related activism, always choose the latter, African American women were very active in the YWCA. The Y and the NCNW had significant overlap in their membership.[81] The Y was also unique for its significant commitment to integration. While many women's volunteer organizations of the 1940s and 1950s claimed to be in favor of integration on a national level, they did not have the commitment or network to enforce racial change around the country. Though by no means fully integrated, the YWCA made the earliest efforts to push its organization in that direction.[82] The Y also helped fuel the civil rights movement by paying the salaries of women like Height and later civil rights activists, such as Doris Dozier Crenshaw, whom the national board sent to Chicago to help with the SCLC's Chicago campaign.[83]

At the same time, the YWCA enabled racial pride and self-determination in its black branches.[84] When hiring Height as her assistant at the Harlem branch, Saunders said that the branch "look[ed] out for our own."[85] The branch was a place at which Height encountered other vibrant bright black women. Anna Arnold Hedgeman, Ella Baker, and Pauli Murray all routinely gathered at this location to discuss politics and culture. Hedgeman helped bring in a steady stream of impressive women speakers to the Y, including Bethune, St. Luke Penny Savings Bank president Maggie Lena Walker, WC president Nannie Helen Burroughs, and cosmetics giant Annie Turnbo Malone.[86] Barbara Ransby has called the Harlem YWCA one of the "dual pillars of Harlem's intellectual and political life for over two decades." In this space, highly educated and worldly black women, such as Height, Baker, and Murray, who were either single or childless, "represented a new model of black womanhood in this era."[87] The YWCA provided a space that challenged gendered expectations of how a woman should live her life. Height's time in Harlem helped her foster her connections to other strong black women leaders.

While working at the Harlem Y, Height became involved in exposing "black slave markets"—labor arrangements in the 1930s in which young black women would stand on designated corners in New York City neighborhoods and be taken for day labor. Height recalled meeting one woman who was tricked into working extra hours; others were left unpaid, and others were sexually assaulted or raped. As an administrator at the Y, Height encountered many young women who came to look for job opportunities but had been unable to find steady work. Through the YWCA, black women organized across class divisions, with domestic workers and teachers working in tandem for the progress of the race.[88] Height tried to help these women as best she could by working through the YWCA, but she also turned to promoting legislation. She worked with Young Communist League workers and offered testimony at a city council meeting, which helped bring light to the problem, although the city council never passed any legislation to eliminate the "slave markets."[89]

It was in this environment of thriving black women's leadership that Height first encountered the National Council of Negro Women. In November 1937, Height, as a staff person at the Harlem YWCA, was chaperoning Eleanor Roosevelt to an NCNW event when Bethune asked her to join the NCNW. Height was immediately appointed to the NCNW's resolutions committee and a year later was the registrar for the annual convention.[90] Height volunteered her time with the NCNW while working full time for the Y, but Bethune urged her to see if the Y would pay for her to work full time for the council. This possibility was forestalled, however, when Height joined the national board of the YWCA and quickly became immersed in creating and preparing for the Interracial Charter. Although she could not work full time with Bethune during this hectic period, the YWCA did let her work as a representative to the council, and she was free to go to NCNW meetings in this capacity.[91] While working for the Y, Height spent most of her free time, including holidays, working as a volunteer for the council.[92]

Height also worked for nearly a decade as the president of Delta Sigma Theta. While president of the national sorority, she helped organize the sorority by hiring an executive director and purchasing a national headquarters.[93] She also focused on opening up the workplace to the professional Delta women. Her work largely echoed Bethune's push to incorporate black women and their programs into American government.[94] However, Height's tenure as Delta's president was not without controversy. While in office, she maneuvered to serve four terms, an unprecedented move.[95] Though some disagreed with Height's tactics, she learned a great deal in both white-dominated and black-led women's groups, which informed her moderate approach within the NCNW.

In late fall 1957, Dorothy Height was elected president of the NCNW. Under Height, the council remained focused on securing economic and political opportunities for black women. Because many middle-class black women taught in black secondary and elementary schools within the state public school system, they risked being fired if they publicly pushed for the right to vote. In one of many instances of this happening to black teachers, Ernestine Denham Talbert of George County, Mississippi, was fired from her job in Greene County, Mississippi, when she registered to vote in 1962. Denham stated that many other blacks and even some whites were supportive of the voter registration efforts in Mississippi in the early 1960s but were afraid to publicly support it out of fear of losing their jobs.[96] While the NCNW attempted to secure the teaching positions of middle-class black educators during the early days of desegregation, it also worked to ensure that there would be an equitable distribution of white and black teachers and administrators in the schools, rather than just focusing on the integration of black students into white schools.[97]

Height also worked hard to financially stabilize the council. When she took office, she inherited an economic mess. Height recalls that on her first day, she received a certified letter calling for immediate payment of a $7,500 loan from the Industrial Bank of Washington. She immediately called her cousin Campbell C. Johnson, who was on the bank board, and the bank allowed the NCNW to pay off the loan in installments.[98] In 1958, the NCNW instituted a Fair Share program to ensure that local council groups paid membership dues in one lump sum. Height also tried to boost the NCNW's potential for programming by creating the Educational Foundation in 1959, which became tax-exempt in 1961 and was led by longtime NCNW member Daisy Lampkin.[99] One of the earliest initiatives of the foundation was the Women Integrating Neighborhood Services (WINS) project, which tried to facilitate communication between white and black women over school integration in hopes that this would strengthen white support for the *Brown* ruling. Under the foundation, the council also fund-raised for a memorial to Mary McLeod Bethune in Lincoln Park, which was initiated in 1958 (see chapter 7). The foundation additionally raised funds for a forty-four-unit low-income apartment building in Washington, D.C., called the Bethune House.[100]

Through the foundation, the council could also raise money to more significantly support other efforts of the civil rights movement. The council sponsored a series of Action Fellowships to help support students whose financial aid had been revoked because of their full-time participation in direct-action civil rights work. Well-known recipients include Howard-based Nonviolent Action Group members Ed Brown, Courtland Cox, and Stokely Carmichael.[101] In the fall of 1964, NCNW pledged to sell six million "Freedom" Christmas cards, featuring a Christmas tree adorned with the different promises of the Civil Rights Act, in order to raise money for the scholar-

ships.[102] In addition to funding Howard students Brown, C
chael, the council donated funds to William Porter, a student
Albany State College for his participation in the movement. After
mitted to Albany State, the council paid his tuition. The council als
tuition of Harvey Gantt and Lucinda Brawley, who were the first
American students to enroll at Clemson College; Marion Barry's graduate
school tuition; and SNCC volunteer Endesha Ida Mae Holland's tuition for a
Mississippi vocational college.[103] By 1966, the NCNW scholarships program
had helped seventy-two young men and women who had risked their lives
and livelihoods for desegregation.[104]

While president of the NCNW, Height came to more fully support the
male-led civil rights movement.[105] On May 12, 1963, Height delivered a
speech in which she lauded the efforts of the Alabama Christian Movement
for Human Rights (ACMHR) and the SCLC direct-action campaign in
Birmingham, which began with sit-ins at "whites-only" lunch counters on
April 3. These groups had organized protest marches on city hall, which were
violently put down by police using hoses and police dogs. Television camera
crews filmed these marches, and people around the country were horrified by
local Birmingham police chief Eugene "Bull" Connor's use of violent tactics
on the peaceful demonstrators, who had children among them. In the wake
of this police brutality on television, President Kennedy sent Assistant Attorney General Burke Marshall to quell the violence. While protesting, King was
arrested on April 13 and wrote his "Letter from Birmingham Jail" in condemnation of not only racist whites but also black and white liberals who claimed
to want to help the movement but refused to take action.

Height also worked with these same male civil rights leaders through the
Taconic Foundation and later the Council for United Civil Rights Leadership
(CUCRL). The Taconic Foundation, a group established in 1958 under the
leadership of white philanthropists Audrey and Stephen Currier, sought to
limit the growing turn toward militancy the civil rights movement and to
unite black civil rights leaders under a banner of moderation. Early in its existence, the Taconic Foundation conducted conversations with the Kennedy
administration on how to push activists toward voter education rather than
toward other direct-action projects.[106] In general, it funded projects that worked
within the existing political and legal system or increased understanding between black and white groups.

As the leader of the only major women's organization in the CUCRL,
Height had different concerns from those of the male delegates. She later
recalled, "Sometimes the men had trouble seeing why I was always linking

desegregation with hunger and children and other social welfare issues."[107] She also tried to unite people across the generation gap. She insisted that SNCC leaders be included in the CUCRL leadership groups.[108] She claimed, "I smile when I recall the meeting at which I suggested including the Student Nonviolent Coordinating Committee (SNCC) in the civil rights leadership. The youthful members of SNCC, full of revolutionary zeal, were using tactics some saw as counterproductive. But I was concerned that the young people were not at the table."[109]

But the male leaders of moderate organizations were not interested in letting the women speak any more than the student activists.[110] As Alabama SCLC activist Doris Dozier Crenshaw recalls, "At that time, women and the role of women was suppressed. And often women were on the back seat, the back burner," of the movement.[111] For instance, the March on Washington leadership indicated very publicly that men were leading the civil rights movement. No woman was invited to make one of the major speeches or to be part of the delegation of leaders to go to the White House.[112] Daisy Bates, the NAACP leader of school desegregation in Little Rock, Arkansas, gave a very short address on behalf of women in the civil rights movement. In response, organizer A. Philip Randolph offered a few comments that only made the patronizing attitude of male organizers more striking. Pauli Murray—feminist, civil rights activist, lawyer, and member of the NCNW—pointed out two months later at the NCNW annual convention that this gesture reflected a "tendency to assign women to a secondary, ornamental or 'honoree' role" in the movement.[113] Thus, rather than merely being a token gesture of solidarity, Randolph's comments highlighted the male leadership's sexist attitudes.[114] Still, despite this treatment, the NCNW sent several hundred women to participate in the March on Washington.[115]

Careful Steps

Just as the council had worked carefully to foster relationships with white-dominated institutions and organizations, it also worked carefully to foster relationships with male-led civil rights organizations. While younger African Americans were pursuing outspoken direct-action activism, the NCNW continued to highlight respectable and "ladylike" behavior in order to combat long-held stereotypes of domineering matriarchs and lascivious temptresses. These stereotypes were still being reinforced by some black scholars at the time. In 1939, sociologist E. Franklin Frazier wrote *The Negro Family in the United States*, pinning the problems of poverty on the structure of black families, which he argued were headed by overpowering black "matriarchs."[116] In 1957, he followed up with *Black Bourgeoisie*, a scathing critique of the black middle class, especially black clubwomen. In it, Frazier wrote, "In fact, in middle-class [Negro] families, especially if the husband has risen in social status through his own efforts and married a member of an 'old' family or a 'society' woman, the husband is likely to play a pitiful role."[117] Adding insult to injury, Frazier went on to say that the black male, frustrated at his lack of power, was likely to pursue extramarital affairs.[118] In both books, Frazier implied that through their domineering roles, black women—whether middle or lower class—harmed their families more than they helped them and thus posed barriers to racial progress.

Many black clubwomen read these attacks on their middle-class "dominance" and were careful not to project such an image. Long before the Moynihan Report of 1965—which blamed the "tangle of pathology" on the breakdown of the nuclear family structure, led by overly powerful mothers—the NCNW provided a forum for such gendered attacks on their power.[119] At the 1960 Silver Anniversary annual meeting, Dr. Hylan Garnet Lewis gave the keynote speech on "Recent Changes and the Negro Family." From 1959 to 1964, Lewis was the director of a childrearing study for the Health and Welfare Council of Washington, D.C. In November 1965, he was appointed cochair for the proposed family section of the White House conference "To Secure These Rights," President Johnson's effort to update Truman's 1947 Civil Rights Commission report. During his 1960 NCNW speech, Lewis echoed Frazier and foreshadowed Daniel Patrick Moynihan's infamous report when he argued that black men should take a larger role in the family as more African Americans moved into the middle class: "Both literally and figuratively—in the past and now—the presence and the role of the Negro male in the Negro family are, too frequently, shadow[s] and without substance sufficient to assure the kind of family life children certainly—and probably in most instances, women— deserve, and a healthy community demands."[120] As civil rights organizations began to focus on the well-being of the race as a whole and the end of segregation, black women in the council put their own needs and concerns behind those of black men who sought increased status in their families and communities.[121]

Black women sometimes articulated these same concerns about the role of domineering women in black families. In 1961, Dorothy Height served as the only black woman on President Kennedy's twenty-six member Commission on the Status of Women. In addition to serving on the main commission, she headed up the Consultation on Problems of Negro Women committee, in which black men and women discussed black women's role in the family, employment, volunteering, and education.[122] According to Duchess Harris, the committee was divided on most issues, but within the discussions about family structure, the group ultimately "blamed Black women for the destruction of the Black family caused by their own 'selfish' academic and professional ambitions." This critique was led by Alice Dunnigan, a high-powered Washington-based black correspondent for the Associated Negro Press; Deborah Wolfe, education chief for the U.S. House of Representatives Committee on Education and Labor; and Inabel Lindsay, dean of Howard University's School of Social Work. These members worried that black men would not be able to assume the role of defender and provider for the family with such overbearing wives, although Harris points out that some on the committee, including Height, resisted Dunnigan's ideas.[123] Still, the committee's final report echoed Dunnigan's findings. While the report pointed to the barriers to education and employment for black men, noting that women often had more education and higher-paying jobs, it also argued that this was "demoralizing" to men and detrimental to children, who would not develop the proper understanding of masculine and feminine roles without "a strong male model." In this "matriarchal type family," the report hypothesized, "is it any wonder that a child may find the man who is 'beating the game' a more tempting model to follow than a hard-working parent stuck in a low-paid job?"[124] In summarizing the committee's findings, Height concluded that "'if the Negro woman has a major underlying concern, it is the status of the Negro man and his position in the community and his need for feeling himself an important person, free and able to make his contribution in the whole society in order that he may strengthen his home.'"[125] This statement was quoted by the black press, including the *Baltimore Afro-American*, shortly after the meeting and then again in the *New York Amsterdam News* shortly before the report's release. It was also included in the conclusion of the committee's report.[126]

Moynihan then used Height's quote in his infamous 1965 report to argue that "the testimony to the effects of these patterns [of matriarchy] in Negro family structure is widespread, and hardly to be doubted."[127] Moynihan's report was highly controversial in that instead of blaming structural problems for black poverty, he cited behavioral problems within the black community, thus placing the blame on the poor themselves, especially black women. Moynihan emphasized the breakdown of the black nuclear family under a domineering mother and an absent father. Although the Consultation on Problems of Negro Women committee had emphasized that it was structural racism that prevented black men from succeeding, and thus thrust black women into the role of head of the household, it had also criticized women who took too large of a role and emphasized that this structure was detrimental to the well-being of black families and communities. Thus, Height's immediate reaction to Moynihan's use of her quote was to reinforce his conclusions by confirming the importance of her own nuclear-family experience to her development.[128] She supported the report further by handing out copies of it to council contacts and making the theme of the November 1965 annual convention exploring the black woman's role in the family. However, after other participants at the NCNW convention criticized Height's support of the report and pointed out the ways that it was deeply problematic, she pulled away from endorsing it. One month after the convention, Moynihan complained that even Dorothy Height had turned on him.[129]

Height was also personally influenced by these concerns of women's dominance. She never married because she wanted to fully pursue her activism without worrying that she was overshadowing a husband. In a series of interviews in the mid-1970s, Height admitted that she had been attracted to and dated some very interesting and dynamic men, but according to Height, they found it difficult to "accept the fact that, you know, that I was a person." Instead, her suitors expected that as a wife, Height would push her own interests to the background in order to promote her husband's interests. While Height initially supported the Moynihan Report, she was also cognizant of the toll that the traditional family structure took on women: "I found it very hard to believe that the Lord intended for one person to subdue herself and become something else just for the love and friendship of another person." She believed that "the over-emphasis on marriage has destroyed so many people," especially vibrant, motivated women who had to take a backseat to their husbands. She also had the example of contemporary activist women in New York and Washington who had never married, were divorced, or never had children.[130] Ultimately, she decided that single life was more fulfilling for what she wanted to accomplish: "I just said to myself, that there are some things that I want to accomplish while I live, and I can't do it if I'm going to be upset by worrying whether or not someone else feels that I'm overshadowing or I'm doing something." This realization brought her much relief.[131]

Still, as the leader of the largest black women's club organization in the country, Height continued to publicly promote a respectable nuclear-family model. She recognized the patronizing attitudes of her male (and even some female) counterparts, but with the voices of Frazier, Lewis, Dunnigan, and later Moynihan resonating in her mind, she also insisted that black women had to support the interests of black men in general.[132] In hindsight, in her 2003

autobiography *Open Wide the Freedom Gates*, Height argued that women's ex-
clusion from the March on Washington leadership was "vital to awakening the
women's movement." She pointed out that the male leaders "were happy to include women in the human family, but there was no question as to who headed
the household!"[133] But in truth, she was not outspoken about the sexism that
she or other black women faced at the time.[134] Instead, as she had always
done, she looked for an alternative strategy to circumvent these limitations.
There was still plenty to be done, with or without the support of men.

The (mostly male) organizers of the 1963 March on Washington had requested that no organizations hold separate meetings after the march. However, recent violence against young protesters pushed Height to violate this
request. Only a few months prior, Height, along with Jeanne Noble, then
president of Delta Sigma Theta, spoke out on WNEW, a popular New York
City radio station, to describe the disturbing details to thousands of listen-
ers.[135] Danielle McGuire has pointed out that when Height and Noble took
to the airwaves in the first week of June, "respectability and reticence, hall-
marks of the black clubwomen's movement in the early twentieth century,
gave way to stark testimony." Both women described how guards had forced
imprisoned women to strip naked and endure these invasive and unsanitary
exams. Height minced no words in calling these examinations rape.[136] A few
days later, members of the NCNW met with eleven other black women's
groups at Holly Knoll near Capahosic, Virginia, and formed a Youth Emergency Fund to place a "spotlight" on the abuse of young women in prisons.
They felt they were forced to do this given the "failure of the Federal officials
to act in the face of the mounting number of complaints of personal and
actual abuses." Height and Noble, now joined by Lena Horne, reiterated their
concerns in a press conference at the *New York Amsterdam News* office on
June 11, the same day that President Kennedy would announce the push for
a Civil Rights Act and the day before Medgar Evers would be killed.[137]
Height repeated their concerns yet again at a gathering of civil rights leaders
in Washington on the morning of Medgar Evers's burial.[138] Although this
testimony disclosed a less-than-respectable topic, Height felt it was the duty
of the NCNW to speak out in defense of these women, especially given
the long history of black women's sexual exploitation. A few days before
Evers's murder, Fannie Lou Hamer, June Johnson, and Annelle Ponder were
beaten and sexually abused in Winona, Mississippi, after being pulled over on
their way back from a citizenship training school in South Carolina.[139] Miss
Bessie Turner of Clarksdale, Unita Blackwell, Faith Holsaert, and countless
others had either been threatened with or received physical and sexual abuse

at the hands of police and jailers.[140] The sexual abuse of black (and some white activist) women pushed the council toward more significant involvement in the civil rights movement.

After the March on Washington, Height brought together a group of women at the Shoreham Hotel on August 29 at a gathering called "After the March— What?"[141] She encouraged women's groups to think about how they could become more involved in the civil rights movement, especially in activities oriented toward women, arguing that they had a special task to look after the concerns of education, childcare, and housing.[142] She also offered a platform for young women activists to describe their stories of voter registration and the horrid conditions they had faced in southern jails. One of the young women who had been present at the meeting was Prathia Hall, a SNCC field secretary who called Height a month later to ask her for help investigating the imprisonment of three hundred youths arrested for supporting a local voter registration drive.[143] According to Height, she and the women at the post–March on Washington meeting "were really trying to build more of a climate of support around these young people, and also to bring to public attention the way they were being treated."[144] Local activists Frederick Reese and Amelia P. Boynton, who had both helped found the Dallas County Voters League in Selma, had organized this 1963 voter registration drive.[145] Boynton was the widow of the county's black agricultural extension agent and an independent businesswoman who owned an employment and insurance agency.[146] Southern black women who owned their own businesses were often able to become more involved in the civil rights movement, especially if their business catered solely to the black community, but the brutal tactics of Selma sheriff Jim Clark discouraged most local blacks from even making the attempt. Boynton bravely fought against injustice but still welcomed outside help.

That help would not come from Washington. The federal government did little in reaction to official violence in Alabama, claiming that its hands were tied by the constitutional limits on federal intervention in state police matters. As John Doar recalled years later, "We weren't going to put policemen down there to guard every SNCC worker wherever he might go. . . . We were going to enforce the law through the standard method of law enforcement, which was to bring actions against persons who interfered with citizens' right to register and to vote."[147] And yet even when black citizens were blocked from registering through violence, the FBI and other federal officials did little to punish those who hindered the process.

Despite the overwhelming conviction within the African American community that black women were less likely to face severe repercussions than were black men, these women were beaten, tortured, and raped for defying white supremacy and aiding the civil rights movement.[148] Black women in America had long been exposed to sexual violence at the hands of slave masters, and once "free," they were still vulnerable to assault while serving as domestic workers. Darlene Clark Hine argues that black women often employed tactics of dissemblance to shield themselves from the cruel yet all-too-common realities of rape and sexual abuse. Instead of speaking out about this experience, many refused to acknowledge it for fear of reinforcing white stereotypes of black women as sexually promiscuous. Silence thus became a form of respectability and an answer to the cruelty inflicted on them. Dissemblance allowed black women to control one aspect of their lives, but it also kept many from protesting their abuse. Not all black women dissembled, however. In fact, civil rights activists Ida B. Wells and Rosa Parks, as well as victim Recy Taylor, refused to dissemble and helped activate the antilynching activism of the late nineteenth century as well as the civil rights work of the mid-twentieth century. When Height and Noble spoke out on WNEW, they were driven by a long-standing "tradition of testimony" of black activist women who were motivated at key moments to speak out against sexual exploitation. These struggles against the rape of black women helped motivate and inspire other civil rights efforts, including the future civil rights work of the NCNW.[149]

IN THE FIRST twenty-five years of its organization, the council focused on opening professional opportunities for African American women and helping to integrate them into liberal America. This provided an important network of black middle-class women, who believed that they bolstered the power of the race when their own power increased. While they were involved in lobbying efforts against discrimination, they were more interested in promoting the leadership of black women both nationally and internationally. Given these targeted goals and its elitist reputation, the council was unable to attract a large grassroots constituency. During the presidencies of Vivian Mason and Dorothy Height, the NCNW began to focus more on direct support of the civil rights movement. This shift began to push its activism away from the staid teas, balls, and cotillions of earlier decades and toward the support of direct-action civil rights activists. Still, the council continued to promote itself as an organization of professional women, thereby maintaining its elite image of "hats and white gloves."[150] While the NCNW supported the civil rights efforts of groups such as CORE, SNCC, and the SCLC—both financially and through lobbying for changes to federal legislation—its members were not yet willing to take off the gloves and get their hands dirty.

CHAPTER TWO

Creating a Ministry of Presence

Setting Up an Interracial Civil Rights Organization, 1963–1964

The young activists' imprisonment in Selma provided a devastating but important opportunity for Height and the national NCNW to become more directly involved in the civil rights movement while still focusing on women and children. But Height was the ultimate strategist. Having worked in the worlds of Christian and white philanthropic organizations, she decided to go down to Selma with another black woman—Dr. Dorothy Ferebee, the former NCNW president—and two white women—Shirley Smith, a Freedom Rider and president of the newly created National Women's Committee on Civil Rights, and Polly Cowan, a white volunteer member of the NCNW. Height first met Cowan at a meeting of the Taconic Foundation and was impressed by her thoughtful commentary on the meeting. Height felt, "If I had been in the same situation, I would have wanted to cover it in the same way."[1] From that moment forward, Height and Cowan became genuine friends, both learning from and treating each other with patience and respect.[2]

The council-sponsored team flew down to Selma on the first Friday of October 1963 to investigate the violence. Members of the Dallas County Voters League were organizing for the Freedom Day voter registration drive for the following Monday, and the police had reacted with characteristic violence.[3] Instead of protecting black demonstrators, Selma sheriff Jim Clark and his police force took pride in encouraging violence against them. Earlier that week, over three hundred ten- to twelve-year-olds had been placed in local jails while trying to help their parents register to vote. The youngsters had been stuffed into jail cells and fed food mixed with sawdust, and prison guards had sexually threatened the female prisoners.[4] This violence at the hands of authorities, coupled with the fact that it had been less than a month since four children had been killed at the 16th Street Baptist Church in Birmingham, pushed the council-sponsored group to investigate and report back to their respective national organizations. While Height and Ferebee focused on meeting with and supporting the young black activists of Selma, Cowan and Smith planned to make contacts with any local white women who might be friendly to the movement.

Height understood the importance of not only using her respectable presence as a middle-class black woman but also working with white women of stature. With the help of these white women, Height and the women of the NCNW were able to bring heightened attention to the problems facing black activists in the South. But Height's civil rights team was still very much upper and middle class. Its focus was on using a respectable interracial presence to try to impress southerners, especially white ones, to openly and publicly support civil rights. The Selma group also hoped that their clout might enrage federal officials enough to change the conditions for black activists in the South. This short trip became the model for Wednesdays in Mississippi, an interracial organization sponsored by the NCNW a half a year later, which brought black and white northern and western women to Mississippi in support of Freedom Summer. Though important in drawing national attention to the conditions African Americans faced in the deep South, these programs of interracial witness in the fall of 1963 and summer of 1964 were limited and seemingly far removed from the dangerous, direct-action daily work of locals like Amelia P. Boynton and SNCC activists like Prathia Hall, who worked on the ground to improve the conditions of African Americans in the Deep South.

Alabama's Police State

The interracial team's first stop on the way to Selma was the Atlanta YWCA, where the women spent three and a half hours making calls to activists in Selma's black community to confirm their plans, but they were unable to get through to any of their contacts. They were told that the numbers they were trying to reach were not working numbers. Only if they made a call through an operator would it go through. As Selma team member Cowan recalls, "We came to the conclusion that in this way all calls could be monitored, . . . as all were to people connected with voter registration either directly or in sympathy with the effort." Even before they had arrived, the group was experiencing the surveillance of Alabama's police state.[5]

While at the Atlanta Y, Dorothy Height set up a meeting with Dorothy Tilly of the Southern Regional Council. Tilly was a southern white woman who had worked for desegregation both through moral suasion in church organizations and through legislation. Height wanted to gain insight into the challenges that the interracial team would face in Selma, but as a white activist, there were limitations to Tilly's knowledge. Tilly's Methodist background inspired her and provided her with tangible opportunities to work interracially, though rarely with African American women having an equal footing. She first worked with the Women's Missionary Society of the Methodist Church. Since the early twentieth century, this organization had encouraged its white female members to help remedy the inferior housing, education, and recreational facilities available to black men and women throughout the South.[6] Tilly next worked with the Commission on Interracial Cooperation (CIC), a biracial group that sought to improve race relations through education, re-search, and persuasion but, like many moderate southern organizations, did not publicly challenge segregation.[7] Through the CIC, Tilly formed a friendship with Mary McLeod Bethune.[8] In the 1930s, Tilly joined Jessie Daniel Ames's Association of Southern Women for the Prevention of Lynching (ASWPL), an organization of white southern women who sought to prevent lynching by fighting it at the local level, and a decade later served as the Southern Re-gional Council's director of women's work.[9] In 1948, she served as a member of President Truman's Committee on Civil Rights, and in 1949, she created a new women's organization called the Fellowship of the Concerned, using her faith to support the fight for justice for black and white southerners. In only one year's time, four thousand women had joined.[10]

The Fellowship of the Concerned continued the legacy of Jesse Daniel Ames's ASWPL by forming a "ministry of presence" of white respectable women to observe the unfair trials of black men charged with the rape of white women in the South. The women also accompanied their black em-ployees to the polls to help them safely vote.[11] These white women sought to knock down racial inequality in a private, personal way. They hoped that by accompanying their maids to the polls, or by sitting in southern courtrooms to remind judges and juries that upstanding white ladies were watching, they might stop the most egregious injustices. Southern white women in the Fellow-ship of the Concerned thus deployed their race and gender to their advantage as activists. Their behavior was not disruptive or offensive, but they reminded white men of their responsibility as "gentlemen" to ensure that justice rather than lawlessness ruled the courtroom. Thus, they believed that the visible display of their femininity and their all-white constituency was essential to the effectiveness of their activism.[12]

The fellowship initially formed to ensure justice for African Americans in southern courtrooms, but in 1953, it began preparing white southerners for the end of segregation by encouraging its mainly female members to teach tolerance to their children, which would ultimately reduce racial prejudice and build a more egalitarian society.[13] This activism remained largely behind the scenes, "effecting social reform under the protective and comfortable guise of domesticity."[14] This personal strategy required only that a woman influence members of her nuclear family and was a relatively safe form of activism for white women in the South who wanted to do "something" but did not want to jeopardize their families economically, socially, or politically. Especially in the 1940s and 1950s, when any progressive action was deemed communist, white activist women learned to hide their "subversive" efforts. As historian Sarah Wilkerson-Freeman argues, their actions often remain "clouded in obscurity in part because women deliberately hid and disguised their most subversive political activity in order to fool, disarm, and outmaneuver their opponents."[15] Even so, white women were sometimes threatened with violence, but far less often than black women. Tilly took into account the reality that few white women would risk alienation from their communities to take a strong public stance against segregation. Although Anne Braden, Lillian Smith, and Virginia Durr had done so, they were dramatic exceptions to the generally united front of white opposition to integration.[16]

Although Tilly's organization was clearly limited in its challenge of segregation, Height was still willing to work with her. Height was not averse to the liberal strategy of promoting civil rights efforts that focused on moral suasion and personal change as activism. Sensing that working with white women was important even when it was limited, Height participated in white-dominated women's organizational efforts. In December 1961, Height served as the only black woman on the President's Commission on the Status of Women (PCSW), although Jeanne Noble, Pauli Murray, and Addie Wyatt sat in on other subcommittees.[17] The larger commission was largely led by labor union women, including the commission's de facto leader Esther Peterson, director of the Women's Bureau. (Eleanor Roosevelt was the PCSW honorary head until her death in 1962.) The work of the PCSW led to the passage of equal pay legislation in 1963 and nondiscrimination laws in the 1960s and 1970s. Like many of the labor union women in the commission, the NCNW opposed the Equal Rights Amendment, seeing it as a danger to black women, who worked in the harshest conditions and needed protective legislation.[18] Still, the white women of the PCSW did little to incorporate the concerns of black women into their agenda. Although Dorothy Height had wanted the conclusions of the special consultation on "the Problems of Negro Women," which she headed (see chapter 1), to be in the final report of the larger commission, only a few references about black women were made, though the report did have a statement on discrimination against black women in employment.[19]

Despite such setbacks, Height and the council continued to be an important presence at other liberal, majority-white women's meetings, including President Kennedy's White House Conference on Civil Rights for women in the summer of 1963. Three hundred white and black women from national volunteer organizations congregated in Washington to discuss what role women's clubs could play in the passage of Kennedy's proposed civil rights bill. Enthused by the excitement generated at this initial conference, this group of clubwomen formed the National Women's Committee on Civil Rights (NWCCR) to act as a clearinghouse for information about the bill. The group was composed mainly of white women from national voluntary organizations—some were integrated, but most allowed their southern branches to remain segregated. The meeting's goals remained largely symbolic.[20] An August 15 pamphlet encouraged committee members to assist with desegregation of schools and to "talk with members of Negro organizations . . . about the kind of citizen support which they think might be helpful. Consult with police officials and religious leaders. Talk to newspaper editors, radio and television editors."[21] Much like Tilly's Fellowship of the Concerned, the NWCCR strategy involved behind-the-scenes efforts that would not disrupt the status quo on a large scale; however, it was never quite clear what the next step would be or how communication would lead to school integration, the right to vote, or social acceptance of blacks by whites.

While most NWCCR white women did not push for any racial change that might disrupt their national organizations, two white participants—Polly Cowan and Shirley Smith, who were both leaders within the organization—pushed the NWCCR to be more forceful in promoting integration in the South.[22] They believed that white southerners were capable of supporting integration and that southern white women's "previous lack of action on behalf of racial justice reflected a want of effort rather than a want of will."[23] But some of the affiliate organizations of the NWCCR, such as the American Association of University Women (AAUW), could not agree on integration as a goal and did not want to risk alienating those constituent organizations that allowed segregation of local branches. As a result, the group was not able to accomplish much and became nearly defunct after Senate passage of the Civil Rights Act on March 30, 1964. Most participants in the NWCCR believed, and perhaps accurately, that Smith and Cowan's notion that a multitude of southern white women secretly supported integration was unrealistic and that more intervention in the South was unlikely to change their minds.[24] But Cowan and Smith remained inspired by the interracial NWCCR meetings and traveled with Height and Ferebee down to Selma. They hoped that they, as northern white women, could serve a unique role in creating communication links with southern whites who had been paralyzed into inaction by fear and misinformation.[25]

Cowan and Smith were in for a rude awakening. On the plane to Alabama, the NCNW team met SNCC's Jim Forman and comedian Dick Gregory, who were also traveling to Selma for the Freedom Day rally. Gregory's pregnant wife had been jailed for her activism in preparation for Freedom Day. When the group landed in Montgomery, Boynton could not fit Height and Ferebee in her car, so the northern interracial group of women rode in Cowan and Smith's rental car to Selma. Height and Ferebee, aware of the danger of traveling interracially, suggested that they pretend to be cooks for their white colleagues. Years later, Cowan described her discomfort with the ruse: "It is difficult to describe how frustrated I felt at the realization that such a pretense was necessary." Ferebee and Height were the second and fourth respective presidents of the NCNW; they had also been the presidents of major national black sororities. Ferebee, a physician, was the medical director of Howard University Health Services. This was one of the first difficult lessons that Cowan would learn in the segregated South.[26] Height, on the other hand, recalled years later that she and Ferebee laughed about the ploy. However, their laughter quickly ceased when they saw two cars pull out behind them; the cars followed them for the rest of the trip.[27]

The four drove to First Baptist Church, where they ultimately interviewed sixty-four of the boys and girls who had been arrested, confirming Prathia Hall's earlier reports of police brutality. The children had indeed been crowded into cells without room to sit on the floor, with no blankets, little water, and food mixed with sawdust and salt.[28] Many of the children's parents were unable to learn the whereabouts of their children. If parents asked about their child's location, they themselves were jailed. One mother introduced Height to her emaciated eleven-year-old daughter, who had a stomach condition that forced her to take special food. While the child was in jail, her mother had not been allowed to see her, but she had brought her special food for the whole week; the guards had never fed it to her. When her daughter was released from jail, she was "skin and bones," and the food was sitting in a corner of the jail, "rotting, filled with maggots and vermin." Other children told stories about eating food mixed with "boll weevil gravy."[29] From these stories, the four visitors came face to face with the ugly reality of police tactics against children and their families in Selma. Sometimes, in order to shield their parents from repercussions of violence, these young people gave false names. Height recalled that during her stay in Selma, she met children who possessed a strength that their parents did (or could) not have. Height recalled a teenager whose mother was having difficulty accepting her daughter's activism. This young woman asked Height, "'What do you do when you're really trying to say to your mother that you are working so that she won't need to be so fearful?'"[30] These young people's sacrifice was even more extraordinary given that the 16th Street Baptist Church in Birmingham had been bombed only three weeks prior. Clearly, white supremacists in Alabama were not beyond injuring and killing black children to maintain the power structure of the state.[31]

Height and Ferebee's presence in Selma signaled the interest and concern of the NCNW in grassroots organizing in the South. They were most concerned with investigating the jail conditions of the black youth in Selma and hoped that they might be able to spread the word about the horrible conditions the children faced. According to Height, the Selma trip was the beginning of the council's "unique involvement in the struggle for freedom in the South."[32] Height and Ferebee later spoke at a rally held at First Baptist Church in preparation for the Freedom Day voter registration drive the following Monday. Height brought greetings from the women of the NCNW, but she also remained distant from the direct-action struggle, claiming that "there is very little that any of us can bring to you. We can only take from you the sense of dedication to the whole cause of freedom and assure you that your sisters and brothers across this land are with you."[33] Despite the council leaders' distance from the direct-action work, local law enforcement did not make the same distinction. Height and Ferebee later learned that they had both been issued a summons for contributing to the delinquency of minors, simply for speaking with the young men and women at the church that night.[34]

Although interested in being a part of the Freedom Day rally, Cowan and Smith feared their presence as white women might not only bring added violence against black civil rights workers but also hurt their efforts to make inroads among local white women. However, when the two white women arrived for the Friday evening event, Jim Forman encouraged them to sit on the stage as well. Smith excused herself from the stage, as she had not received permission from the NWCCR, her sponsoring organization, but Cowan had no similar excuse. Cowan admitted later that she was initially hesitant but also excited by the energy of the rally, and she wanted to show her support as a white northerner.[35] Not only did Cowan sit on the stage, but after Height spoke, she got up and offered a few words on behalf of civil rights supporters in New York.

The rally ended around 10:30 P.M., but the NCNW women stayed so the girls who had been jailed could tell the NCNW women "things they could say to women that they didn't or couldn't say to men." Cowan recalled the warden threatening the 12- to 16-year-old girls that if they didn't behave, he would let the male prisoners into their cells. The girls did not remove their clothes that night.[36] Height recalled a similar story, saying that the teenage girls "huddled themselves up so that if an effort was made to attack any, they could all fight back as a group."[37] The northern white women were horrified that the guards had not only starved the prisoners but also sexually threatened the young girls. However, as Height already knew, this was far from extraordinary.

After an hour, though, SNCC photographer Danny Lyon strongly suggested that it was time to leave, and he urged the women to keep their eyes down and follow him. Cowan noticed that there was still a large gathering of teenage boys standing on the church porch. She later realized that they would have to stay on the porch until someone picked them up in a car. If they attempted to walk home, they faced being harassed or even killed. But most adults were hesitant to drive them home because they themselves could be charged with contributing to the delinquency of a minor or even suffer violent reprisals.[38] Such intimidation was common. Cowan recalled her astonishment: "How can you keep your eyes down when you're beset by curiosity? I didn't know we [were] going to confront an army. But we were." Fifty helmeted state troopers waited in the churchyard. She continued, "They stood in clumps. It was dark—only one dim street light—so I couldn't see them all at first. . . . These men had been issued pistols, carbines, riot guns, submachine guns, tear gas and cattle prods." The effect of this intimidation was formidable. She concluded, "The bright orange helmets and arm bands added to the impression that this was an invasion. And invasion against what? Teenagers and women."[39] These were the forces that black civil rights activists in the Deep South faced as they insisted on equal access to voting and education for themselves and their communities.

Anguished Liberals

Ferebee and Height returned north the next day, but they encouraged Cowan and Smith to stay to try to make inroads in the local white community. The white women stayed to meet with two self-described "anguished liberal" southern white women (recommended by Tilly)—Rosa Miller Joyce, the daughter of former Alabama senator Sam Hobbs, and Kathrine Cothran, director of Christian education at Selma First Presbyterian Church.[40] Cowan and Smith were eager to speak with these interested white women in hopes that they might support local black-led civil rights efforts. But as Cowan and Smith discovered, Joyce and Cothran were frustrated by earlier efforts to work with the local white and black communities, and were also frightened about repercussions if they became publicly involved in the movement. Although their racial ideas were relatively conservative, these women had pushed for integration of the First Presbyterian Church. They believed that their church had made great progress by allowing four black girls to sit in the balcony. However, when the local paper reported that the church had "integrated," it caused an uproar that led the Presbyterian elders to abandon their "open door" policy. Joyce and Cothran feared that their beloved pastor would resign over the elders' decision and be replaced by an avid segregationist.

The two women were also concerned about other efforts related to school integration and voter registration. Like most whites in the Deep South at the time, Joyce and Cothran suspected that voter registration activism was communist inspired, and they had little sympathy for African American activists if that was indeed the case.[41] They also claimed that they had tried to work with local whites, but when one of them asked the mayor what she could do to help with integration, he had told her, "Go home and lock your door until it's over. Nothing is going to make us change around here."[42] They also had little luck working with local black activists. Joyce had tried to talk to members of First Baptist Church, but the preacher told her that he had nothing to do with the movement. He made it clear he did not want to be involved personally out of concern for his safety and livelihood. Given the propensity of whites to attack civil rights workers in Alabama, the black preacher of First Baptist Church had good reason to be suspicious of any whites in the community, even those claiming to want to help with integration. But as Cowan noted, Joyce "felt the door shut in her face on both sides."[43]

Smith and Cowan helped Joyce and Cothran develop a limited plan of action—to meet in a black woman's home to discuss racial issues—as they did not want to risk their own safety by inviting blacks into their homes. Thus, black women continued to bear the burden of fostering interracialism and the risks that ensued.[44] Joyce and Cothran, in turn, informed their northern visitors that "no one wanted any outside help," and if information about their meeting with Cowan and Smith got out, it would ruin any chance for communication and progress within the local white community.[45] Cowan and Smith still felt that while limited, this was a step in the right direction. But the following morning, the *Selma Times Reporter* revealed that Smith and Cowan had attended the Freedom Day rally at First Baptist Church. After reading the newspaper, the two southerners felt betrayed by their northern guests, who had seemed concerned for their well-being but had been so public in their support of the black community. As a result, the two white women from

Selma refused to proceed with their plans to offer further support to the local black freedom struggle. Indeed, they decided to cancel a meeting with Dorothy Tilly the following Monday without informing her. Instead, they left the frail eighty-year-old activist stranded at the airport. When Tilly called to see why no one had arrived to pick her up, Cothran replied, " 'We have been betrayed. These women, Mrs. Polly and Shirley, told us they came because they were interested in this community. But they have been with *those* people' " (emphasis in original).[46]

These were the tremendous obstacles that local black leaders like Amelia Boynton faced in trying to solicit the aid of local whites. However, instead of giving up on the white Selma community, Cowan believed that there might still be hope for white activists to become involved, as long as they could stay behind the scenes. Immediately following the trip, Cowan wrote, "I think we must conclude from this experience that it is best if women go into these communities quietly and anonymously." Cowan and Smith had become swept up in the excitement of the Freedom Day rally and had alienated the very women they had hoped to convince to join their efforts. But instead of concluding that these women's continued adherence to white supremacy made the situation hopeless, Cowan altered her strategy so as not to offend them. She and Smith decided that any future activities targeting white southern women needed to be done in a quiet, unobtrusive way; otherwise, they might refuse to help.[47] In making this decision, Cowan and Smith believed that they were taking the only course of action that would slowly build a climate of support for the black freedom struggle among white women, though it involved catering to the concerns of local whites at the expense of taking a public stand against segregation.[48]

While Joyce and Cothran feared social and economic reprisals, black women in Selma faced much higher risks for their activism. After all, it was young black women in Selma who had been jailed and sexually threatened by prison guards for their activism, while adult women faced equally frightening and dangerous repercussions. When a group of black women who worked at Dunn's Rest Home in Selma tried to register to vote shortly after the NCNW-led group returned home, Dr. Dunn fired one and beat another on her back and across her face with an electric cattle prod.[49] Meanwhile, on Freedom Day itself, the FBI simply observed as protesters were accosted and arrested by Sheriff Jim Clark on the federal courthouse steps.[50] Although the Selma NCNW team did not directly witness these incidents, they heard stories about these types of brutal attacks on black southern women. While this reinforced the NCNW activists' belief that something had to be done, it also made clear the cost of high-risk public activism.

While their activism was not usually considered "high risk," some southern white women involved in interracial efforts became victims of dangerous emotional, physical, and sexual threats, in addition to finding themselves socially and economically ostracized. Jane Schutt, who was a member of the Mississippi State Advisory Committee of the U.S. Commission on Civil Rights, received numerous threatening phone calls, and a cross was burned and dynamite was thrown on her front lawn.[51] Another white woman from Maryland, Anne Karro, was arrested in Danville, Virginia, for carrying a placard that read "No more segregation" and passing out voter registration flyers. This upper-middle-class white mother of three was thrown into the Danville jail. Five days later, she was taken from her cell and led to a room where she was to be "examined." Without consulting her, the jailer drew blood from her arm. Next, an unidentified white man asked her if he could do a "pelvic exam." She objected, which caused quite a stir, since she was the first person to ever resist the examination. Karro wrote, "The matron said in a low voice to the jailer that nobody had objected before in the time she had been there, and if this objection was allowed there would be trouble with others. The jailer then threatened: 'If you don't let him do it, the doctor will have to.' 'I want to speak to my lawyer,' I repeated. We were then returned to our cells."[52] As the wife of a prominent attorney, Karro knew and insisted on her rights. While black women had privately endured physical and sexual abuse for centuries, Karro demanded a public response. She sent written testimony of her experience to the U.S. Senate, the American Medical Association, and newspapers in New York and Philadelphia. She thus used her power as an upper-middle-class white woman to enrage Americans like her.[53] Karro recognized the part classism and racism played in setting a higher priority for wealthy white women's suffering over that of black women and used this awareness to gain support for campaigns to stop the sexual abuse of all women—black and white—in jails.

Cadillac Crowd

After returning from Selma, Cowan began to develop an idea for a new type of civil rights organization based on the Selma trip. With Dorothy Height's encouragement, she began to brainstorm how white women like herself could be most useful to black freedom efforts. In a letter written from London on

November 14, 1963, titled "Women in the Civil Rights Movement, Variations on a Theme," Cowan began to formulate a plan for a "Cadillac Crowd" of upper-middle-class women, whose class status would offer them protection from harassment and violence.[54] She believed that the elite status of all four participants in Selma—black and white—had shielded them from violence from the police and the local white community.[55] Cowan asked, "Could we organize a group of wealthy and powerful women (women of influence, connections, stature in their communities) who would go to several troubled areas simultaneously[?]" Perhaps, she thought, southerners would reevaluate their beliefs about "beatnik" civil rights workers if they saw a new model of civil rights worker. In order to knock down such stereotypes, she would overwhelm southern women with an ostentatious display of integrated wealth and respectability. She continued, "I would recommend chauffeur driven cars to be sent South ahead of an airplane arrival by the women. Or, in the case of women who live within driving distance and have status symbol cars of their own, they might drive themselves." She thought that the "distinguished look of the car's occupants will almost certainly put some fear into the power structure at the local level."[56]

Cowan's plan of having cars filled with interracial teams of wealthy women drive around the South seems vastly out of touch with the reality of racial violence that she had just witnessed in Selma, but the plan made sense given Cowan's background. As an affluent heiress of the Spiegel mail-order business, who was also Jewish, Cowan had experienced discrimination but also understood the power of affluence in challenging inequality. In addition, like Mary McLeod Bethune, Polly's young husband, Louis (and Polly by proxy), became involved in the world of government, working with the dollar-a-year executives in the Roosevelt administration during World War II. Afterward, Louis moved up in the private sphere, first producing *The $64,000 Question* and then moving on to be president of CBS TV. Polly continued to enjoy a privileged lifestyle, with access to a wide range of cultural events and part-time professional opportunities, but she also felt frustrated at times by the corporate company she and Louis kept. As her children have remarked, Polly was different from the other business wives: she had an "equal passion for fashion and social justice."[57] She did not see her participation in high society and social justice as competing but rather as enabling great change. She had also been involved in progressive causes in the 1930s and later attempted to aid Jewish refugees from the Holocaust. She had wanted to help more and remained haunted by the Holocaust. This served as an impetus to become more involved in all types of social justice issues. As her son Paul recalled, "Her feelings about the Holocaust also imbued her—and [her children]—with a secular messianism: a deep commitment to the belief that we had a lifelong debt to the six million dead." She encouraged her children to fight not only anti-Semitism but all forms of injustice.[58] She donated much time and money to the NCNW and even sat on its executive board.

Cowan had access to centers of power and wanted to use her influence to support the civil rights cause on behalf of the NCNW, for which she was now volunteering regularly. In her November letter, she envisioned groups of three to five women traveling south in "Truth squad cars" filled with influential female reporters, including Inez Robb, Marya Mannes, Mary McGrory, and Doris Fleeson, who she believed could report on what was happening. They would not only be a visible and respectable presence but also be able to circulate information about the movement between the South and the North. She continued, "The car's owner (for example Mrs. Marshall Field) [along with] a friend who is [a] trained observer (like Mrs. Field's friend Lillian Helman [sic]) plus a Negro woman of importance (of whom Mrs. Field has many as friends)." Cowan knew that she could rely on her networks of prominent white acquaintances to engage in this type of activism. Elite women would move around the South together, waving their white gloves in the face of Jim Crow. "Groups like this would be duplicated—sometimes two or three cars to one town, sometimes to adjacent towns, sometimes one car full to one town," Cowan suggested, "all to be carefully assessed in terms of the situation in the area."[59] She envisioned affluent black and white women bridging racial and regional gaps by stressing their similar prominence.

Of course, middle-class black women had long been involved in struggles for black freedom and did not need interracial projects to inspire them to action. The women of the NCNW had long worked in both direct and indirect ways to fight against inequality. Black women like Rosa Parks, Daisy Bates, Anna Arnold Hedgeman, and Ella Baker had taken central roles in the southern fight for desegregation. Much like middle-class white northern women, black women wanted to become involved in the movement, but unlike white women, they faced more severe repercussions, and no matter what they did, their skin color marked them as inferior by mainstream American society.

From this initial idea, Cowan developed her plans for what would become Wednesdays in Mississippi (WIMS). She wrote that her Selma trip should serve as a model for other interracial groups to open dialogue in communities "where the communication has never existed or where it has broken down."[60] The participants would witness what was happening in the movement and open lines of communication for southern white women who wanted to help but did not know with whom to talk or what to say. She wrote, "The raison d'être for these women being in troubled spots should be the same as Mrs. Tilly's Fellowship of the Concerned: because they care, they want to know the truth, they want to help."[61] They would become, in Cowan's mind, a "ministry of presence," to bring light to white southerners struggling to support integration.[62]

Like a Long-Handled Spoon

While Cowan was working on creating a project that would bring affluent white and black northerners down to the South, Height maintained her focus on investigating police brutality against young activists and reaffirmed her commitment for the council to become more actively involved in student-led civil rights activism. In addition to its support for activist scholarships, the NCNW invited students to speak at its 1963 national convention that November. Height invited Susie Goodwillie, a white representative working for both the NWCCR and the NCNW, to speak about a tutorial program for middle and high school students. In addition, two SNCC students—Mr. Charles Jones and Miss Bobbi Yancy, southern campus coordinator of SNCC—spoke about the efforts of the students since the sit-ins in 1960. Yancy spoke of the isolation, short staffing, and difficulties faced by SNCC workers. Likewise, Jones mentioned the difficulties and the frustration with the "comfortable professional Negro." He called on the council to remember the students in the South who are often hungry, homeless, and in danger but willing to risk their lives for black equality. After these three presentations, NCNW women broke into discussion groups. One table proposed giving up vacations and giving that travel money to SNCC; another table suggested that one council woman be in touch with SNCC students in every area of their work and deliver supplies to them. The women present also raised $100 in cash on the spot for SNCC.[63]

Height also continued to encourage black and white clubwomen to help investigate the police brutality against civil rights activists. She presented her report about her Selma trip, especially the treatment of the young imprisoned activists, to the national board of the YWCA that fall. This presentation resulted in the creation of the Women's Inter-Organization Council, formed out of the NCNW, the YWCA, the National Council of Catholic Women, the National Council of Jewish Women, the National Council of Catholic Women, and United Church Women.[64] These groups decided to organize an "off-the-record" meeting in Atlanta for the following spring to discuss police brutality against women.[65] This conference took place at the Americana Motor Hotel in Atlanta, with its original purpose being to bring together black and white women from around the South to discuss how to protect young girls in jail.[66]

The Atlanta meeting also offered black and white women an opportunity to discuss their fears about the civil rights struggle, the implementation of judicial decisions and legislation, and reprisals against those who attempted to fight for justice. Still, many of the white southern delegates present at the March 1964 meeting could not bring themselves to address civil rights, as that phrase had been associated with the direct-action efforts of groups like SNCC, the SCLC, and CORE, and seemed too controversial.[67] Instead, as Cowan noted in her observations of the Atlanta meeting, "The women would come together because it was too difficult to say no to a problem of humanity," as children and young adults were the target of mistreatment and abuse.[68] Black and white southern women could discuss the health and well-being of children who had been jailed, but "civil rights" was too highly charged a topic for the white attendees to be the official reason for the meeting.

Some of the women attending the meeting also had misgivings about the impending Freedom Summer voter registration project planned for Mississippi that year.[69] Freedom Summer was a project of the Council of Federated Organizations, or COFO, a coalition founded as an ad hoc group before the Freedom Rides in May 1961 but which became a formal organization in February 1962 to work on direct action and voter registration. COFO in Mississippi drew together SNCC, CORE, the SCLC, and the Mississippi state office of the NAACP.[70] As Cowan learned more about Freedom Summer, she believed that it might be the opportunity they had been waiting for to implement her idea of sending teams of upper-middle-class volunteers to the South.

Both the black and white southern women at the Atlanta conference expressed concerns about the backlash that might result with the Freedom Summer students' arrival. Fear drove the decisions of these middle-class black and white women. In an informal report that Cowan wrote in response to the official "stuffy" report of the March meeting, she spoke about this fear among participants. When the women were asked at the last session if they wanted to exchange names and contact information, there was a resounding no. And when a woman at the meeting tried to take a picture of a presiding officer and a panel of women, some of the participants jumped, as though they had been caught doing something illicit, and begged the photographer to destroy the picture.[71] Even some middle-class black southerners felt threatened by the recent direct-action civil rights activism of SNCC. Many black men and women had been working for a long time in the South before the arrival of the youth organization.[72] Some also believed that as established middle-class southern blacks, they—not the working-class, student, or northern activists—should be the ones directing racial change. Others resisted COFO out of fear. Theirs was a precarious position within southern society; they wanted to hold on to what little power they had under white supremacy.[73]

And yet despite its caution and secrecy, the Atlanta inter-organizational meeting was personally transformative for the participants, especially the white southerners. Black and white women did everything together in the safety of this private meeting. They sat, conversed, and ate together. In the process, the white women were exposed to the true brutality that black women, even these highly respectable clubwomen, faced daily. The interracial group heard stories about participant Mrs. A. G. Gaston of Birmingham, who had a bomb detonated at her house; the employees of Dr. Dunn's rest home in Selma, who had been beaten and fired for voter registration; and cases of forced sterilization in Sunflower County, Mississippi. Both Height and Cowan believed that southern white women could not help but be influenced by even this brief exposure to middle-class black women's experiences. Cowan concluded, "They listened to the telling manner in which one Negro woman after another put the case for her community. It will be impossible for these white women ever again to discuss the relative mentality of white and Negro."[74]

Clarie Collins Harvey—a black businesswoman from Jackson, founder of Womanpower Unlimited (WU), and member of Church Women United (CWU)—and Jane Schutt—the white former president of the Mississippi branch of the CWU, who sat on the United Civil Rights Commission in the late 1950s—told the meeting that this was the first time that black and white Jacksonians had sat together as equals.[75] They also asked for a group to come in from the North and stir up Mississippi as if with a long-handled spoon. Dorothy Height recalls that Harvey asked for northern women to visit Mississippi during the upcoming summer "to act as a quieting influence by going into areas that are racially tense, to try to build bridges of communication between us, between our black and white communities, to be a ministry of presence among us." She stressed, "It would be of tremendous help to us."[76]

Even as Harvey requested outsiders to come "stir things up," she was looking for northerners to add support and money to the southern movement rather than take charge. For the previous three years, Harvey had been leading WU, a Jackson-based organization that fed, clothed, and brought provisions to the Freedom Riders who had been jailed in Parchman penitentiary.

Many members of WU ran businesses in their own community and were thus not subject to white economic reprisals. WU members highlighted their role as mothers, hoping perhaps that cloaking their efforts in the respectability of motherhood would serve as protection. According to Morris, despite Harvey having no children of her own, her "first response demonstrated a 'mothering' instinct—to help these activists in a practical way that would sustain them in their ensuing struggle."[77] While WU initially provided basic needs for the jailed Freedom Riders, it soon expanded its activism as more civil rights activists, including students who entered Mississippi during voter registration campaigns, arrived. Establishing a flexible movement and fluid leadership, the organization fostered the creation of wider activist networks as it continued to provide practical aid.[78] Thus, Jackson's middle-class black community engaged in civil rights efforts well before the Freedom Summer student volunteers or Cowan's Cadillac Crowd arrived.

WU engaged in interracial activism as well. The Interracial Prayer Fellowship Committee sought to foster and encourage cooperation between WU members and sympathetic white women in Jackson. In addition, the organization set up a Chain of Friendship of over three hundred white women around the country who supported its efforts. These "friends" were asked to exert their "influence" in a variety of ways. First the WU asked for the women's prayers and then for their financial support. It also hoped these "friends" could help by lobbying state and federal legislators and patronizing businesses that were active in supporting the movement. They also hoped that white northern women in national organizations like the YWCA or CWU might be able to convince white women in southern branches of the clubs to "fulfill their humanist agenda . . . to improve race relations" and support the local movement.[79]

After receiving the invitation from Harvey, Cowan was thrilled that there might be an opportunity to implement her plan for a Cadillac Crowd. The NCNW—the only black-led, black-majority organization in attendance at the Atlanta meeting—was the only organization that offered to be a national sponsor for Cowan's project. While the other women's groups present at the March meeting allowed Cowan to include their organization's name with the phrase "in association with members of," Church Women United refused to be included, although some members went out on their own.[80] Although it is unclear why CWU had this particular attitude toward Cowan's project, most likely it viewed the project as outside of the interest of the national organization. Much like the difficulties faced by the NWCCR, most national women's organizations still believed that sponsoring interracial projects focused on integration and voter registration was too controversial a goal and might alienate southern chapters.[81] The council's support revealed that once again, black women bore the burden of fostering interracialism. But Height and the NCNW also had much to gain from the sponsorship of this proposed project. The Cadillac Crowd project would be a national project of the council, with funding provided mostly by the participants themselves and money raised through NCNW's tax-exempt Educational Foundation. The project participants were socially conscious black and white women, often with personal ties that might directly benefit the council financially as well as raise visibility for the council's activities on the national level. Perhaps most importantly, the project provided the council with an opportunity to see the movement in the Magnolia State firsthand, and it could claim that it was directly involved in Freedom Summer and the larger civil rights struggle.

With Height's support, Cowan and Smith went to Jackson two months after the Atlanta meeting to make sure that there was still interest in sending teams of observers and to establish contacts for the project.[82] While some local women had concerns about WIMS coming to Jackson, most believed it was at least worth a try, saying, "Try it—try anything." Cowan felt that WIMS's job was not only to be a witness but to transgress the "cotton curtain" by bringing outside news and information to the Jackson women, especially the more progressive members of the white community.[83] Height and Cowan both believed in the importance of this alternative civil rights project, and they began recruiting staff and participants for the summer trips. Much like Cowan's initial vision articulated in her November 1963 letter, interracial and interfaith teams of between five and seven women would travel from northern cities to smaller towns in Mississippi for a total of three days. She hoped that women of prominence would both inspire and financially and socially support Mississippi activists, black and white. But as requested by local black and white middle-class women, they would move behind the scenes to establish contacts on a personal basis only.[84] Thus, from the beginning, the council's first direct-action project was structured not around offering highly public support for the COFO project but around quietly supporting it on a personal basis. Height began to recruit black clubwomen for the project, while Cowan and Smith began to search for white participants to bring this vision of an integrated "behind the scenes" project to life.[85]

ALTHOUGH THE COUNCIL had been involved in a few projects related to civil rights, most of its work until the summer of 1963 was in support of other organizations. At its post–March on Washington meeting in late August,

Dorothy Height made contact with Prathia Hall, who was working on voter registration in Selma. Height then took an interracial team of elite club-women to witness and speak out against the violence against imprisoned teenagers. This model of interracial witnessing drew on Cold War liberal activism that promoted both interracialism and personal moral transformations of whites in order to combat discrimination. After the Selma trip, Polly Cowan and Dorothy Height brainstormed how elite black and white women might use the tactic of personal witness to support the direct-action efforts of student activists, such as those in Selma. Then, at an inter-organizational meeting in March, Clarie Collins Harvey invited Cowan to bring her teams of observers to work in support of the COFO-directed Freedom Summer project. Unlike the other majority-white organizations represented at the March meeting, the NCNW embraced the project wholeheartedly. Thus, while NCNW women were taking off their gloves to work in a more direct way in the movement, they still believed in the power of interracial activism and of personal change as a form of civil rights activism. NCNW women also continued to promote themselves as elite women in hopes that this might help inspire more white southern women to join the larger civil rights cause.

CHAPTER THREE

High Heels on the Ground

The Power of Personal Witness, 1964

As Boston civil rights leader Ruth Batson sat in a planning meeting with other members of the newly formed civil rights organization Wednesdays in Mississippi (WIMS), she pondered whether to take part in their Mississippi project. While SNCC was committed to fighting white supremacy publicly during Freedom Summer, WIMS seemed more concerned with making white locals feel comfortable with the most modest forms of social change. Boston WIMS leader Laya Wiesner, wife of the dean of sciences (and soon to be president) of the Massachusetts Institute of Technology, explained to Batson that unlike the student and local activists of SNCC, WIMS members would attempt to support moderate women in Mississippi. In order to do so, they must remain inconspicuous: rather than visibly challenging Jim Crow, they would travel in segregated vehicles and stay in segregated housing. Although Batson understood that both she and the people in Mississippi would be safer if she adhered to the status quo, she questioned the strategy, especially when hundreds of black and white student volunteers—and the black residents who housed them—refused to abide by segregationist norms.[1]

Batson had fought against white supremacy in Boston, working in the city's Roxbury district schools to ensure that her daughter received the same educational opportunities as whites. She was also the chair of the Massachusetts Committee Against Discrimination, a delegate to the 1964 Democratic National Convention, and the education chairman of the Massachusetts NAACP. She considered herself a firebrand, and others concurred.[2] She had fought for integration for herself, for her daughter, and for her community; she did not want to adhere to the unjust rules of white Mississippi.

Ultimately, however, since she had never been to Mississippi, she decided that seeing Freedom Summer in person was worth some capitulation. Once in Jackson, Batson traveled in segregated cars and stayed separately from the white women of the team. Doris Wilson, the black WIMS staffer in Jackson, talked with Batson during her first trip to Mississippi. Wilson echoed Wiesner, reminding Batson that the WIMS delegates were not there as "testers" but to support local black and white women behind the scenes. Although Batson was still skeptical, she was impressed by Wilson, a social worker and longtime leader in the YWCA, and thought that if Wilson recommended it, then perhaps there was some value in the strategy.[3] While in Mississippi, she also visited freedom schools, community centers, and mass rallies, meeting with black and white, activist and non-activist, men and women. She heard the personal accounts of those in the heart of the struggle.

Despite Batson's initial concerns, by the end of her trip she felt that the journey had been worth her time. Seeing the severity of southern racial problems up close profoundly affected her. In the team debriefing, Batson claimed, "This was the most meaningful thing that I've ever done. I've never been South before. I had no idea of what the problem was, even though you think you know." As a self-proclaimed "red hot Civil Rights worker," Batson thought that she understood the obstacles facing civil rights workers in the South. Instead, the WIMS trip revealed such an "enormous problem" facing Mississippians that "I began to feel that actually I'm not doing too much." An energized Batson returned to Massachusetts and immediately pushed the Massachusetts Democratic National Convention delegates to support the Mississippi Freedom Democratic Party (MFDP). Her personal WIMS experience helped lend credibility to the cause. She said, "When I stood up there and I said to them [the Massachusetts delegates to the DNC], 'Now I just got back from Mississippi,' well you know . . . it made all the difference in the world. Because they're used to people talking about what happens in the South when you haven't been there."[4]

Although Batson originally thought that she would be betraying her convictions by going on a trip that mandated public segregation, she came to feel that the brief, three-day trip was life changing. The council's first major civil rights project was not nearly as daring as the activist work of SNCC, as it simply brought elite white and black women to Mississippi to view what was happening on the ground in Freedom Summer and report back to their northern communities. But it also provided an opportunity to open dialogue privately between black and white southern and northern women of all faiths. As Tiyi Morris has argued, even though the WIMS strategy seemed relatively moderate, and two-thirds of its participants were white, this "belies the fact that WIMS is rooted in Black women's community activism and is representative of Black women's social and political organizing traditions." Harvey, who represented the local black women's group Womanpower Unlimited, was the one who first requested outsiders to come stir things up in her hometown, and WIMS helped extend the WU network beyond the state of Mississippi. Like WIMS, WU wanted to make personal connections among blacks and whites nationally through its Chain of Friendship, and it felt that cultivating these types of personal relationships with black and white women would aid the local organization and the Black Freedom Movement more broadly. As Morris argues, "WIMS demonstrates Black women's acumen for political organizing in that they understood the necessity of women's contributions for the success of the civil rights movement and the necessary connection between local and national civil rights agendas."[5] Both Harvey and Height understood that while moderate, fostering private interracial dialogues and support still served a purpose.

WIMS was also transformative for most of the forty-eight women who traveled to Mississippi that summer through the council project. Many of them said that their short trips profoundly altered their ideas about Mississippi and the nation at large. Most importantly for the NCNW, participants fostered relationships with women and men in the Mississippi movement who then made the council fully aware of the severity of segregation in the most racially violent state in the country. The personal connections forged that summer also began to lay the groundwork for NCNW work in Mississippi that would come to alter the organization's purpose, strategy, and identity as the largest black women's organization in the country.

WIMS Angels

After confirming the decision to go to Mississippi in late May, Height, Cowan, and Smith had only eight weeks to organize what would become Wednesdays in Mississippi.[6] WIMS leaders began to seek out friends and acquaintances as applicants for the project. Beginning in mid-July, teams of between five and seven women—white and black; Jewish, Catholic, and Protestant; elite and middle-class—traveled down to Jackson on a Tuesday; visited a smaller town, such as Hattiesburg, Canton, Meridian, Vicksburg, and Ruleville, on Wednesday, and returned home on Thursday. They planned to visit for only three days to accommodate the northerners' busy schedules and also to not be too great of a burden on their southern hosts.[7] The northern women came from New York, Boston, Chicago, Minneapolis, northern New Jersey, and Washington, D.C. Height and Cowan hired three highly accomplished staff members who stayed in Jackson to organize WIMS. The black staff member, Doris Wilson, was a former employee of the YWCA and held a master's degree in social work from Case Western Reserve. Height believed that Wilson's YWCA connection would enable her to work with both white and black directors of the organization in Jackson.[8] The first white staff member was Susie Goodwillie, a program assistant for the NCNW and the NWCCR. The second white staff member was Diane Vivell, a Stanford University law student and a Woodrow Wilson Stanford Law Fellow, who volunteered for WIMS during the summer. The three WIMS staff persons attended the first orientation session for COFO volunteers at Western College for Women in Oxford, Ohio, during the third week of June. At this orientation session, they learned about voter registration, community activism, and how to brace themselves for a beating so that it would not be fatal. Unfortunately, these preparatory steps could not save James Chaney, Andrew Goodman, and Mickey Schwerner, three COFO activists who were declared missing while Goodwillie and the others were attending the orientation.

Of course, the three staffers needed the help of local women—or "angels," as they were called by Height and Cowan. Clarie Collins Harvey, the black Jackson woman who first called for northern women to come to Mississippi to help stir them up with a long-handled spoon, was the most prominent black WIMS angel. She had impressive professional and activist credentials. She was born in Meridian, Mississippi, in 1916 and attended eleventh grade through her freshman year of college at Tougaloo College, a private Methodist college in Jackson, and transferred to Spelman College in 1934, where she received a bachelor's degree in economics. In 1939, she attended the World Conference of Christian Youth in Amsterdam, Holland, at the age of twenty-three. That same year her father died, leaving Harvey's mother and herself as business associates of her family's funeral and insurance companies. In 1940, she was a cofounder of the black Farish Street YWCA (also known as the Branch Y). In 1943, she married Martin Luther Harvey Jr., who became the dean of student affairs at Southern University in Baton Rouge. They never had any children. She was one of the founders of State Mutual Savings and Loan Association, a black enterprise that later became a multimillion-dollar financial institution.[9]

Harvey was an influential activist in the 1960s, but she was also solidly middle class. From 1960 to 1970, she served on the Mississippi State Advisory Committee to the U.S. Commission on Civil Rights. She was a member of Women Strike for Peace, as well as a member of the board of the Southern Regional Council in 1965. From 1971 to 1974, she was chosen as national president of Church Women United, which represented thirty million women at the time. In 1974, she received the Churchwoman of the Year award from the Religious Heritage of America Foundation, and Mississippi governor William Waller declared December 30, 1974, Clarie Collins Harvey Day.[10] Other women of the black community who aided WIMS were leaders of WU and the Jackson YWCA, including Thelma Sanders, who owned her own dress shop; Lillie Belle Jones, director of the Branch Y in Jackson, Mississippi; and Aurelia Young, wife of attorney Jack Young.[11]

White southern women had also developed their own progressive organizations before the arrival and during the first summer of WIMS, but in order to attract other women, they felt that they had to remain segregated. One such local segregated organization was Mississippians for Public Education (MPE), an all-white women's group formed in anticipation of forced integration of the public schools in the fall of 1964.[12] This nonprofit group was organized to help keep Mississippi's public school system open without interruption. Although most of MPE's members favored integration as the end goal, they feared that promoting this message too strongly would be too disruptive. Founding member Winifred Green said that fear of economic and social reprisals against members prevented MPE from integrating. As she said, the thought at the time was, "If you break the community mores [of segregation], you would be excluded, and that worked very well for white people for a long time."[13] Instead, MPE maintained that keeping the public schools open was its end goal, regardless of who attended these schools, and that it was concerned about the economic drain that would result when whites sent their children to private schools. MPE members like Esther Ethridge, the wife of Thomas Ethridge, a former Mississippi state senator and U.S. attorney, even spoke against integration, explaining, " 'There are a lot of people like me who are not for integration. But we would rather see the schools stay open and our children get an education.' "[14] Members tried to convince women to join by putting their argument in economic terms. The head of the organization, Mary-Ann Henderson, summarized these arguments succinctly: vouchers for private schools would bankrupt the state, the private schools would not be accredited, and inadequate schools would spring up around the state.[15]

Privately, MPE women met with women for coffee and to quietly convince them to send their children to public school. They encouraged them to put pressure on the state to keep the schools open and pointed out that Mississippi should follow the constitution of the United States. They placed full-page ads in newspapers, passed out brochures, and set up billboards around the state urging people to continue to send their children to public schools. They avoided large meetings so as not to attract attention from the Klan or the Citizens' Council, which might, according to Green, "terrorize women who were considering taking the right moral position on it." Overall, "It was working quietly, but not secretively. . . . We wanted our existence known, we just didn't want to be put in a situation where we could let others take control of meetings."[16] Green estimates that over the duration of MPE's tenure, it contacted over a thousand white southern women, many who continued to send their children to public schools long after the majority of their white neighbors sent their children to private academies after federal courts forced Mississippi to integrate in the late 1960s and 1970s.

Despite MPE's segregated status, WIMS sensed that its underlying motive was to support integration, and so it worked with MPE that summer. Cowan focused on the northern and southern women's common concern for the education of their children. As Cowan told the women of MPE, "We are not just northerners visiting the South; we are parents, who must act upon our concern—now intensified by our own direct confrontation—that children everywhere in the United States must be able to grow up, to acquire education, and to build their lives without living constantly in the presence of fear."[17] Like WIMS, the women of MPE "moved quietly" in "loose knit chapters."[18] Much like Dorothy Tilly's Fellowship of the Concerned, MPE shielded its activism under its segregated status in hopes that it would keep violent resistance at bay. These efforts, however, came at a cost to black activism. Woman-power Unlimited had difficulty finding more than a few local whites who would work with the organization.[19] In addition, despite MPE's decision to remain segregated to ensure members' safety, its efforts were in vain. By the time WIMS arrived in Mississippi, the Citizens' Council had already begun a "Dial for Truth" campaign against MPE, in which callers could dial in and hear about how MPE favored integration, and it continued to harass the women of MPE well into the late 1960s.[20]

In addition to WU and MPE, WIMS developed connections to other southern black and white clubwomen through local affiliates of national organizations in Jackson. One of the most active of these organizations that attracted both black and white southerners was Church Women United (CWU). When speaking about her decision to become involved in the struggle to end segregation in Mississippi, white Jacksonian and CWU leader Jane Schutt insisted that "it was very much a matter of Christian conviction that this was something that I should do."[21] Jean Benjamin, a member of the first WIMS team in 1964, remarked about Schutt, "This woman is the embodiment of true Christianity, the way it was meant to be. You just know it when you talk to her. She just glows. It comes out of her face. Everything she says is very simple, but the face is there, and she looks like a saint."[22] Schutt had a significant impact on civil rights in Mississippi. Like many of the southern white women who worked with WIMS, she was not originally from the Magnolia State. She had grown up in Washington, D.C., attended George Washington

University for three years, and got married in 1934. Her husband's career carried her across the South.[23] In 1959, having long been inspired by ecumenical Christianity, she became the president of CWU of Mississippi.[24] During her tenure, the organization released a statement claiming that it favored a policy of separate races working harmoniously together in a Christian manner. While this policy was interpreted by Mississippians to support segregation, Schutt argued that the resolution was more open-ended. She later claimed that the national CWU and the National Council of Churches, which was its sponsoring organization, were in favor of a more integrationist policy. Indeed, recognizing Schutt's views on the matter, the Mississippi State Advisory Committee to the U.S. Commission on Civil Rights invited her to become a member.[25] In the summer of 1963, after submitting the advisory committee's interim report, she spoke in front of the U.S. Senate subcommittee on behalf of the civil rights bill. After her appearance in front of the Senate, the Citizens' Council placed greater economic pressure on her husband's business; in response, she resigned as the advisory committee's chairman, though she continued to work under the radar in a subcommittee of the commission.[26] She joined the Mississippi Council on Human Relations, continued working for CWU, and became one of the only white members of WU's Interracial Prayer Fellowship.[27]

In addition to WU and CWU, the YWCA provided crucial black and white southern support for the WIMS project. Dorothy Height recognized that "a lot of enlightened white southerners . . . were part of the YWCA, [and] the YWCA was their way of getting to [work on social and racial justice]."[28] When Cowan was drafting her plan to create WIMS, she interacted most often with members of the Y in Jackson. Although the national YWCA pledged to become an interracial organization in 1946 (with Dorothy Height's guidance), the Mississippi branches remained segregated, with a main campus and a branch campus. The two sometimes held interracial meetings, but the facilities remained separate, including in Jackson, where Y leaders promised in the late 1950s to include more local board members who favored integration. The national YWCA struggled with the tension between autonomy for local and district branches and enforcement of the national organization's Interracial Charter.[29] Still, the Jackson YWCA was deemed one of the most progressive institutions in the city.

Ann Hewitt was perhaps the most important white WIMS angel. Like Schutt, Hewitt became involved with WIMS through her connections to Church Women United.[30] She later allowed WIMS staff members Goodwillie and Vivell to use her car, and she laundered payment for their summer housing in the Magnolia Towers apartment complex. Hewitt also helped find accommodations for white women in homes by the end of the 1964 trips and during the 1965 trips. She was born in Chicago, Illinois, and moved to Mississippi, where her mother had grown up, when she was a small girl. Hewitt and her mother, Helene Alford, both joined CWU. Alford was the chairperson of the Negro Women's Conference of the Presbyterian Church in the 1930s and 1940s, which held its conference at Jackson State College every summer. Most importantly, though, Ann Hewitt was a widow, and her children were both grown; thus, she and her children were subject to fewer serious economic reprisals.[31] While WIMS promoted itself as an organization that ripped the hole through the cotton curtain, Harvey, Schutt, Hewitt, and the women of Womanpower Unlimited had already been working to promote equality for black Mississippians; however, they still welcomed outside help from the eager northern WIMS members.

High-Level Women

WIMS staff members Wilson, Goodwillie, and Vivell arrived in Jackson on a humid June 27 and immediately began their clandestine work. The white staff members were picked up by Ann Hewitt's daughter Helene and her husband, Jack. They were then transported to the Magnolia Towers, where Hewitt had helped pay for the white staff members' rent, claiming that they were her "daughters," so as not to draw attention to the project. The girls told locals that they were writing a cookbook for Chilmark Press, Lou Cowan's publishing company. They hoped that this ruse would keep them from drawing attention from the Citizens' Council. The staff members also tried to adhere to what they understood to be southern mores. They went to church on Sundays and Wednesdays. They also wore dresses and white gloves.[32] Wilson, on the other hand, stayed with Ernestine Lipscomb, a librarian at Jackson State College. When Lipscomb's mother became fearful that they might be bombed for hosting an outsider, Wilson moved to stay with Lucilla Price, a local social worker. But Price also was scared, and refused to leave her driveway light on for fear that she would be shot while driving into her garage, as Medgar Evers had been the year before.[33] The women had tense moments as they avoided publicity while trying to set up logistics for the teams of women who would soon be arriving in Mississippi. Ultimately, with the help of these local Mississippi angels, the staff members arranged the visits of seven interracial teams, with the first team arriving on Tuesday, July 7, and the last leaving on Thursday, August 20.

Although a generation older, the teams of black and white women whom Dorothy Height and Polly Cowan recruited for Wednesdays in Mississippi resembled the COFO Freedom Summer students in political and social beliefs as well as economic means. The average Freedom Summer volunteer's family income was nearly 50 percent higher than the national median and nearly six times that of the average nonwhite family income in Mississippi at the time.[34] Freedom Summer volunteers had to be able to pay their own way south and be well connected to politicians and influential businessmen around the country. Unsurprisingly, five WIMS members had children who were Freedom Summer volunteers.[35] One major difference between the Freedom Summer volunteers and WIMS, however, was that one-third of the WIMS volunteers were black, while only one-tenth of the Freedom Summer student volunteers were black. But overall, both black and white WIMS women were at least middle, many even upper, class.

The WIMS leadership hoped to use the prominence of its team members to advance the agenda of the civil rights movement. In a letter to David Hunter, manager of the philanthropic Stern Family Fund, Shirley Smith, NWCCR chair and fellow white member of the 1963 Selma team, described the recruitment of participants for WIMS, arguing, "There has been a conscious effort to build a multiplier effect into every trip. This has been done by having women on each team who are in key positions in national women's organizations and who can do effective follow-up, both this summer and in the months ahead." She then went on to list the impressive team members, including Height; Geraldine Woods, president of Delta Sigma Theta; and Pearl Willen, president of the National Council of Jewish Women (see appendix 1 for a full list of the 1964 women). Smith believed that all these women would "be vital communicators to thousands of women across the United States vis a vis [sic] their Wednesday in Mississippi."[36]

The emphasis on women with ties to respected national organizations was complemented by links to corporate power. As Smith noted further, "On every team we have also tried to have the wife of a significant American businessman," highlighting that the wife of the president of United Artists, the wife of the president of Baltimore Life Insurance, and the wife of the vice president of Minnesota Mining had all agreed to participate.[37] Unlike the COFO student activists, who often tried to display their solidarity to the local people by donning the clothing and living in the communities of the black working class, Smith, Cowan, and Height highlighted their prominence, hoping that the class and social status of their participants would make white southerners more receptive to supporting integration efforts with black women.[38]

Although the NCNW publicly sponsored WIMS, it did not contribute a large amount of money to the effort. Initially, WIMS members either paid for their own trips or were sponsored by the organizations they represented.[39] The group also solicited donations from individuals and philanthropic organizations. For the 1964 trip, the Presbyterian Commission on Religion and Race contributed $500, while individuals—including Mrs. Jeanette Boddie, Miss Jewell Hines, and Mrs. Mary Cushing Niles (the team member whose husband was the president of Baltimore Life Insurance)—contributed a total of $687. But the largest donors were the Louis and Pauline Cowan Foundation and the Stern Family Fund.[40] The Cowan Foundation donated a total of $2,417, or over 36 percent of total funding for the 1964 trips. The Stern Family Fund donated $3,000, or 45 percent of total contributions. Jerome Weisner— husband of WIMS team member Laya Wiesner, dean of sciences at (and later president of) the Massachusetts Institute of Technology, and science adviser to John F. Kennedy—was a director of the Stern Family Fund.[41] Jerome Wiesner had encouraged Cowan to apply for funding for WIMS through the fund. Within a few days of sending their request for money to the president of the fund, the executive director sent WIMS back a check.[42] The money to fund the project thus mainly came from affluent, liberal whites and the progressive foundations they established. Because of Cowan's financial investment in and willingness to pour her time, energy, and attention into the project, Height gave her a lot of liberty to design the project in the way she wanted.

Height and Cowan were both members of the first WIMS team, but they sought out additional participants who were as respectable as themselves and their staff. The second black member of the first team, Marian Bruce Logan, fit the bill. As a young woman, Logan had developed a defiant spirit, and she continuously pushed against racial injustice in her lifetime. This was clear from the very beginning of her WIMS journey. Under the blank space for race on her WIMS application, Logan wrote "HUMAN! (Negro . . . if you insist)."[43] At the same time, she had no problem writing "housewife" as her profession on that same application. For many black women, who had to work outside the home more often than white women, the ability to be a housewife was a privilege. After all, Logan was not solely a housewife. She had been a cabaret singer in her youth, and as an adult, she served on multiple commissions devoted to progressive causes. She was once the only northern board member for the Southern Christian Leadership Conference, acting as the New York coordinator for the SCLC.[44] She was president of the women's auxiliary to the Manhattan Central Medical Society, a member of the NAACP

Legal Defense Fund, and a member of Harlem Youth Opportunities Unlimited (HARYOU). She was married to Dr. Arthur Logan, a board member of
the Urban League and prominent member of the SCLC. According to Height,
Logan was not particularly religious; indeed, the space in her WIMS application
for religion was left blank, which distinguished her from the others selected,
whom Height viewed as having "deep religious conviction," like herself.[45]

Like Cowan and Logan, New York team member Jean Kortright Benjamin
had also left organized religion behind. She was born in China and then moved
with her parents to England, their home country.[46] Although Kortright grew
up as a member of the Church of England, her active church attendance ended
after she moved to the United States. She attended the University of Lausanne
in Switzerland for her bachelor's degree. She moved to the United States, became an American citizen, and met and married Robert S. Benjamin, who was
chairman of the United Artists Corporation.[47] As the wife of a prominent businessman, Mrs. Benjamin was involved in many liberal organizations, such as
the League of Women Voters, the Girl Scouts, the Red Cross, and the National
Council of Women. Yet she also had an independent career, working for *Life*
magazine as a reporter and then the Department of State for several years.
Like Height and many of the WIMS women, she was very much a world trav-
eler and activist by the time of the WIMS trips.

Anne McGlinchy was the most mysterious of the first team members, as
she left behind fewer records than her teammates. She was active in the
Brooklyn branch of the National Council of Catholic Women and the Social
Action Committee of the Catholic Interracial Council and thus shared a religious commitment to social justice.[48] Yet in many ways she broke the mold
for a typical WIMS participant. First, she was not married. Most WIMS participants were married, and they often defined their status through their husbands, even if they had careers of their own. Second, McGlinchy was a retired
high school history teacher from Brooklyn, who lacked the wealth and status
of her WIMS coworkers. Third, she was Catholic. The Catholic Church was
much less open to working with interfaith projects, and its parishioners were
less likely to embrace progressive social change than were other religious
groups.[49] Indeed, throughout WIMS's history, Cowan had a much harder
time recruiting and working with Catholic women—in both the North and
the South—than with Protestant or Jewish women.

Although the ideal of the homemaker loomed large in the 1950s and early
1960s, the reality was far different for most American women, especially black
women.[50] Many of the WIMS women worked outside the home. About two-
thirds of WIMS participants listed an occupation on their applications. Twenty-

eight of the original forty-eight were professional workers, but this included a much larger percentage of black women than white.[51] Unlike the majority of black women in the United States, the black WIMS women were middle, even upper, class. Of the sixteen black women who attended the WIMS trips in 1964, most were employed in elite professions (see appendix 1). Etta Moten Barnett was an actress who played Bess in *Porgy and Bess* in Chicago. Her husband was Claude Barnett, founder of the Associated Negro Press. Flossie Dedmond was an associate professor of English at Coppin State College in Baltimore. Mary Kyle was a reporter. Florynce Kennedy was an attorney in New York City. Flaxie Pinkett owned a Washington, D.C., real estate and insurance business, which she inherited from her father; Beryl Morris worked as a lieutenant for the Department of Corrections of New York State's Bedford Prison for Women; and Edith Savage worked as a supervisor in a youth correctional facility in Trenton. These African American participants continued a long legacy of combining work and activism. The historical legacy of black women working for wages in contrast to white women created one of the most important differences separating the two groups.[52] Yet the black WIMS members, unlike the majority of black American women who worked as farmers, domestic servants, and cooks, worked in middle- and upper-class jobs as businesswomen, educators, and entertainers.[53]

White women, on the other hand, had a much lower level of paid employment. Of the thirty-one white women who traveled with WIMS in 1964, seventeen filled in the space for "occupation" with "homemaker" or "housewife." Much like the black professionals of WIMS, the white professionals were educators, executives in voluntary organizations, or workers in mass media. Alice Ryerson was a school psychologist; Marjorie Dammann was a public relations assistant to Victor Weingarten and president of the Jewish Family Service of New York; Hannah Levin was an assistant professor of psychology at Rutgers University–Newark; Sister Catherine John Flynn was a teacher at Immaculate Heart College in Los Angeles; and Helen Meyner, wife of the former governor of New Jersey, was a newspaper columnist for the *Newark Star-Ledger*. Both black and white women were also well educated. Of the forty-eight who traveled with the 1964 WIMS team, thirty-eight held bachelor's degrees and one a bachelor of laws, nine held master's degrees, four gained PhDs, and one an EdD. Only four did not attend college, and four others attended but did not graduate.[54]

Black and white WIMS women were also united by their overwhelming participation in voluntary organizations.[55] Both groups of WIMS women served as presidents or former presidents of progressive volunteer organizations such as CWU, the YWCA, the American Association of University Women, the League of Women Voters, the American Red Cross, and the National Council of Women. Most of the black participants belonged not only to one of the above organizations but also to the NCNW, the NAACP, the Urban League, and black service sororities such as Delta Sigma Theta or Alpha Kappa Alpha. Two black women were or had been executive staff members of these national organizations: Dr. Geraldine P. Woods served as president of Delta Sigma Theta from 1963 to 1967, and Arnetta G. Wallace had been the president of Alpha Kappa Alpha from 1953 to 1958. Many others were presidents of local chapters of black sororities. Ilza Williams was the president of the Zeta Nu Omega branch of Alpha Kappa Alpha in Westchester County from 1962 to 1967. They also took prominent roles within coed organizations as well. Ruth Batson was a member and eventual chairperson of the Massachusetts Commission Against Discrimination from 1963 to 1966. White WIMS women were also active in voluntary groups. Narcissa Swift King was the chairperson of the Women's Board of the Chicago Urban League; Frances Haight was the president of International Social Service in Geneva and the vice president of Citizens Committee for Children; Ethel Haserodt was the executive director of the Passaic YWCA; Pearl Willen was the president of the National Council of Jewish Women; Margaret "Peggy" Roach called herself a "social action secretary" and was an executive assistant of the National Council of Catholic Women.

The fact that many women in WIMS were the wives of major business executives reaffirmed the postwar liberal notion that racial equality and business could go hand in hand.[56] During the Cold War, this helped WIMS justify its presence as an organization that supported fundamental American beliefs in both racial equality and capitalism. There was an added advantage to including businessmen's wives in a civil rights project. In the Cold War era, many southerners conflated integration with communism.[57] Indeed, as Jackson WIMS angel Hewitt affirmed, "Anything national [or international] in Mississippi was communistic. That's the mindset."[58] WIMS leaders hoped that their corporate credentials could successfully block any suspicion that the group was communist.

WIMS's initial efforts fit neatly within existing liberal women's voluntary initiatives—in the North and the South—in which well-to-do families donated goods and contributed time to assist the less fortunate. Indeed, volunteer religious activities were generally deemed to be part of the private sphere, seen as the realm of women and off-limits to regulation by the state. WIMS's original program reflected this deeply personal volunteer focus. In a letter dated July 27, 1964, Smith wrote to the Stern Family Fund, describing some of the concrete actions that WIMS was taking in Mississippi. For instance, after traveling south, Jean Benjamin encouraged her local social action organization—the Great Neck (Long Island, N.Y.) Human Relations Council— to adopt the Hattiesburg Freedom Schools, after which the council sent books to Hattiesburg, Mississippi, Freedom School students. A "food merchant," secured by Cowan, donated 750 pounds of food to Vicksburg for distribution to Freedom School workers and host families. WIMS also sent shipments of clothing and art supplies to Freedom Schools and community centers.[59] In the same letter, Smith notes that another member was keeping Robert Mc-Namara advised on the activities of the Freedom Schools. She thus implied that the members of the group were using their personal connections with influential politicians to advocate for the efforts of civil rights activists.[60] However, this liberal strategy ultimately did not lead to systemic change. Individual women, no matter how affluent or influential, had limited power to combat racial and class oppression in America. While Height and Harvey certainly knew better, Cowan assumed that only ignorance and lack of education stopped white southern women from joining the movement.[61] Increased interracial contact promoted by WIMS might help in reducing individual fears and misunderstandings, but it could only chip away at the physical, emotional, and economic harm that black Mississippians faced daily.

The Possibilities of Personal Witness

As soon as the plane carrying the first WIMS team touched the ground in Mississippi, the women separated from one another.[62] The black women traveled with Wilson and stayed with local black families, while the white women were picked up by Goodwillie and Vivell and shuttled to the Sun-n-Sand Motel.[63] On their first evening, white members of the New York City team met with the all-white Jackson League of Women Voters (LWV), headed by Jane Schutt. The LWV had recently invited a speaker from the UN, now deemed subversive by the Citizens' Council for its commitment to international human rights. In response, the Citizens' Council sent letters to the husbands of LWV members, threating their businesses and jobs. Two-thirds of the Jackson LWV women left the organization after the Citizens' Council's attack. This was the environment that the white progressives faced in Mississippi.[64]

Meanwhile, black southern women faced even more severe threats. On their first day in Mississippi, Logan and Height went with Clarie Harvey to eat at the recently integrated Sun-n-Sand Motel. While the women recalled being courteously seated, their waitress was hostile and threw the silverware at them, reluctantly took their order, and refused to fetch a pack of matches for Logan. The women waited so long for their food that Height decided she had better let the WIMS staff know that they were fine. While the waitress was making nasty comments, the black waitstaff began to appear around the women, "as though for protection." The manager then came to their table and asked whether they were from Jackson. When Harvey answered yes for the group, he probed further, "Aren't you afraid that you'd find yourself in a riot?" He could not believe that three black women dared to visit the restaurant, even though the motel (and its restaurant) had been recently desegregated in the wake of the Civil Rights Act. As the women left the restaurant, the black staff lined up once again.[65]

The next morning, the whole team traveled to Hattiesburg, where together they visited a Freedom School at Mount Zion Baptist Church. Cowan and Height had chosen Hattiesburg as the town to visit outside Jackson because they had been advised that it was relatively safe.[66] However, after the team's morning visit to the school, the group was eating lunch at Mount Zion when a car zipped by and someone threw a Molotov cocktail in front of the church. The bottle did not blow up, and when those inside heard what had happened, they sang the "Hallelujah" chorus.[67] The Reverend Bob Beech, the white head of the interracial Ministers Project in Hattiesburg, spoke with local police after the incident. Later that evening, instead of arresting the perpetrator, police arrested Beech and put him in jail. The Justice Department informed Cowan that Beech had been thrown in jail on a bogus charge of overdrawing his account and had been fined $2,500.[68]

Despite Height's and Cowan's efforts to find safe towns for WIMS visits, the women still faced threats. The climates in Jackson and Hattiesburg were saturated with fear. In Hattiesburg, no white southern women would meet with WIMS. After the trip, Cowan reported, "We did not see any white women in Hattiesburg. Every effort was made, and it broke down. There is one white woman who works on voter registration but at the last minute, she was afraid to see us because it was bright daylight and she can't move around except at night."[69] While Cowan consistently pointed out the fear expressed by white southerners, that fear was most likely motivated more by concerns about social and economic reprisals than physical danger. It was generally black Mississippians who became involved in the movement who had reason to fear for their lives. While Cowan tried to accommodate local women's fears by meeting with them secretly, the odds that white women would commit themselves to social integration were still extremely low.

After visiting Hattiesburg, the first team met with local civil rights leaders and then headed back to Jackson, but they arrived too late to worship with an Interracial Prayer Fellowship group. The WIMS women did, however, attend a Womanpower Unlimited (WU) meeting, at which they learned that women from the Jackson Jewish community had worked with WU in the past and had recently provided the food for a July 4 COFO picnic. Still, these white women were not public in their support, as they transported food and supplies in the evening, when they were less likely to be seen. At the time of the WIMS trip, Womanpower Unlimited had only two white participants out of a group of over thirty members. Likewise, the Interracial Prayer Fellowship that met right before the WU meeting had far fewer white than black members.[70]

WIMS participants did sympathize with the fear of both black and white southern women. Team 3's Flossie Dedmond, a black professor at Morgan State and a member of Alpha Kappa Alpha, the YWCA, and CORE, remarked, "Everybody's afraid of the other fellow. The whites are afraid of the whites. The Negroes are afraid of the Negroes—afraid to trust them. And the whites . . . and Negroes are mutually afraid of each other."[71] Trude Lash, a white WIMS team member from Team 5, spoke with Dr. I. S. Sanders, a black principal in Jackson whose wife, Thelma Sanders, owned a dress shop and was a leader in Womanpower Unlimited. Dr. Sanders told Lash that the black middle class also feared the direct-action freedom movement. Lash said, "He felt . . . that the fear has been so inbred into everyone that they no longer wait until something is actually threatening, but the knowledge . . . the feeling that this is going to be so . . . makes them much less able to do things."[72] Sanders did say that because he and his wife were in secure economic positions, they could be more involved in the movement, but that most teachers and superintendents wanted nothing to do with the movement. Many members of the black middle class were teachers, principals, or superintendents in state-funded education and risked losing their jobs if they openly challenged white supremacy in Jackson or Mississippi's smaller towns. By the late 1950s, the Mississippi State Sovereignty Commission was investigating and intimidating black teachers by monitoring their "loyalty" to segregated education.[73]

Black WIMS members also experienced some trauma while in Mississippi. Ruth Hurd Minor from New Jersey recalled the incredible toll that the short trip took on her physically and emotionally. Minor, a middle-class northern black woman living in the suburban community of Roselle, New Jersey, worked for the public school system and was a member of the Urban League, the American Association of University Women, the League of

Women Voters, and many other women's volunteer organizations. But the experience of going to Mississippi deeply affected her. She wrote that when returning home to her relieved husband and children, she shook so much that she was unable to hold a pen steady or drink a cup of coffee. "I was visibly gripped and shaken remembering the manifestations of the delicate balance of terror in Mississippi Negroes and whites because of the efforts being made 'to alter the course of that state's movement into a totally 'closed society.[']"[74] In this overwhelmingly fearful environment, Height and Cowan believed that a personal approach would be most effective to help the women of Mississippi themselves. The personal witness of WIMS trips helped open up dialogue between women as well as build support for the COFO-led projects of Freedom Summer. By the end of the seventh trip in 1964, Cowan estimated that WIMS interacted with over 150 black and 100 white women in Mississippi. According to Cowan, they had been "immeasurably cheering to the COFO staff and workers" of the Freedom Summer voter registration project.[75] Indeed, Marian Logan received a standing ovation at an NAACP mass meeting in Jackson for coming to Mississippi.[76] Frances Haight and Flo Kennedy from New York's Team 5 insisted that their team to Ruleville was welcomed.[77] WIMS women had also expressed their admiration for these same activists to skeptical white and black Mississippians, in hopes that it would help diminish negative feelings and suspicion of them.[78] Some of the participants highlighted their own personal connections to the COFO students. Jean Davis, president of the Chicago-area Girl Scouts, defended her daughter's decision to be a volunteer during Freedom Summer.[79]

In addition to supporting the COFO-led efforts, the teams sent books and other supplies to community centers. WIMS donated so many books that the book project required its own coordinators.[80] Ilza Williams also sent Canton MFDP leader Annie Devine money for her child to go to college, while Trude Lash and Claudia Heckscher set up a program in New York City to sell quilts made by women in the Mississippi Delta.[81] When the home of Thelma and I. S. Sanders—Florynce Kennedy's Jackson host family—was bombed two months after the WIMS trip, Kennedy hosted a fund-raiser for the couple.[82] These types of activities emphasized the importance of personal connections created through WIMS visits.

WIMS also worked to open the lines of communication between local activists and organizations that could provide those activists with support. Sister Catherine John of the Holy Sisters of Mary in Los Angeles traveled with the Boston team and visited the Holy Child Jesus Mission in Canton, Mississippi. Although the parochial school served black children, WIMS members described it as an "island" separated from the local community. Sister Catherine John's visit led the sisters of the school to meet members of the surrounding African American community for the first time, and WIMS brought movement leaders Annie Devine and George Raymond to the school to work out a plan so that Freedom Summer volunteers might use the school's facilities.[83] The following summer, the school opened its doors for a Head Start program.[84] And then in the summer of 1966, it offered shelter to hundreds of marchers in the Meredith March Against Fear.[85]

Holy Child Jesus Mission quickly became an important part of the black freedom struggle. When the Mississippi Highway Patrol attacked the 1966 Meredith march protesters with "riot grenade irritating agents" as they tried to place their tents on the grounds of McNeal Elementary School in Canton, Holy Child served as a triage unit for the many who struggled to breathe and see through the blinding poison gas. Later, a mass meeting of seven hundred gathered at Holy Child Jesus Mission's auditorium to announce the blackout and boycott that followed Carmichael's utterance of "Black Power" just a few days prior. Later that evening, four hundred of the bruised and battered protesters, whose tents had been confiscated by Mississippi authorities, lay down on blankets on the concrete floor of the school's auditorium to sleep. They would sleep there one more night before leaving Canton.[86] It was WIMS that first opened up the line of communication between local activists and this school, which would become a crucial site for the black freedom struggle.

WIMS visits enabled individual participants to personally witness major civil rights projects, meet with their leaders, and experience personal transformations of their racial understanding. Black New Yorker Marian Logan commented during the team debriefing, "You really feel [the news of violence against civil rights activists] because you've been part of the situation or a community for no matter how short of time it was."[87] White WIMS participant Gerry Kohlenberg experienced a similar change: "And . . . in talking to the people I've talked to, I feel that I am—I was where they are in terms of being nice white liberals, and I can't explain why I'm not quite where they are anymore, except that I'm not."[88] Another white participant—Ethel Haserodt, executive director of the YWCA of Clifton and Passaic, New Jersey—wrote Dorothy Height to thank her for being included in the WIMS project, pointing out how the experience had opened her eyes: "No matter how much I had read and heard about the difficulty of getting Negroes registered I simply did not know the depth to which our so called American democracy had degraded." She had not understood "the extent to which reprisals are a way of life in Mississippi," and the huge obstacles and violence that blacks faced daily.[89] During her trip debriefing, Marjorie Dammann expressed her shock and distress that a sixty-year-old woman with seven children had her welfare check slashed from $67 to $49 after receiving a few materials from the COFO Freedom Summer project. While Dammann was appalled that this had happened in Mississippi, Kennedy, Lash, and Heckscher pointed out that the welfare policy was the same around the country, even in their own northern backyards.[90] Through the experience of WIMS, its northern members learned about the plight of poor women across the United States, including in their own northern communities.

After experiencing these personal transformations, WIMS women became more involved in civil rights projects in their own communities. Ethel Haserodt began speaking in front of local businesspeople and club organizations to discuss ways to open educational, economic, and dialogue opportunities for blacks in her northern community.[91] Ruth Batson and Laya Wiesner returned to Boston and set up a new interracial organization to support a program to bus children from the inner city of Boston to the wealthier suburbs. The program was launched in fall 1966 and named the Metropolitan Council for Educational Opportunity (METCO), and Wiesner served on its board of directors. Much like WIMS, METCO functioned on a private, small-scale basis, and was shielded from the vitriolic criticism of court-ordered busing in Boston in the 1970s.[92]

WIMS members also began to advocate for the nationwide support of SNCC, COFO, and the MFDP—and women in Mississippi more broadly. As noted earlier, Ruth Batson pushed the Massachusetts delegation to the Democratic National Convention to support MFDP's challenge. Team member Frances Haight noted that the work environment for black welfare workers became more difficult after 1954's *Brown v. Board of Education* decision. Haight recounted her conversation with the black supervisor of child welfare for black children in Hinds County, Mississippi. The supervisor could not attend any professional meetings in Mississippi or the Deep South, and her only professional communication occurred when she traveled to the North. This woman also claimed that Burt Beck, assistant director of the National Association of Social Workers, bypassed her and her agency when he visited Mississippi. Haight exclaimed immediately after her trip that she planned to "get on the telephone and call up this man and tell him what [she thought]."[93]

Finally, WIMS leaders used the project to influence civil rights legislation. On August 15, 1964, three days before the final WIMS 1964 team left New Jersey for Mississippi, Dorothy Height and Polly Cowan testified on behalf of

Wednesdays in Mississippi to the U.S. Commission on Civil Rights in Jackson. They used the personal stories of the WIMS women to show the level of violence that existed in Mississippi. Thus, WIMS's encounters in the South had some impact on the policies of the federal government. This meeting was closed to the press and public, but the commission included a transcript in its report the following year. Height and Cowan shared stories of the harassment and violence participants experienced, whether from private persons or local officials; of the protection (or lack thereof) provided by state and local law enforcement; and finally of WIMS's relationship with the FBI and the Department of Justice. In addition to testifying, Cowan submitted a six-page, single-spaced report to the commission, in which she described what she felt the women had accomplished that summer. Cowan was proud of the range of women that the WIMS members met. She believed that WIMS had opened conversations among women in the South who would not have spoken to one another otherwise.[94]

Limitations

During their trips to Mississippi, black and white WIMS members interacted and learned a great deal about one another; however, occasional tensions developed among them as well. For instance, in the debriefing that followed the first team's visit, WIMS leader Polly Cowan called herself a "white Negro." Cowan was not black, but she had worked with the NCNW for nearly a year and was the head of Wednesdays in Mississippi. Marian Logan shot back almost immediately with a simple yet effective, "No, you're not."[95] Logan wanted to stop Cowan from assuming that just because she was a white supporter of the civil rights movement she could claim such a title. Other white WIMS women also still had much to learn. Marjorie Dammann credited Freedom Summer student activists for work that local Mississippians had been engaged in for a long time, claiming, "These people in the Delta have been awakened to their own identity, their own significance and . . . the part that they can play in their own destiny."[96] She thus implied that it took the influx of mostly white northern students to push black people in the Delta to recognize their own worth. Yet other WIMS women—both white and black— felt comfortable correcting their fellow team members. White participant Trude Lash reminded Dammann that the movement had begun with local female leaders who were pivotal to Mississippi's black freedom struggle long before the students' arrival. Lash argued, "I think we have to be very careful because you remember Mrs. Johnson, who is the head of the movement in

Ruleville[,] and Mrs. Williams and . . . Mrs. Hicks and Mrs. Hamer . . . have been working ever since Bob Moses came around."[97] Here, too, WIMS provided important spaces for white and black women to learn from one another.

Black and white WIMS women also did not always agree on what issues were most important to civil rights efforts. Some WIMS women were especially concerned about the dress and appearance of the student activists. Dammann, for example, was impressed that female students wore skirts. She commented as well about how clean their blouses, dresses, and hands were.[98] Dammann was a white social worker from New York, who was also a public relations worker for Victor Weingarten—PR consultant for Stephen Currier, president and founder of the Taconic Foundation—and on the advisory board of the Urban League of Westchester. Like many other northern WIMS women, Dammann placed a high value on the appearance of the activists. Jean Benjamin, a white member of the New York team, expressed anguish at the irreverent dress of a boy from Mississippi. Though he had already been jailed, he still walked daringly around Hattiesburg with a T-shirt with "CORE" on the front and "FREEDOM NOW" on the back. Benjamin wrote in her reflection paper, "As much as I admire this boy's courage, I felt strongly that this was going too far. Surely it is unwise to 'ask for trouble' in this way when there is a solid job of work to be done." While thinking about this one young black Mississippian's T-shirt, Benjamin wrote about her disdain for the student activists' appearance in general: "Can't they be persuaded that they are harming the cause by looking so dirty and sloppy? . . . They would make so much better an impression in the South if they took the trouble to be better groomed.[99] Benjamin felt that change might be possible with a more "respectable" appearance. Some WIMS women felt that at the very least, students should acknowledge the southern code of passive respectability and try to live within it. Yet these WIMS sentiments did not go unchallenged. Black WIMS participants Ruth Batson and Florynce Kennedy pointed out that activists' outfits should be irrelevant in the struggle for justice, given that black Mississippians were discriminated against regardless of what they wore.[100]

WIMS members also sometimes disagreed about the best methods for fighting racial discrimination. Some WIMS women advocated for getting the best and brightest Mississippians out of the South and bringing them north for "good" educations. Claudia Heckscher, a white member of Team 5, suggested that sixteen-year-olds be brought to the North to improve their educations and opportunity; Trude Lash chimed in that "there's absolutely no chance for them—this was addressed by everybody—for a good education in Mississippi." Kennedy responded, "It isn't education they need alone, you see? The teachers are educated. You see what education does for many of them."[101] As Kennedy's biographer Sherie Randolph has argued, Kennedy was "most interested in troubling the falsehood of white northerners' racial tolerance and acceptance," which most of her white team members believed.[102] Kennedy insisted that the problem was not a lack of education on the part of black southern teachers but rather the racist system that provided unequal facilities and terrorized those who insisted on equality. She thought it was important for youth to stay involved locally instead of pursuing an education far away from the heart of activism.[103]

WIMS was also limited in fostering interracialism in Mississippi. Not only were the travel and housing accommodations segregated, but many of the group activities were segregated or unevenly integrated. Haight was disappointed while visiting the local COFO office because her team of four white and two black women was joined by six additional white visitors from the YWCA, the Westport Connecticut Society of Friends, and the University of Mississippi. Thus, COFO workers who met with the "interracial" WIMS team on this occasion found themselves talking to a mostly white group. In addition, she pointed out that her team saw a Freedom School only when it was closed. The COFO school in Ruleville did open for a special day so that the visitors could observe what it normally did, but Haight and the rest of the team felt that this setup was contrived, intended to entertain the visitors rather than offer an honest portrayal of the school's programs.[104] Finally, even within the WIMS project, black and white participants often did not know one another before embarking on their trips. When Ruth Batson's hostess asked her about the white women on her team, Batson was disappointed that she could not tell her much about them because she did not know them herself. She could not even say what they did for a living. Her host then pointed out a great irony of the project: Why was it OK for her to come to Mississippi to open up lines of communication when none seemed to exist between white and black communities in Boston? Batson and her host wondered how WIMS participants might transfer what they learned in Mississippi back home.[105]

Finally, coming face to face with such severe racial discrimination in Mississippi, black WIMS women began to question the power of personal witness. Beryl Morris noted that she "just had no idea of the problem. I've read about it, . . . seen it on television, but to actually go down and walk on Mississippi soil . . . , just to feel practically invisible" to whites.[106] In Mississippi, black WIMS women were exposed to a new level of racism that they had never before experienced. This deep discrimination convinced Ilza Williams that perhaps the problems in Mississippi were too severe to be fixed by the liberal strategy of changing the hearts and minds of white southerners. Williams said that her three-day trip made her a better person, but it also made her aware that the problems were so deep that they could not be solved regionally. Williams believed that whether WIMS teams stayed three days or three months, their strategy was insufficient. As she commented in her debriefing, "You believe that this is America and you know that if you speak out long enough, and if you speak to the right persons, you feel that you have a solution. But I just got the feeling that in Mississippi, everything was so dead." Williams believed that they had found Mississippi dead on arrival and that they would have to leave it that way as well.[107]

Some of the southern white women also questioned the helpfulness of a project like WIMS. Winifred Green—a member of Mississippians for Public Education, who worked closely with Constance Curry of the American Friends Service Committee—did not understand the effectiveness of WIMS's efforts until she saw the connections created in the project lead to the poverty projects in the Mississippi Delta a few years later. "I truly confess I, at one time, thought[,] I wish they would stay home and send the money," she said, but also acknowledged that she did not know much about WIMS's purpose in that first year. Instead, she went to meet with the women on Wednesday mornings to speak about MPE. She and fellow white Mississippian Patt Derian joked with each other that their roles were to be "the white women of goodwill." Green did comment that she believed that WIMS had the greatest impact on its northern participants, who witnessed the Freedom Summer firsthand and contributed more money and time to the movement afterward.[108]

THOUGH LIMITED, the WIMS strategy of bringing teams of individual women down to Mississippi did open the eyes of northern women, provide crucial support to the COFO-led Freedom Summer project, and extend the national network of interracial support for the Mississippi Black Freedom Movement. While hardly radical, WIMS visits facilitated understanding between women of different races, religions, regions, and classes when division was the norm at the time. Thus, these visits provided a spark for social justice in an environment of great fear and violence against anyone who became involved in the movement. Most importantly for the future of the NCNW, WIMS's personal witness helped lay down connections between Mississippi activists and council members, which would serve to fundamentally alter the direction of the organization. The council made contact with Fannie Lou Hamer, Annie Devine, Thelma Sanders, George Raymond, and other local activists. In 1964, there were no active local sections of the council in Mississippi. The inroads made with local Mississippi workers would later bear fruit in strengthening and expanding the council's presence in Mississippi, making it one of the NCNW's strongest membership states by the 1970s. The council also furthered its reputation as a bona fide civil rights organization through its testimony in front of the U.S. Commission on Civil Rights. Thus, as it built its communication network with women on the ground, the council was also expanding its national civil rights presence.

CHAPTER FOUR

We Have, Happily, Gone beyond the Chitchat over Tea Cups Stage

Moving beyond Dialogue, 1965–1966

Following Freedom Summer, black Mississippians challenged white supremacy more directly than ever before. The Mississippi Freedom Democratic Party, which had registered hundreds of voters in 1964, leveled the strongest attack. That August, the group sent a delegation of sixty-four black and four white delegates to challenge the legitimacy of the all-white Mississippi delegation at the Democratic National Convention (DNC) in Atlantic City. President Johnson expected the convention to be his shining moment, since he had no competition as the Democratic nominee. But the MFDP raised questions about the legitimacy of the convention itself. Fannie Lou Hamer's speech before the DNC's Credentials Committee on August 22 was particularly compelling. Before a national television audience, Hamer testified to the horrible beating that she endured after her arrest in Winona, Mississippi. President Johnson quickly organized an impromptu press conference interrupting her televised speech, but he could not silence the larger issues that she raised—police brutality, sexual assault, disenfranchisement, poverty, and endemic violence against African Americans in the Magnolia state. Worried about alienating white southern Democrats, Johnson refused to seat the MFDP. Instead, he sent Hubert Humphrey, long viewed as a friend to civil rights workers, to plead for political compromise by offering the group two at-large seats. Ultimately, with prominent women civil rights activists Fannie Lou Hamer, Annie Devine, and Victoria Gray Adams leading the way, MFDP members refused to give any legitimacy to a system that they felt unfairly excluded blacks from the voting process in Mississippi, and they rejected the offer.[1]

The MFDP's actions at the DNC in Atlantic City marked a significant shift in the civil rights movement. Delegates challenged northern white liberals not only to transform the institutions that sustained political equality but also to become more involved in supporting programs launched by blacks, including the poor, in Mississippi.[2] During the summer of 1964, Wednesdays in Mississippi had worked with many MFDP leaders, including

Hamer, Devine, and Gray. WIMS team members had also attended some of the MFDP meetings, and some, like Batson, offered political support afterward.[3] Now they had to decide how to respond to the Atlantic City challenge.

Despite WIMS's support of MFDP leaders when visiting Mississippi that summer, they said little about the organization after the convention.[4] WIMS did reimagine its role in the freedom struggle in important ways, but members—both black and white—continued to develop programs that were distinct from the increasingly grassroots efforts of groups like SNCC and the MFDP. Two days before Hamer's speech, the final WIMS 1964 team returned to New Jersey. Edith Savage, a WIMS 1964 participant who was also the supervisor of the Mercer County Youth House—a juvenile correctional facility—and a member of the NAACP, CWU, and the Trenton YWCA, was one of two black members of her seven-person New Jersey team. In a letter dated September 13, Savage recommended that future WIMS programs should consider "the strong need of trained social workers for the purpose of health and welfare needs [and] the general concern for the health of the children of Mississippi." She also advocated a "People-to-People program," in which a northern family would sponsor a southern black family for ten dollars a month, the amount that they could make and still receive welfare. Finally, she called for efforts to "induce the Federal Government to intervene by sending members of the Peace Corps to train adults in special skills in order to increase their earning power."[5]

Height and Cowan took up Savage's suggestions and focused on building a future WIMS that highlighted its members' expertise as teachers, social workers, and scholars in fields related to child development. While such programs were useful, they continued to promote a form of uplift that placed WIMS members as experts and local Mississippians as clients. This strategy continued to remain removed from SNCC's and the MFDP's encouragement of organic leadership that emerged from local and often impoverished communities. In this way, WIMS mirrored larger and more established civil rights organizations, like the NAACP and the Southern Christian Leadership Conference, which relied on a circle of seasoned leaders. What differentiated WIMS from these more formal groups, however, was its insistence on female leadership, women's expertise, and paying special attention to women and children in Mississippi. In 1965, WIMS sought to redefine itself as an organization of experts and then, in 1966, as a group to address racial inequality in the North. As it worked on new projects, WIMS—and the NCNW as its sponsoring organization—realized the limitations of a liberal personal strategy focused on building interracial dialogue and promoting elite expertise.

IN THE FALL OF 1964, WIMS was not the only organization considering its future and how to restructure. On September 18, 1964, the National Council of Churches called together civil rights leaders in New York City to discuss the future of the movement. According to John Dittmer, "White liberals and black moderates wasted no time in moving to undermine the SNCC-led COFO coalition."[6] SNCC was largely missing from this meeting, as the group's main leaders were on a tour of Africa. Instead, leaders of the NAACP, CORE, and the SCLC, along with a large number of white activists (who constituted a majority of the meeting), condemned what they saw as the divisive tactics of SNCC, the MFDP, and COFO. Heads of more established organizations, such as the SCLC's Andrew Young, called for the "development of a 'structure of cooperation.'"[7] Freedom Summer visionary Allard Lowenstein even encouraged a more centralized structure for civil rights activities occurring in the South. Moving away from SNCC's leaderless model, he argued that the movement now needed "'structured democracy[,] not amorphous democracy.'"[8] And so in the fall and winter of 1964, officials in mainstream liberal groups, such as the NAACP, the National Council of Churches, and Americans for Democratic Action, were moving to "isolate SNCC, COFO, and the MFDP and to create a new leadership base in Mississippi."[9] While this might have promoted efficiency, it replaced new grassroots leaders with more traditional leaders, including ministers and middle-class club leaders.

Meanwhile, race rebellions in New York City, Rochester, Jersey City, Chicago, and Philadelphia rocked communities around the country that summer. Through violent confrontations and other means, black communities began to question their traditional deference to white and middle-class authority. For many mainstream civil rights activists—both black and white—this was a disheartening development. Calls for "structure" and for "experts" offered one way for northern leaders to maintain their presence in the southern movement without necessarily challenging segregation in their own backyards and for southern moderates to reclaim their leadership roles in the face of more militant groups. WIMS women followed the moderate path, focusing on maintaining control over their project and assisting the poor in Mississippi through teacher training and other social service work. The following year, WIMS worked on investigating violations of the Civil Rights Act, assisted with desegregation of schools, and worked with Head Start, continuing to adhere to personal witness and uplift as a means for facilitating integration.

Throughout the second year of the project, however, WIMS leadership began to learn of the limitations of these approaches.

The NCNW, as WIMS's sponsoring organization, continued to embrace the interracial project. In her opening remarks at the 1964 NCNW annual conference, Dorothy Height introduced WIMS as a council-sponsored project to establish a "ministry of presence" in Mississippi. WIMS also took up a prominent space in the annual convention's program with a corresponding daylong convention that celebrated its impact over the summer and planned an agenda for continued civil rights work. Delegates of the WIMS project were guests of the convention, though some—like Marie Barksdale and Polly Cowan—were also Council members.[10] Most importantly, the WIMS visits to Mississippi helped push the NCNW to focus more on what could be done about poverty in the Magnolia State. Although Cowan was not initially sure if WIMS would send groups of women for another summer to Mississippi, the enthusiasm of conference participants, as well as other southern women who wrote letters of thanks to WIMS staff, pushed her to begin planning for a subsequent summer. As Height and Cowan later insisted, southern women felt that "WIMS-1964 started something invaluable, something which, though just begun, possessed a great deal of potential for wide and significant expansion." Even while working in support of COFO and the MFDP, WIMS maintained its distance from their grassroots work. According to WIMS leadership, the southern women "felt that with extended civil rights activity in Mississippi during the summer [of] 1965[,] the presence of an 'eminently respectable' group of persons who could not be branded 'activist' would be needed more than ever to supplant violence with reason."[11] While Height and Cowan decided to plan for another WIMS summer, they continued to highlight their participants' elite status.

And yet the women of the NCNW also wanted to become more involved in fighting poverty. More Americans had become increasingly aware of poverty thanks to several important studies published in the early 1960s. In his 1962 book *The Other America: Poverty in the United States*, Michael Harrington pointed out that although the United States was a wealthy nation, within its shadow lay a large indigent population. Harrington and other scholars proposed that the federal government provide financial resources and infrastructure to end poverty.[12] The Johnson administration took note. On January 8, 1964, just a little over a month after taking office, President Johnson announced that his administration would fight a "War on Poverty." His efforts to combat economic injustice greatly expanded the Kennedy administration's approach to civil rights. Now the federal government sought to make American society more equal in education, housing, and employment for all Americans. Johnson proposed creating a "Great Society" based on a liberal notion of universal equality.[13]

The NCNW was poised for action. The November 1964 annual convention's theme was "The Challenge of Poverty," and workbook materials included a report on *The Other America*, facts about poverty in the United States, and a brief paper from War on Poverty consultant Elizabeth Wickenden.[14] Task groups explored how the council could help through Job Corps, community action, and voter registration.[15] Still, the council's extensive poverty work was on the horizon but not yet realized. The NCNW continued to work on projects through its tax-exempt Educational Foundation, including a voter registration telephone bank through New York City's WMCA radio station, with 115 volunteers assisting with information about how to register to vote; a mobile health clinic for migrant workers; and a Friends of the Juvenile Court program. While important, these projects only scratched the surface of what the national council could do for civil rights and poverty. Much of the fund-raising arm of the Educational Foundation's money was tied up in raising money to erect a statue for Mary McLeod Bethune in Lincoln Park (see chapter 7), with only a small amount going to the poor. WIMS, as the national council's main civil rights outreach project at the time, began to lay the foundation for later poverty work in Mississippi.

Height and Cowan took pride in WIMS's achievements that summer and began publicizing its accomplishments to influential politicians and donors. That winter they invited Edith Green, Oregon congresswoman who was a longtime supporter of civil rights and who had stood in solidarity with the MFDP in its Atlantic City challenge, and Don Edwards, a California congressman whose son had been a Freedom Summer volunteer, to a benefit held for WIMS. They also sent material on WIMS to Maurine Neuberger, a senator from Oregon.[16] In promoting WIMS, Height and Cowan claimed this work as women's activism, different from the nascent feminist movement but with one similar aim—to take women's activism seriously and to highlight it as being equally important to men's.

WIMS also used its connections on the ground in Mississippi to ensure that Title VI of the Civil Rights Act, which prevents discrimination from any programs receiving federal funding, was being enforced in Mississippi, since the state received $750 million annually in federal assistance.[17] Cowan very much appreciated the "insider" information from southern white women like Hewitt, Patt Derian, and Florence Gooch, who had been crucial to the success of WIMS in 1964. For the local black women who were too afraid of reprisals to report violations of the Civil Rights Act directly to the federal government, the New York–based WIMS office sent the complaints to the appropriate federal agency. As a result, WIMS intervened in several cases in Mississippi. As early as October 1964, Cowan wrote Robert Weaver— administrator of the federal Housing and Home Finance Agency (and later the first secretary of the Department of Housing and Urban Development)—to inform him that the local housing authority had doubled the rent of Annie Devine, the Canton MFDP leader who had worked with WIMS in the summer of 1964, most likely because of her voter registration activity. Cowan wrote, "I am writing to express our concern, to let you know that we care deeply and that we will continue to watch the situation carefully, with high hopes that you will be able to correct this particular injustice and prevent any future occurrences of this kind."[18] She acknowledged that the Commission on Civil Rights already knew about this situation, but she wanted to add the voice of WIMS to the case.

Head Start

In the spring, WIMS began planning its next summer trip. Although announced earlier as an initiative, on March 8 Johnson made public the "President's Report to the Nation on Poverty," in which he revealed plans to spend $50 million on Head Start classes in the summer of 1965. With only four months before the project was set to begin, Office of Economic Opportunity (OEO) director Sargent Shriver frantically wrote thirty-five thousand letters to public health directors, school superintendents, mayors, and social service commissioners to announce the program. He also contacted the three hundred poorest counties in the country to alert them to funding opportunities for Head Start, with an application deadline of April 15. The OEO wanted programs that would help children grow and develop, so they had to offer educational lessons as well as health and social services. The programs would be financed by the OEO up to 90 percent of their cost; 10 percent had to be provided by the local community in cash or kind by providing space, equipment, utilities, or personnel.

Despite the short notice, the response to Shriver's call for applications was overwhelming. Many of the staff members who sorted through the flood of applications were not qualified to assess the proposals, which led to a great disparity in the quality of programs offered.[19] One scholar has noted that the "hectic pace led some observers to call the entire operation 'Project Rush-Rush.'"[20] Indeed, OEO staff member Polly Greenberg remembers the reckless way in which projects were approved, with OEO funding approximately 82 percent of all proposals. By mid-May, Johnson announced that twenty-five hundred Head Start programs would operate eleven thousand Child Development Centers, serving 530,000 children. The cost totaled $84 million, or $150 per student in the eight-week program. Edward Zigler, a member of the Head Start planning team, recalled that Deputy Director Jules Sugarman assured him that they would cut any unsuccessful programs, but the OEO had a difficult time cutting funding for any Head Start programs.[21]

While the hectic pace of funding Head Start applications was disorienting to many government workers, the OEO's emphasis on "maximum feasible participation" of the poor was even more so. Although the OEO sent out a booklet saying that the summer projects needed well-trained professionals, it also encouraged parents and community members to become involved as volunteers or paid employees of the centers. Although most Head Start programs functioned without controversy, the Child Development Group of Mississippi (CDGM)—with its focus on empowering the poorest Mississippians—made national headlines. Northern and Mississippi civil rights workers joined together with Mary Holmes Junior College to create the largest Head Start program, running eighty-four centers (out of Mount Beulah Community Center) to serve six thousand children. Although this project was honored as the best in the nation, critics of CDGM claimed that the teachers, many of whom were poor and black, were unqualified. Senator John Stennis, the junior senator from Mississippi and a member of the Senate Appropriations Committee, opposed funding CDGM because he believed it was supporting the MFDP and because it placed federal dollars in the hands of poor black Mississippians, with no state oversight.[22]

Head Start gave WIMS a new focus and purpose. In late winter, Height and Cowan sought to learn more about Head Start from academic experts and disseminate that knowledge to Mississippians as well as future WIMS participants.[23] In early March, Cowan flew to Jackson and stayed with Patt Derian, another white supporter who had been active in WIMS and in Mississippians for Public Education. She met with local women to discuss how to create Head Start programs and how the WIMS 1965 team could be most helpful.[24] In a letter to a woman interested in participating in the next WIMS summer, Susie Goodwillie wrote, "As you may know, our role in Mississippi will be somewhat expanded this year. We have, happily, gone beyond the chitchat over tea cups stage."[25] On April 2, just two days after Goodwillie sent her letter, William Taylor of the U.S. Commission on Civil Rights agreed that while WIMS's ministry of presence had been important the previous summer, now "additional efforts should be made to bring to the South persons best able to communicate needed skills, in education, welfare, and community organization."[26] The WIMS staff took heed and recruited only women who they believed possessed such skills. In early summer, Goodwillie wrote to the wife of the dean of humanities at the Rhode Island School of Design, rejecting her application to join WIMS. Goodwillie noted that while she had much life experience as a mother and housewife, WIMS now needed women with professional education and particular areas of expertise.[27] Despite the group's previous emphasis on participants' intuitive feminine bridge-building ethic, WIMS now sought members who had formal training in social work and education.[28]

Those who were chosen for teams in 1965 were asked to bring their unique talents to Mississippi.[29] With Head Start "desperate for trained people in the field of Education," Goodwillie stressed, "our team will be doing all they can to contribute needed skills and expertise to the HEAD START projects in Mississippi."[30] The women who would travel with WIMS in 1965 would offer assistance as teachers and even as lawyers in some projects. Goodwillie also mentioned that they hoped to have one member of each team who was a qualified speaker and who would talk on any subject of choice—except civil rights, as Cowan believed whites might be turned off by a discussion of civil rights—to attend these events. Cowan wanted to attract an interracial audience that would learn something about education, social work, or youth programs from a black northern expert.[31] WIMS also helped Head Start by working to bring white teachers to Mississippi Head Start programs that were all black and thus at risk of losing their federal funding. In a letter dated June 16, 1965, a WIMS staffperson quoted Jackson-based Derian in saying that more than anything, Head Start " 'just needed white faces in those classrooms so desperately . . . we'll need everybody.' "[32]

Individual WIMS members also became involved in the fight to help save Head Start funding for CDGM. Members worked with CDGM-supporting organization the Citizens' Crusade Against Poverty (CCAP) to assist War on Poverty projects at risk of being attacked by local governments. The organization was chaired by United Auto Workers (UAW) leader Walter Reuther (who ironically had played a major role in destroying the MFDP Atlantic City challenge) and included representatives from a range of progressive organizations.[33] On June 2, 1965, the executive committee of the CCAP met to discuss how it could best assist projects that "were designated as among those most likely to need citizen organizations support."[34] Many WIMS members attended CCAP meetings as unaffiliated individuals. On June 9, Cowan,

Goodwillie, Caroline Smith, and Oceola Walden (the latter two working as Mississippi staff persons during the summer of 1965) participated in a CCAP meeting to discuss Head Start. When Senator Stennis pressured Shriver and the OEO to withdraw funding for CDGM one year later, the CCAP spearheaded the campaign to reverse the decision.[35]

Cowan continued to seek women for the 1965 summer who would not be too public in their condemnation of segregation. She wanted WIMS participants who "could communicate without arousing hostility, who could listen as well as talk, who were aware of the national scope of social ills that concerned them, and who were committed to resolving civil rights problems in the North as well as the South."[36] She remained committed to the view that respectability—in the form of demure feminine behavior and dress—was a crucial strategy, suggesting a wardrobe that included "light weight dresses, one medium dressy dress, a sweater or thin jacket, for air conditioned cars and homes, comfortable walking shoes and a pair of dressy shoes, a rain coat, 'wash and dry' cloths (you may have to 'freshen up' on the fly), [and] white gloves."[37]

In addition to the women's appearance, the structure of the second year of summer visits was very similar to the previous one. Seven teams from seven cities—New York, Philadelphia, New Jersey, Chicago, Washington, Minneapolis, and Boston—traveled to Mississippi between July 6 and August 26. Before the teams visited, WIMS sent four art teachers from Boston to provide advice to Head Start instructors on incorporating art projects into their classrooms. Each team flew to Jackson, where they were met by new staff members Oceola Walden—a black social worker from Albany, Georgia—and Caroline Smith—a white writer and research analyst from Philadelphia, Pennsylvania.[38] Some groups stayed to work with Jackson's Head Start program, while others traveled to other projects in smaller towns. During the summer, forty-eight women went to Mississippi with organized WIMS teams, while six others went on special assignments. The women visited Jackson, Greenwood, Greenville, Oxford, and Philadelphia, Mississippi.

As experts, WIMS members met with southern counterparts in professional organizations. For black southern women who had been excluded from local professional groups, WIMS provided an important conduit to national organizations. During one trip, three black northern social workers met with three white and five black southern social workers to hear the southerners' concerns and tell them about the resources available through the National Association of Social Workers. In addition, two WIMS librarians met with black and white officials to find ways to facilitate the integration of libraries and improve these facilities in Mississippi. They also spoke with staff and leaders in the Mississippi Library Commission, the executive secretary of the state association of Negro teachers, a librarian at Jackson State College, librarians from the public school system, the head of the Jackson Municipal Library System, and the chairman of National Library Week for Mississippi. Finally, Dr. Anne Keller, a pediatrician from Philadelphia, met with doctors from the Jackson Medical Committee on Human Rights (MCHR)—a team of mostly white northern medical professionals who came to Mississippi to aid the civil rights activists during Freedom Summer and later civil rights demonstrations. Upon her return, she was able to secure equipment and supplies to send to Mississippi.[39]

That summer, WIMS contributed its expertise primarily in the fields of educational instruction and psychology. It worked closely with the Jackson Head Start program, directed by Esther Sampson—a black Womanpower Unlimited member and WIMS angel—and Ann Hewitt, the white assistant director and arguably the most important local white WIMS angel. The Jackson Head Start board became integrated after another 1964 WIMS angel Patt Derian insisted that the board include equal numbers of white and black members.[40] Still, the Jackson Head Start program, like many others around the country, suffered from a lack of local support. The state refused to let any schools, black or white, be used for the integrated Head Start projects. Instead, the projects had to be run out of black churches, parochial schools, community centers, and one Unitarian church (no other white churches agreed to host the projects). Despite these handicaps, the Jackson program alone included twelve hundred children in eighty classes in eighteen Head Start centers. This was a welcome addition in a state with no kindergartens or compulsory school law.[41]

Although they aided projects around the state, WIMS members did not have universally positive responses to their work with Head Start. Carol Guyer of the New York team expressed some frustration: "Yes, I . . . felt that in Jackson . . . we were fifth wheels, that they were courteous to us, but that they were so busy, the people who were involved in Head Start, for instance . . . obviously were burdened by our presence there."[42] The skills of Guyer, chairperson of the Contemporary Arts Committee in New York, and of Jean Dillinger, chairperson of the Christian World Missions of CWU, were of little use to Jackson Head Start, which put them to work organizing the medical records of the registrants. However, Guyer and Dillinger also concluded that this was "all they needed anybody to do. They didn't want anyone to come in and teach at that point. They had to get their records straight."[43] The two team members felt that their job was not to impose their expert advice on the centers but to offer help according to the Mississippians' needs. Guyer claimed in her debriefing, "One has [to be] prepared just to serve as they see fit, really, and to forget what you think your own . . . qualifications are and just to serve as needed."[44]

In addition to the Jackson Head Start program, WIMS aided the state-wide CDGM program by serving as "resource teachers" to help integrate the programs and provide guidance—but not instruction—to the children.[45] CDGM was revolutionary in that it not only educated preschool and kindergarten children but also employed their parents, embracing the concept of "maximum feasible participation" of the poor. In some cases, men and women could make four times what they usually made as a domestic or an agricultural worker.[46] Children received regular meals, healthcare, and love.[47] In the spring, WIMS leaders had attended an initial organizing meeting of CDGM and then observed its efforts over the summer.[48] Rae Cohn, a member of the National Board of the Women's International League for Peace and Freedom and the Philadelphia team, stated in a brief report that the Child Development Group was fantastic in that its "emphasis is placed on the community around the child, by encouraging mothers to take an interest through the PTA."[49] She recommended that more funding be given to this organization. While one woman described the Mount Beulah projects as "disorganized organization," most pointed out that it met the needs at hand, providing education, food, and happiness to students and staff.[50] Sylvia Pechman, a presenter at the 1965 NCNW conference, reported that she thought the program at Mount Beulah was "splendid" and "should be revived and should receive better public relations and support."[51]

However, WIMS's organizational support of CDGM was limited, and most white WIMS women seemed to question CDGM, while the black WIMS participants seemed more complimentary of its methods. At the same annual meeting where Pechman commended CDGM, other WIMS women emphasized the importance of using the Jackson Head Start program—an integrated, middle-class operation run by WIMS women Sampson and Hewitt—as a model, "so that the national image of southern Head Start programs would begin to change."[52] Patt Derian—who was on the board of the Jackson Head Start program and supporter of the middle-class interracial political group Mississippi Action for Progress—felt that the thing that the children needed most was not more money or better books but a speech therapist, "as so many children speak a dialect, distorting ordinary words." Another white participant, Dr. Gertrude Hunter, concurred with Derian's assessment that the speech of the youth was "one of the greatest problems" and a "result of poverty and cultural deprivation."[53] Cowan had also refused to take an organizational stand in favor of local grassroots organizations like CDGM or the MFDP, claiming that WIMS had "been asked by F-D-P to act, over and over and over again. . . . But so far . . . I haven't seen, at any rate, a group activity. And individually, of course, anybody must and should do any thing they want." Instead, as an organization, Cowan saw WIMS's mission as working with the full spectrum of Head Start and civil rights activities and not giving all of its organizational support to CDGM or the MFDP.[54]

WIMS's emphasis on expertise was likely alienating to the grassroots, and often poor women of CDGM. Initially, Head Start did not even require teachers to have formal credentials, such as licenses or degrees.[55] Teachers in the first summer were called "teacher trainees," and they did not need college degrees or teacher certificates—only to enjoy being around children and be able to read at the eighth-grade level.[56] CDGM circumvented lines of formal authority within the state to enable poor people to access federal dollars directly.[57] It also encouraged local people to share ideas for how to best implement the Head Start program. "These types of discussions were important," Head Start historian Crystal Sanders writes, "because poor people had the opportunity to design their own curriculum and policies rather than be handed a set of instructions from experts."[58] Thus, CDGM's philosophy that the people under the heel were fit to teach was foreign to most of the highly educated, highly credentialed women of WIMS.

While not grassroots or radical, WIMS did push boundaries in other ways, especially by challenging sexism in the movement, including within Head Start, through the presence of female experts. Sanders has shown how important black women were to CDGM. Black women greatly outnumbered black men as directors, teachers, cooks, aides, and secretaries.[59] They also infused the program with their energy and commitment to quality education, displaying both "activist mothering" and "other mothering."[60] CDGM women leaders resisted Moynihan's notion of matriarchy through their leadership, but they still had to deal with sexist ideology. For example, founding director Tom Levin stressed the need for women to defer to male authority figures in front of children at the Head Start program.

While CDGM was able to envision working-class men as experts, it could not fully break out of the gendered expectation that a healthy familial relationship centered around a patriarchal structure. In her book *The Devil Has Slippery Shoes*, written in 1968 following the collapse of CDGM's Head Start program, CDGM leader Polly Greenberg was clearly influenced by Daniel Patrick Moynihan's and E. Franklin Frazier's psychological explanation for black dysfunction—the same explanation that had circumscribed Height's actions within the council a few years earlier. Greenberg wrote that black communities lacked strong male authority figures. She concluded, "Potent men of this kind were not in most homes to block infantile fantasies, the search for magical fulfillment through a powerful mother, waves of rage at frustration and disappointment, and unlikely aspirations that resulted in feelings of complete inadequacy and inaction." She continued by arguing that this created a cycle of poverty. "Passive men produced passive little boys who sought powerful mothers and wives, who married passive men and produced passive little boys."[61] Greenberg and Levin both believed that the answer lay in restricting black women's power within these communities. Greenberg points out that Tom Levin concluded that "it was neither stimulation nor male teachers CDGM most needed, but opportunities for children to see virile male members of *their* communities functioning in significant roles, and women from *their* communities working creatively instead of dominatingly with these men."[62] WIMS's insistence on female expertise challenged this attitude.

Continued Challenges of Desegregation

In addition to working with Head Start, WIMS women as well as other NCNW women participated as educational experts at two desegregation institutes at the University of Mississippi. Over 120 teachers, principals, and superintendents attended these sessions. The program sought to disseminate information about desegregation to a mostly white audience, aid participants in creating school policies, and create a program designed to assist schools affected by desegregation.[63] Kate Wilkinson, assistant director of the institutes, was completing a master's degree at the University of Mississippi and had also been a white southern WIMS angel in 1964. Wilkinson encouraged WIMS members to serve as experts during the two days before or after their "Wednesday" in Mississippi, and staff members at the desegregation institutes were delighted to have their assistance.[64]

Six 1965 WIMS team members and four additional NCNW women—including Dorothy Height; Dr. Jeanne Noble, a black NYU faculty member in the School of Education; and Ellen Tarry, a black award-winning children's author—presented at the institutes. Tarry was delighted at the opportunity to speak before a southern audience about her writing: "For once, I did not have to apologize for my southern accent!" She found it exciting to tell this nearly all-white group about the moment when she decided to become a writer: "I discovered that my Negro students at old Slater School in Birmingham lacked the capacity to dream because they were not sure that Negro children had the right to conjure up visions of faraway places with strange-sounding names." At the end of her speech, two black teachers expressed their appreciation for her presentation and her books.[65] According to WIMS's final report, "For the first time, the [white] teacher-students were exposed to prominent Negroes and they were impressed by them."[66]

However, Height also emphasized to institute participants that while they might be impressed with her and her fellow presenters, she shared the discrimination faced by all black Americans, stating, "Other Negroes and I stand alike as we try to be served in a hotel or a restaurant. I'm no higher than the one who is farthest down because we are really indeed equal when it comes to justice and to voting." Thus, Height insisted on drawing a link between herself and the poorest black Mississippians in front of this audience. Many of the white participants claimed that they would never hold the same prejudiced views after meeting these NCNW women. Ole Miss graduate student and institute staff member Gabe Beard from the University of Mississippi confirmed the positive effect that the women "from Yankeeland" had on the integrated group of educators. According to Beard, it was the first time that she and many of the white teachers had ever been involved with black teachers in any significant way. Seeing elite, professional black women "had to impact them because they'd never seen people like this. . . . They'd never seen [such] educated, brilliant black folks."[67] Still, while the desegregation institutes were a positive step in the right direction for school integration, much more would be necessary before schools around the state would truly be integrated.[68]

While there had been some great successes in fostering further integration through WIMS in 1965, there had been some serious disappointments as well. Perhaps most disheartening, the local YWCA was more resistant to working interracially in 1965 than it had been the previous year. New York WIMS team Ellen Dammond, a black national YWCA board member, met with YWCA members in Jackson.[69] Following Dammond's visit, the YWCA's southern district coordinator requested that WIMS no longer use the YWCA's facilities for their meetings, and that "anything you do from now on must be one to one, face to face, individual meetings."[70] At the same time, Marguerite Cassell of the Chicago team met with Barbara Barnes, the white executive director of the Central Mississippi YWCA, who had been working with WIMS for well over a year; Cassell "served mostly as a crying shoulder for [her]." Still,

Cowan pointed out that while the group could no longer use YWCA facilities for group meetings, the WIMS visits, especially Dammond's trip, pushed the national YWCA to pay more attention to Jackson and recognize the need for stronger integration efforts there.[71] The Jackson YWCA was finally desegregated in 1968.[72]

WIMS continued to have difficulty meeting with southern Catholic and Jewish women in 1965 than it had the previous summer. The southern women became more resistant after reading a confidential report of northern WIMS participants' reflections of the previous summer.[73] After her unsuccessful trip in 1965, Gladys Zales, a member of the New York team and the Hadassah National Board, wrote that she found the Jackson Jewish women as racist as the non-Jewish women. Unlike previous participants, Zales was unwilling to believe her co-worshippers in Mississippi who claimed that their experience was as harsh as that of the black community. Zales's host had tried to explain to her the difficult position of Jews in Jackson, where they were a very small minority: about 120 families out of a city of 250,000. They, too, faced discrimination and were ultimately fighting to care for their families in a hostile community. Zales was not convinced. She stated, "I'm sorry to say that this isn't true. . . . There's just race hatred. [Jewish Jacksonians] are as southern as any of the other southerners, and it was very disheartening for me. I found it very disheartening."[74] The previous summer, the Jewish community had remained closed to 1964 WIMS members until two women from the Chicago team were housed with Elaine Crystal, a local Mississippi Jewish leader.[75] WIMS members also met with Rabbi Nussbaum and his wife, as well as with the president of the temple and his wife, Mr. and Mrs. Stamm. According to Cowan, the two Chicago members expressed the same point of view as Zales and received the same defensive reaction.[76] Still, Nussbaum and Stamm did have good reason to be fearful and defensive of outsiders' visits. Just two years later, on September 18, 1967, the Ku Klux Klan would bomb the brand-new Temple Beth Israel, the only synagogue in Jackson. And two months after that attack, the KKK would bomb Nussbaum's house while he and his wife were inside. Although no one was injured in the blasts, the attack made clear that there were real threats against Jewish families in Jackson.[77] Ultimately, WIMS's visits may have opened up some new lines of understanding, as the Jackson Jewish women later claimed that Zales's visit had helped change their perspective on racism in Jackson.[78]

Southern Catholic women also continued to be difficult to recruit. Ellen Tarry, the black storyteller from New York, met with Father Bernard Law, then chair of the Mississippi Council for Human Relations, who said that there was virtually no interracial Catholic movement in the state.[79] However, WIMS did have great success in 1965, working closely with the Pax Christi mission after women from the Washington, D.C., team stayed overnight at the mission in Greenwood. Pax Christi had been established by Franciscan missionary Father Nathaniel Machesky in the mid-twentieth century, and by the time WIMS arrived, director Kate Foote Jordan attended to both white and black communities in Mississippi.[80] In the summer of 1965, the mission ran a Head Start program with fifty summer volunteers from eighteen states. When they returned to Jackson, the WIMS group spoke with local Catholic women who, with WIMS encouragement, later visited the Pax Christi mission to view the civil rights activities there.[81]

WIMS members continued to find their trips life-changing. Jean Dillinger, a member of the Philadelphia team who traveled from California to join the group, wrote, "For those of us who were able to go to Mississippi, it was an invaluable experience both in terms of our own reactions, and of our ability to do some interpreting of the situation to our friends."[82] They had gone as experts, but the WIMS trips challenged many of the ideas they had brought with them. But such transformations no longer satisfied Cowan. Although these women had gone south to offer their expertise, Cowan noted that too little had actually been accomplished. She said, "I think one of the problems that we've had up to now is there's been too much observing and too little work."[83] Both Cowan and Height began to think about new directions for WIMS.

WIMS after 1965

At the end of the 1965 trips, Cowan once again was not sure whether the WIMS project should continue, and she asked funders and other influential backers to offer their opinions, sent out her "Final Report" on WIMS's activities to influential politicians (including Vice President Hubert Humphrey) and liberal businesspeople, and continued looking for other ways to raise money. Trenton participant Edith Savage organized a benefit concert to help raise money for WIMS that October. Coretta Scott King, a close friend of Savage, sang in exchange for two-thirds of the funds going to the SCLC. Initially, Savage asked Cowan if she would speak during intermission, but Cowan, as a white activist, believed that Dorothy Height, as the black leader of the NCNW—WIMS's parent organization—would be a better speaker for the event and encouraged Savage to ask her instead. Height agreed and gave a "splendid" presentation, according to Cowan. The benefit raised $7,000, but only one-third of it ended up in WIMS hands.[84] While the event raised money to pay for the activist projects of the previous summer, Cowan and Height waited until the NC-NW's November meeting to determine WIMS's future.

The theme for the 1965 NCNW annual conference, in the wake of the Moynihan Report, was "The Negro Woman in the U.S.A.: New Roles in Family and Community Responsibility." The convention was cosponsored by the U.S. Department of Labor, and many women from prominent governmental organizations participated. Once again, the NCNW offered WIMS a primetime slot at the conference, with a separate session, titled Women in Community Relations, where members reported on their experiences during the summers of 1964 and 1965.[85] The women present debated what would be the most effective use of WIMS womanpower and resources in the future, and they discussed ideas ranging from opening "lines of communication" in other parts of the South or the North to helping poverty initiatives acquire federal funding.[86] Although there were various ideas offered, the consensus was that interracial activities were still valuable and that the organization should continue to work—but now in the North.

WIMS leadership hoped that the project's non-confrontational approach could stave off white backlash in communities that were recently rocked by race rebellions. During the 1950s and early 1960s, Americans were fixated on stories of racial violence in the South, but problems had also been growing in the North and West for a long time. Since the early twentieth century, African Americans had left the South in large numbers to find economic opportunities in northern cities. However, by the late 1950s, these areas were becoming deindustrialized, as many manufacturers moved their factories to the South or overseas. Thus, southern migrants now faced high unemployment as well as ongoing problems with housing and schools. In addition to deindustrialization in the North, other companies started moving to industrial parks in the suburbs, where large numbers of white ethnic residents provided a ready workforce. Meanwhile, in urban areas, few blacks served on police forces, which often brutalized African Americans. Segregation, unemployment, and discrimination were the reality for blacks living in American cities in the mid-1960s, and violent uprisings erupted in many of these areas to protest their living conditions.[87] Concerns with white backlash intensified in the summer of 1965, when race rebellions once again arose in urban areas, the worst occurring in Watts, Los Angeles, in August. Watts residents faced high levels of unemployment, police brutality, and substandard housing and schools. By the end of the rebellion, there were thirty-four people dead, one thousand injured, and four thousand arrested, and more than $35 million in property had been damaged. Sixteen thousand National Guard soldiers, Los

Angeles police officers, and California Highway Patrol officers were on hand to put down the approximately thirty-five thousand active rioters.[88] Reacting to such devastation, Cowan and Height became more convinced of the need for WIMS programs outside the South.[89]

Although former participants had enthusiastically endorsed WIMS at the November NCNW conference, when asked again a few weeks later, many of the white northern participants reacted with ambivalence to the idea of developing programs in their own communities.[90] In early winter 1966, Cowan sent out a questionnaire to 1964 and 1965 WIMS participants, asking if they might be able to work on a training institute in their town or city or participate in or host a WIMS team for four days or longer. She then asked them if they felt that their community should be on the northern WIMS list and whether they would be willing to assist a project in their hometown. Some of the white women, such as Ethel Hasserodt—an enthusiastic participant of the 1964 trips—said that they could indeed help with a northern project, but many of the other white women insisted that they were unsure of their schedules in the summer and that they expected to be very busy with other activities, many related to social justice. Jean Davis, a white housewife from Winnetka, Illinois, involved in the League of Women Voters, the YWCA, the Girl Scouts, and Church Women United, described her activism in Chicago. She had been chairing her church's benevolence committee, which was working closely with Martin Luther King Jr.'s Chicago campaign. She concluded, "I truly don't know whether there is a place for WIMS here—my 'opposition' stemmed, I think, from my concern as to where WIMS could do the most good with the least effort or change in format." Other white participants, including Anne E. Keller from Philadelphia, expressed similar concerns. While she believed there was still a need to direct attention to Mississippi, "I see a real danger in a group like this getting 'delusions of grandeur' and spreading itself very thin. I would think it could function in Mississippi for the next million years without running out of work to be done." Similarly, Marjorie Dammann from New York City claimed there was simply no need for a WIMS project in her community.[91]

Yet other WIMS participants, especially the black women, applauded the initiative. To the inquiry "Do you think that your own community should be on the list of the 10 to 12 communities which will be named in our proposal?" Floynce Kennedy of New York answered "Absolutely." Kennedy believed that she could be most useful in teaching about "government and business delinquency in race and civil rights matters," as well as "consumer pressure," and that her community could benefit from concentrating on "voter and consumer education," "economics and politics of wars against wars against poverty," and "attention to youth groups and more cooperation with them especially regarding . . . [the] priority of war over national problems and projects." Edith Savage affirmed the need for WIMS in Trenton. She wrote, "Our town needs this bridge of communications, we have a problem of Negro and white women (and men) not working together in our community at this time. . . . I feel middle class negro [sic] and white women working together would increase concern and bring about new ideas." Overall, black WIMS members, even ones as radical as Kennedy, believed that there was still much value in trying to educate northern whites about the racist structures of power in their communities, and they tended to be more in favor of moving WIMS operations to the North than were their white counterparts.[92]

Despite the white respondents' ambivalent response, WIMS moved ahead with plans for projects in Boston and Paterson, New Jersey. Both had been at the center of contentious debates over school integration. Paterson had also been the site of a race rebellion in 1964 and continued to suffer from massive white flight. Boston, however, was to be WIMS's first northern test case. As WIMS staffmembers had done in Mississippi during the previous two summers, they again sought to work with middle-class women. They described the potential participants of the northern workshops as "citizens, mothers and community leaders [who] are concerned about civil rights and human relations." And they again stressed the importance of "outsiders" as a "catalyst" even while acknowledging the importance of being invited by local residents. WIMS hoped that as these middle-class women worked together, they could expand their efforts to disadvantaged community members "who will then take increasing responsibility as they understand their role in relation to mutual concerns."[93] WIMS's statement reveals a paternalistic assumption of racial and class uplift, still embraced by many American liberals at the time, that WIMS participants could teach disadvantaged women how to "take increasing responsibility" for their economic, social, and political choices, and that informal conversation was still a valuable means of transforming race relations.[94]

Cowan and her staff first met with representatives from liberal organizations in Boston (such as the YWCA and the NCNW), the Catholic Interracial Council, the Urban League, and the American Jewish Committee in late winter 1966. At these meetings, the black and white Bostonians resisted the whole idea of "building bridges." Black women from Roxbury especially resented Cowan's implied notion that they were the ones who needed to "learn" something from middle-class white women in the city and that their community was the one needing "help." WIMS staff again acknowledged the limitations of their racial understanding. They wrote in a report of a meeting at Ruth Batson's house, "It became obvious immediately that the WIMS sheet that we had prepared was much too naive for the sophisticated audience assembled." Questioning WIMS's own strategy, they continued, "The Negro women reacted to our wording with reasonable hostility, and pointed out their objections to the stratification of our 'middle class.' They also pointed out the errors of concentrating our work in Roxbury, instead of South Boston, or other areas where the bigotry exists." The Roxbury women were hostile to the idea that "outsiders" needed to come in to help them, pointing out that they had been working for years on trying to establish interracial organizations but had encountered significant resistance from the white Catholic community. The black participants in the discussion pointed out the subtle racist, classist, and gendered assumptions underlying WIMS's focus on individual change and pointed to the prejudice of white Bostonians and structural corruption as the main problems. Cowan and her staff, to their credit, recognized the limitations of their own assumptions by acknowledging these women's ideas as "sophisticated" and even justified their hostility toward the project as "reasonable."[95]

Cowan and WIMS leaders, including Ruth Batson, tried to make inroads at that meeting with twenty-five black and white local activists at Batson's home. They did not succeed. Like the black leaders of Roxbury, the progressive white and black Catholic women at Batson's house rejected Cowan's project, arguing that WIMS leaders had little to teach them. When Cowan suggested bringing in Mississippi Catholic activist Kate Foote Jordan, the Boston women argued that she was too much "on the missionary level to be applicable in Boston."[96] Thus, the women displayed their sense of regional superiority, feeling that very little could be learned from southern Catholics, especially from a small parish in Mississippi. One black Catholic activist, Muriel Snowden, also suggested that WIMS branch out to reach Catholics in areas other than Roxbury.[97]

Although many participants rejected WIMS, Batson, who had been at the forefront of activism in Roxbury, came to its defense. She pointed out that it was WIMS that enabled her to set up this meeting between black women and the Catholic Interracial Council, and she pointed out that communication between the races in Boston was still poor.[98] WIMS staff then broke the women into smaller groups, later claiming that "a great many misunderstandings were settled in the small groups, before the meeting resumed, and warmth overcame the hostility," with the meeting ultimately opening up lines of communication.[99] However, subsequent meetings did not yield any significant results. Ultimately, the Boston women told WIMS staff that they "saw no point in 'talking to themselves,' and felt that it was much more important to 'do' than to 'talk.'" Cowan and her staff thus concluded that bringing teams to Boston was a lost cause, but they pledged that WIMS would help build local white support for Operation Exodus, a grassroots school-busing plan for Roxbury; recruit more sponsors for local Head Start programs; try to open more public and private housing for black Bostonians; and work with Catholic officials to reduce the impact of Louise Day Hicks, the Boston School Committee member who opposed busing and redistricting to foster school desegregation.[100] Unfortunately, as busing became an even larger issue in Boston, racial relations simmered and eventually exploded in the 1970s.

In many ways, WIMS's failure in Boston marked the beginning of the end of its liberal dialogue strategy. Northern women had pointed out two fundamental flaws with the WIMS approach: first, by setting up a conversation between supposed "equal" parties, it assumed that racism lay as much within the black community as within the white; and second, it placed the burden of accounting for large-scale systematic unemployment, poverty, and substandard schools and housing on black participants. The problems in the late 1960s were simply too great and too entrenched to fix by informal personal communication and education. And yet, as Ruth Batson pointed out, for a brief moment, WIMS exposed white and black women to the other's point of view.

WIMS had better success in Paterson, a city in northern New Jersey that staff described as "decaying" due to white flight, political corruption, and poor housing.[101] During the NCNW's 1965 convention, Madie Horne—Passaic County's NCNW president—had heard about WIMS's efforts in the South and requested that the group initiate a workshop in Paterson in the upcoming year. She gathered three local women to lead a September workshop: Bessie Jamison, a black executive of the Paterson Task Force, a local poverty program funded by the OEO; Marion Rauschenbach, a white member of the Paterson Task Force and president of the Passaic County Community Council; and Florence Brawer, a white housewife with a degree in business administration.[102] Joining the three local leaders were 1964 WIMS team members Ilza Williams and Trude Lash. Horne chaired the session, and Cowan moderated the panel. The call for participants stressed that women needed to learn to be sympathetic to the needs of others by highlighting similarities and minimizing differences, especially about women wanting the same things for their children.[103] The conversation ranged over a variety of topics, including education, welfare, housing, health care, and the lack of meaningful communication between black and white residents. Over 130 women attended at least some part of the day-long conference.[104] While initially targeting middle-class women, the inclusion of the task force women meant that the Paterson conferences provided a setting for poor black women in the community to voice their concerns and be listened to with respect, which had traditionally been denied them. According to the post-conference report, white female participants especially learned that "it was time to work *with*, not *for* these people. . . . They [white and black women] had come together to work from a common base. As citizens of the same city they were concerned . . . about the same things [and] seeking similar solutions" (emphasis in original).[105]

At the end of the workshops, the participants formed the Women's Council for Community Service. WIMS staff acknowledged their excitement but also anxieties, as this group brought women together across not only racial and religious lines but also class lines. WIMS believed that white women had learned the necessity of listening to black women, both the middle-class NCNW women and poorer women, but they were noticeably uncomfortable with the outspoken and "more militant" working-class black women of the Paterson Task Force. Staff feared that the contingent from the task force would dominate and destroy the newly formed and more moderate Women's Council.[106] WIMS's initial mission in Paterson was to stave off white backlash by increasing communication between middle-class blacks and whites. Thus, staff lamented the militancy of black women who wanted the coalition to produce tangible poverty projects for the black community; while the middle-class black women of the NCNW fit WIMS's model, the task force women did not. Though the organization wanted to foster dialogue, it was hesitant to have the poor be the ones directing the conversation.

Still, changes were occurring within WIMS, the NCNW, and the nation more broadly. Head Start and the growing War on Poverty as well as the growing militancy of black women in the North forced WIMS to question the effectiveness of its personal approach. "The day has gone when we can solve problems by ourselves. We must deal with problems by tackling the system which has created the individual's problems and his hopelessness," stated WIMS's observations from Paterson.[107] The experiences both in Mississippi in 1965 and in northern cities in 1966 also suggested the limitations of interracialism as a goal and interpersonal dialogue and relationship building as long-term civil rights strategies.[108] While WIMS women made many inroads in promoting understanding, they also responded to the changing mood of the black freedom struggle. After its limited success in the North, WIMS began to subsume its public identity under that of the NCNW, promoting black women's advancement over interracialism. WIMS and the council also began to shift away from viewing the elite moderate black woman as the best spokesperson for the race. Ultimately, this change signaled the end of WIMS and the beginning of a new direction in the larger NCNW.

FIGURE 1 The closing dinner marking the retirement of Mary McLeod Bethune in November 1949. Second president Dr. Dorothy Ferebee is to Bethune's left, while third president Vivian Mason is to her right. On the far right of the photograph is fourth president Dorothy Height, who served as NCNW president from 1957 to 1998. (Photograph by Fred Harris, courtesy of the Mary McLeod Bethune Council House National Historic Site, National Archives for Black Women's History. NCNW Records, series 14, #0056.)

FIGURE 2 NCNW leaders' conference in Daytona Beach, Florida, April 1952. In the top row, Dorothy Height is second from left and Edith Sampson is on the far right. In the bottom row, Vivian Mason is second from left and Mary McLeod Bethune is third from left. (Photograph by Beach Photo Service, courtesy of Beach Photo and the Mary McLeod Bethune Council House National Historic Site, National Archives for Black Women's History. NCNW Records, series 14, #0080.)

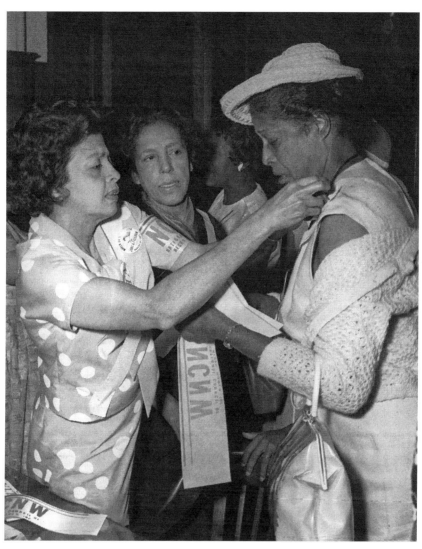

FIGURE 3   NCNW women preparing for the March on Washington at the 1318 Vermont Avenue, Washington, D.C., headquarters. Several hundred NCNW women participated in the March. (Photograph by Fred Harris, courtesy of the Mary McLeod Bethune Council House National Historic Site, National Archives for Black Women's History. NCNW Records, series 14, #1462.)

FIGURE 4 1964 Wednesdays in Mississippi Team #3 from the Washington, D.C., area. Women from left to right are Dorothy Height, Wilhelmina (Billie) Hetzel, Flaxie Pinkett, Margaret Roach, Justine Randers-Pehrson, and Flossie Dedmond. (Photograph by unidentified photographer, courtesy of the Mary McLeod Bethune Council House National Historic Site, National Archives for Black Women's History. NCNW Records, series 14, #1043.)

FIGURE 5 Left to right: Fannie Lou Hamer, Dorothy Height, and Polly Cowan at the 32nd NCNW annual convention, November 1967. (Photograph by unidentified photographer, courtesy of the Mary McLeod Bethune Council House National Historic Site, National Archives for Black Women's History. NCNW Records, series 14, #1285.)

FIGURE 6 Dorothy Height as the only woman at a meeting of civil rights leaders the day after Martin Luther King's assassination. Left to right, attendees include: Seated, Hon. Thurgood Marshall, President Lyndon B. Johnson, Clarence Mitchell. Standing, Roy Wilkins, Secretary Robert Weaver, Congressman William McCulloch (obscured), Hubert Humphrey, unknown (obscured), unknown, Height, Mayor Walter Washington, unknown (obscured), Whitney Young, Walter Fauntroy, Bayard Rustin, unknown, unknown, unknown (obscured), Rev. Leon Sullivan. (Photograph by Yoichi Okamoto, from LBJ Presidential Library, #A6016-18.)

FIGURE 7 NCNW representatives visiting a pig bank site in the Mississippi Delta. (Photograph by unidentified photographer, courtesy of the Mary McLeod Bethune Council House National Historic Site, National Archives for Black Women's History. NCNW Records, series 15, Subseries 4, Folder 19, #0003.)

FIGURE 8 NCNW leadership laying a wreath at the Mary McLeod Bethune statue in Lincoln Park. (Photograph by unidentified photographer, courtesy of the Mary McLeod Bethune Council House National Historic Site, National Archives for Black Women's History. NCNW Records, series 14, #0484.)

FIGURE 9 International seminar participants at the Dorothy Height Community Center in the Eastgate community in Cleveland, Mississippi, in July 1975. Women from left to right: Christabel Zondo, Lenora Moragne, Ruth Minor, Kay Fitts, unknown, Victoria Mojekwu, Diana Opondo, and Elizabeth Nkomeshya. (Photograph by unidentified photographer, courtesy of the Mary McLeod Bethune Council House National Historic Site, National Archives for Black Women's History. NCNW Records, series 14, #1512.)

FIGURE 10 International seminar group at Howard University, 1975. From left to right: Maida Springer Kemp, Dr. Mae King, Anne Turpeau, Nancy Moatlhodi, Dovey Davis, unknown, Emma Agyepong, Dorothy Height, Nellie Okello, Diana Opondo, and Salimatu Diallo. (Photograph by Jim Wells, courtesy of James L. Wells III and the Mary McLeod Bethune Council House National Historic Site, National Archives for Black Women's History. NCNW Records, series 14, #1506.)

CHAPTER FIVE

You Know about What It's Like to Need a Good House

The Changing Face of the Expert, 1966–1970

On November 18, 1966, Unita Blackwell, a SNCC, CDGM, and MFDP leader, sat in the conference room at the Jackson, Mississippi, Farish Street YWCA building with about sixty other women.[1] A representative of the Jackson NCNW and Coleman Miller, head of the social service community section of CDGM, had invited her to come to the Branch Y, which served as the black YWCA—still segregated in practice—for a workshop about alleviating poverty in Mississippi.[2] The NCNW women, Blackwell, and other participants later met at the Heidelberg Hotel, which had been integrated two years earlier with the passage of the Civil Rights Act.

Blackwell didn't know much about the NCNW, but as someone who had worked with SNCC, the MFDP, and CDGM, she noted the out-of-touch approach of the initial conversations of the workshop. As she recalled in an interview a year and a half later, "So, we went to the meeting, and I just couldn't stand it, you know. 'Cause it was just some bunch of little biddies sittin' there, what I call these 'highly elites,' you know. And they didn't know what in the world was going on in the community, but they was there, you know, talking about flowers and beautification programs and all this other kind of stuff, which you know wasn't even hittin' nowhere what we was talking about."[3] Blackwell was so frustrated by this meeting that she got up to leave and return to her small Delta hometown of Mayersville. But on her way out, Doris Dozier, a recent NCNW staff member who had also been a member of many different civil rights organizations in the early 1960s, stopped her and pleaded with her to stay. Dozier then asked if there was any way that they could channel the meeting "into really getting down to something, you know, what is happening in the communities and what should be done."[4] After Dozier's appeal, Blackwell decided to stay. This was the first of two meetings sponsored by the NCNW in the winter of 1966–67 to determine what poor Mississippians wanted. By the end of the second workshop two months later, the participants had developed tangible proposals for better housing, childcare, and government aid.

As Blackwell's quote suggests, the NCNW had not always been in touch with the concerns of grassroots women of Mississippi. As a middle-class organization, the council had difficulty establishing itself as a civil rights organization devoted to serving the needs of the total black community. But in the 1960s, this meant that the NCNW played catch-up to other national civil rights organizations that had been active in community-based projects in the 1950s and 1960s. Its reputation as a middle-class organization in the 1950s and early 1960s hurt its ability to recruit the "masses of black women"—especially youth who "distrusted its middle-aged constituency" and the council's integrated projects, including WIMS.[5] While not as young as many of the college activists (she was around thirty at the time), Blackwell had cut her activist teeth in organizations energized by youth and radicals, and she had been present as these organizations debated the role of whites in the movement. She, too, may have distrusted the council's integrationist tendencies as well as its elitism.

But by the mid-1960s, the NCNW came to embrace a new definition for "expert." During Wednesdays in Mississippi, the NCNW had identified upper-middle-class black and white women as the leaders through which to help with the black freedom struggle, but just a few years later, it had changed direction. On July 1, 1967, less than eight months after Blackwell's initial encounter with the NCNW, Dorothy Height appointed Blackwell codirector of a new low-income home ownership program, that by 1975 had help build 18,761 Turnkey III homes for poor people around the country.[6] As Blackwell recalls in her autobiography, when Dorothy Height told Blackwell that she would be a good person to work with housing expert Dorothy Duke on the project, Blackwell stated that she didn't know a thing about housing. "Well, you know about what it's like to need a good house," Height responded. "Now, that's the gospel truth," said Blackwell.[7]

Height, like many other civil rights leaders involved in community development in the late 1960s, came to recognize and appreciate the power of local women in the rural South and the urban North, the same way that SNCC, the MFDP, and CDGM activists had previously done. Charles Sherrod referred to these women, who were willing to support the SNCC volunteers during their voter registration efforts, as "'mama[s]'": "'She is usually a militant woman in the community, outspoken, understanding, and willing to catch hell, having already caught her share.'"[8] But these grassroots women also possessed a local knowledge of their own experience that came to redefine the council's notion of "expert."

Taking a page from SNCC's strategy of integrating local people, the council hired Blackwell to reach out to Mississippi community members because she understood their plight. Height took Blackwell under her wing, bringing her places in Mississippi where she hoped to increase the council's presence. Blackwell recalled, "I had to get me some lists together to find out who's in this town. 'Why is we goin' there?' . . . I asked her, and she started doin' that. She got her secretary to run it out to me . . . and then I sent it back to her, and I told her this is the lady that you want to talk to or that is the man you want to talk to." Height appreciated Blackwell's know-how so much that she hired her as a senior staff member of the council.[9] Unlike Sherrod, the council did not label these women "mamas" but instead designated them as formal leaders. In a 1966 initiative targeting black women volunteers—Project Womanpower— the council referred to these women as the "vanguard," recognizing their importance through this formal title.

Height did not develop an appreciation for local women's expertise solely on account of SNCC's and CDGM's admiration. Instead, she was undoubtedly influenced by the federal government's War on Poverty, which called for "maximum feasible participation" of the poor.[10] She was also moved by the shift in mood of the black freedom struggle away from integrationist tactics and toward a more separatist approach. Thus, it was hardly a coincidence that Height began, in 1966, to implement programs that would incorporate more local black women into the constituency and leadership of her organization. Like many other civil rights organizations at the time, which stressed local control of antipoverty projects, the council acquired this new sense of expert, but at the same time did not completely let go of the former one. In their new Turnkey III housing program, Height paired Blackwell with Dorothy Duke, an upperclass white housing specialist from Lorain, Ohio.[11] In this sense, Height had found a successful strategy in using both her former integrationist tactics and her growing respect for community development led by the black poor.

The NCNW's now more capacious definition of "expert" bestowed a new level of power on individuals representing previously marginalized groups in the late 1960s. This newly acquired status for these individuals altered both the NCNW and the identities of the people themselves, who were now being placed at the center of (previously inaccessible) policy debates. For instance, through her council connections, Unita Blackwell worked with first lady Pat Nixon on housing. After her time with the council, Blackwell ran for mayor of her hometown and became the first female black mayor in Mississippi, serving for a total of twenty years. She served on numerous political boards, including President Carter's Presidential Advisory Committee on Women; traveled on diplomatic trips to China, India, Latin America, Africa, and Europe; and received a MacArthur Fellowship in 1992. An exceptional individual on her own, she also learned how to work within political systems while at the council. She has credited Dorothy Height with teaching her that "if I approached people, even the most highly placed leaders, on their level as an equal, most of them would receive me as an equal."[12] But there were also moments of frustration for these new experts. In a 1967 debriefing, Blackwell mentioned how difficult it had been for her to work with a former Citizens' Council man who had to learn how to say "Negro" in front of her.[13]

The NCNW also questioned what needed to happen within its own organization as the country seemed to be dividing between black separatists and more moderate black and white liberals. In the summer of 1965, the council had become more involved with the War on Poverty, sending WIMS teams to aid in efforts with Head Start and contributing services to Women in Community Service's work with Job Corps (see chapter 7). Many local NCNW chapters also helped with Head Start, including one in Queens that had a $25,000 grant from the OEO. NCNW local groups also set up childcare centers in Greensboro, North Carolina; Hackensack, New Jersey; and Brooklyn, New York.[14] Then, in spring 1966, SNCC ousted its more moderate executive director, John Lewis, in favor of the more radical Stokely Carmichael. With the election of Carmichael and the reelections of Ruby Doris Smith Robinson and Cleveland Sellers, SNCC signaled its desire to move in a more militant direction.[15] And then in June 1966, local Mississippians began embracing the rallying cry of "Black Power" during James Meredith's March Against Fear.

This new rhetoric frightened more moderate civil rights leaders. Martin Luther King, who was on the Mississippi march as well, embraced many of the goals of Black Power and agreed with the sentiments of people like Carmichael, but he feared the backlash of the white community, including both civil rights supporters and enemies. The leaders on the march could not agree on what slogan they should use as a whole—the SCLC's slogan "Freedom Now" or SNCC's "Black Power."[16] The march ended on June 26 with a rally of fifteen thousand people in Jackson. But noticeably, the NCNW did not attend in any official capacity.[17] Instead, Height called together the leaders of the council for an urgent meeting the second week of July at a retreat center in Capahosic, Virginia. It was at that meeting that she and the other leaders of the NCNW decided in what direction to take the NCNW following the more militant moves of the black freedom struggle in general. Height emphasized the need for overall unity as a national organization, stating, "Every one of us around this room could make a twenty-minute speech on the National Council of Negro Women, but do we have a group mind about the National Council of Negro Women?"[18] Several tape recordings of the two-day meeting show that while the request was for unity, the discussion was not always unified. Members expressed everything from NCNW board member and WIMS leader Polly Cowan's white liberal integrationist rejection of Black Power, to a desire to better understand the meaning of the phrase. What did unite the meeting was its defensive tone—members of the council felt attacked because of their class, age, or stance on integration.

Height began the meeting by acknowledging the difficult situation that moderate organizations were having as the tide turned more separatist and militant. Height stated, "Part of what we are caught up in today with the struggle between SNCC, and SCLC, and NAACP and all the rest of this . . . is the problem of the generations."[19] But she was well aware that the problem also included differences of class and ideology, and she defended (and appeared defensive about) the NCNW's approach, claiming, "We're in a day when status is in revolution." She continued, "We spell our own doom because what has happened in the War on Poverty is that at last the people farthest down, if you want to call it that, are now awakened just as around the world the have-not nations have awakened." Far from seeing this new development as positive, Height continued, "And so what we're up against in the ghettos especially is the fact that the rest have made up their minds that if they don't have it, they can at least make everyone else so uncomfortable that they won't enjoy what they do have."[20] Height voiced her frustration with those who questioned "establishment" women who might "enjoy the luncheons and the teas, and those who have some social skills." She argued that black, brown, and white moderates were justifiably frustrated by this radicalism.[21] Far from wholeheartedly embracing the new direction of the movement, Height struggled with the turn toward more grassroots and radical control of the movement. She felt that there were dangers with letting people with little formal education lead the black freedom struggle, arguing, "When you say to people well that's not a very sensible way to approach this, they couldn't care less because: a) they have nothing to lose. [b)] They have nothing to protect."[22] But sensing that she must reform the council, given the social climate, Height called for greater integration of membership along class lines.[23]

This July meeting in Capahosic, Virginia, began the transformation of the NCNW's mission. At the beginning of the meeting, Height acknowledged her frustration at being misunderstood by the youth, white liberals, and poor black communities in America. But by the end of the meeting, the NCNW had created consensus. As part of its new vision, the organization changed its articles of incorporation and began working toward bringing in more black grassroots women. At the November 1966 annual convention, the NCNW's program goals included recruiting and training black women for participation and leadership within community service organizations, developing cooperative and independent projects, "work[ing] for legislative enforcement and administrative and legal action to protect civil rights and to combat poverty," and, most significantly, broadening the base of women participating in these activities.[24]

Workshops in Mississippi

Around the same time as the November annual convention, Dorothy Height and Polly Cowan discussed ways that WIMS could change to complement the council's larger shift in strategy.[25] In late 1966, after its failure in Boston and minimally successful work in Paterson, Wednesdays in Mississippi became Workshops in Mississippi and redefined itself as a liaison organization between black women in Mississippi and government agencies distributing War on Poverty funds. The new WIMS subsumed its public identity under that of the black-directed NCNW, thus enabling the sub-organization to build up a strong coalition of black women activists in Mississippi instead of focusing on facilitating interracialism. WIMS now used its fund-raising abilities, political connections, and experience with social activism to help design and support a series of NCNW workshops to be led and attended by local Mississippi women. These workshops, slated to begin in November 1966, would be different from the Wednesdays in Mississippi activities of the previous two years. WIMS was now offering funding and staff—including Cowan and Ann Hewitt—to support these efforts, yet no white and only a handful of the northern black participants from the previous two years, such as Marie Barksdale and Ruth Batson, acted as consultants for the new workshops. Despite its black woman constituency, WIMS sought out the aid of white faculty from the University of Mississippi's 1965 desegregation institutes, including women's dean Katherine Rea, education professor Roscoe Boyer, and sociology professor Julian Tatum, as well as white graduate students Kate Wilkinson and Gabe Beard, from the departments of education and sociology at Ole Miss. With such white southern scholars providing consultation at the November 1966 workshop, it was hardly surprising that Blackwell found it alienating.

WIMS was not yet fully sensitive to the concerns of women like Blackwell, but it would soon be. In preparation for the November workshop, Height sent a call out to the black women leaders of Mississippi to join together for a planning session that would identify their concerns for their communities. She invited an impressive group of activist women from across the state, including Mrs. Jeanette Smith and Mrs. Natalie Mason, who, as the wives of

NAACP leaders, had worked hard in the background of the civil rights movement. Height also included many civil rights trailblazers, including Annie Devine of Canton and Jessie Mosley of Jackson, to discuss job training, childcare, and consumer education. She also encouraged the women from Mississippi to write her with other suggestions for the conference.[26] Although Noelle Henry, wife of Aaron Henry, could not leave her small family pharmacy to attend the first workshop, she did write to Height that "when this organization speaks, it can be said, 'This is the voice of Negro women in Mississippi.'"[27] Further suggesting the tremendous interest in uniting black women in the state around a common cause, fifty-three women representing fourteen towns showed up, even though only twenty-five signed up ahead of time.[28] The women represented a wide range of black Mississippians. Nine of the women were community organizers, fourteen had been working with Head Start, eleven were teachers, four were social workers, one was a librarian, and several worked for social agencies.[29] Women from all areas of Mississippi attended. Height chaired the conference, with Cowan as director. This first workshop still maintained some sense of the traditional expert, with the Ole Miss white steering committee and Height chairing the event. As previously mentioned, Blackwell pointed out that this meeting started out in a manner irrelevant to poor black Mississippians, who had little in the way of food, education, and housing. But again, women like Doris Dozier, representing the council, were able to convince Blackwell and others to stay.

By the end of the workshop, the local women had taken control of the workshop and begun brainstorming on "what the National Council of Negro Women can do" for them. Task force leaders included Smith, Devine, and Blackwell.[30] These local leaders stressed to the workshop organizers that women's involvement in activism was influenced by resources—for instance, if they didn't have the money to travel or for food, they could not volunteer in their community. Thus, for the second workshop, impoverished women would need travel stipends. Also, the women of Mississippi encouraged WIMS and the NCNW to carefully consider what they meant by "local" concerns, reminding them that the wealthier areas of Mississippi, such as Jackson and the Gulf Coast, had different problems from those of the rural Delta.[31]

Two months later, WIMS set up a second workshop in Oxford, Mississippi, which reflected this change in direction. This time, Boston WIMS activist Batson was the workshop chairperson, and local black women had an even stronger leadership presence. Devine and Mosley, representing Canton and Jackson respectively, were co-chairs of the conference, with a host of local leaders on the steering committee. Forty-three women came from across the state to learn from consultants how best to apply for federal grants to help their local communities. Of the forty-three women attending this workshop, only twelve had a regular source of income. The women represented a range of places, with eight from rural communities with populations under 2,500, three from small towns with populations between 2,500 and 10,000, and eight from cities with populations over 10,000.[32] Consultants came from the Women's Bureau of the Department of Labor, the Office of Economic Opportunity, and the Department of Agriculture to lend their assistance in helping the women write War on Poverty project proposals. According to the workshop report, the consultants from these agencies were skeptical that much could be done in three days, but by the end of the grant-writing conference, WIMS helped local women create plans for a childcare center in Ruleville; a school breakfast and gym uniform program in Canton, which served twelve hundred children in the 1967–68 school year; and a day care serving unwed mothers in Okolona.[33]

After the Oxford workshop, participants went back to their home communities and conducted additional gatherings to inquire about local needs. In Laurel, Elizabeth Malone reported that she met with three hundred people locally and that childcare was something desperately needed in her town. Other women, like Devine in Canton and Willa T. Raspberry in Okolona, reported that in addition to working on community projects, there was now a deep desire among women in their hometowns to become a part of the NCNW, and some of the women began organizing sections. The women also requested that the NCNW continue to sponsor workshops around the state to help facilitate their fledgling grant programs.[34]

Workshops in Mississippi also served as a liaison not only to open dialogue between the poor and government agents but also to expose the problematic ways that government employees interacted with the poor. When Lillian Palmer, a white federal extension agent of the U.S. Department of Agriculture from Mississippi State University, spoke in front of the Oxford conference about how to stretch one's income through budgeting, she implied both that poor women had enough money to consider budgeting and that poverty was a product of their own fiscal irresponsibility. The poor women attending the conference pointed out that many of them made less money than Palmer's assumed lowest salary for a budgeting family—thus teaching the government "expert." Cowan went one step further by taping the presentation. After Palmer's insulting presentation, Fannie Lou Hamer became so angry that she nearly left the meeting. As Cowan recalled, "I thought we'd lost her for NCNW." Yet Cowan was able to appease Hamer by promising that she would play the tape for high-ranking officials at the U.S. Department of Agriculture. As the wealthy, politically connected wife of Lou Cowan, Polly Cowan used her clout to publicize Palmer's presentation. The Department of Agriculture later used the recording to teach its future agents the right and wrong ways to address welfare recipients.[35]

Influenced by Palmer's problematic assumptions about the Mississippi poor, WIMS sponsored a third workshop, "Closing the Communication Gap," later that summer in Indianola, the county seat of Hamer's Sunflower County. Although Cowan and WIMS staff had written the proposal for the workshop, WIMS continued to subsume its identity under that of the NCNW, referring to itself a few times as "the National Council of Negro Women's Workshops in Mississippi," but more often as simply "the NCNW" in its official report.[36] Cowan and the WIMS staff, most of whom were white, kept the focus on the black women, both as participants and as leaders, while asking the question, "How can we get better relationships in the future than we have had in the past?"[37] WIMS and the NCNW hoped that they could continue the dialogue between the rural poor and government agents, especially those from the U.S. Department of Agriculture, and they believed that the government officials could learn much from the interaction.

Height again moderated the workshop, while the NCNW leaders, including some WIMS staff members, asked Hamer, whom they paid to be the Sunflower County coordinator, to select the twenty community experts. Then, in a diplomatic move acknowledging the board of Sunflower County Progress, Inc. (SCPI)—the local white-dominated Community Action Program—WIMS asked the board to select eleven more rural poor women to join. The NCNW then chose a few consultants from this group of women. WIMS made sure to pay the participants from the rural community as consultants, in case local white officials questioned the women's authority. By insisting that all participants of the Sunflower County workshop be labeled as consultants, WIMS established the rural poor as leaders in that county, paying them for their expertise and making it feasible for them to attend. Workshops also paid for each rural woman's stay in a motel for two days.[38] In total, thirty-one women from rural communities; nine members of the SCPI; and fifteen members of federal, state, and local agencies—including the OEO, the Farmers Home Administration, the Soil Conservation Service, the Sunflower County Welfare Department, the Mississippi Employment Service, and the Social Security Commission—attended.[39] The OEO newsletter *Rural Opportunities* noted, "It's all part of the cooperation that can be developed between poor communities, CAA's [Community Action Agencies] and the Technical

Action Panels in order to get services where they belong—to the low-income people."[40] The council sought to establish communication between elite and poor and between black and white people.

Like black residents of this county, whites were also circumscribed by the race divide, having learned to act condescendingly and sometimes violently toward black Mississippians.[41] According to WIMS, the white staff of the motel, which housed the workshop participants, agreed to comply with the Civil Rights Act and let the participants stay, but they were frightened for their own safety, as angry segregationists might attack them as well. However, as a WIMS staff member wrote, "Our [white] Mississippi Workshop Coordinator [Ann Hewitt] who had made the physical arrangements, served as a model for the [white] motel-keepers in her consistent use of courtesy titles, her concern that each woman be housed comfortably. The natural sincerity of her respectful manner gave every local woman a new confidence."[42] Workshop staff member Helen Rachlin, who was present at the meeting, confirmed this, saying that Ann Hewitt had helped desegregate the motel: "The hotel took us, but there was a demonstration in front of the hotel, but Ann got rid of them. She didn't care who she shook her finger at."[43] The report continued by attributing the success of the workshop to the network established by Wednesdays in Mississippi: "The contacts and skills growing out of team visits and Workshops over these years has built confidence, understanding and cooperation with government, with the white community and among Negro women."[44]

At the event, the black women of the Delta aired their grievances to government officials, including white representatives, while the council ensured participants' safety. Dorothy Height encouraged the women to avoid using the first person and instead speak collectively about their concerns for their communities, to make them less likely to suffer any reprisals.[45] With this strategy in place, the women testified about the horrible conditions they had endured. One woman testified that she had so many holes in her roof that she had to put on full rain gear inside her house when it rained. Another explained that her family had to sleep in scarves and winter clothes to combat the lack of heat in their home. And another woman told officials about how her home had so many gaping holes that there was no place where she could not see outside (and this was not because of windows). Rachlin recalled one poignant moment vividly, in which a government official was explaining all the programs that the War on Poverty was implementing on behalf of the poor, including the newly expanded food stamp program, which cost a small fee. He argued that food stamps were so cheap that surely they were affordable to all people. One woman stood up and said, "Mister, we ain't got nothing," stopping the official in his tracks and showing the limitations of the food stamp program in helping the poorest people in Mississippi.[46]

The council helped legitimize poor black women's stories in front of white officials. Sunflower County clerk Jack Harper was initially skeptical of the workshop but decided to attend out of curiosity. Over the course of the two-day meeting, he began to see the value in the conference, but when a young woman testified that she had been unknowingly sterilized in a local hospital after giving birth, a procedure so common that it was nicknamed a "Mississippi appendectomy," Harper interrupted, claiming that this was flatly untrue.[47] Height supported this local woman's story in her regal, calm matter when she responded, "In our experience it was hard to get fifty black women together without someone telling that story." By the end of the two days, Harper had learned a great deal and even gave thanks to Height for the conference that "brought us together." In this instance, a man who had previously seen these testimonies as false came to reevaluate his own biases and even became a "friend" of the council.[48]

But this workshop was not without its costs. Workshops in Mississippi had received a grant from the OEO for the workshop, but just before it convened, Mississippi governor Paul Johnson vetoed the grant.[49] WIMS went ahead and hosted the event, unsure of whether the governor's veto would go through. Cowan and WIMS then spent a month waiting to see if they would have to pay for the workshop. As Cowan wrote, "It was a successful workshop— the report is just being written—and we may go broke over it, but I think it was worth it."[50] Indeed, they almost did go broke; Johnson was able to successfully block the funding for the workshop, and WIMS had to pay $4,000 for the entire workshop. The organization spent several tense months fundraising to cover this debt.[51] Thus, while the NCNW publicly sponsored the workshop, WIMS women scrambled behind the scenes to ensure that poor women of the Delta would have opportunities to design programs that would aid them directly.

A little over a month after the conference, Height, Blackwell, and Cowan met to discuss the progress of Workshops in Mississippi. Gone were the discussions about the direction of Wednesdays/Workshops in Mississippi and with it the defensiveness about what a middle-class women's organization could do for local people. Instead, WIMS had found its stride by helping Mississippi residents learn about the programs available to them and teaching government officials the reality of how their own programs affected the poor. In the process, the poor themselves became the respected teachers within the organization. By drawing on their connections with wealthy benefactors and government officials, WIMS provided a safe space for Mississippi women who would otherwise not be treated with dignity by government officials or be encouraged to articulate their concerns.[52] These workshops also helped bring Mississippi women together and harness the national power of the council. Height pointed out how helpful the council could be for women in Mississippi: "I think what really we're saying is—is we're talking about political strength and the use of . . . power—we have to learn what it is [that] produces some kind of—of leverage . . . we're part of a national effort."[53] Appropriating the power inherent in the national network of women, the council and its sub-organization, WIMS, were able to use their clout with local officials, contractors, and builders in Mississippi as well as threaten to contact officials in Washington if any of them did not comply with federal law.[54]

Project Womanpower

While WIMS targeted women in Mississippi, the council was working toward building up another system of workshops throughout the nation. In May 1966, the NCNW received tax-free status retroactively to December 1965. Then, in early July, the Ford Foundation officially announced that it would fund NCNW's proposed Project Womanpower with a $300,000 grant. Project Womanpower planned to identify local black women leaders, train them in grant writing and volunteer service, and then set them on the task of building up local volunteer efforts in their own communities. The NCNW proposed to the Ford Foundation that their ninety vanguard women would then help train six thousand more women for community service. In addition, the NCNW hoped to build interest in the organization.[55] In internal letters, Ford Foundation officers acknowledged that the council's goals were ambitious but recognized that even if the NCNW achieved half of what it set out to do, it would still be a success.[56]

With its new tax-exempt status and the Ford Foundation funds, the NCNW could hire staff members for Project Womanpower rather than rely on volunteers, as it had in the past.[57] When selecting staff, the NCNW "made a conscious and deliberate effort to break with more traditional patterns of leadership that tend to be politically and socially conservative" and engage young activist women in their program.[58] The staff that the council hired for Project Womanpower reads like a who's who of young activist women from SNCC, CORE, the SCLC, and SDS, including Prathia Hall, who served as assistant director; Merble Harrington Reagon, research assistant; Frances Beal, administrative assistant; Doris Dozier, southern field representative; and Gwendolyn R. Simmons, who had been a leader of Freedom Summer in Laurel, midwestern field representative (see appendix 3). As Beal said in a 2005 interview, "NCNW hired people who had been in SNCC. Almost all the people had been in SNCC, so it was like an act, we were young Turks in the group. But she [Dorothy Height] always listened. She always had an open ear."[59] Crenshaw likewise recalls that Dorothy Height "didn't close her door to any of them," regardless of how militant. She worked with Stokely Carmichael and met with Malcolm X.[60] Although Height and many of the other members of the council pursued a more moderate public path, they were still "interested in [supporting] their people and their work."[61] Merble Reagon agrees that although the council was known as a group of women who hosted teas and cotillions and wore white gloves and hats, most council members fully supported the younger activists and their civil rights work. Height likely felt that this new staff, would also help build interest in the council. "I think that Dorothy Height understood that because of the people that she hired for the staff, that inevitably different kinds of women would come into the organization because their perception of it might change in ways that would make a difference to them."[62]

The council provided paychecks to these young women and allowed them to work for their other activist causes.[63] In 1968, while working at the council, Frances Beal created the Black Women's Liberation Caucus within SNCC. One year later, the group split off from SNCC to become the independent Black Women's Alliance, and in 1970, it became the Third World Women's Alliance (TWWA). TWWA was a feminist, anti-imperialist, antiracist organization grounded in socialist principles. Kimberly Springer has pointed out how difficult it was for radical black feminist and socialist groups to gain funding from mainstream American women's and African American organizations. Thus, the paycheck that Beal took home from her work at the council was even more important to the survival of the TWWA.[64]

The council also provided a setting through which to strengthen black women's power. Although the council had a conservative reputation fueled by its sorority constituency who enjoyed teas and other social events, many of the new, younger staff knew of and respected NCNW founder Mary McLeod Bethune and believed that even the elite council was still concerned for the welfare of the total black community, including the radical women.[65] Reagon was particularly excited at the opportunity to work for a nationwide black women's organization, as the civil rights organizations that she had already worked for—SDS and the Northern Student Movement—were majority white. Though she would have never joined a sorority and was "definitely not interested in Cotillions or teas," she still perceived the women of the NCNW as "women like myself" and was looking forward to working around the country with this woman-led project.[66]

Also, although Height was not outspoken against the sexism that women faced in the movement, she was certainly aware of it and was willing to support younger women in their activist efforts.[67] As the calls for Black Power in the mid-1960s grew stronger, so, too, did the "black macho rhetoric" of the movement. Prathia Hall and the other women who came to work for the council around 1966 and 1967 may have been fleeing such a stifling environment.[68] Others believed that they could do a lot of good through council work. When Dorothy Height approached Simmons, the SNCC Atlanta project was falling apart, and Simmons was excited at the prospect of organizing black women for social change. This new project seemed to take advantage of her skills to train women to be community organizers. For her, she thought, "This is not a break from civil rights work; this is a continuation of the work that you've been doing and that you're committed to." After all, as Simmons pointed out, even though black women often didn't get credit for civil rights work, they were the courageous backbone of the Mississippi movement. As she noted, the women that she encountered during her days working within SNCC were daring, bold, and "put the A-A-A-A in bad." She was excited at the idea that this project, sponsored by the NCNW, would finally recognize women's role in their communities and help them come together to bolster their power in community activism.[69]

Much like in Workshops in Mississippi, Project Womanpower's success depended on identifying and using the power of the local leadership. The first step of the Project Womanpower grant was to hire field staff who could then identify vanguard women. Dozier was one of the first staff members hired and was able to attend the first Workshop in Mississippi in November 1966 as a Project Womanpower representative.[70] However, most of the rest of the staff was not hired until spring 1967.[71] Later that summer, the staff, forty-five vanguard women, and women from Kenya, Lesotho, Nigeria, and Sierra Leone, joined together for a conference at Airlie House in Warrenton, Virginia. There they learned about and discussed African American history, relationships between black men and women, community action, consumer education, and economic cooperatives. Vanguard women came from all walks of life, including some clubwomen from NCNW-affiliated organizations and others from grassroots organizations. Project Womanpower staff hoped that the vanguard women would then create volunteer projects in their own communities and also join the NCNW. According to a Project Woman-power report, the conference was "electric" for the women, with many stay-ing up late into the night to plan conferences and projects to draw in women from their communities.[72] Simmons agrees that Airlie House was "phenome-nal." For her, it was exciting to see powerful black women activists from around the country come together to share their thoughts on community activism while also learning about black history and culture. "Those were powerful gatherings, as I remember and I . . . remember us having major . . . break-throughs with people having insights into things that they just had no knowl-edge of."[73] Reagon agrees that Project Womanpower was a "safe space," where women could address civil rights issues and discrimination against women "in an unapologetic way."[74]

The vanguard women then began organizing community service insti-tutes in their own hometowns in hopes of recruiting more volunteers. As Rea-gon recalls, "In every instance . . . we would take our cues from the women who lived in a particular locality." Reagon would then do research about the different areas targeted by Project Womanpower and try to learn more about what was needed by black women in those locales.[75] The first Project Wom-anpower community service institute took place in Macon County, Alabama, a little over a week after the Airlie House conference, as over seventy women congregated at the Tuskegee Institute. Crenshaw recalls that Vera Foster, the wife of the president of Tuskegee, invited her into her home and helped her bring together a wide spectrum of black women in the region. Indeed, as a result of Foster and Crenshaw's hard work, women came from mainly rural areas to find a way to continue the Head Start program in that area, as well as start a candy cooperative, a vegetable canning cooperative, and a credit union. The women discussed creating a traveling thrift store, where clothes could be remade and sold for $.25 to cover the cost of the program. A new council chapter was also created.[76]

By the middle of the fall, vanguard women, with the help of research as-sistants and the field staff, had sponsored community institutes around the country. In Lorain, Ohio, Simmons and four vanguard women established a new section of the NCNW; created a consumer workshop; launched a black history program for local youth; and brought forty-six women together for a two-day community service institute to establish a welfare union, coopera-tive programs, and job training. Simmons recalls how eager these women were to launch a project.[77] In Crawfordville, Georgia, two hundred women attended a community institute that centered around how to boost participation in a local clothes-making cooperative, which helped quadruple the women's salaries.

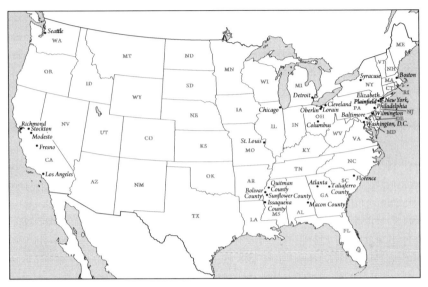

Project Womanpower Community Service Institutes, 1967–68

Eighty-six Issaquena County, Mississippi, women—teachers, cotton workers, and domestics—were bused to the nearest facility for their conference at Mount Beulah College to discuss welfare, education, and black history. In Harlem, seventy-six women discussed joining the local NCNW section and becoming more involved at the local NCNW-sponsored Bethune Center. In Elizabeth, New Jersey, thirty women discussed the need for low-cost housing and childcare. Most of the women at the community service institutes looked to the NCNW as a way to continue their poverty programs and community service work, and most expressed their desire to set up NCNW sections in their area.[78]

In its second year, Project Womanpower expanded further, especially to target cities in the Midwest and West. Ultimately, the program trained 117 vanguard women from all walks of life. These women held institutes in over thirty areas of the country, including the rural South; small urban areas, such as Plainfield, New Jersey; and large urban areas, such as Watts, Los Angeles (see map). Between thirty to three hundred people attended each seminar to discuss food production, housing, consumer education, and day care. One of the most important—and popular—parts of the program was the black heritage kit created by historian John Henrik Clarke, which was distributed to all the women who participated in the program. This kit included information on black history, especially stories of black liberation. Historians Clarke, T. C. Baird, and James Campbell also became instructors for both of the vanguard training conferences, with the understanding that their history lessons would be shared further at the institutes.[79] As one woman from Mississippi wrote, "The session I liked best was the one on black history, because it told me so much about myself and my people."[80]

Project Womanpower also helped transform many of its participants' sense of self. While women were the backbone of the civil rights movement, many of them felt uncomfortable speaking at the public meetings. Crenshaw recalls that in order to speak with many of the women in the Deep South, she had to go through their husbands. Simmons recalls that even the most courageous black women activists—such as Elberta Spinks of Laurel, who housed Simmons during Freedom Summer and helped set up a support network for twenty-two SNCC activists—were uncomfortable taking charge. According to Simmons, Spinks insisted that "we have to put the men up there; we have to prop up our men, because they should be the leaders." Not all the women involved believed this, but Simmons recalls having to address this reluctance of the vanguard women to becoming formal leaders.[81] With the release of the Moynihan Report just a year before the beginning of Project Womanpower, the women discussed both their feelings about "matriarchy" and the health of the black family. Project Womanpower helped address the shame that black women associated with being too powerful in their families, allowing women around the country to move beyond the myths perpetuated by the Moynihan Report and other critics at the time.[82]

The final report for Project Womanpower suggests that the NCNW had come a long way as an organization in understanding and learning about the needs of poor women in just two years. In its final recommendations, Project Womanpower stated first that "bread and butter pressures" on women—such as securing money for a ride to the project location—made it difficult for them to sustain their volunteer activities. Second, the NCNW recognized that "an indigenous local coordinator . . . is vitally important to sustain the ground work, once laid, and to help local groups gain momentum in community service and community action." And finally, the NCNW found that the Project Womanpower staff needed to stay for a long time in order to offer help to the local vanguard coordinator.[83] These were all findings that suggested that the NCNW had spent a large amount of time around the local activists and come to appreciate the full needs of the community leaders. Still, the two-year-long grant project was too short to make a lasting impact in all the communities that it touched. The structure of Project Womanpower was meant to support black women in their creation of community organizations, not sustain their projects for the long term. Simmons has suggested though, that just as SNCC has been used as a community-organizing model by the Black Lives Matter and Dream Defenders movements, Project Womanpower could be a good model for organizing people in social movements.[84]

Many of the Project Womanpower staff women and participants remained connected to the council. As previously mentioned, Beal stayed on with the NCNW, eventually publishing its newsletter, the *Black Woman's Voice*. The council job paid Beal's bills while she worked for more radical causes. Prathia Hall also stayed on with the council and would later direct another training program, and Merble Reagon became the director of a new career center in the 1970s (see chapter 7). With the help of these younger staff members, but also influenced by the shift in the mood of the black freedom struggle, the NCNW adopted a more radical stance in the late 1960s. Height learned a great deal from Beal and the other "young Turks." In a 1975 interview, she stated, "I think what many blacks who have had my kind of training and experience with many whites don't realize is that black young people have a whole lot to be angry about."[85] Behind the scenes, these young Turks were educating Height, who then went on to implement several black self-directed projects to help poor women. They encouraged the council to think about unifying black women along class lines. As late as May 1966, the council used a letterhead with a logo of what appears to be five to six properly dressed women standing between olive branches. The slogan was "Faith, Leadership, Culture."[86] A few new logos appeared in the late 1960s, but by 1970, a new logo was developed by pan-Africanist artist Herman Kofi Bailey. This logo was designed especially to grace the cover of the new *Black Woman's Voice* newspaper in 1971 but was later adopted by the council. Beal explained how during her time at the NCNW, she and the other young staffwomen helped the council develop a new black nationalist logo, including a "prim-looking woman, . . . one woman with an Afro, another with an African dress—to see the kind of different women that existed," and a new motto of "Commitment, Unity, and Self Reliance."[87] Thus, the council's public material reflected this new approach.

The confident tone of the Project Womanpower final report stands in stark contrast to Height's fearful comments in Capahosic two years earlier. Instead, the report points out that Hamer and Blackwell, who had recently become leaders of the national NCNW programs, brought "a richness of knowledge and experience in dealing with economic and social issues and with the poor" to these organizations. They spoke in front of the national convention in November 1967, along with a number of other vanguard women attending the conference, offering perspectives on their projects, especially grassroots cooperatives that they had been working on with the help of Project Womanpower. The authors of Project Womanpower's final report proudly wrote that despite the council's middle-class image, "Project Womanpower provided a unique opportunity for women to test and to learn ways of making the 'unity of purpose—unity of action' slogan become a reality." Unlike earlier efforts at integration, such as in Wednesdays in Mississippi, now the council was focused on unifying black women, hoping to develop "a greater sense of self-acceptance and black consciousness" more than anything else.[88] Project Womanpower helped facilitate a profound change in the council. Reagon estimates that the project had an impact on thousands of women, and believes that it helped change the direction of the council by drawing in women who had not previously been a part of it.[89]

The Commission on Community Cooperation

While Workshops in Mississippi began to address the problems of women in the South, and Project Womanpower united black women across the country, a new interracial organization under the NCNW purview promoted poor black women as experts in the North. In July 1967, after years of tension resulting from a lack of sufficient housing, education, and job opportunities and the disruption of black neighborhoods through urban renewal, black residents of Newark, New Jersey, angrily protested. Cowan, director of both Wednesdays and Workshops in Mississippi, responded to the violence the best way she knew—by organizing a communication-building workshop. She chose to do this not through WIMS but through a new organization that she and Dorothy Height had founded in early 1966, the Commission on Community Cooperation (CCC). The CCC was very similar to WIMS in using the idea of building bridges of understanding, but its name did not limit its activism to one state. Like WIMS, it was a sub-organization of the NCNW.[90] Helen Rachlin, a white Jewish NCNW volunteer, became the organization's director, and Cowan served as chair.[91] By the time of the Newark rebellions, the CCC had already begun working on a job-training program in New York City as well as a consumer workshop in Indianapolis.

The problems in these urban areas seemed overwhelming. On the evening of July 12, 1967, police arrested and severely beat a black cab driver named John Smith in Newark's Central Ward. Neighborhood residents saw police dragging Smith's body into the police station and quickly congregated in front of the building, demanding to see Smith. In frustration, they threw bricks, bottles, and Molotov cocktails at the precinct. The police eventually moved into the crowd of protesters and began to beat them as well.[92] As Ko-mozi Woodard writes, at this point, for the black community, "the nonviolent phase of the struggle was over."[93] For five days, angry and exhausted black citizens of Newark fought against the injustices of the city that had plagued them for decades. They looted and set fire to businesses owned by whites who had charged too much or treated them poorly. Meanwhile, believing that snipers were attacking them, the mostly white police force and National Guard shot back at innocent citizens with indiscriminate violence. By the end of the revolt, thousands of dollars worth in property had been destroyed, hundreds were injured, and at least twenty-three people had been killed. Twenty-one of those killed were black; two were children.[94]

Residents of Newark responded in different ways in the aftermath of the violence. Members of the black community tried to recover from the enormous devastation wrought in their neighborhoods. Though it had already been gaining a foothold in the North before the rebellions, black nationalism quickly gained greater attention in Newark.[95] At the same time, arguing that the city was no longer safe for them, many white residents and businesses moved out to the suburbs. As the National Advisory Commission on Civil Disorders argued, the country was not moving toward integration but was instead "moving toward two societies, one black, one white—separate and unequal."[96] The Kerner Commission explicitly laid the blame for the rebellion on the racism of Newark's white politicians, businesspeople, and residents, stating clearly: "What white Americans have never fully understood—but what the Negro can never forget—is that white society is deeply implicated in the ghetto. White institutions created it, white institutions maintain it, and white society condones it."[97]

Despite the longtime lack of white Americans' acknowledgment of racism and its toll on black Americans, Cowan and Rachlin believed that Newark might still welcome an interracial project for local residents. They thus designed a special project for Newark—the Program for Housewives—which involved a series of workshops titled "What's Happening to My World?"[98] Black and white lower-middle-class housewives would meet one another and discuss their common interests related to the well-being of their families and the community. The primary goal of the workshops was to promote communication between women of different races. A secondary goal was to encourage these women to support, and possibly volunteer in, racial integration projects in local schools and community organizations. During the planning stages, women from Paterson, New Jersey, also requested that the CCC continue the work already begun with WIMS the previous year. Between 1967 and 1969, Newark hosted three workshop series and Paterson, two.[99] Participants listened, sometimes screamed, and even cried as they sat next to women from different races and classes, but even when they disagreed with one another, they were forced to hear the other side of the story. Over the course of the workshops, the white women heard a litany of racist experiences that black women faced on a daily basis. By the end of the workshops, many of the white women claimed that they had changed their opinions and ideas about racially charged topics such as welfare, education, and police brutality. Much like with Workshops in Mississippi and Project Womanpower, the black participants in these council-sponsored workshops emerged as the experts.

Even as the council worked on new initiatives that placed more emphasis on empowering poor black women, it did not abandon its interest in interracial work. The leaders of the CCC felt that their organization was the ideal vehicle for educating women who were embracing white backlash in Newark. An internal NCNW planning document explained: "Under our auspices as a Negro organization and as a women's organization committed to the total community, [the CCC] can do a great deal to develop new insights, new approaches to problems and new ways of working."[100] In many ways, the proposal to enact cross-racial projects under the umbrella of a black female organization challenged the expected leadership of many white-led interracial organizations in the North. Although Cowan and Rachlin were white, Madie Horne, chairwoman for the Newark workshops, was black; and one of the two chairwomen of the Paterson series of workshops was black. And although white women still held a slight numerical edge in leadership positions in these workshops, the presence of black leaders as well as outspoken black participants dramatically transformed the dynamics of these programs.

While leadership was visibly integrated, rank-and-file participation was much more divided. Once the CCC began to recruit women for the workshop, the leaders employed the tactics that they thought would best attract "middle American" housewives to their project. According to an internal document, the CCC believed that ethnic white women "work[ed] hard to maintain [their] homes and families,"[101] valuing their role as family caretaker above all others. Thus, the organization tried to appeal to this presumed interest. As Rachlin later stated to workshop participants, "There are always panels of experts who express their opinions on something and . . . sometimes we [women] know very well that we know more than the experts because it's our day to day experience but we never get the chance to speak."[102] These women viewed themselves as community "experts" because they understood the social organization of community.[103]

While the CCC attracted white middle-American housewives, it had much more trouble attracting black middle-class women to the housewives program. Many white ethnic housewives traditionally stayed home during the day, but black women had to work out of financial necessity, so midday workshops did not fit their schedules.[104] Because the CCC insisted on hosting their workshop for "housewives," most of the African American women who could participate were either marginally employed or unemployed and on welfare. Thus, the workshop provided an excellent forum for impoverished black women to debunk many myths that white middle-class American women harbored.

The CCC's first workshop series was held in late 1967 at the Rutgers University Student Center in Newark. In order to facilitate the gathering, the workshop offered day care to participants and a $100 stipend. By offering these incentives, the CCC was able to recruit a wide variety of women, from mothers to retirees. Women came from every Newark ward and were evenly divided between black and white, with a significant number of women coming from blue-collar families and others coming from white collar and professional families. Rachlin and the other CCC leaders were proud of the diversity of the participants.[105] They hoped that through this diversity, the women could clearly see the participants' universal respectability. Rachlin wrote on the first day, "Each participant was carefully groomed, making it impossible to distinguish the PTA officer from the welfare mother."[106] Although Rachlin employed her own stereotyped, paternalistic assumptions about the "typical" appearances of women of different classes and races, she also pointed to the ways in which women who held stereotypes began to rethink their assumptions. The women had to interact with one another throughout the day. Not only did they talk about issues in the discussion sections, but they also spoke with one another at lunch and in other informal gatherings. These moments of exposure were crucial to white women's learning.

In addition to exposure, the women focused on learning by doing. They went on field trips, where they witnessed the efforts of community organizations outside the areas in which they lived. They visited the Child Services Association, the Essex County Youth House, and the Urban League in inner-city Newark. They were also given homework to interact with neighbors and observe racism within their communities. One homework assignment called for the women to speak with their family members about their ideas about race. Another assignment had them visit different stores to compare prices and discuss the results back at the workshop. The wealthier women soon learned what poorer women had always known—that goods were more expensive in the poorer areas of Newark. Through these activities, the white women engaged in consciousness-raising about their own racism.

Despite the growing knowledge of participants, it did not always lead to consensus. The women differed in their views about welfare, the police, and education. In one heated incident regarding welfare, one middle-class black woman stood up and cited welfare abuses such as "furniture bought for them with taxpayers money . . . wall-to-wall carpeting . . . free medical care when I pay cold cash." At the end of her tirade, she claimed, "Don't expect life to be handed to you on a silver platter!"[107] A welfare rights activist then stood up to argue that it was societal conditions that made welfare a necessity. Another participant shot back, "They have babies, over and over. . . . If a woman is well enough to get all these illegitimate babies, she's well enough to go out and get a job. . . . Women should start learning morals!"[108]

The women fought back and forth, black and white on both sides of the issue, until one woman stood up. Visibly shaken by the conversation revolving around the economic system that she relied on, she stood up and said, "W-E-L-F-A-R-E. I hate the word. My children hate the word. But without the welfare we couldn't live." According to Rachlin, the whole room was shaken by this experience. The women suddenly realized that they were speaking about workshop participants, just like themselves, who were forced into financial situations in which welfare was a necessity. "I didn't mean you," said the woman who first led the attack. "Who did you mean, then?" the mother on welfare replied.[109] Confrontations like these, though uncomfortable and tense, became opportunities for some women to learn from the poor and be accountable to them.

Subsequent workshops in Paterson also helped shatter many whites' misconceptions. During a field trip to a children's shelter, the white women responded that they were appalled at the poor conditions there. Some of the black participants commented that this situation was minor in comparison to the way that the shelter handled discipline. They told their white counterparts that the shelter actually locked up children to punish them. The white women did not believe her, but one week later, a story about a boy who had been locked in his room at the shelter for eight days because he was caught smoking hit the headlines. According to the CCC report, the white women began to understand why black women were often hostile to government institutions that (the white women now realized) allowed, and perhaps encouraged, the abuse of black children.[110] According to Emily Schneider, a psychology researcher who came to evaluate the Paterson workshop, 41 percent of white participants felt that the workshop had helped transform their attitudes about blacks.[111] (Helen Rachlin commented that the black participants in Paterson were far more knowledgeable about racial inequality in the city, and only about 9 percent changed their minds about whites.) Overall, 76 percent of the Paterson participants said that they had "gained knowledge, the majority specifying new information about concrete problems such as welfare, education, government processes and consumer problems."[112]

In addition to rethinking their views, white and black women developed tangible personal relationships with one another. At the conclusion of the program, alumnae groups and individuals met every week to touch base and discuss plans for new projects. Additionally, some women visited one another in their own homes. Though this hardly seems like activism, for some, it was a big step; and as they developed closer relationships with the women of the workshop, they began to question their prejudices. One white woman from the first Paterson workshop began carpooling with a fellow participant from a low-income black neighborhood. According to the CCC internal reflection report, the woman stated, "I'm not afraid to go in there since I know Mary lives there."[113] Acting on behalf of the community as mothers also was empowering for both black and white women. As they listened to the black mothers talk about their concerns for their family, white women questioned contemporary racist stereotypes of them as uncaring, inattentive mothers, and of their families as dysfunctional.[114]

Finally, the women, both black and white, experienced personal empowerment as activists. Simply being active outside the home had been an important experience for some of the participants, including one black woman in Newark who attended only the first session of the workshop. Rachlin and the others figured that she had not gotten much out of her short experience. However, at the end of the workshop, she reappeared to tell the group that her one day with the CCC had "taught her how to listen and work through differences" in her new job. Several other women became involved in community projects.[115] While the CCC workshops were not as innovative or dynamic as other contemporary programs in Newark in combating discrimination, they helped to gently push white residents to question their own racist ideas and complicity in a system of violence against black residents, and they exposed white housewives to black female leadership in a significant way.

WHILE NOT WITHOUT their limitations, the workshops sponsored by the NCNW in the mid-1960s revealed profound changes that were occurring within the organization at the time. Through Workshops in Mississippi, Project Womanpower, and the Commission for Community Cooperation's efforts, the formerly elite-focused black women's organization began to transition away from viewing a middle- or upper-class, college-educated woman as an expert to appreciating the "wisdom of the pinched toe and empty belly."[116] These new initiatives helped push the council in a new direction. Not only did women on both sides of the class and racial divide alter their attitudes toward one another at these workshops, but the council began to shift its national program to design and implement projects that gave the black working poor food, shelter, and day care. The council then used these plans to implement domestic development projects around the country but especially in America's poorest, most racially violent state: Mississippi.

CHAPTER SIX

But If You Have a Pig in Your Backyard . . . Nobody Can Push You Around

Black Self-Help and Community Survival, 1967–1975

In 1968, Thelma Barnes—a popular black candidate who had served in the Greenville-based Delta Ministry for several years—lost a bid for Congress to Thomas Abernethy, a known segregationist. Later, Dorothy Height asked Fannie Lou Hamer how Barnes had lost even in Washington County, which had a 70 percent black electorate. Hamer pointed out that some black residents had been threatened and others had been bribed away from voting with $20 or promises of new jobs. Hamer concluded, " 'You see, Miss Height, down where we are, food is used as a political weapon. But if you have a pig in your backyard, if you have some vegetables in your garden, you can feed yourself and your family, and nobody can push you around.' "[1] In addition to the economic intimidation and poverty that blacks continued to face in the late 1960s, the benefits of both the Civil Rights Act and the Voting Rights Act were slow to reach the people of the Mississippi Delta. In 1966, the Mississippi legislature had divided the region up in such a way as to ensure that each congressional district had a white majority.[2] The MFDP, in which both Barnes and Hamer were heavily involved, was well aware of the political chicanery that black candidates faced after the passage of the Civil Rights and Voting Rights acts. In 1965, the MFDP initiated a suit to challenge Mississippi's drawing of its legislative district lines to dilute the black vote. Peggy Jean Connor, a beautician in Hattiesburg and a local activist who had served as COFO's secretary-treasurer and the MFDP's executive secretary, lent her name to the court case as plaintiff. Fourteen years later, the Supreme Court ruled in favor of Connor, and black representation rose dramatically.[3]

The council, however, was not involved in legal action like the NAACP or the MFDP. Instead, with Hamer's words resonating in her mind, Height took the first steps to create a pig bank for Hamer's nascent Freedom Farm Cooperative, seeking a way to transcend Mississippi's legal barriers by providing black women and men in the Delta with food, shelter, and day care. A 1969 progress report of the council's "Self-Help Campaign Against Hunger" stated that the Sunflower County pig farm began "based on the thesis that a people who have the means to serve themselves not only can begin to relieve the terribl[e] problems of starvation but also with dignity and freedom can begin to break the chain of political oppression."[4] In providing these basic necessities, the council was responding to the imperatives of Delta women themselves. In a series of workshops sponsored by the NCNW in 1966 and 1967, poor black Mississippians had made plans to implement these kinds of projects. As the 1969 report pointed out, participants in an NCNW-sponsored workshop in Mound Bayou, Mississippi, pointed out that they could not wait for the federal government to provide them with the bare essentials of life, emphasizing that " 'there is an urgent need for food *now!*' " (emphasis in original).[5] The council implemented self-help projects that would not only furnish Mississippians with the necessities of life, which they were not receiving under existing state or federal War on Poverty programs, but also offer them employment, training opportunities, and possibly political independence. Much like many Black Power initiatives at the time, self-help became a call to arms for the council's work in Mississippi beginning in 1967.

In its proclamations of self-help, the council continued to emphasize individual and community change as the means to eradicate racism and poverty. This community-level self-help approach remained appealing not only for advocates of Black Power, who called for increasing black independence from mainstream America, but also for government officials in the War on Poverty, who, while seeking to alleviate poverty, quickly began to rein in federal funding for antipoverty projects in whatever way possible.[6] Political leaders were more than happy to place a large portion of the burden for new poverty initiatives onto voluntary organizations like the NCNW (and the philanthropic organizations that funded them). The council also tried to incorporate the private sector, as it sought out contracts with local businesses, even though these were often led by avowed white supremacists. Finally, the council employed conservative rhetoric to counter popular stereotypes of blacks, especially black women's dependency, when justifying its projects. Height repeatedly stressed that it was not that these women and men did not want to work; it was that they could not find work—or, if they could, it did not pay them enough to live.[7]

As it implemented domestic development projects around the country, but especially in Mississippi, the NCNW walked a fine line between appeasing proponents of Black Power, who called for self-determination, and conciliating white funders who questioned the wisdom of placing the black poor in leadership positions (as Height herself had done just a year prior at the Capahosic executive board meeting). The council claimed that it was simply providing poor communities across America with the tools for self-sufficiency, but it helped create such self-sufficiency through a network of philanthropic supporters from both the private and the public sphere to overcome deficiencies in federal, state, and local aid. It also walked a fine line between bringing more activist members into the council and appeasing its more established members, while also consulting with mainstream American white leaders, who still resisted black community control.

Combating Hunger

The three-month-old pigs arrived on October 10, 1968, to great fanfare.[8] Under its new program, Hunger, USA, the council had been working since the summer to purchase fifty white Yorkshire gilts and five brown Jersey boars for a pig bank for Hamer's farm. The NCNW purchased the pigs for $25 each from the Heifer Project (later to become Heifer International) with the help of Willis McAlpin, a retired farmer in Iowa.[9] Over time, each pig gave birth to about five litters and produced around six to eight piglets per litter. Each family that owned a pig then donated two pigs back to the pig bank, replenishing the supply. By 1973, the pig bank had produced three thousand pigs.[10] As one grateful recipient remarked that year, "Every time I kill them hogs, I think about the National Council of Negro Women . . . and if Miss Height and your [group had not] come down here, [we] wouldn't have this meat."[11] The council also bought thousands of dollars' worth of wire and posts to help make individual pens for the pigs. For a long time, the council also supplied the feed for the pigs.[12]

In addition, Fannie Lou Hamer purchased about forty acres for a Freedom Farm in Ruleville, on which she might be able to grow vegetables for the hungry in the area. The NCNW provided turnip, mustard, kale, and collard green seeds for her small farm. Other gifts in kind that the council donated to the farm were six soil tillers, a full-size tractor, a tool storage house, and a 21-cubic-foot freezer.[13] In the first year of the Freedom Farm, the council helped raise and harvest these crops and then helped can approximately two thousand pounds of vegetables. The council also helped secure additional resources for the community farm and pig bank. One New York–based NCNW woman who served on a foundation board began to seek funds from her foundation to pay for a community center near Hamer's Freedom Farm, and another NCNW woman petitioned her sorority to pay for the farm tools.[14] The council estimated that over three hundred people were involved in this initial effort. Eventually, through the help of other groups, Hamer's Freedom Farm grew to nearly seven hundred acres.[15]

In Bolivar County, Mississippi, in that same fall of 1968, the council provided seeds for five more community gardens in Rosedale, Shelby, Mound Bayou, Cleveland, and Gunnison. Community farmers grew collards, cabbage, turnips, onions, spinach, mustard greens, and kale. Gunnison alone canned over one thousand pounds of food and froze another fifteen hundred pounds. In the spring, the council helped plant peas, string beans, okra, corn, and potatoes.[16] And in Macon County, Alabama, after a Project Womanpower meeting there, Mrs. Consuello Harper of the local NCNW began to help organize a community farm. In 1969, the council purchased $67 worth of seeds and $60 of fertilizer for this farm. A representative of each of the sixty-four families who received these materials had to sign a pledge that they would plant, cultivate, can, and then share their crop with others.[17]

Crucial to its success in these cooperative efforts was the council's reliance on local leadership, which helped maintain communication between the rural communities and the national NCNW. As discussed in chapter 5, the council had become much more sensitive to the importance of incorporating local leaders—and their expertise—into its projects. Hamer, the NCNW's main Delta contact, was perhaps the most well respected local activist in all of Mississippi. The NCNW hired her as a field organizer, and she helped set up the pig bank by recruiting and then screening applicants and reporting back to Height. Hamer "tried to make every effort to try to help these families become self-sufficient," and the council appreciated her efforts on behalf of the national organization.[18]

However, the council's aid in procuring food was not meant to last indefinitely. Height had hoped that from the initial council contributions, the pig farm could become self-sustaining. Although Hamer highly prized this program for giving the participants "a new sense of pride and security," activists Charles McLaurin and L. C. Dorsey have both pointed out the limitations of the pig bank.[19] The pig bank was on its demise by the mid-1970s. Dorsey said that it was "'not a good project,'" as it had only lasted a few years. She also claimed that "'no real farmers would ever have come up with anything that crazy,'" calling it a "'[Dorothy] Height problem.'"[20] McLaurin agreed that many of the pig bank members never fulfilled their pledge of returning two piglets to the litter.[21] However, McLaurin believed that the pig bank had served its purpose. People continued to have pigs from the project until at least 1976, and contrary to Dorsey's assessment, McLaurin felt that the project ended not because of its inherent weaknesses but because most people in the area no longer needed it. According to McLaurin, by the late 1970s, many people had begun to receive a regular paycheck thanks to the efforts of Head Start and the community action work in the area, so they dropped the pig bank project when they were no longer desperate for meat.[22] In her work on cooperative economic thought and practices, Jessica Gordon Nembhard has argued that the pig bank was the most successful part of Hamer's Freedom Farm, "perhaps because it was the best capitalized, was relatively self-contained, was not capital- or labor-intensive, was run by women, and did not depend much on the weather."[23] Although it did not last long after Hamer's death, the pig project fed many people, who desperately needed the meat at the time.[24]

Providing Shelter

At the Mississippi workshops in 1966 and 1967, women from across Mississippi had revealed not only the profound hunger they faced on a daily basis but also the horrific conditions they faced in housing. Many poor women lived in unsafe substandard housing.[25] The council sought a solution to this problem and established a housing initiative to implement the federal low-income homeownership program Turnkey III, which brought together a local private builder, the local housing authority, and a home buyer to help low-income people slowly purchase their federally subsidized homes, instead of renting. The buyer would not have to provide a down payment for the home but could use "sweat equity," or an agreement to do his or her own home repairs as well as place the first $250–$350 of homeownership payments into a fund that could be drawn on for repairs or new appliances. After fulfilling this initial payment, 20 percent of the buyer's income would go toward paying off the mortgage of the home. After twenty-five to thirty years of this steady payment, participants would own their homes.[26]

While this program certainly gave many people an opportunity to own their own homes, it could not help the very poorest Mississippians, since the potential home buyer needed to have sufficient income to put at least 20 percent toward the mortgage to qualify.[27] However, the attention on housing conditions that Turnkey III brought to many communities forced local housing authorities to become more accountable to the low-income and poor residents in their area. In addition, moving those people who could afford the small payments away from renting to the homeownership project helped create a ripple effect, in which the very poor could be moved out of shelters and into the public housing vacated by the Turnkey III residents.[28] Based on its experience with Turnkey III, the council would create and then lead a task-force under HUD secretary George Romney that successfully raised the percentage of homeownership programs sponsored by federal public housing.

The NCNW's Turnkey III program was born after a fortuitous meeting between HUD general counsel Joseph Burstein and Dorothy Duke, a feisty white NCNW staff member, who had worked on a housing project for the elderly with HUD in Lorain, Ohio. Duke, who was heavily involved in women's club and civic organizations, had also worked with both Workshops in Mississippi and Project Womanpower in the spring of 1967.[29] Burstein had already been working on strengthening governmental housing authorities' relationship with private builders (through the Turnkey I program) and private management (through Turnkey II). When Burstein met with the council, he was enthusiastic to find a way to facilitate homeownership through Turnkey III, and the council became the "outside agent" necessary to help Burstein put his idea into practice.[30]

While Burstein wanted to increase the privatization of public housing, the council wanted to ensure that Turnkey III would help local people take ownership over their communities. Since Turnkey III relied on a private builder and the local housing authority—two groups that were rarely friendly to black Americans—the council tried to give as much power as possible to the low-income potential homeowners. Crucial to the council's strategy was to set up community participation committees (CPCs) and home buyers associations, first to help screen and train potential homeowners, and then to manage and maintain their homes, respectively. The CPC in the first Turnkey III community in Gulfport was composed of the local NCNW section and the Harrison County Civic Action Committee, a local CAP.[31] The council envisioned itself as the body to recruit participants, train potential homeowners, manage the program, and work on the program's development.[32] Ford Foundation evaluators later criticized the council for giving too much power to the community participation committees it help set up. However, these same evaluators—like many critics of the War on Poverty programs at the time—seemed more interested in the financial solvency and sustainability of the program than its community empowerment potential.[33]

In order to maximize both community participation in and the technical expertise of the project, Height appointed Blackwell, the firebrand from Mayersville, Mississippi, who had threatened to leave the 1966 Jackson Workshops in Mississippi meeting because it lacked relevance, to work with Duke. During that Jackson workshop, Blackwell had impressed Height and other council members with her strong leadership and willingness to help the council rethink its activism in Mississippi along local lines. Blackwell also possessed experience working with SNCC and the MFDP. According to a 1973 Ford Foundation report on the NCNW Turnkey III project, "Combining political sophistication and folksy wile, Mrs. Blackwell is regarded proudly by the poor blacks and establishment whites alike as a very capable and effective individual."[34] She was the leader whom Height selected to appeal to local Mississippi communities. She helped Height identify key leaders with whom to work on the project. Together Height and Blackwell traveled around the state and the country. Blackwell recalled that Height would tell her which town they were traveling to and give Blackwell a list of names of leaders in the town. In return, Blackwell would tell her whom she needed to consult (see chapter 5). Height appreciated Blackwell's know-how so much that she hired her as senior staff of the NCNW.[35]

After winning tax-exempt status in May 1966, the council used its connections with governmental and philanthropic organizations to help find funding for the project. The OEO granted $45,000 to the council in mid-1967 to begin work on the pilot project for Turnkey III and then another $89,000 less than a year later for continued work on the first Gulfport community. The Ford Foundation granted the council $330,000 in October 1968 and another $315,000 in October 1970 as it began to set up more housing communities.[36] In February 1973, the Ford Foundation gave the NCNW $110,000 (for a total of $755,000) to help incorporate Turnkey III as an official program in federal and state housing.[37] The council worked with the local housing authorities, home builders, and banks around the country. As Height recalls about the early planning for Turnkey III projects in Mississippi, "For the first time in state history public officials and private businesspeople sat in conference with representatives of a national black women's organization to discuss—as equals—how to meet the housing needs of the state's poorest black people."[38] However, these partnerships were often strained.

The NCNW was very interested in working with the local housing authority despite the difficulties that it posed. In planning for NCNW's first housing community, Dorothy Duke wanted to find a local builder and work with the local housing authority to ensure the success of the community. Francis Collins—a well-respected third-generation builder on the Mississippi Gulf Coast, known for his progressive views on race—agreed to build the subdivision and helped convince Albert E. Rushing, the director of the local branch of the Mississippi Regional Housing Authority, to take up the project.[39] When announcing the Gulfport project, HUD secretary Robert Weaver found it so appealing that he advised President Johnson to make an announcement highlighting the "role of private enterprise in developing housing for low-income families," since the NCNW, a private volunteer organization; the National Association of Home Builders; and Thiokol Chemical Corporation had collaborated on the project.[40]

Secretary Weaver publicly announced the project in February 1968. He felt it was " 'one of the most promising innovations' " in public housing, yet HUD did not initially rush to sponsor the program, despite Burstein's HUD appointment.[41] It was the OEO that gave the council more money to work further on the creation of a citizen participation committee and to counsel the home buyers in homeownership.[42] However, the NCNW was not allowed to be the main nongovernmental partner in this project. HUD had also brought in the Thiokol Chemical Corporation, based in Utah, to screen and train potential home buyers after they were approved.[43] Thiokol was a curious partner. It was a chemical company that had produced materials for both civilian and military purposes since the mid-1940s. By the 1960s, almost two-thirds of its business came from defense contracts. Its long history in producing rocket fuel for military purposes likely helped it secure War on Poverty government contracts.[44] For the company's participation in the project, it received $40,000 from HUD and $45,000 from the local Gulfport housing authority. Ironically, a chemical company involved in defense contracting was deemed a more qualified organization to train potential homeowners than the council, which had long been interested in the needs of the black community. Apparently the company's race and gender makeup, as well as its defense contracting connections, played a role in the decision to offer Thiokol the job of training homeowners, thus reducing the council's control over that part of the project.

Once Secretary Weaver and the OEO announced the Gulfport program, other cities interested in developing Turnkey III projects contacted the council as the "unofficial information center and technical advisor on the program." An external Ford Foundation report in 1973 claims that as the requests from other localities piled up, the council was "spread thin with responsibilities in widely separated localities and a whirlwind national consulting effort."[45] The council then approached the Ford Foundation to help continue its efforts with Turnkey III; it was especially interested in funding to help with preoccupancy training.[46] The council envisioned its role as translator of the needs of the poor to the government and business leaders in control of the money, and by September 1968, the Ford Foundation had given the council the first of its grants to both maintain the projects begun under the OEO grants and continue to spread the Turnkey III idea around the country.[47]

One of the first housing authorities to contact the council in the spring of 1968 was the St. Louis Housing Authority. Already under considerable scrutiny for a rent strike of tenants and the failing public housing project of Pruitt-Igoe (which would be demolished in a highly publicized television spot four years later), St. Louis was looking for new options. With council help, the builder and housing authority received approval for eighty-two townhouse units, a community center, and a high-rise development for senior citizens. The racially mixed, working-class local community erupted in protest, not wanting yet another failed high-rise. The council then created a parallel community group to approve of the project, thus throwing out the sentiments of the many locals who disagreed with the project. The council's efforts, however, were for naught, as the training contract that they were seeking was awarded instead to a local mortgage company reviled by the black community for its exploitative practices. The council left this project a little over a year later.[48]

From the spring of 1968 through the end of 1969, the council was met with opposition in its efforts to set up other homeownership projects around the country. In Dallas, the council set up a CPC to help with implementing a one-thousand-unit Turnkey III project, only to lose the training contract for the project. In San Antonio, despite the NCNW's best efforts, the local white community blocked plans for another community. Local council affiliate Delta Sigma Theta and the League of Women Voters tried to reassure local whites that they had nothing to fear, but the city council ultimately vetoed the project. Additional efforts in Elizabeth, New Jersey, also failed when the Newark mayor rejected the potential site as unsafe. In Raleigh, North Carolina, Dorothy Duke helped set up a CPC in May 1968. The council helped the CPC with tenant selection and screening, and eventually gained some funding for training from HUD (though the vast majority of the money went to Thiokol after a politician pressured HUD to give the contract to the chemical company). Ultimately the training in Raleigh continued under the direction of the University of North Carolina, with no input from the NCNW.[49] In Oklahoma City, the council provided information for a potential project but did not do much beyond that.[50]

The council had a bit more influence with its Turnkey III project in Indianola, Mississippi, named Southgate. When the council met in Indianola for its "Closing the Communication Gap" workshop in June 1967, Colonel Jack Harper told participants that there was no infrastructure to set up a local housing project because there was no local housing authority. In addition, any public housing project would have to be voted on by public referendum, something that whites, who continued to hold the majority of political power in the Mississippi Delta, would not support. Joseph Burstein proposed that a project could be created under Turnkey IV, built on the leasing program of public housing (Section 23), and would thus not be required to have the public referendum approval.[51] A local economic development group, the South Delta Economic Development District (SDEDD), took charge as the de facto housing authority, and the council finally won contracts to do the pre- and post-occupancy training of homebuyers.[52] Later developments in Cleveland and Moorehead, Mississippi, however, excluded the council from their training programs, though the Eastgate community center in Cleveland named its building after Dorothy Height in honor of the initiating role that the NCNW played.[53]

But Southgate was not a total success. Charles McLaurin pointed out that the NCNW "got the money for the housing, . . . but then the [local white] political power . . . set up the terms."[54] The community was established outside Indianola's city lines. For Owen Brooks, this was initially a strength. The NCNW went directly to local leaders like Hamer, Joe Harris, and Amzie Moore and their organizational affiliates when setting up the homeownership projects. According to Brooks, "Those municipalities [in Indianola, Cleveland, and Moorehead] had no interest in building low-cost housing for any of the poor black people in their areas" before the council-sponsored efforts. "So this was an alternative that enabled low-cost housing to be built, in important areas of the state[,] as models that could be repeated when and if some of those municipalities gave in and organized municipal housing authorities on their own. So it was a good effort."[55] However, a few decades later, this made for difficult times in securing services and political power for residents. McLaurin had to go to court around 1985 to ensure that Southgate became incorporated into Indianola in order to strengthen black voting power and to secure basic infrastructure services from the city. In addition, even at the time of the establishment of the homeownership projects in the Delta, McLaurin was skeptical that anyone would be able to own their homes through these projects. McLaurin told Joe Harris, the rural outreach person for the NCNW at the outset of the project, that "these people ain't never going to own these houses . . . it took me a day to read [the contract]." Indeed, even for those residents who were close to homeownership, when the homes changed hands, the new owners had to start making payments all over again. For those who were lucky enough to complete the payments to own their homes, when the house changed hands, the new owners had to pay heavy taxes that they were often not prepared to pay.[56]

The council envisioned its role as the mouthpiece for the local black community, and it was able to have a significant role in Gulfport, yet even there it had limited access to continued community involvement after occupancy.

The council's major role in Turnkey III was in initiating the program and providing information about the housing projects that had already begun to be built. In addition, the council worked on tenant selection. Despite its efforts, however, the council had limited involvement with the projects once the initial setup period was over.[57] Although the council had become a trusted part of the black communities in which it had set up projects, it was accused by local housing authorities of bringing "an air of moral superiority to discussions" and being "a divisive force in the sense that it set the community and the home buyers in an adversary position to the authority." A few Ford Foundation evaluators saw this as "the combative spirit of community action" and believed it unproductive, but the council saw itself as trying to gain maximum resources for the neighborhood residents. The NCNW wanted to allow home buyers to pay their mortgage payments late and to allow large families to move in. Although this may not have been financially efficient, it was what the community actually needed.[58]

The council quickly gained a reputation among housing authorities of being strongly pro-resident, at the expense of the local housing authority. In the Delta, SDEDD, the de-facto housing authority, criticized the council's Indianola training program as "leaning too much to community organization and too little to the practical problems of prospective home buyers" and that the NCNW-initiated home buyers association was "difficult to work with and overly independent."[59] A Turnkey III project developed in Columbus, Ohio, worried that the council would form a community participation committee and fight the authority " 'every step of the way.' "[60] Columbus did not invite the council to participate further in the project. SDEDD claimed that the NCNW had fostered a spirit of hostility in the projects it was involved in, but this was likely due to its insistence that the community have a voice equal to that of the builder and the housing authority. While the council was invested in the home buyers associations, many housing authorities found them problematic and did not include them.[61] However, in 1974, the U.S. General Accounting Office (GAO) found that strong pre- and post-occupancy training programs and home buyers associations—two parts of the project that the NCNW had been most involved in before 1974—were crucial to the success of the program.[62]

With so many setbacks in trying to establish Turnkey III communities, the council moved away from setting up new projects and instead began to institutionalize Turnkey III as a permanent project in HUD. Turnkey III was initially created by Burstein and the NCNW as a creative interpretation of existing legislation rather than its own program. On July 10, 1970, the council convened a meeting with a handful of housing-related and civic organizations, including the National Association of Home Builders, the National Tenants Organization, the National Urban League, and the Rural Housing Alliance.[63] The conference resulted in an increased commitment from HUD and the creation of a task force to investigate homeownership in public housing. Height became the chairperson of this new task force, which helped push HUD to allocate more money toward homeownership. HUD ultimately accepted the task force's recommendation that it allocate 10 percent of its units to homeownership in 1971 and 15 percent in 1972.[64]

The council believed that as an independent, nongovernmental organization, it provided a crucial role in the establishment of homeownership in public housing. "Contracting the community organization and development work out to private or non-profit firms has merit, but there must be a system for quality control. In the end, perhaps, there can be no substitute for the NCNW or comparable organizations functioning as watchdogs to see that the job is done well." The council was proud of its role in the Turnkey III projects: "It is worthy of note that a national voluntary organization of black women was able to take an expressed need of poor families, convert it to an idea, nourish it, prod the authorities into producing it, and stay with the product until it became accepted nationally." They had helped make "the American dream of homeownership" a reality for poor men and women around the country.[65]

In March 1974, through the efforts of the Height-led task force and HUD, Turnkey III became law. Congress amended Section 5(c) of the United States Housing Act of 1937 with Section 201(a) of the Housing and Community Development Act of 1974. This statute provides that home buyers would continue to receive federal subsidies even after the title was transferred from the government to the occupant as private owner. In today's federal housing guidelines, Turnkey III is still active, and the council's influence is still noticeable. One of the most important recommendations in the Turnkey III guidelines refers to creating a community participation committee in each new project "to assist the community and the LHA [local housing authority] in the development and support of the Turnkey III program." The guidelines go on to state that the CPC "shall be a voluntary group comprised of representatives of the low-income population primarily and may also include representatives of community service organizations." Thus, the council's concern in helping to build a CPC in each community to ensure that potential home buyers have a voice in their communities has lived on to the present.[66]

As it had done during Wednesdays in Mississippi and subsequent workshops around the country, the NCNW worked to facilitate communication between diverse groups in order to get maximum results for local black communities. Now the council was building bridges primarily between government officials and the local community. One example of this bridge building occurred when a key builder for Turnkey III, who was white, needed housing information on properties in the black section of Greenville, Mississippi, but could not find the information. He asked the NCNW for help. Dorothy Duke then called Thelma Barnes, the Delta Ministry and Head Start community leader who had run for Congress in 1968. But Barnes had only spoken to the builder one previous time, and she needed the NCNW to introduce her. The NCNW complied, and the builder was able to acquire the information he needed to proceed with the construction of low-income housing units. Duke claimed that although Barnes and the builder lived only about ten blocks away from each other in Greenville, "to be able to converse on a problem of intense interest to both, a bridge had to be established through an N.C.N.W. staff person that was traversed at least 5 times in less than 4 hours." Later, both called the NCNW contact to tell her how positive the conversation had been and how they planned on meeting independently to discuss future housing programs to help the black community.[67] Here, and in many other situations, the council opened dialogues between government officials, community activists, and businesspeople to get things done.

Another council role was to help train potential home buyers in home-maintenance skills, legal and financial knowledge of homeownership, and self-government. While many people balked at the idea that black homeowners needed training, Gray-Wiseman recalls that the instruction was helpful. She, along with her mother, Youther Lee Keyes, had been instrumental in civil rights activities in North Gulfport, and had helped with the site development and recruitment of home buyers. She had also helped train the potential home buyers to clean their new homes. As she recalls, "Before anybody moved in, again we had to go through how to clean and what to do because a lot of these people came out of places, Lord you just don't want to know." Many of these new home buyers had come from rental units that lacked electricity and running water, and many had never seen the kinds of appliances that were in these new homes; therefore, Gray-Wiseman believed that the training was crucial to helping the new home buyers.[68]

The NCNW housing program, however, was not without its problems. The Gulfport project, for instance, experienced problems from the very beginning. The Gulf Coast–based builder Francis Collins was known for his progressive views on race, but he had convinced the less progressive head of the local housing authority, Albert Rushing, to work with the Forest Heights development. A few years into the project, Rushing seemed to be doing everything in his power to prevent the maintenance of the Gulfport community, even though he was being paid by HUD to do just that. He took $20,000 a year from HUD for administrative purposes related to the project, yet he continually blocked requests to help fix up the property. When HUD officials questioned him about this, he chose to return money to HUD rather than fulfill his contract to assist the community. Collins ended up doing the job that Rushing was supposed to do and cleaned up the property on his own. However, GAO evaluators still found clogged drainage systems, broken-down play areas, and unkempt common grounds.[69] Ford Foundation evaluators thought that the local housing authority's hands-off attitude suggested that it hoped the project would fail. Rushing joked to the GAO evaluators in 1973 that he would sell the Gulfport project to them for $10.[70] While the council was proud of its efforts in bringing all types of southerners together—even those like Rushing—the hostility of these types of officials stood in the way of its success. Rushing blamed the NCNW for the failure to properly train the residents of Gulfport. Collins did not blame the NCNW for the community's failure, but he did take a swipe at the council by telling Ford Foundation evaluators that his own company would have done a better job than the NCNW at training.[71]

However, Collins, in his role as builder, could have done a better job. Since the Gulfport housing units were put up in less than a year, the homes' foundations did not have time to properly settle. Some of the building materials were cheap and were already falling apart after five years. The ⅜-inch walls were too thin to handle the wear and tear of family life. While these problems were not so different from those of other quickly built subdivisions at the time, the residents of Forest Heights were rightfully concerned that their twenty-five-year investment would be worthless by the time their mortgage was paid off. While the homeowners were responsible for fixing small things in their homes, patching holes in the walls, painting exteriors, and fulfilling larger maintenance needs were the responsibility of the local housing authority, which remained intransigent. When the Forest Heights residents requested a ditch to be rebuilt and fenced in because it was perpetually clogged and bred poisonous snakes, Rushing allegedly refused to put up a fence because "those people would throw debris over it into the ditch and the fence would make the ditch more difficult to clean."[72]

The project also suffered from vacant properties, which later became vandalized. The council wanted the local housing authority to have less stringent requirements for income so that more people—both above and under the limit—might purchase a home. However, the 1974 GAO report insisted that HUD must maintain its standards for income, regardless of whether there were vacancies. Unsurprisingly, Rushing blamed the vacancies on the "bad reputation" of the project.[73] By March 1974, thirteen units were unoccupied, and 37 percent of the original families had moved out. This was likely in response to deterioration of the homes, lack of upkeep of the common spaces, and property vacancies causing the value of the homes to diminish. In some cases, these property owners were making payments meant for a home appraised at a higher price. Although some of this was the result of homeowner neglect, much of the situation was due to the local housing authority's negligence. One indication of the pride and efforts of the residents who were committed to staying in the community is that the Gulfport project had one of the lowest percentages of delinquent payments of all the Turnkey III projects, with only 17 percent of payments late in 1972.[74]

Although there were problems with the program, the homes in Forest Heights were better than anything else that poor residents in North Gulfport had access to at the time. "Housing then was pretty rough and rugged," noted Gray-Wiseman. Hired by the NCNW at the start of the project to complete a survey of the housing needs in the area, she found families with as many as six children and two adults living in a single-room home. Some families would use a slop jar, sleep on one pallet on the floor, and keep their perishable foods in a tub covered with ice. Many homes lacked running water. Through Turnkey III, many poor people in Mississippi finally had a permanent and sound structure in which to live. As Fannie Lou Hamer remarked in 1973, while speaking with a new homeowner, "It's a wonderful experience . . . when you can . . . quit looking through the floor down under the house."[75] Not only had the council made homeownership a new reality for many poor Mississippians, but it had included home buyers in the planning of the project from the very beginning, giving them ownership of the project.

Most of the residents who moved into Forest Heights were thrilled to be there. In 1969, the subdivision was saved from flooding by the heroic efforts of Ike Thomas, who risked his life during Hurricane Camille to close the floodgates that protected the community. According to Height, when asked by HUD secretary Romney why he had been so brave, Thomas commented that "for the first time in their lives, they had something of their own."[76] Mary Spinks-Thigpen has lived in Forest Heights for forty-five years, ever since she moved into a three-bedroom home with her husband, daughter, and son. While the people who chose to move into Forest Heights were "determined and exceptional" people to begin with, she notes that growing up in the community strengthened everyone as well. She also points out that many young residents of Forest Heights have gone on to get their doctorates and other advanced degrees. The community has produced nurses, managers, bankers, teachers, NFL and NBA players, chefs, physical therapists, business-people, CPAs, teachers, police officers, cosmetologists, barbers, and small-business owners. She has emphasized that it was the strong community that helped build the character of its youth. "We are a closed-in community. . . . We [had only] one way [to drive or walk] in and one way out, so we all knew each other[,] and most would help each other." This meant that community members could encourage and reprimand one another's children. "We meant well when we talked to our children; we wanted them to be the best."[77] Third-generation Forest Heights resident Kewanna Riley agrees with this senti-ment: "One of the things that I truly loved is that everybody raised everybody's children. It really was like growing up having dozens of grandparents and countless parents and aunts and uncles because everyone really looked out for everyone else. There would be days when my mom would cook a meal and all of my brother's friends would come over to the house to eat."[78]

Forest Heights became much more than a subdivision; it became a commu-nity. "We would have neighborhood cleanups . . . or block parties where we would really just celebrate the true essence of life and love[,] and there would be children everywhere and food being cooked on the grill and just so much going on in the community at the time," Riley said.[79] Riley's own success bespeaks the value of the community. She became the Southeastern Regional Boys & Girls Club Youth of the Year in 2003, Miss Tougaloo College in 2006–7, Gulfport Chamber of Commerce Elementary Teacher of the Year in 2014–15, and Harrison County School District Teacher of the Year in 2015–16. She attributes her success to growing up in a proud, independent black com-munity, formed around strong extended families. Both Spinks-Thigpen and Riley pointed out the importance of having strong families in the community.[80] Although single women were welcomed into the community, priority was given to married couples.[81] Any unmarried couple that lived together had to get married before moving in so as to ensure survival benefits for their children. By 1970, twenty-five of the home buyers at Gulfport became legally married in order to move in. Men and women who were separated and single or who had remarried had to provide evidence of divorce from their first spouse.[82]

The NCNW fought to keep black families together, whether or not they fit the nuclear family mold. The council was proud of its efforts in pushing for the housing authority to accept single mothers into the homeownership program. Thiokol later confirmed the benefits of adding this demographic, writing, "The majority of single parent heads of families have been very successful at Gulfport."[83] The NCNW also fought to allow a family, whose teenage daughter became pregnant while the family was applying for their Turnkey III home, to still move in. The local housing authority considered any minor who had a child to no longer be a minor and therefore now considered the family a two-family home and thus ineligible. The housing authority later admitted to the Thiokol staff that "the ruling in this matter was made because of the tendency of minorities to have illegitimate children." The NCNW, Thiokol, and the selection committee for Forest Heights all attempted to appeal this racist and sexist ruling, but to no avail.[84] While the council pushed for compassion and consideration in these types of situations, the housing authority still had the ability to disqualify candidates.

While those who remained in Forest Heights are evidence of the strength of the community, reaching and maintaining homeownership was a challenge. Those residents who finally came to own their homes after twenty-five years would sometimes have a deed-burning ceremony to celebrate the new ownership. Many could not believe they were finally homeowners, given how many years they had been making payments, but they reveled in the accomplishment.[85] Others—like Spinks-Thigpen, who paid off her mortgage in the late 1980s—chose to celebrate privately, out of respect for those who were still working on completing their mortgage.[86] However, paying off the mortgage did not always result in ownership for perpetuity. When their parents died, children were sometimes surprised by and unable to pay the taxes on the home.[87] In addition, the whole community was flooded in 2005 during Hurricane Katrina. Presidents Bush and Clinton visited the proud neighborhood and vowed to rebuild it, awarding the NCNW $750,000 to restore the community.[88] For this task, the council also worked with Habitat for Humanity.[89] In 2008, the restoration project was nearly finished with the help of the Jimmy and Rosalynn Carter Work Project, and a year later, the community received a levee to help with drainage in the area.[90]

Although they did not oversee the creation of or training for the vast majority of Turnkey III projects that were developed after the Gulfport project, the council deserves credit for building interest in and momentum for the federal program, which helped many low-income Americans own their own homes. By 1972, 85 municipalities around the country were managing 6,637 completed Turnkey III units, were in the process of building 6,439 more, and had 5,685 more units at the preconstruction or application phase. The estimated total worth of these 18,761 units was $407 million.[91] The council brought together private businesspeople, philanthropists, and voluntary organizations as well as governmental organizations to create this project. A variety of constituencies now had a mutual interest in the success of this project, which gave many working poor families the chance to own a home for the first time.

Raising the Next Generation

In addition to working on hunger and housing, the council tried to aid impoverished working mothers by providing free day-care facilities for them. One of its most ambitious projects was in Okolona, Mississippi, the county seat of Chickasaw County, located in the northeastern corner of the state. Besides being the county seat, Okolona was best known as the home of Okolona College, founded in 1904 by Dr. Wallace Battle to be an industrial training school for African American students. In 1921, the school was taken over by the Episcopal Church and became an official college in 1934, but it closed in 1965.[92] After the college closed its doors, the NCNW tried to establish a day care for unwed mothers on the former campus. The council first developed the idea for the Okolona Project after the Oxford Mississippi Training Workshop in January 1967.[93] The NCNW tried to be sensitive to community needs.[94] As one council staffperson reflected following that workshop, "We went into the communities[,] and we said go to the [people,] talk with them, and bring to us the things you need to have done—the priorities."[95] In 1968, the NCNW responded to the priorities suggested by local leaders and applied for funding under Title X for a home for unwed mothers on the former college campus. The council proposed that the former college become a home for about two hundred girls, including full-time housing for forty to fifty girls between the ages of fourteen and sixteen during their first pregnancy. The NCNW planned to offer participants a wide array of educational, economic, medical, psychological, and vocational services in the hope that it might help them secure and maintain a job. Continuing its role in social uplift, the council also planned on training these young women in ways that it deemed socially appropriate. The 1968 proposal stated that each young woman would be trained "for meaningful and appropriate roles as individuals and for responsible parent roles in relation to her child." In addition, the council promised that the broader local community, including whites, would have input into how the home functioned.[96]

The NCNW also wanted to use the childcare program established at Okolona to conduct research into the reality of life for single teenage mothers. The council hoped that it could provide some data for how best to serve this fast-growing demographic in the rural South and that the data could then be used to aid in developing other programs for young women.[97] The council received funds from the federal government, including the U.S. Department of Health, Education, and Welfare; from private foundations, such as the Irwin Sweeney Miller Foundation; and from businesses, including IBM, which donated typewriters and keypunch machines, and the Merck Corporation, which donated pharmaceuticals.[98]

While the NCNW received tentative approval to move forward with plans for the Okolona home in the summer of 1968, its funding was revoked that fall by the federal government after local congressman Thomas Abernethy complained that supporting the project would be encouraging prostitution. Instead of publicly defending these women, the council shied away from engaging in a battle with Abernethy, which would have likely resulted in a loss, given Abernethy's national prominence, and certainly resulted in a public discussion of black women's sexuality. Instead of taking on such a fight, the council decided to quietly alter their project and create a nonresidential childcare center instead. After this change, the NCNW continued to receive funding from various sources, including the federal government and eventually the Appalachian Regional Council. The childcare center opened in 1970 and employed some of the single mothers whom Height had originally hoped to include as residents of the home. These mothers took care of fifty children, their own and others.[99]

Spearheading the effort to create the childcare center was Willa Tucker Raspberry, a middle-class leader in Okolona, who had attended the Oxford Workshop in Mississippi in January 1967. Born in 1906 in Monroe County, a northern county on the border with Alabama, on land that her former slave grandfather had purchased after the Civil War, Raspberry had experienced both the pride and the challenges that came from being a landowning descendant of slaves in Mississippi. The oldest child of a school principal, Willa excelled in school. After high school, she attended a brief teacher-training program at Fisk and became a teacher at a Rosenwald school in Friendship, Mississippi.[100] After meeting and then marrying her husband, who was also a teacher at this school, she moved to her husband's hometown of Okolona to be both a teacher and a librarian at Okolona Industrial School and later college. After the college closed, she became pivotal in establishing the day-care center. For Raspberry, having community involvement, both white and black, was key to the childcare center's success, arguing that it had done a great deal to bring the black and white communities in Okolona together. Raspberry went so far as to argue that after the establishment of the Okolona day care, whites were much more respectful to blacks.[101]

Okolona was not the only day care to arise from the council's workshops in the late 1960s. The NCNW set up the Fannie Lou Hamer childcare center in 1970, to enable low-income mothers of infants and toddlers to work full time in an NCNW-supported garment factory in nearby Doddsville.[102] Thirty children, ages six months to three years, attended the center, which stayed open from 8:00 A.M. to 8:00 P.M. to accommodate the two shifts at the factory. The children received nutritious food throughout the day, as well as comprehensive medical examinations from local doctors. Only one staff accommodated both shifts.[103] Ultimately, the Doddsville factory shut down due to a lack of marketing for goods, few external resources to help fund the enterprise, and the racism of the surrounding community.[104] Although the garment factory and childcare center no longer exist, the childcare center continued to operate until the early 2000s with the support of the NCNW.[105]

The Fannie Lou Hamer childcare center and Doddsville factory project were overseen by several local black leaders, including Hamer, Joe Harris, Sally Mae Carther, and Miles Foster, all leaders of self-sufficiency work in the Delta. Included on the board of directors were Head Start teachers Juanita Harvey and Ruby David; Gilbert Mockabee, assistant principal of Drew High School; Mr. H. R. Smith, principal of Ruleville Central High School; and Dr. L. F. Packer, a local dentist. This governing board included professional local residents who were working with federal government programs, state-supervised public schools, and private businesses. Together they were responsible for the center's "proper function."[106] The childcare center also benefited from some government participation, as it received help in food planning from the State Department of Public Health and Agriculture.[107] The center was initially run by the Delta Opportunities Corporation, a community action agency of the Office of Economic Opportunity, with the NCNW serving as a "delegate agency" for the OEO. As a delegate agency, the council agreed to run the childcare center, provide family services, and manage the finances.[108]

The Jackson NCNW also built a childcare center for low-income working mothers under the direction of Dr. Jessie Mosley, a Womanpower Unlimited founder and NCNW leader in Mississippi from the late 1960s until her death. Mosley liked to brag that the children blossomed after attending her center; not only did it provide the children with shelter and love, but it also instilled black pride in their heritage. Mosley began pushing for black Mississippians to know their history long before it became popular in the late 1960s. In 1950, she wrote *The Negro in Mississippi History*, and she later fought to create and direct the Smith Robertson Museum and Cultural Center in Jackson, devoted to the preservation of African American history and culture.[109] As of 1975, the childcare center was open twenty-four hours a day, with volunteer efforts from retired teachers in Jackson. According to Height, the center received no public funding, functioning strictly through volunteer efforts and private funding.[110] This childcare center also became a day camp in the summer for the children of working moms until it closed in 1989.[111]

THROUGHOUT THE LATE 1960s and early 1970s, the NCNW proposed solutions to a wide range of problems that relied on a combination of private, public, and volunteer efforts to promote black self-help. Recognizing that the federal government was no longer able or willing to serve as the primary vehicle for programs addressing poverty, civil rights, and gender equality, the organization relied increasingly on private foundations and corporations to aid its volunteer efforts. And yet more radical activists, who took less of a mainstream approach to activism, still valued the council's antipoverty work. As stated at the beginning of this book, former Delta Ministry leader Owen Brooks held Height in high regard and felt that the compromises she sometimes made were worth it for the good of black community development.[112] Charles McLaurin, who worked with both the Fannie Lou Hamer childcare center and the later Women's Opportunity Program (see chapter 7), has said, "I know these projects [of the Council] were effective because they got results." In addition, young women who had first worked with SNCC, COFO, and the MFDP went on to work in the council. "[The NCNW] was certainly effective in providing training and leadership for women," McLaurin stated.[113]

Mississippi women were also appreciative. In one recording of a 1974 meeting, a local woman stood up and told the assembled NCNW leaders, "We as black women appreciate [the] talent in all these women who have come [to] us and help[ed] us to make these inroads." She acknowledged that perhaps many years later Mississippi women themselves would have been able to accomplish what had been done, "but it wouldn't have been done this soon without them. And we'll always remember that."[114] Mississippi civil rights leaders Unita Blackwell and Fannie Lou Hamer agreed, claiming that even though by the late 1960s student groups such as SNCC, CORE, and COFO "were long gone," the NCNW maintained a significant presence in Mississippi.[115] By providing the pigs and seeds for farm cooperatives, housing, and day care, the council helped alleviate some of the suffering of black communities in Mississippi. Not only did this provide much-needed resources to impoverished women and men, but it also helped to boost interest in the council.

CHAPTER SEVEN

The Power of Four Million Women

Growing the Council, 1967–1980

On July 10, 1974, after sixteen long years of fund-raising efforts, the NCNW successfully unveiled a twelve-foot-tall bronze figure of founder Mary McLeod Bethune in Lincoln Park, Washington, D.C. This was the first memorial of either an African American *or* a female leader on public land in the nation's capital.[1] The council wanted the statue of Bethune to stand opposite the controversial Emancipation Group statue, sculpted in 1876 by Thomas Ball, which depicts Abraham Lincoln standing above (and presumably freeing) a kneeling slave. Unlike the Emancipation Group statue, which has been criticized (even at the time of its founding) for perpetuating racist notions of black dependency and inferiority, the image of Bethune (who was only a year old when Ball's statue was completed) represents African Americans' ability to free themselves and triumph despite great odds. For the council, raising the money to erect this statue represented a monumental achievement (literally), displayed its prominence, and affirmed its ability to be self-reliant.[2]

Although there had been a strong fund-raising push in the early 1960s, the effort waned as other civil rights projects took precedence. Then, in the late 1960s and 1970s, the council re-embraced the statue project, emphasizing that it was part of *their* struggle as black women to celebrate their beloved founder. In fact, the NCNW solicited memories from black women of the moments in their lives when they had felt the most proud. The council promised that these recollections would "live on with the memory of a great woman" as they would be placed inside the statue.[3] Dorothy Height was also responding to heightened black nationalism, affirming the importance of black pride and self-reliance but rejecting the misogyny that was adopted by many of these groups.[4] From the stage on the statue's dedication day, Height proclaimed that the Bethune statue was "a symbol of the kind of partnership that has to take place in our own country of men and women, of people of all backgrounds," but she went on to point out that this memorial would offer recognition of the great heritage and contribution of black Americans as well as a "new awakening and recognition of the contribution of women in society." She continued, "Who could bring them better together than a woman who is also Black, knowing the meaning of double jeopardy?"[5] Height likely learned the phrase "double jeopardy" from activist Frances Beal, who had first coined the phrase while working for the NCNW.

Since the time of Project Womanpower and Workshops in Mississippi, the council had been shifting its purpose. Instead of focusing on opening up opportunities for professional black women, it created poverty projects. Instead of facilitating conversations between white and black middle-class women, it asked the poor what projects were needed and how best to implement them. It had put food on tables, roofs over heads, and children in loving childcare centers. Now it wanted something in return for this effort. The council took advantage of the heightened visibility that its poverty programming brought and promoted itself as the voice of all black women, both rich and poor. To increase programming and membership, the council attempted in 1969 to push members of its affiliate organizations to become direct members of the NCNW as well. It also pushed for the creation of more local sections. The council hoped that this would grow its membership base and help fill the council's coffers. At the same time, the council experienced great prestige in the 1970s, as it was consulted by the federal government as the organization that best understood not only the needs of black women but also the needs of women in general; in this capacity, the council conducted research for and submitted a major HUD-sponsored report, *Women and Housing*. This was indeed the National Council of Negro Women's hour.

Put "Ma in the Park"

The bronze statue to Bethune is impressive. Sculpted by Robert Berks, who was renowned for his larger-than-life bronze sculptures that look like they have been modeled out of globs of clay, Bethune gazes into the distant future and holds in her left hand her legacy (in the form of a scroll), which she is passing to a young boy while a young girl looks on. The figure of Bethune herself stands twelve feet tall and weighs about 2,000 pounds, while the children's figures are about nine feet tall and 1,000 pounds each.[6] Encircling the base of the statue is an adaptation of Proverbs 31:31: "Let her works praise her," as well as an excerpt from her last will and testament. Art historian Kirk Savage has pointed out that "Berks clearly intended the Bethune monument to be in dialogue with the Freedmen's Memorial [another name for the Emancipation Group statue]," as both Lincoln and Bethune are standing upright with outstretched arms with scrolls in hand. Whereas the Emancipation Group depicts a standing and fully clothed Lincoln freeing a kneeling, nearly naked slave, Bethune, in her usual respectable garb, stands proudly and looks off into the distance, all the while offering hope to the children close by. Savage comments that "the figures look weighty and brittle at the same time, as if the traditional solidity of Ball's figures was no longer credible in a world unsettled by enormous social, political, and racial transformations."[7] Bethune's image symbolizes the end of the racial hierarchy so apparent in Thomas Ball's statue.

To make this dialogue between the two statues even clearer, Dorothy Height and the council insisted that the original Emancipation Group statue be turned around, so as to turn Lincoln away from the Capitol building and have him instead face Bethune; by July 1970, Lincoln had been repositioned.[8] While working to fund-raise for the statue project, Height had encountered some white leaders who were concerned that Bethune's statue might actually look better than Lincoln's. But as she said at a planning committee meeting in January 1974, "We got Mr. Lincoln turned around before they all got alert to that."[9] In addition to changing the direction of the Emancipation Group statue, the council helped clean up the surrounding park. The NCNW also wanted to make sure that the local community was consulted and would benefit from the new sculpture's placement.[10] Task force members hoped that the statue would give a sense of pride to the local, predominantly black neighborhood.[11] Indeed, on the night before the official unveiling ceremony, locals came together to welcome Bethune to the neighborhood with drumming, flutes, and other instruments.[12]

The day chosen for the statue's official unveiling was the ninety-ninth anniversary of Bethune's birth. Mayor-commissioner Walter Washington, the first black appointed mayor of Washington, D.C., proclaimed it Mary McLeod Bethune Day. Eighteen thousand people, including representatives from over 125 organizations, met at the site of the park to commemorate Bethune's life and view the statue.[13] On the platform at the unveiling ceremony that day were Dr. Richard V. Moore, the president of Bethune-Cookman College; Congresswoman Shirley Chisholm; Congressman Andrew Young; Coretta Scott King; and actors Cicely Tyson and Roscoe Lee Browne. President Richard Nixon—then embroiled in the Watergate impeachment investigation—did not attend the ceremony but sent his congratulations to the council on successfully establishing the memorial for a leader who "will remain an inspiration for all of us."[14]

At the end of the program at the statue site, the Bethune-Cookman College band very symbolically marched in salute not to the former U.S. president but to Bethune. The band then led a number of smaller corps, which had traveled from all over the nation, as they marched from Lincoln Park to the steps of the Capitol. A parade of thousands followed the bands. Upon arrival at the

Capitol, the group was met by Vice President Gerald Ford; Speaker of the House Carl Albert; and the highest-ranking female military general at the time, Major Jeanne M. Holm, who awarded prizes to the best marching corps. Congresswoman Barbara Jordan, master of ceremonies for this part of the commemoration, greeted the NCNW members and thanked them for their extensive efforts to memorialize Bethune. Representatives of the governors of thirty-one states as well as Washington, D.C., and the Virgin Islands sent flags and proclamations of support for the creation of the statue and the celebration of a day in Bethune's honor.

Although the day was magnificent—even in spite of the July humidity and heat—the road to establishing this statue had not always been so rosy. The council had introduced legislation to erect the statue in 1958, hoping that it would be completed in five years for the one hundredth anniversary of the Emancipation Proclamation. They had to assure Congress that no federal funds would be used to pay for the memorial (although one hundred years prior, Congress had paid for the base of the Emancipation Group statue), but the process took much longer than originally expected.[15]

The council first had to raise political support for the project by working with people across the political spectrum. In 1958, Mr. Dolphin Thompson, a public relations worker in Washington, first urged Height to set up a statue to Bethune to serve as a proud contrast to the Emancipation Group statue. Height and Mabel Staupers—nursing leader, World War II–era civil rights pioneer, and charter member of the council—then approached Ohio Republican Frances Bolton, a longtime friend of Bethune, with the idea for a memorial. Bolton introduced the bill to the House of Representatives in August 1959.[16] Height and Staupers then walked the halls of Congress to raise support, even reaching out to more conservative legislators, including Senator George A. Smathers. Although Height called him a "fine southern gentleman" in her 2003 autobiography, Smathers had signed the Southern Manifesto, pledging to fight against *Brown v. Board of Education*, and refused to sign the Civil Rights Act of 1964, among other things. But Height worked behind the scenes with Smathers, who confided to her that he could not have been elected to the House of Representatives in 1947 without Bethune's help. According to Height, Smathers told the council that he could not take the public lead in supporting this project in the Senate, for he would not be reelected. Instead, he found another senator to introduce the bill and then helped secure votes behind the scenes to put the statue in Lincoln Park.[17] The efforts of Bolton and Smathers ultimately bore fruit. In the summer of 1960, the 86th Congress passed the joint resolution approving the Bethune statue for installation in Lincoln Park, and President Eisenhower signed the bill into law.

In addition to raising political support, the council had to fund-raise. The joint resolution stated that the federal government would not pay a cent for the statue. Therefore, the role of raising the $400,000 necessary to establish this statue fell to the voluntary efforts of the NCNW. Council members raised money on the local level. They sold boxes to NCNW members for a dollar, and then asked those members to fill the boxes with coins to put "Ma in the Park." They also asked members to contribute a dollar on special days in February called "Sweetheart Dollar Days," in honor of Bethune's favorite song: "Let Me Call You Sweetheart." In another push, the council created a group called the Committee of 400, in which each member pledged to raise $1,000. External groups helped as well, including the United Methodist Church, which provided $100,000.[18] Even Jacqueline Kennedy offered her support for the fund-raising for the statue.[19]

The council slowed down its fund-raising at the height of its civil rights efforts in the mid-1960s. Dorothy Height recalls in her autobiography, "Even our own were asking, 'Should we give to a monument, or should we help raise bond money to get Dr. King out of jail?'"[20] Height and other members of the council felt that there were more important ways to spend money when so many activists were being jailed, attacked, and even killed while pursuing voting rights, school integration, and poverty work. But there is more to this story. Deborah G. White has pointed out that during the civil rights movement of the 1950s and 1960s, the council placed black women's concerns behind those of black men, as they felt that "black women were served when the race was."[21] Hence, the council's fund-raising for a statue to their female leader took a backseat as male-led youth and radical groups consumed the attention (and dollars) of supporters around the country.

But fund-raising for the statue was revived in the late 1960s and early 1970s, a time of growing national support for women's rights and leaders. In 1972, Congresswoman Barbara Jordan won a seat in the House of Representatives, and Shirley Chisholm became the first black woman to run for president. The council was also invigorated by its roles at this time in aiding women with housing, hunger, and job training. Most significantly, the NCNW sponsored a black women's unity drive that helped identify and augment direct membership and move the council's identity away from that of an umbrella organization that united affiliated organizations to that of an organization that united women directly under the council banner. This drive was chaired by actor Ruby Dee and ultimately brought in thousands of new members and boosted total outreach of the council to four million women.

Building the Membership of Black Women

Seven years before the statue's unveiling, the council began to rethink its membership structure amid growing tensions within the organization and larger society. In July 1967, dozens of people were killed in the Newark rebellions. Less than one month later, on August 11, 1967, Detroit erupted as well, and forty-three persons were killed and over one thousand injured, most by the National Guard. Dorothy Height sent an urgent telegram to all twenty-four NCNW affiliate heads. She gave the women a little over a month to make plans for a three-day conference in September to discuss how the council could provide a unified response to the rebellions, calling the gathering "extremely critical."[22] Although the council had already done some soul searching at its Capahosic conference after the 1966 Meredith March Against Fear, it now sought to respond in a unified way to the crisis facing black urban areas around the country, hoping to take a "backward look at our programs and projects to assess whether they are truly relevant to the needs of the present."[23]

The September conference's final report, "It Is Two Minutes to Midnight," highlighted the grim reality facing most American black women at that time. While more black women worked than white women, they were in low-paying, low-status jobs. Three-fifths of nonwhite women worked in households or in another form of service employment and made a little over $1,000 a year. A high proportion of nonwhite women also headed households, which were economically disadvantaged.[24] The council used this conference to encourage its affiliates to be more sensitive to the needs of black women in their local communities. By the time Height called this national meeting, Project Womanpower was a year old and Workshops in Mississippi had just finished its "Closing the Communication Gap Workshop." These workshops had opened the eyes of many in the NCNW, but the council still remained a national organization influenced most by its elite affiliate groups, and it pushed for programs at the local level that might embrace "blackness" not just for women and children but also to help the total black family, especially "so that black men can walk in freedom and equality without crutches."[25] Based on its nascent efforts in poverty work, the council believed that its newly formed national staff could help local councils or local affiliate chapters design programs to help the poor. Once the national staff had set up a project, it could then fade away and let local leadership take charge of the project.[26]

There was also a financial incentive for the council to create more programming at the local level. The ongoing Project Womanpower and Workshops in Mississippi had revealed what was possible with increased poverty work on the ground: community members became impressed with the council and wanted to join the organization directly. Project Womanpower especially helped the council expand its work at the local level by increasing field staff; developing training and materials related to the council; and uniting the NCNW, its affiliates, and other community groups on the ground.[27] During the years of Project Womanpower, from 1966 to 1968, the NCNW grew by forty-seven new local sections, with a 58 percent increase in individual memberships. Growth in membership during this period was greatest in the Mississippi Delta, where membership in the Sunflower County section alone doubled from 125 to 250 members in just a few months. Membership increased so dramatically during this period that the NCNW created a simplified booklet explaining how to establish a new section so that any women, "regardless of their educational level," could use it.[28]

A few months later, upon the recommendation of the executive board, the NCNW annual convention voted to alter the council's policy for annual dues. The convention reduced annual dues from $5 to $2 in impoverished areas and allowed half that amount to stay in the local treasury; moreover, in exceptional cases, in which women could not even afford that amount, they could join for free. Workshops in Mississippi and Project Womanpower helped highlight the council's strengthened commitment "to concentrate attention on problems of the poor and women in the black [c]ommunity who have been outside the mainstream of influence and power."[29] The council also furthered its work to help the poor through its support for the SCLC's Poor People's Campaign. In the wake of Martin Luther King's assassination, Ralph Abernathy took up leadership of the SCLC and the campaign.[30] The council encouraged all section presidents, national officers, and affiliated organizations to become active in the Poor People's march locally by supporting the campaign's caravan with food and housing (if in the path of the caravan's march to Washington), write letters to Congress to show support for the Poor People's Campaign, and "identify your Section with the cause of the elimination of poverty and racism by publicizing your action."[31] Notably, Height called for a visible stand in favor of welfare rights for women, encouraging council members to organize simultaneous local marches during the Poor

People's Campaign on May 12, Mother's Day, to "[speak] out against the welfare amendments passed by Congress against the best interest of both welfare mothers and their children."[32] On June 19, 1968, the council participated in the Poor People's Campaign Solidarity Day.[33]

At the 1968 national convention held in Los Angeles that fall, the council repeated its call to fight against the poverty facing black women even more forcefully. The meeting opened with Dorothy Height addressing the convention by asking, "Who are we? What are we doing? Where are we? How do we respond to the Voices and Needs in the Quest for Truth and Beauty in Blackness?" (emphasis in original). The council then broke attendees into six groups for sensitivity training led by women, including some who had worked within Project Womanpower. The training session lasted four to five hours on the first day, and the groups continued to meet on the subsequent three mornings. Attendees also visited sites in Los Angeles committed to community development. As a report of the conference claimed, the council wanted to avoid a "purely 'look-see' experience" and hoped that attendees would gain ideas for local projects that they could continue in their home communities.[34]

Increasingly committed to publicly aligning themselves with the poor, the council again stressed its proximity to them. The Los Angeles conference pointed out that black women constituted over half of domestic workers and farm laborers, one-fourth of laundry workers, and one-fifth of cooks and janitors, and that nearly one in four black women headed households. As they were learning from their self-help work in Mississippi, black women could not wait for federal, state, or local governments to promote black well-being. The council's activism emphasized this connection to poor women not only by pushing for the creation of childcare centers but also by examining the specific concerns of household employees, 64 percent of whom in 1968 were nonwhite and nonsalaried. The council continued to push for increasing rights for these particularly vulnerable women.[35]

The push to increase work on the local level became institutionalized shortly thereafter. In July 1969, the executive committee of the NCNW met in Nassau in the Bahamas for a national conference for affiliate organizations. At this historic conference, the affiliate heads voted to adopt an amendment to the Constitution that would restructure the council and push all women belonging to its affiliate organizations to also join the NCNW as direct members. This move was intended to help boost programming and visibility for the council but also to raise funds. Upon becoming president, Height had implemented a fair-share program to make local sections pay extra dues, or a "fair share" of $200 a year, but she never insisted on an additional amount from the affiliate organizations. Until the 1970s affiliate organizations paid only between $100 and $500, depending on their membership size, annually to the council. However, after 1969, the council approved the new plan, in which each individual member of an affiliated organization would pay dues to the council directly.[36]

The Nassau convention also embraced a much more radical tone. The Nixon administration, which had been in place for six months, seemed to be doing everything in its power to roll back the progress made in school desegregation, voting rights, welfare rights, and other programs within the War on Poverty. The conferees claimed that they had previously "failed to recognize" the federal government's role in blocking progress for black communities. The executive committee indicated its change of heart as it sympathized with the more militant, youth-led movement: "Now, we understand better what our black youth have been saying to us."[37] They went on to state that they would do everything in their power to help black communities "by any means necessary," using Malcolm X's own words.[38] A few months later, the NCNW's proposed resolutions for its annual national conference sought to add "to develop a strong black women's movement dedicated to the achievement of full liberation for black Americans" to its mission statement, reasoning that it wanted to build membership to "develop the strategies for basic change in the conditions of black people in America."[39] Gone were appeals for interracialism; instead, the national council strengthened itself by broadening and then consolidating its power as a black woman's organization seeking liberation for black communities, families, and women.

In this year, the council announced another historic shift. Recognizing the problems that the black community would face when the increasingly conservative federal government transferred responsibilities to state governments, it changed its sub-organization from a regional to a state model.[40] Through this new structure, the NCNW hoped to strengthen its power at the state level, while also working as a "watchdog" against any state policies damaging to African Americans.[41] Under this new structure, the council pushed the new state convener to help shed the NCNW's identity as an elite membership organization and instead embrace poverty programming, encouraging them to develop new sections that were "issue-oriented," not "status oriented."[42]

In order to raise membership to fill in this new state mechanism, the council tried a few different tactics. The first was a Black Women's Unity Drive chaired by Ruby Dee in December 1970.[43] With the approval of the council's affiliated organizations, this drive pushed women of those organizations to follow through on becoming direct members of the council, in hopes of building the council's fund-raising and programming power. As part of this membership drive, which continued well into the mid-1970s, the council created a filmstrip called *The Power in Four Million Women*, which emphasized its work on hunger, housing, day care, and employment. The NCNW also sought to draw new members into the council by showing the effectiveness of its new programming for alleviating black poverty, with unity serving as the rallying cry of the campaign.[44] Dee claimed, " 'We must revitalize our people. Those among us who have achieved a degree of prosperity cannot disassociate ourselves from the poor.' "[45] Ironically, as the council pushed to bring in poorer women, class diversity within the local sections became less of a priority. At the thirty-fifth annual convention in 1971, a task force even suggested that "multiplicity and full diversity need not be achieved in every group. New sections may be built around vocations or special interests etc. The diversity will be realized as the number of sections in a given community coordinate their efforts and work with each other."[46]

At the same time that the NCNW highlighted its connection to poverty work, it continued to draw on the elite connections of some of its members. Although it had employed grassroots and radical women like Blackwell, Hamer, and Beal, the council continued to stress the importance of the financial and educational status of some of its members. This stance contrasted with the more fluid and experiential-based concept of "expert" it embraced in its work in Mississippi. In 1969, at the same convention where it affirmed the new direct-membership policy, the NCNW proposed creating a Resources and Development Committee to provide elite members of the organization with a more central role. In justifying the move, council leaders noted, "Over the years, NCNW has acquired some degree of sophistication with respect to funding. We recognize a positive role for those supporters of NCNW whose stature on the American scene is so prestigious as to either attract direct contributions or to be able to influence the funding of our various programs as they are developed." The council wanted to ensure that these prestigious individuals be allowed to remain in the council, even if they could only serve in a "limited capacity," asserting that "this is how they can best serve the Council."[47]

The NCNW thus continued to strengthen its alliances with powerful people, not alienate them, as it called for the unity of all black women, rich and poor. At that same annual meeting, council leaders also proposed reducing the size of the board of directors, claiming that having two hundred women on the board made it difficult to meet and conduct business. As a result, the board would now include only the officers of the NCNW,

presidents of affiliated organizations, chairwomen of the standing committees, and five members elected at large by the convention. The presidents of
the young adult and junior sections as well as the presidents of the local sections were thus removed from their national leadership posts.[48] While this
certainly made the organization more efficient, it also made it less democratic.

In addition to broadening the base of membership (while shrinking its
leadership), the council fully professionalized itself in the mid-1960s. After
the council became tax-exempt in May 1966, it began to hire staff, mostly for
grant-funded projects, which were now much more plentiful given the new
tax status.[49] From 1935 to 1942, the council was a completely volunteer organization. In 1942, the council hired its first paid executive secretary, Jeanetta
Welch-Brown; a stenographer; and a clerk. These positions remained more
or less the same until 1966. By 1981, the council had 160 paid staff members.[50]
In the late 1960s and early 1970s, the NCNW hired some of the most vibrant
black women organizers in the country, including Frances Beal, Doris Dozier,
Merble Harrington Reagon, Prathia Hall, and Gloria Richardson Dandridge,
who was hired in 1973.[51]

Having this staff certainly helped the council operate more effectively
around the country, but as seen in Project Womanpower and the self-help
projects in Mississippi, these staff positions also provided new opportunities
for young activist women and the local poor to make a salary while also working on other pursuits. Project Womanpower staff member Merble Reagon
pursued a law degree at New York University School of Law while working
for the council in the 1970s. As Reagon explains, she did not want to practice
law, but she wanted an advanced degree to give further credibility to the work
that she was already doing with the council.[52] As previously mentioned, Beal
joined the NCNW staff in 1966 and worked as an administrative assistant for
Project Womanpower, then stayed on to work in a variety of NCNW positions. As Beal recalls, "Dorothy used to turn a blind eye to all of the extra
work that some of her more activist staff was up to," but it allowed for more
radical views to permeate the generally staid organization. While working for
the NCNW, Height also allowed Beal to work on publishing *Triple Jeopardy*
when at the council's headquarters in New York. As Beal recalls, "We used to
lay out the Third World Women's Alliance newspapers there because they
had access to this huge room where other big meetings used to take place."
The council tried to help these young staff members in other ways as well.
Height continued to pay Beal a full-time salary even after she had to reduce
her hours at the council in order to begin working full time as a professor at
Richmond College in 1972.[53]

To facilitate these major structural changes, the NCNW sought support from philanthropic sources. From 1971 to 1974, the Rockefeller Brothers Fund and the Ford Foundation together gave the NCNW $600,000 to sponsor a three-year membership drive and leadership training program for NCNW staff and volunteers. Height tagged Hall—the former SNCC field secretary whose telephone call first brought Height and three others to Selma in 1963, and who worked as an assistant director of Project Womanpower—as the director of this three-year project.[54] An external Ford Foundation report of the program was impressed by the council's selection of Hall, noting her strong activist credentials from her time with SNCC and Project Womanpower. The transition to the NCNW was not always easy for Hall. A private Ford Foundation report claimed that Hall's move "required a significant change in orientation both physically and philosophically," as she was "an activist accustomed to direct approaches to problems, [who] was committed to fundamental changes which she considered necessary but which would mean radical change to the NCNW operation." But as Height had done with the young activist staff of Project Womanpower, she encouraged Hall's vision. She wanted Hall to "develop her ideas for the metamorphosis of NCNW into an activist organization" concerned with the well-being of local black concerns around the country.[55] The first year of the grant project focused on recruiting new members, especially those who were interested in creative ways for black women to unite to work for change. According to the Ford Foundation report, in the first year of the program, "the Council's image evolved from 'reliable but unexciting to one of new vibrance [*sic*] and vitality." The sessions brought in younger, more active women, "bridg[ing] socio-economic gaps [by] bringing together women from varied economic backgrounds and social circumstances."[56]

This new direction, however, was not easy for everyone in the NCNW to accept. Some older members of the council lamented the new direction the NCNW had taken since the late 1960s and dug their heels in to stay committed to the former structure and orientation that focused on hosting social events and fund-raising rather than actively engaging in poverty work. In Miami and St. Louis, there were now two types of sections: "activist" and "conservative." The Ford Foundation report revealed that disagreements within sections in Chicago had led to a "hopscotching of leaders who, after becoming dissatisfied with one section, will organize a new group where they can better assert their views." While this did increase the number of sections, it led to infighting that reduced efficiency within the national organization and revealed the limitations of the council's efforts to embrace poor and activist black women.[57]

Even Height had some trouble adjusting to her loss of control over recruitment and training efforts. In 1971, in anticipation of the National Convention, project director Hall called a preconvention leadership conference in Puerto Rico to introduce council staff (administrative, programming, and clerical), consultants, and a few volunteers to one another. This was the first staff meeting that the council had called since 1967. The convention was supposed to focus on staff cohesiveness, management training, and strategies for building up the council, especially locally. When Hall sensed that staff members were holding back some criticisms of the organization because Height and Jeanne Noble—NCNW vice president and Ford Foundation consultant—were watching, she requested that they not attend after the first session. This turned out to be a mistake. After this, the relationship between Height and Hall, who had worked with the council for over five years at that point, deteriorated. However, three external consultants found that staff members did indeed feel that there were serious problems with the structure of the national staff, especially concerning an "imprecise relationship to the president and a problem of authority versus responsibility." External reviewers felt that Hall and her staff brought new energy and accountability to the NCNW and should have been incorporated as an "integral part" of the council.[58] Both Height and Noble believed in altering the mission and the scope of the council, but only as long as they remained firmly in charge.

Height recommended a reevaluation of the structure and staffing of the training institute at the end of that year. The following spring, Hall was unable to push through her desired programming in Mississippi and Alabama because of pushback from Height. Finally, in July 1972, Height fired Hall, claiming that her pregnancy had "resulted in poor attendance and inefficient performance." After Hall was fired, Noble took over as interim director through the end of the year.[59] Noble tried to resuscitate the program, hiring new part-time staff for the project. However, staff members were now in short supply, and volunteers seemed reluctant to be involved. As the Ford Foundation report states, "NCNW was trying to invent a new wheel but lacked the necessary tools," as they were putting the cart before the horse. The council needed better programming in order to recruit, not the other way around.[60] After all, the council's success in gaining members in Mississippi followed its poverty work there rather than preceded it. The council's own report of its activities acknowledged the limitations of the training institute project: "'A training institute cannot assume a messianic drive, seeking to teach new truth and then train people to actualize the truth.'"[61] While the program did increase direct members from affiliated organizations, it came nowhere near the goal of 200,000 new direct members proposed for this project.[62]

Despite these setbacks, there were still successes in the council's recruitment efforts in the 1970s. The training program helped train new members and bring in new paid and volunteer leaders within the organization, including Gloria Richardson Dandridge, who was hired to be associate director of the leadership development and training program in 1973.[63] It also helped shift the council from a regionally organized field structure to a state-based organization headed by a state convener. In addition, the program provided training materials to help women across the country set up council sections and new poverty projects.[64] Along with the Black Women's Unity Drive chaired by Dee, this grant helped boost the council's numbers in the early 1970s. In 1971, the council had 6,169 members in its local sections and 5,917 direct members, many from affiliate organizations, for a total of 12,086. By March 11, 1974, the council had 22,277 direct members, with 140 local sections organizing in 32 states. While the 1974 direct council membership growth was far below what was projected in the grant, the council had nearly doubled its number of direct members from local sections, affiliated organizations, and general memberships.[65] In May 1974, the council sponsored a massive Black Women's Unity Day—a national program taking place in sixty-eight cities—to bring more black churchwomen into the council.[66] By 1981, the council had two hundred local sections.[67]

In Mississippi, the council grew most dramatically, thanks largely to its poverty programs and the work of dedicated members like Jessie Mosley, who, as the first Mississippi state convener, traveled throughout the state helping to organize new sections for the council. Mosley had been the long-standing treasurer of Womanpower Unlimited.[68] While Mosley's home base of Jackson had an active council section in the late 1940s and early 1950s, the section had not been active since that point. Clarie Collins Harvey, founder of WU, had been an active member of the Jackson Metropolitan Council in the late 1940s, so she certainly had familiarity with the council.[69] According to WU scholar Tiyi Morris, Height had told Harvey in 1964 that there was no need for the council to push to establish a section again in Jackson because "Womanpower was already doing what the NCNW would do."[70] However, once WU was on the decline, the women became part of the council, as they decided that moving into the NCNW would afford them the most opportunity to become part of a larger black women's organization. According to Morris, the group chose to join the NCNW because "the Council embraced

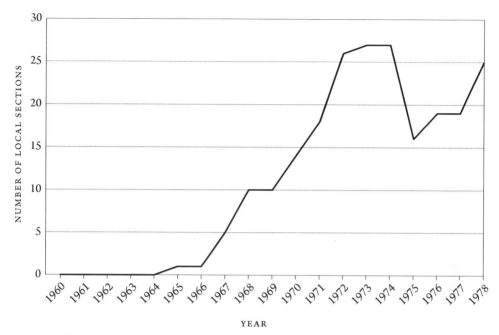

YEAR

Local growth of Mississippi National Council of Negro Women in the 1960s and 1970s. Sources: NCNW Registers and/or Rosters from 1960 through 1978, as found in Series 13, Folders 65 through 79, NCNWP.

interracial cooperation and an international humanist focus that was central to Womanpower's philosophy" and because of NCNW's recent shift to more concern for grassroots programming. The Jackson section of the NCNW organized in 1967, with Mosley as section president.[71]

As Jackson section president and then Mississippi convener for twenty-five years, Mosley was tireless in her efforts to build NCNW programming and membership in Mississippi.[72] The Jackson section established a child-care center that functioned as a camp in the summer and also helped organize household workers.[73] Through Mosley's efforts, the poverty projects that aided so many women, and the membership drives, the number of sections in Mississippi grew dramatically, jumping from zero in 1961–64 to five (Okolona, Greenwood, Jackson, Oxford, and Moss Point) by 1967 (see graph).[74] By 1973, the council had twenty-seven sections in Mississippi. At the end of the decade, the council still had twenty-five sections in the state.[75] This is even more remarkable considering that each section needed fifty members to be chartered. Mississippi was filled with vibrant, engaged women interested in building the local power of the council. In 1981, forty-eight women chartered a bus to attend the annual meeting of the national council. These women constituted the largest statewide delegation of the conference. While in Washington, the Mississippi group attended workshops and gained resources to increase their efforts at the local level.[76] Clearly the increased programming of the NCNW in Mississippi had helped build the power of the national organization.

The turn to increased direct membership, the Black Women's Unity Drive, and the leadership training institute were all focused on uniting the power of black women. This focus on the specific concerns of black women sometimes placed the NCNW at odds with the majority-white feminist movement. Although members of the council and others who had participated in council-related activities—such as Pauli Murray, Fannie Lou Hamer, and Flo Kennedy—were heavily involved in the foundation and early growth of the National Organization for Women, the council was hesitant to fully embrace a white-dominated women's liberation movement.[77] While Dorothy Height participated in feminist activities, such as being a speaker at the Women's Strike for Equality in August 1970 and joining the National Women's Political Caucus (along with NCNW members Vivian Mason and Hamer) in 1971, she still insisted that black women's concerns differed from white women's and that they be considered separately.[78] In this way, the council was very similar to other black women's organizations, which felt that they could not ignore racism as they sought to combat sexism.

The council insisted on bolstering its own power as an organization of people who were both black and women. Height sent Doris Dozier Crenshaw as an NCNW representative to a feminist gathering with Gloria Steinem and Bella Abzug, but as Crenshaw recalls, "That was about the extent of it for me and the feminist movement. I mean, we were so busy with the stuff going on around here in the South . . . we kind of stayed engaged with that 'cause I was [talking] with men and women [about] discrimination and oppression." To Crenshaw, the problem of poverty in the black community was more pressing than the concerns of women's liberation.[79] Beal recalls that while the NCNW pushed for the advancement of girls, it never spoke of women's liberation. Many black women, including the young activists working for the council, were hesitant to use the word "feminist." Beal stated, "Too many white women thought that when they were speaking about women's equality they were speaking for all women, and spoke in those terms." Beal did not use the term "feminist" to describe herself because "right from the beginning we [black women activists] were dealing with a race and gender integration." In addition,

Beal was concerned with class: "Even though it wasn't explicitly articulated, our viewpoint was that we had to build a movement that was based on the poor black women, not on the more qualified black women."[80] Throughout the 1970s, the council kept its focus on building childcare centers, community farms, and housing, as a way to best help black women. While the council had long worked to open up professional opportunities for women, it was also concerned with the well-being of the race. In December 1977, at an advisory board meeting of the newly created NCNW International Division, a board member asked Height about the relationship between the council and women's liberation. Height stated that the "NCNW's real concern was the family[,] which we reach through women," and then quickly closed the meeting.[81] As so many scholars who study black women's history have shown, black women have long been concerned not only with their own advancement but with the advancement of black families and communities. The council was no exception.[82]

The NCNW also differed at times with white-dominated women's groups on other feminist issues. In 1971, the executive committee voted against including an endorsement of the Equal Rights Amendment, but by 1977, the council had reversed its position. With respect to abortion, most black organizations remained ambivalent in the 1970s because of their concerns about forced sterilizations of black women and the fears of genocide expressed by Black Panthers and other black nationalist organizations. Yet some African American activists, including Beal, were strong in their support for the need for reproductive control. Beal had nearly died from an illegal abortion, and a close friend of hers had died. While some black nationalist men claimed that abortion was killing black communities, other black activists, like Beal, insisted that "no, without a right to abortion, very good people are being murdered by these backstreet abortionists."[83] Through her editorship at *Black Woman's Voice*, Beal helped push council women to better understand their own female anatomy and reckon with the changes to abortion law after the passage of *Roe v. Wade*. As she recalls, the respectable council was "very reticent around the reproductive rights questions," and Dorothy Height "took a lot of heat" for allowing Beal to publish articles about women's anatomy, access to birth control, and abortion in the official newsletter of the NCNW. However, Beal believes that council leadership was "happy that we were there to raise those questions when they couldn't yet," because it was such a private thing for black women in the council to talk about sex and reproductive rights at the time.[84] With Beal's pushing, the NCNW recognized that black women had the highest annual rate of illegal abortions and were the primary victims of forced sterilization. The 1971 annual convention's "Commitments for Action" included an endorsement of the Black Women's Task Force of the Women's National Abortion Action Coalition, which not only fought against restrictive abortion laws but also kept tabs on sterilization policies around the country "that promote[d] Black genocide."[85] In 1973, Minnie Lee and Mary Alice Relf were sterilized using federal funding and without the informed consent of their parents. In testimony that echoed Height's and Noble's highly publicized condemnation of the rape of civil rights workers ten years earlier, Height held a press conference, speaking on behalf of fourteen women's, religious, and population-control organizations, urging that federal law prohibit the use of federal funds to perform sterilizations on minors, such as the Relfs, who were fourteen and twelve (respectively).[86] The council had certainly worked in private spaces to combat sexual exploitation of black and poor women, but once again, it was calling for its end in a highly publicized testimony.

The council also became more outspoken in its criticism of governmental responses to racism in the early 1970s. While a moderate organization, the council took more radical stances in this period relating to race. The council spoke out against the FBI assassinations of Black Panthers Fred Hampton and Mark Clark in Chicago and the deaths of prisoners in San Quentin and Attica prisons in its 1971 national conference resolutions, which point to the council's frustration and the need to shift direction. The November 1971 resolutions also called for the release on bail of California professor Angela Davis for medical and legal reasons, movement of her trial site to San Francisco, and continued support for her defense.[87] In early August 1970, seventeen-year-old Jonathan Jackson smuggled guns into a Marin County, California, courtroom and took three jurors, an assistant district attorney, and the courtroom judge as hostages. Although Jackson and two of the three convicts who helped with the takeover were killed by police, the judge was killed as well. Later, police found that the guns used in the takeover were registered to Davis. She was accused of kidnapping, criminal conspiracy, and murder. She fled California, fearing for her life, but was later arrested and held in a small windowless cell for over a year.[88] While the NCNW resolution demanded that Davis be treated more fairly while awaiting her trial, it also stated that in recent months the legal system had taken "an implacable *adversary* role in relationship to Black Americans, with institutional emphasis being disproportionately directed to maintenance of unassailable authority lines at the price of inadequate consideration of other priorities" (emphasis in original). The NCNW then continued with the resolution, "As women who are aware of the multiple dimensions of struggle—physical, moral, and intellectual—we do not believe that a strong and wise nation need[s] to fear its young rebels, but rather to understand their despair." The resolution went on, "Prolonged attempts to destroy them, increasing in recklessness and employment of the massive and ruthless powers of the state, can only lead to disaster for all of us, we believe."[89] The NCNW's public support of Davis and other black prisoners differed from that of other women's groups, which were hesitant to embrace the liberation of Davis as a feminist issue. The NCNW's support reveals the complexities of the council as a black moderate women's organization in the early 1970s.[90]

Women and Employment

While the council embraced poverty work and sought to increase its network of committed women, it also tried to help them find employment. The council had long been interested in lobbying for legislation to aid black professional women, but now it became more involved in finding jobs for the poor. One of the council's main initiatives during the War on Poverty was its work with WICS to partner with Job Corps. The council had first made ties to the other major national women's organizations in WICS—the NCJW, the NCCW, and CWU—at a secret interorganizational meeting in Atlanta in March 1964 (see chapter 2). From this meeting, WICS arose by the end of that year. Later, the American GI Forum Women's Auxiliary and the League of United Latin American Citizens joined the group as well. By 1972, the organization was responsible for placing 49,000 young women into Job Corps and had provided additional training opportunities for 200,000 more.[91]

The most significant of the council's projects for employment was its establishment of the Women's Center for Education and Career Advancement (WCECA) in 1970 in New York City. Merble Reagon, Polly Cowan, Helen Rachlin, Ann Hewitt (who had since moved to New York to be closer to her daughter), and other representatives of the NCNW and the NCJW came together to brainstorm how they might be most helpful to women in New York City. After working together on multiple NCNW projects, the women had noticed that most of them had gone to one of the Seven Sisters schools, and that this experience had empowered them in multiple ways.[92] The group had then approached Height with the idea of creating a career center that would help women at the bottom of the career ladder in corporate America get training and learn how to advocate on their own behalf for better salaries. Of equal importance, the group felt that these women should be encouraged to enjoy the cultural opportunities of Manhattan, such as going to the theater, museums, and iconic venues with their children on the weekend. As Reagon, who has served as executive director of the WCECA since its founding in 1970, recalls, "Our idea was for them to feel a greater ownership for the opportunities that the city offered, not just our program, but everything." The advisory group wanted to boost these women's sense of entitlement not only to having a higher salary or better job but also to taking advantage of the city in the same way that the advisory group members had. They also wanted to make sure to house the program on Pace College's campus, to make the women feel comfortable going in and out of a college setting. Height embraced the project immediately.[93]

The WCECA was funded with help from both government and private organizations, including the U.S. Office of Education, the U.S. Department of Labor, and the Andrew W. Mellon Foundation, in addition to Pace College.[94] The center also received significant corporate support from AT&T and Chase Manhattan Bank. In its first few years, the WCECA helped train young women in typing, office management, record keeping, and additional secretarial skills. NCNW volunteers and staff helped with tutoring and staffing the center, while Pace College teachers taught the classes. Courses were tuition-free for students.[95] In the center's first few years, it had already made great strides in helping black women in New York boost their training and salaries. One woman had been a clerk for four years for a bank. She needed training in shorthand and was able to receive a course at the center. While still enrolled at the center, she passed a typing test and was promoted to secretary, earning over $1,100 more (the equivalent of over $6,000 today). Another woman took shorthand courses at the center and subsequently boosted her salary by nearly $1,500. Despite a strict attendance policy (which was difficult for mothers who were working full time), two-thirds of the women who began the program completed it. By the end of the first four semesters, two hundred students had finished the program, and three-fifths had been promoted or had moved to better jobs. Other students were able to complete their high school diplomas or move on to college full time.[96]

A primary goal of the WCECA was to let women define their own needs. In its first three years, the center was focused on helping women upgrade their clerical skills, but the administrators realized that these women could not make further advances within their companies. To do so, they needed to earn a college degree. So the center shifted its focus and began a program to develop a two-year Liberal Arts/Business Associate degree, which would teach women business skills and also give them classes in liberal arts. While corporations were initially resistant to paying for their employees to pursue this degree, many eventually changed their minds. The WCECA hoped that this degree would be a starting point for women to eventually pursue the second half of a four-year degree on their own. After three years, Pace College adopted the program, which ran for twenty years. In addition to the pilot degree program, the WCECA worked on programs for displaced homemakers, women in debt, women in need of computer skills, and senior women who had lost their jobs in the recession of 2008, just to name a few.[97]

After the election of Ronald Reagan, the WCECA and the council had to sever their formal relationship. As Merble Reagon recalls, the council had several million dollars in government grants on the eve of Reagan's election, but within a few days of his inauguration, Reagan attacked civil rights organizations' funding. Almost immediately, the council lost most of its government grant funding. In response, Height requested that certain programs, such as the women's center, split off from the council and seek tax-exempt status in their own states. The WCECA did so and also turned to private funding. Despite the fact that the center was no longer receiving funding and formal support from the council, it continued to foster its relationship with the NCNW through the 2000s. From its founding to the end of its direct-service programming in 2015, the WCECA had helped forty thousand women. Since ending its direct programming, the center works with New York City to help residents determine their economic standing. In 2000, the WCECA developed a web-based self-sufficiency calculator for New York City, which uses geographic location, number of people in the family, and salary to determine whether a family is working at a surplus or a deficit. WCECA also created the Self-Sufficiency Standard for New York City, and WCECA published the third edition of the standard in 2010. Their calculator also continues to be updated and has been used by thousands of New York City area caseworkers, counselors, and pay-equity campaigns to raise awareness about the difficulties facing poor women in their quest for financial security.[98] Reagon credits the council for teaching her the value of listening to people in order to better understand their needs, and this has helped her in her forty-seven years as WCECA director. "I think that I received an education that I never would have received otherwise around these issues of equity and economic self-sufficiency," she has said. "[The Council and its projects] taught me very valuable lessons about communicating with people."[99]

In July 1973, the NCNW also started Operation Cope, to provide vocational training to single mothers with little formal schooling but many responsibilities as a mother, homemaker, worker, and citizen. The U.S. Office of Education, under the Adult Education Act, funded the program, in which mothers would attend sessions at a neighborhood center where "each woman improves her skills in basic math and communication, [and] studies money management, consumer habits, health and nutrition, and family planning." In its first year, 180 women "helped to move themselves and their families into happier, more stable and productive lives."[100] Clearly, the council still embraced racial uplift as a means to improve the lives of black women, but it also sought to help make these women self-reliant by helping them find employment. Later, the NCNW also recommended that black women seek out trade schools sponsored by unions that offered black women training for skilled jobs. At the 1973 NCNW annual conference, participants resolved that "the guarantee of a job is a basic *right*, and the fight for human dignity and equality is not won without jobs for all." Thus, as an organization, the council offered its support for the Humphrey-Hawkins Full Employment Bill of 1976.[101] In the spring of 1974, the council reiterated its call for full employment, stating that "*for us, unemployment at any rate is unacceptable*" (emphasis in original). While the council believed that a job was a means to self-sufficiency, it also believed that the federal government should help to make more jobs available, especially for black women whom it saw as being victimized by the regressive employment policies of the Nixon administration.[102]

The council also continued to work in Mississippi to find job opportunities. As part of a comprehensive self-help program for the women of Mississippi, the council, along with the Delta Opportunities Corporation, based in Greenville, and Southern Rural Action, helped set up the Doddsville factory, which employed twenty-five women, while their children stayed at the Fannie Lou Hamer day care. The NCNW, along with community members who donated their time and labor, covered the bulk of the costs in setting up the factory, as well as the childcare center, for $35,000. Not only did the council provide stipends for ten weeks of training, but it provided a transportation stipend for the women as well. It was trying to take care of the total needs of the community.[103] Unfortunately, the Doddsville factory did not survive long due to the lack of a market for goods and resistance from local whites. But the council did not abandon Mississippi. In 1979, the council established the Women's Opportunity Program to help rural women gain their GED and then train them for different professions, including nurses' aides, in Mayersville, Okolona, and Greenville. Charles McLaurin was a rural outreach team member for this project, building interest in the program and finding out what it was that the people themselves needed.[104]

While the council supported job training and educational opportunities for even the poorest women, it had no initiatives to bolster the power of welfare women. It supported welfare reform in the pages of the *Black Woman's Voice* and asked local sections to help stop the maligning of black women on welfare, insisting especially that local welfare "workers maintain sensitivity and understanding of the needs of poor people." It urged members to educate black women about their rights to welfare and to provide job training and public service jobs for women on welfare.[105] While the NCNW had come a long way since its silence around Senator Long's remarks in 1967 (see introduction), it still did not focus on helping black welfare mothers through a national program. Beal insisted that while the Third World Women's Alliance sought out a relationship with the National Welfare Rights Organization (NWRO), the NCNW never had a relationship with the NWRO.[106] With programs that promoted job training, the NCNW sought to find a middle ground amid the conservative turn of the federal government. However, the NWRO, while it provided speakers and consultants for council events, never became an affiliate organization of the council.

Women and Incarceration

While the council was interested in helping poor black communities, it was also willing to follow the flow of available federal funding. Height and the council looked for sponsorship for their poverty projects around the country, and there was increasing funding available to combat juvenile delinquency and black crime in the late 1960s. As both Naomi Murakawa and Elizabeth Hinton have convincingly shown, liberal leaders of the 1960s were interested in combating the supposed crime and pathology of black communities by increasing funding for programs to stave off black criminality.[107] Far from criticizing this punitive turn, the NCNW and its members had participated in efforts to prevent juvenile delinquency in black communities. Marjorie M. Lawson, who was one of Bethune's protégés and general counsel for the NCNW, was the first black woman to be appointed to a local Washington, D.C., court when John F. Kennedy appointed her to the juvenile court bench in 1962.[108] In 1963, the council started its Friends of the Juvenile Court program, to provide volunteer services to young women brought to court (and their family members) and to introduce them to the community services available to them.[109] However, it is not fair to characterize the council as embracing a notion of black criminality. Rather, the council wanted to help the black community through rehabilitation instead of institutionalization of young girls who had been accused and convicted of crimes. Unfortunately, the council's programs sometimes gave credence to the notion of black youth as delinquent. As Naomi Murakawa writes, "The combination of a meager welfare state but a capacious carceral state had led interest groups to rely on criminal justice for social change." While Murakawa is referring to antiviolence movements using existing institutions and domestic violence courts to help their efforts, the NCNW used the new crime prevention programs of the federal government to fund some of its programs to bolster NCNW's power in the black community and bring aid to youth.[110]

In September 1966, at the same time that the council began Project Womanpower, the NCNW received $154,000 for Volunteers Unlimited, a two-year project sponsored by the Office of Juvenile Delinquency and Youth Development and the U.S. Department of Health, Education, and Welfare.[111] Although the NCNW wanted to use this program as a way to train black women for more effective leadership skills in community volunteering (much as it had done with Project Womanpower), it would be training women to volunteer and "better serve disadvantaged girls in their communities by opening doors of opportunity and providing services which were previously unknown to and/or unavailable to them." The project worked with women in Miami; Danville, Virginia; and Minneapolis.[112] Ultimately, the project trained 180 black women for volunteer service with young women ages thirteen to seventeen. In addition, the project hoped to broaden the NCNW's reach into the black community and dispel the elitist reputation of the council by building bridges between low- and middle-income black women.[113] In Danville, the program volunteers quickly identified that the young women needed more recreational facilities to prevent loitering. The initial volunteers recruited more volunteers to become a fifty-person-strong Youth Service Corps. In Miami, the women volunteered at a home for girls to help teach the young women personal care, history, music, and religion. In Minneapolis, the volunteers looked for and tried to combat the "patterns and tendencies of predelinquency."[114] In seeking the "patterns" of delinquency, this NCNW project mimicked other liberal efforts to seek out and eliminate so-called black pathology. While well intentioned, this ultimately led to more surveillance and policing of black communities, which then contributed to heightened incarceration.[115] However, the council could not foresee the implications of such a program. Instead, it believed that it was a way not only to reach out and help young black women with federal funding but also to train more women for community service, while also building up the council's power in local communities.

The council continued to enlist the federal government's help in correcting and preventing delinquency among girls, while trying to boost its presence in black communities. The NCNW developed a program the following year named Operation Sisters United, which was funded by the Law Enforcement Assistance Administration (LEAA) of the U.S. Department of Justice. The LEAA was created by the Law Enforcement Assistance Act of 1965 as the Office of Law Enforcement Assistance, but it was renamed and expanded under the Safe Streets Act of 1968.[116] The acts of 1965 and 1968 were a push by President Johnson to embrace a war on crime simultaneous with the War on Poverty.[117] The LEAA was the same organization that helped fuel a massive increase in the militarization of state police forces by enabling them to buy more helicopters, patrol cars, and riot gear, which was often used against black citizens.[118] For instance, the LEAA helped Louisiana purchase a tank, which was then used to storm the New Orleans Black Panther Party headquarters.[119]

A pilot program of Operation Sisters United was established in Washington, D.C., in 1972. By 1975, the program had established chapters in Greenville, Mississippi; St. Thomas, Virgin Islands; and Dayton, Ohio; and by 1980, the program was in ten cities in addition to Washington, D.C.[120] By 1981, the program had received $4 million from the LEAA.[121] Operation Sisters United paired an NCNW member with an at-risk young girl, who would otherwise have been sent to juvenile detention, to establish a one-on-one relationship. By 1979, over six hundred girls had participated in the program, which helped the girls with recreational activities, health information sessions, counseling, mentoring, academic tutoring, vocational training, and black history programs.[122] The program ended shortly after the 1981 convention, as a result of the LEAA being disbanded after Reagan's election.[123] As a moderate organization seeking funding from federal sources, the council embraced the federal government's efforts to modernize the criminal justice system through the LEAA, but as a black women's organization, it hoped it would have the opportunity to shape policy and protect black children from institutionalization by working within the system. Indeed, the program, while costly, yielded results. From 1972 to 1976, Operation Sisters United had a recidivism rate of only 2 percent.[124] External evaluators also commented on the success of the program in delivering services to the teenagers, though evaluators did comment that the NCNW program needed more working-class volunteers.[125] However, the council's impact was small and short lived in comparison to the carceral legacy left by the war on crime and the rise of mass incarceration.[126]

The Power of the National Network

Drawing on its growing experience in poverty, hunger, and housing initiatives, the council began to promote itself as an organization with expertise in public policy around these issues. On a national level, the council called for immediate changes in food apportionment for poor women and children. In early June 1969, the council organized a preliminary meeting in anticipation of a National Convocation on Hunger to take place two months before President Nixon's White House Conference on Food, Nutrition, and Health planned for December. The council's press release announcing the preliminary meeting and subsequent convocation stated what it had heard at local workshops around the country: that despite many gains in federal policy, more was needed. Stated simply, "The hungry cannot—and we will not—wait." At this June gathering, the women discussed school lunch and breakfast programs, infant and maternal feeding and health, food stamp legislation, the medical and psychological implications of hunger, and the role of self-help and other cooperative programs in eradicating hunger.[127]

The council pointed to its work in Mississippi to make its case for increasing funding to combat hunger. It highlighted the Mississippi Delta, home of Senator Eastland and Fannie Lou Hamer, as one of the sites of the most egregious wealth disparities, with Eastland being paid $277,364 in federal subsidies in 1967 to not plant cotton acreage, while the average child of the Delta received only $9 a month in federal welfare.[128] The council then went on to condemn the "penny-pinching by Congress, sabotage by state and local officials particularly in the South, apathetic administration by the U.S. Department of Agriculture, and interference by the Congressional farm committees" as leaving the poor with far too little food in their pantries and bellies.[129]

Over seventy-four organizations, including some affiliates of the council, helped sponsor the council-organized hunger conference in June. Sponsors ranged from the American Academy of Pediatrics to the Boy Scouts to the NWRO. Notably, over one-quarter of the organizations were specifically women's organizations, while several more—such as the American Nurses' Association, the American Home Economics Association, and the NWRO—were concerned with women's occupations and interests.[130] Women discussed their role in securing food for themselves and their families and were well represented at this national meeting. The H. J. Heinz Company and the Carnation Company were major sponsors of the event.[131]

Instead of holding a subsequent national convocation on hunger that fall, the council decided to host a series of twenty workshops in cities around the country to try to get local feedback in time for the White House conference in December.[132] Height, vice chairperson of the conference's Voluntary Action by Women Task Force, then combined the findings of the workshops into a report to be submitted to the president.[133] At its national convention that year, the NCNW hosted a session led by Jean Mayer, special consultant to the president and director of the White House conference, to be held just two weeks later. This gave the council an opportunity to share its findings from both the June meeting and the nationwide workshops. With hunger on its mind, the council also issued a statement of support for the November 15 moratorium to end the war in Vietnam by linking its decision to protest the war to diminishing funds for the War on Poverty to combat hunger.[134]

The council was willing to explore multiple types of solutions to poverty, even if it meant using the aid of corporate America, like Heinz and Carnation. The council also stressed the importance of private groups and individuals in creating change. Suggestions included fund-raising marches to bring more money to local communities and increasing volunteer power.[135] The council, cognizant of the political limitations of the Nixon administration and state governments, believed that these were ways to accomplish the most in the current political atmosphere. The council promised to push the larger White House conference to address the socioeconomic causes of hunger rather than making assumptions about personal failure.[136] The NCNW loudly protested the reduction in availability of food stamps and the prohibitive costs associated with them from the late 1960s through the 1970s.[137] It continued to focus its work on poverty programming and legislation reform, spearheading another meeting three years later titled "The First Black Women's Institute: 1972 Hunger Convocation." 1,500 women attended the convocation, which was chaired by Marian Anderson. Notable distinguished guests of the meeting included Shirley Chisholm, Coretta Scott King, and Nikki Giovanni.[138] Then, in 1974, it further organized its national efforts by creating the Food for People Network, a coalition of 109 national women's groups "whose membership is working for reform of federal food policies and also to make local governments more responsive to the plight of hungry people under their jurisdiction." They lobbied for food stamp reform, federal programs to help children in schools and day cares, food for the elderly, food subsidy reform, and a repeal of food taxes.[139]

But the council became even more prominent in the area of housing with its national visibility after establishing the Turnkey III project in Gulfport. In 1974, the NCNW spearheaded a massive investigation into the problem of discrimination against women in housing. Under contract with the OEO and

HUD from the summer of 1974 through the following June, the council held hearings in Atlanta, St. Louis, San Antonio, San Francisco, and New York City to document the discrimination women across the country had faced while seeking housing. That material was then compiled into *Women and Housing: A Report on Sex Discrimination in Five American Cities*, published in 1975, which was to be used by HUD's equal opportunity staff.[140] In addition to documenting discrimination, an added goal of the grant was to encourage the private sector's role in eliminating discrimination.[141] Height chaired the hearings, and Dorothy Duke was the overall project coordinator for the report.[142]

The project began with the creation of an ad hoc committee in each of the areas where the hearings would take place. The council relied on its strong links with other women's organizations and invited one hundred leaders of these groups to Washington for a workshop about the project. The council envisioned each local commission as "the voice of women in the local community." These local committees then took the lead in planning the hearings, during which women of all races, ages, and religions came to recount the discrimination they had faced. In addition to organizing the local hearings, the council also held two-day post-hearing workshops in the hopes of increasing public awareness. The council hoped that its efforts would help reduce discrimination against women in housing at the local level by fostering a closer relationship with the private sector.[143]

WITH ITS ACHIEVEMENT of tax-exempt status in 1966, the NCNW was able to apply for grants and bolster its poverty programming around the country. It also sought out—and won—funding to grow its direct membership. In the 1970s, the council tried to recruit members who were vastly different from those who enjoyed teas and cotillions. Instead, it wanted all types of women to join the council, and it facilitated changes in membership dues to help encourage this. But it was the grassroots-led poverty programming of the late 1960s that did the most to help the council attract new membership. In addition to building its direct membership, the council was able to leverage its poverty work in Mississippi to gain federal and private grants to create new programming, take important positions of authority in federal hunger and housing campaigns, and expand its national network of influence. With this strengthened membership and reputation, the NCNW became a major voice for all black women in America.

CHAPTER EIGHT

Mississippi, Who Has Been the Taillight, Can Now Be the Headlight

The Council's International Work, 1975–1985

As one of the most powerful African American women representing the United States at the United Nations World Conference on Women in Copenhagen in July 1980, Dorothy Height believed that she could play a major role in sensitizing Western feminists to the needs of women of color around the world. Together with fellow U.S. delegates Alexis Herman, director of the Women's Bureau of the U.S. Department of Labor, and Sarah Ragle Weddington, special assistant to President Carter for women's affairs, Height helped draft a resolution on racial equality. The resulting statement that Herman presented insisted that in matters related to promoting equality for women globally, "dealing with sexism alone would not be enough. Racism had to be included" as well. According to Height, there was much rejoicing from women of color around the world at the introduction of the resolution.[1] Since 1975, Height had been overseeing the growth of the NCNW's International Division, which worked closely with women in southern and western Africa. She had fostered relationships with her sisters of color around the world, and had even helped many of them come to the conference. The council had won a $60,000 grant from the Africa Bureau of the United States Agency for International Development (USAID) to help fund the trips of twenty women "holding mid-level management or leadership positions in women's bureaus, ministries or women's organizations" in Mauritania, the Gambia, Mali, Senegal, Kenya, Tanzania, Togo, Sierra Leone, Burundi, Lesotho, and Ghana.[2] Influenced by these ties, Height tried to use her voice to sensitize the West to consider racism as part of the fight against women's inequality as well.

But Height's efforts would be derailed. According to Height, sinister "political operatives of the Eastern Bloc" sabotaged the U.S. delegation's resolution by trying to insert the phrase "Zionism is racism." State department officials urged Height and other members of the delegation to use their influence to prevent the phrase from being added to the resolution. Height moved from "individual to individual to establish rapport" with the African women. She believed that the respect that many of these women felt toward the

YWCA and the NCNW, the two organizations that she was most closely affiliated with, might influence them to vote against adding the new amendment. But her efforts were unsuccessful, and the phrase was added. In the meantime, both the U.S. House of Representatives and the Senate passed their own resolutions stating that the U.S. delegation was not to support any resolution that included references to "Zionism," and Congress condemned what it viewed as the "politicization of the convention." Thus, the U.S. delegation ultimately withdrew its support for the resolution.[3] As Height recalled, "It was one time when hard-line nationalist politics won, beating out our deepest convictions and careful coalition-building."[4] Notably, in her autobiography Height did not criticize the State Department officials or members of Congress that had pushed her to reject the resolution. Instead, she criticized the Soviet women who she felt had swayed her African allies.

Even if Height had wanted to criticize the State Department and the congressional resolutions, she could not. Her organization had flourished under federal funding over the past five years. USAID spent over $800,000 from 1975 to 1980 for the council to implement a special conference for women of African descent at the 1975 International Women's Year (IWY) conference, pay for the creation of NCNW's International Division, and help the council implement self-help projects for women of African descent. In 1980, the council won another sizable grant, bringing the total funds received from USAID by 1985 to about $1.7 million. USAID had shifted its focus in the 1970s to providing aid directly to poor, rural, and female beneficiaries, and the council fit in nicely with this shift. As the self-proclaimed "natural allies of southern African women," the council was able to successfully promote itself as a nongovernmental organization with a strong network of women of African descent, but USAID also had much to gain from the relationship.[5]

The council, an American liberal organization committed to volunteer work, stressed that established systems of American democracy and capitalism were the best political tools to combat discrimination against women of color. Unlike organizations that criticized USAID at the time, the NCNW accepted the organization's money. In the process, it gained greater influence over U.S. and UN human rights projects and policy abroad in the 1970s than did USAID's radical critics.[6] This relationship helped fund the NCNW as an organization of African American women and enabled it to increase its network of influence around the world. This enlarged network also helped the council bring local self-help and training projects, much like those it had established in Mississippi, to women around the world. But at times this meant that it had to make political compromises, even at the expense of criticizing racism at home and abroad and fighting for systemic change. While scholars have criticized USAID and the nongovernmental organizations (NGOs) it has sponsored as imperialist, others have pointed out that some good has been produced by these organizations.[7] And although the NCNW was sometimes reluctant to openly criticize U.S. foreign policy, this certainly did not make it an arm of U.S. imperialism and did not preclude it from helping women on their own terms. One of the most pressing issues that the NCNW felt compelled to speak out against was the political situation in South Africa. During its international work, African women working with the council consistently requested that the NCNW use its large network of women of African descent to compel the U.S. government to help end apartheid. The NCNW publicly criticized apartheid policy in 1976 after participating in the Black Leadership Conference on Southern Africa; called for investigations into human rights violations against women and children political prisoners in the region; and sat on the board of TransAfrica, a lobbying group that pushed Congress to end economic partnerships with South Africa in the late 1970s and 1980s.[8] In addition to making public statements supportive of the black majority efforts in South Africa to end apartheid, the council worked to bring resources to women in countries economically dependent on South Africa, while also extending its network of influence abroad.

Postwar Ambassadors

From the time of its founding, the NCNW had been concerned with the role of human rights for people of African descent around the world. The council also wanted to make sure that black women were included in post–World War II committees to help determine how to best ensure those rights. Although no blacks were appointed to the official U.S. delegation of the April 1945 United Nations Conference on International Organization (UNCIO) meeting in San Francisco, Bethune fought hard to be a consultant-observer, and she was finally added, along with Walter White and W. E. B. DuBois, as delegates from the NAACP. Together, these three tried to push for an international bill of rights that might hasten an end to colonialism and racism.[9] Although technically representing the NAACP, Bethune also spoke on behalf of the NCNW, and she emphasized the importance of having black women take a significant role in rebuilding the postwar world. This new confidence and push for women's relevance was bolstered by the efforts of Mabel Staupers and Bethune in pushing for more access to jobs during World War II (see chapter 1).[10] NCNW members Eunice Hunton Carter, Dorothy Ferebee, and

Edith Sampson also attended the San Francisco meeting as observers. The council was one of the first organizations to seek accreditation for UN observer status.[11] In this capacity, the NCNW observers attended meetings of committees most closely related to their interests as black women, including the Economic and Social Council (ECOSOC) and the Commission on the Status of Women (CSW). The council was also part of Women United for the United Nations, a group of thirty-seven organizations committed to the welfare of women, and it has remained proud of its UN observer status to the present day.[12]

In the early postwar period, the council insisted on being included in new postwar women's international groups devoted to promoting human rights. Bethune pushed for NCNW representatives to become part of the Committee on Women in World Affairs (CWWA), a women's organization first created during World War II but devoted to placing American women in positions in the State Department and international organizations in the postwar period. Bethune urged the CWWA to help her place prominent NCNW members Merze Tate, a government professor at Morgan State, and labor leader Maida Springer in leadership positions.[13] In October 1946, the NCNW attended the International Assembly of Women, sponsored by Eleanor Roosevelt, which sought to bring together women from various nations to discuss economic, social, and political issues. Bethune and third president Vivian Mason tried to ensure that more women of African descent from around the world attended these types of international meetings.[14] In addition, council women traveled to many international conferences. In 1947, members attended conferences in Haiti, Mexico, Latin America, Paris, London, and Switzerland. By 1948, women from around the world had become honorary members of the council, including Jawaharlal Nehru's sister and Indian diplomat Vijaya Lakshmi Pandit.[15]

In the early postwar years, the council also maintained alliances with left-leaning anticolonial organizations like the Council on African Affairs (CAA). Bethune was a prominent member of the CAA. NCNW leader Eunice Hunton Carter was the sister of Alphaeus Hunton, who was an open communist and education director of the CAA. Vivian Mason, who would go on to become the third president of the NCNW, was a member of the Congress of American Women (CAW), the American affiliate of the Women's International Democratic Federation—an antifascist, interracial, progressive organization that included Soviet women.[16] Historian Julie Gallagher has argued that these connections show that the council, while a respectable liberal organization, "was also capable of holding a more complex—at times even radical perspective—that critiqued the economic and political structures in the United States and in Africa."[17] Through these groups, the NCNW aligned itself with the anticolonial positions of women of African descent in the early postwar years.

However, this alliance with the left could not outlast the Red Scare. With NCNW leaders Bethune, Ferebee, Mason, and Ada Jackson all suspected of being communist at some point during the postwar period (see chapter 1), the NCNW felt pressure to silence its more radical tendencies by the late 1940s and instead tout its Americanist credentials.[18] Dorothy Height recalls that the NCNW faced a rough time as an organization during the height of anticommunism. The council was harassed, and people in the Deep South were terrified of joining the organization. They wanted to support the council but feared retribution, and so they would send anonymous money orders.[19] In response to these types of attacks, the council—like other organizations— shifted to the right in its international activism. In a clear example of this shift, in 1955 the council, now under the leadership of Mason, decided to sponsor the African Children's Feeding Scheme, an organization that provided free meals to schoolchildren in South Africa. As Nicholas Grant has argued, within this project, the council rarely linked U.S. racism to South Africa's. Also, its work "lacked any specific critique of the U.S. government's cold war extensive diplomatic, economic, and strategic connections with the National Party that many in the State Department believed represented an important bulwark against the potential spread of communism in southern Africa."[20] The council turned away from supporting more radical efforts during this re- pressive time. Still, the NCNW did expand its network to international women, especially under Mason's presidency. The NCNW invited women from Ghana, Nigeria, Liberia, Ethiopia, the Sudan, and South Africa to visit the NCNW headquarters and become members of the organization. When the Bantu Women's League established the National Council of African Women (NCAW) in South Africa in 1940, Bethune encouraged the organ- ization to become a part of the NCNW. Although the NCAW did not join as an affiliate organization, Mason invited leaders of the NCAW to the council's 1956 meeting.[21]

Despite its early alliances with left-leaning groups, the NCNW at the height of the Cold War publicly committed to fighting communism, even if it meant silencing more radical black activists. No council member became more infamous for her efforts on behalf of American propaganda than Edith Sampson, a prominent Chicago attorney who was later elected as a judge on the Chicago municipal court (and thus became the first black woman elected to the Illinois bench) in 1962. In 1949, Sampson participated as an NCNW-sponsored delegate in the seventy-two-day *America's Town Meeting of the Air*, a worldwide diplomatic tour, created by American radio host and producer George Denny, that sent prominent American private citizens around the world to dispel communist propaganda. Representatives from twenty-six other national organizations also embarked on the trip. Initially Denny and the State Department wanted Bethune to go, but her health was failing. After asking other NCNW leaders who were too busy planning other events to go, Bethune recommended Sampson, largely because she was willing to put out the $5,000 to pay her own way.[22] Sampson became infamous while participating in the tour for telling international audiences misleading stories about the high standard of living enjoyed by black Americans. However, she believed that the tour offered her an opportunity to be an "exponent of truth whether painful or pleasing" and that she was not simply a puppet of the State Department.[23] Other organizations in the group included labor unions and liberal volunteer organizations, such as the AFL, the CIO, the AAUW, the LWV, and the NAACP, as well as the more conservative Lions Clubs International and the Better Business Bureau (BBB). Sampson was so palatable to the conglomerate that its members elected her the delegation's president. Her loyalty to the U.S. government had its rewards. In the fall of 1950, Truman appointed Sampson as a U.S. delegate to the UN General Assembly.[24] While Sampson was a member of the UN and traveled around the world, she never strayed from her devotion to America, even as she sometimes hurt the African American freedom struggle in the process.[25]

Sampson tried to undermine black activists who more openly criticized American racism abroad. While in New Delhi as part of the town meeting, she claimed that Paul Robeson, whom the United States was trying to deny a passport for his communist sympathizing, represented a "'lunatic fringe in America'" whereas she represented the NCNW, a much larger and more mainstream constituency. As Laville argues, Sampson built her argument against Robeson as one of a group versus an individual. She presented "Robeson's lack of group affiliation . . . as evidence of his lack of claim to be representative of African-Americans."[26] Therefore, council members like Sampson and their wide network of moderate African American women became even more valuable to American diplomatic missions during the Cold War, highlighting their adherence to democracy and capitalism while slandering others marked as communists.

In another famous incident two years later, Sampson challenged the *We Charge Genocide* pamphlet put out by the Civil Rights Congress (CRC).

Sampson went before audiences in Scandinavia as a promoter of American capitalism to downplay the effects of systemic racism in America. Instead, she told audiences that nothing stood in the way of African Americans voting and achieving the American dream of owning expensive cars and homes and sending their children to the finest schools. State Department officials congratulated themselves on their decision to have Sampson be a spokesperson to counter the CRC's report of genocide against African Americans. Meanwhile, members of the black press, including reporters from the *Crisis*, denounced her ridiculous and dishonest sentiments about the state of black America.[27]

Like Sampson, Dorothy Height played a significant role in international delegations to promote American democracy and capitalism. As a YWCA leader and Delta Sigma Theta president, Height was invited to be a visiting professor at the Delhi School of Social Work in India in 1952, during a time of great political debates over land reform. While there, she visited Travancore, a communist province with the highest number of unemployed college graduates in India. The students "challenged whether or not social work was an opiate of the people, whether or not even the school itself wasn't a Western way of keeping them."[28] Though Height felt challenged by these questions, she maintained her loyalty to America and anticommunism. While in Travancore, she visited the Soviet consulate and was offended at a video that depicted a "very ignorant" farmworker as a typical black American. Height tried to assure her Indian students that this man was "not characteristic" while also not downplaying the United States' racial inequality. While this made her even more suspicious of communism, she also realized that people in India and China were following communism not for the political ideology but as a means to social change.[29]

As a black woman representing the United States, Height often found herself in the awkward position of defending her country, despite its widespread racial segregation and discrimination. After Richard Nixon had been poorly received in the spring of 1958 in Latin America, George Denny sent another group of Americans to help rebuild the United States' image throughout South America. Denny helped create the group of thirty-five Americans, of which Height and Sampson were the only two black delegates. The group visited Peru, Chile, Argentina, Uruguay, Brazil, and Colombia. Although not a governmental group, the meetings received encouragement from the U.S. government, and the embassies of different countries received the group.[30]

When the white delegates tried to lead the discussions, locals begged to hear instead from the two black women. Yet when students in Montevideo pointed to the school closings in Prince Edward County, Virginia, as evidence that the United States was intent on depriving all black children of an education, Height found herself arguing that Prince Edward County was the exception instead of the rule. She defended her nation, pointing to the fact that she and Sampson, who had been educated in the North, did not go to segregated schools, thus using their own examples, which largely misrepresented their experiences, as evidence of the progress being made in America. The students from Montevideo were so intrigued by Height and her pro-American message that many of them asked her to speak at their university. She also conducted interviews with radio stations and local newspapers, which asked for her and Sampson's take not only on race but on foreign policy. According to Height, she and Sampson sought to promote "a real discussion" with the people of the countries, but instead they both downplayed the effects of racism in the United States, much to the delight of the State Department.[31] Members of the Central Intelligence Agency (CIA) at the American embassy in Uruguay thanked Height and Sampson for defusing the anti-American climate there, including one operative who said that he now felt safe bringing his American family to stay with him.[32]

Height felt proud not only of this mollifying role but also of her role in educating the other white Americans on the trip. The delegation spent several weeks traveling around these nations and Height believed that she and Sampson had helped contextualize many of the racial issues that South American citizens had been reading about, but they also taught the other U.S. delegates. As she recalled, "To me the most satisfying part of the whole trip was to recognize the extent to which most of those white Americans had never been in a situation where people of color, in another part of the world, were hating them for their racial policy, or were questioning them because of the racial policy, or were trying to ask, 'Well, why did you drop the bomb on Hiroshima? Why didn't you drop it on Germany?'" For many of the whites in the delegation, this was the first time they had felt put on the spot about their country's racial attitudes. Through these visits, Height helped chip away at white supremacy.[33] However, Height, Sampson, and the other women of the council did not challenge American supremacy and, in the process, made excuses for Jim Crow in front of an international audience.

In 1960, as West African nations were gaining their independence, Height participated in another nongovernmental, anticommunist initiative called the Committee of Correspondence, "inspired by Thomas Jefferson's notion that people could change the world if they kept in good correspondence."[34] This group, however, was composed only of women. The Committee of Correspondence began in 1952 from a call to action by Rose Parsons, former American regional director of the Red Cross, in order to counter what the group saw as the communist propaganda of the Women's International Democratic Federation—a group that the council had previously worked with in the immediate postwar period. What began as a spinoff group from Women United for the United Nations quickly severed ties and called itself the "Anonymous Committee" before adopting its official title. The committee tried to counter communist propaganda by writing personal letters and sending newsletters to friends and their acquaintances in countries around the world.[35] This organization was actually funded by the Dearborn Foundation—a CIA front—from January 1953 through 1967. From 1954 to 1966, the Dearborn Foundation contributed $587,500.[36]

One wonders how much Height knew of the CIA connection, if at all. She claims that the organization was funded by "foundations" and that her task was to "discuss how can women be more helpful in their community, to get out those things that they were concerned about, to see how we could work at that."[37] The African women who worked with the Committee of Correspondence came from the Girl Guides, Red Cross, YWCA, and other groups friendly to Western organizations. In Ghana and Nigeria, Height worked with market women who had created their own women's organizations. Height also visited Guinea two years after the country had declared its independence from France and been spitefully cut off from aid and support from its former colonizer. As Height recalls, "S[é]kou Touré was in the process of changing the money, so that was the first place where the American dollar wasn't worth anything. They were changing all the money, and they were trying to recover from the way the French had left them."[38] She went on to speak with women's groups to "find out what they needed in training, but also doing some training." She went on to Sierra Leone, Ghana, Nigeria, and Liberia. She witnessed the last speech before independence in Nigeria in 1960. Height met with prominent women in Nigeria to establish the Nigerian Council of Women at Ibadan.[39]

Having been inspired by the trip, Height joined the male leaders of major civil rights organizations—Roy Wilkins, Whitney Young, A. Philip Randolph, Martin Luther King, and James Farmer—to create the Call Committee for the newly formed American Negro Leadership Conference on Africa (ANLCA) in 1962. Whereas the left-leaning Afrocentric CAA (which Bethune and Eunice Hunton Carter had been prominent members of only a decade prior) had become more critical of the United States' foreign policy, the newly formed ANLCA sought to be a more moderate voice.[40] The ANLCA was the group through which the NCNW was most active internationally in the 1960s, and it stressed that Americans of African descent should take an active role in trying to influence U.S. policy in Africa. The group also tried to influence the U.S. government to give more economic aid to the continent, suggesting that it was the best way to block the spread of communism there. They also encouraged the U.S. government to include more high-level black employees in the U.S. Foreign Service and censured it for criticizing apartheid in South Africa but not enforcing sanctions to follow through on that criticism.[41]

Through the Committee of Correspondence, Height developed a close relationship with Chief Simeon Olaosebikan Adebo, then the Nigerian minister of finance, who later became Nigeria's delegate to the United Nations. Adebo helped Height meet important leaders throughout West Africa, including Sir Ademola, the chief justice of Nigeria. When the ANLCA later met with Adebo, the group expressed concern over apartheid and U.S. business dealings with South Africa. However, Adebo encouraged them to watch U.S. policies regarding the use of raw materials in southern and central Africa, where withholding food and resources was used as a political tool.[42] This idea of food as a political weapon likely influenced Height's later efforts to establish a pig farm in Mississippi (see chapter 6). Adebo also openly criticized the racial climate in the United States, arguing that even New York was a racially hostile location for UN delegates such as himself.[43] Height's experience with the ANLCA and delegates like Adebo inspired both her and her co-activists to focus not only on altering the political structure of South Africa but also on the economic dependency of these areas.

In her autobiography, Height claims that her international travels also opened her eyes to the commonality of women of color's concerns around the world. "Whether affluent or needy, living in the northern industrialized world or the developing South, educated or illiterate, we all want to improve the quality of life for our loved ones and our communities." The ANLCA also emphasized its shared history with people abroad. At its first major conference in November 1962, the group vowed to " 'rededicate and reaffirm our ethnic bond with and historic concerns for the peoples of Africa and our complete solidarity with their aspirations for freedom, human rights, and independence.' "[44] Thus, mainstream African American civil rights leaders claimed a solidarity with and a historic commitment to the concerns of Africans, and believed that this should push them to play a greater role in weighing in on U.S. foreign policy decisions in the area. However, as scholar Edward Erhagbe writes, the ANLCA was not a permanent organization and only existed through its sponsorship of biannual conferences. It was much more "concilia-tory" and "elitist," and it "did not antagonize the government," as other more radical groups like the CAA did. This meant that the group was often "plead[ing] instead of demand[ing]" action from the government. Ultimately, scholars have concluded that the ANLCA was ineffective in altering U.S. policy toward Africa in the 1960s, with the exception of appointing more African American diplomats.[45] But the NCNW took its commitment to peoples of African de-scent one step further. As the 1960s drew to a close and both black nationalism and the feminist movement grew more powerful in the United States, Height sought to build an international network of black women and help them through training, education, and increased political participation, not only lo-cally but also abroad.[46]

International Women's Year

While the UN had always been interested in combating discrimination against women—the international organization had included it as a goal in its charter and created a Commission on the Status of Women (CSW)—its inter-est in women in development efforts picked up in the early 1970s.[47] In 1970, the CSW helped urge the UN General Assembly to pass a resolution to push for the total integration of women in development. That same year, noted economist Ester Boserup published a now classic study, *Woman's Role in Eco-nomic Development*, which pointed out how contemporary theories about ag-ricultural development failed to measure or respond to women's economic activity. Then, in 1971, USAID published an abstract of her book in its *Devel-opment Digest*, which was sent across the world. This helped spread her ideas further.[48] The following year, the UN General Assembly called for 1975 to be International Women's Year.

The United States followed suit. Many second-wave feminists who were also interested in development began to meet to discuss the effect of economic development on women and found that contrary to its intended outcome, development efforts actually made life harder for many women around the world. This viewpoint helped push U.S. Information Agency officer Mildred Marcy to call for inclusion of women in the soon-to-be-revised U.S. Foreign Assistance Act. Behind the scenes, Marcy secured support for the act, but then asked Republican senator Charles Percy to introduce the amendment, since he would help gain wider support for the measure. The Percy Amend-ment, which stressed the need for women to become major decision-makers in and beneficiaries of development initiatives, was passed in 1973.[49]

The mind-set of international development work was changing as well. As scholar Robert Clark states, foreign aid began to be more concerned with helping individuals and their communities and less about building infrastructure in the 1960s and early 1970s.[50] Marxist movements around the world, Vatican II liberation theology, and the U.S. War on Poverty helped make developed nations more aware of the needs of the poor. The World Bank also tried to get involved. In the early 1960s, it had focused on investing in business development, believing that wealth would trickle down to the poor, and generally avoided offering loans to poor countries deemed uncreditworthy. Under the leadership of George Woods, a New York investment banker, the World Bank began to offer some loans to support education, health, and sanitation projects, instead of solely infrastructure projects, which it deemed most useful to a country's economic growth. The World Bank also shifted its focus away from funding large projects and adopted "Basic Human Needs" as a priority.[51] Woods's successor in 1968, Robert McNamara, took Woods's experiment in funding even further as he questioned trickle-down theory and instead "sought ways of enabling the poor to participate in growth-oriented activities."[52] Moving away from infrastructure and industrialization as priorities, the World Bank attempted to alleviate poverty, including in the long-neglected areas of rural development, education, nutrition, and health.[53] The NCNW's own shift from its elite network of women to a group concerned for the needs of the total community, including the rural poor, fit nicely with the shifting global attitude toward participatory planning of women in development in the mid-1970s.

By the 1970s, the council had already become a part of many international women's groups, such as the International Council of Women, the Pan-Pacific and South-East Asia Women's Association, and the U.S. National Commission for UNESCO. Its members also served on UNESCO and UNICEF.[54] It had also been a prominent member of the ANLCA, interested in promoting African interests. The council looked for a way to link its rural development projects in the U.S. South to international work. In 1973, it sponsored a one-day conference for women from Africa, Latin America, and the Caribbean. At the conference, the council showed the filmstrip *The Power of Four Million Women*. In 1974, a Croissant Rouge official in Mauritania called on the council to aid the organization in relief efforts driven by women and children following droughts in the Sahel.[55] The council was also instrumental in setting up the National Council of Women in Liberia and Nigeria.[56]

Responding to the new Percy Amendment, the NCNW applied for funding to create a formal International Division within the council. The council highlighted its efforts in the rural South, especially the pig bank, the housing program, the day-care center, and the Doddsville garment factory, as evidence of its ability to help women become self-sufficient in rural areas. It then pointed out how it had helped women in the poorest region of the poorest state in the United States, and could likewise be responsible for food production and skills training for women around the world.[57]

The first step of the council's international work in the 1970s was to create the infrastructure for its future international work by organizing a conference for women of African descent concurrent with the International Women's Year (IWY) conference. In May 1975, NCNW won a $100,000 grant from USAID and then had one month to organize everything and find women to participate.[58] The council relied on its contacts with other international or well-known national women's organizations. Leaders made contacts with missionaries and clubwomen who would be attending the IWY conference and received recommendations from the organizers of the larger conference to find speakers and participants. This meant that the women of the group, while living in impoverished countries, had significant status in their home countries and were often not poor themselves (see appendix 4). Attendees included Siga Sene, midwife and vice president of the Economic and Social Council in Senegal; Elizabeth Mulenje Nkomeshya, a tribal chieftain from Zambia; Emma Agyepong, a YWCA regional secretary in Ghana; Nesta Patrick, president of the Caribbean Women's Association from Trinidad and Tobago; and Doris Johnson, the first female president of the Senate in the Bahamas. Every delegate was a highly educated working woman, not only skilled in her own craft but often involved in local, national, or international politics as well.[59]

Through this conference, the NCNW sought to create a global network of women of African descent from fifteen countries "to implement International Women's Year goals through self-help activities." Although the NCNW had expected thirty women to participate, between fifty and sixty women actually joined the sessions at the conference. Unlike the official IWY conference, at which there were too many people for the women to meet, this NCNW-sponsored conference, much like its workshops over the past decade, gave participants the opportunity to speak directly with one another. Meeting together allowed the women to discuss not only their cultural differences but also their commonalities, and this was empowering.[60] In addition, this was a group focused only on the needs of women of African descent, often the targets of aid but not the actors themselves. This smaller conference provided the opportunity for these women to vocalize their needs and to develop plans of action for their own countries.

The objectives of this international conference shared some of the characteristics of council projects in the 1960s, including Wednesdays in Mississippi's concern with building personal relationships and Project Womanpower's focus on self-help. USAID appreciated the council's emphasis on self-help projects, as well as the consistently moderate tone of its activism. Unlike many of the female delegates of the larger IWY conference, who reacted angrily to the fact that Daniel Parker, the male director of USAID, headed the U.S. delegation to the conference, Height did not voice criticism. "My position was, and still is, that the delegations to an official international body are designated by the heads of their governments," Height said, "and once that is done, and you get on territory outside of the United States, there's no need of standing at the door and saying, 'We demand another delegation.'" In her characteristic pragmatism, Height also pointed out the advantages of having male leaders at the conference: in many countries, "they were the ones who had to take a stand." Height felt that women who believed that the International Women's Year initiative was intended to be an international feminist movement were wrong. For her, the year was intended to bring about an "equality of partnership and opportunity of men and women" and to bring resources from governments and the private sectors of business and industry to open opportunities for women.[61] While Height and the council's ultimate goal was the empowerment of women around the world, she was willing to work within the structures of capitalism. In this way, the NCNW was not a radical group, trying to overthrow unequal structures that locked the developing world in poverty. However, in bringing women around the world together, the NCNW provided a network to help chip away at the inequalities of racism and sexism that these women faced, in one form or another.

The NCNW-sponsored conference of women at the Mexico City conference united around the concept of women's economic "self-help," with women of African descent themselves shaping the meaning of this phrase. For instance, Ruby Duncan, the prominent welfare-rights activist, attended the council-sponsored IWY conference. For Duncan, who had moved from the cotton fields of the Mississippi Delta to Las Vegas, "self-help" meant that a woman should receive some income so that she could stay at home with her children, educate them, and attend to them before sending them to a school of the mother's choice. Other attendees from less developed parts of the world felt that a nutritious diet, a convenient water and firewood supply, and a source of income would be enough.[62] This was not a conservative vision of self-help for the poor to pull themselves up by their bootstraps, nor was this the self-help of the Black Panther Party, which advocated an isolationist and nationalist response to racism within the United States. Instead, the women of this conference shaped their vision of self-help as one in which they would be able to help themselves by giving and receiving training to work in food production or traditional handicrafts; promoting girls' education—both formal and informal; and pushing for their governments to recognize the special role of women in society.

Fundamental to the conference participants' idea of "self-help" was increasing their livelihood in the hopes that it would help them enter the "economic mainstream" of their home countries. This version of self-help reflected the council's efforts at job creation through WICS and the job-training centers that it had helped establish around the country. It also reflected the council's interest in making gainful employment possible for black women worldwide. Three conference sessions addressing the economic barriers women faced were "Women and Trade Unions," "Women at Work," and "Third World Craftswomen and Development," with the final session being the largest and most well-attended. In order to move into the economic mainstream, the seminar recommended that women involve themselves in small-scale industry and management through international cooperatives. Participants expected that these handiwork cooperatives could build women's economic and, ultimately, political power.

Recognizing the limitations of their governments in providing these types of resources, the attendees recommended that these rural development projects for women be led by NGOs—which attendees saw as an alternative to government and friendly to women, even though NGOs, like the NCNW, had received much money from their own governments for their projects. Conference participants believed that women would have a better chance of avoiding government corruption, inefficiency, and discrimination by appealing to NGOs to provide them with job training and the marketing advice necessary to help them earn an income.

Attendees also discussed the need for literacy. These elite foreign delegates, most of whom had bachelor's degrees and some of whom had advanced degrees, believed that with education, women would demand better resources, opportunities, and treatment from their governments. They believed that not only formal education but also skills training could make women "more effective as public influences." Again, nongovernmental alternatives were recommended to help with this training. By the end of the conference, the women agreed that voluntary, extra-governmental organizations would be best to provide leadership development and political education programs as well as scholarships, internships, and study tours in order to "improve their expertise in community development techniques" for women.[63] As with the council's previous work in self-help, this had an element of racial uplift as well. The women of the IWY council-sponsored conference were the elite in their communities, but they had been working among the poor as well, and they sought to find additional solutions to the poverty in their home countries.

But reflecting the council's long commitment to engaging both the private and the public sector, delegates also agreed that the government should have some role in ensuring the well-being of these women. Attendees agreed that their own governments should take responsibility for establishing housing for low-income people. They also advocated that governments stop downplaying women's economic role in food production and include them in their calculations of the gross national product. The fact that the council's major funding for its International Division would come through the United States' main international aid body suggests that it believed in the power of government as well.

In addition, although plenty of self-identified feminists attended this concurrent conference for women of African descent, it challenged assumptions and priorities of feminists from the developed world. Because sterilization campaigns from both governmental and volunteer organizations had tried to control the bodies of minority women around the world, conference members rejected a Western feminist platform advocating birth control, or "family planning." Instead, Dr. James Carter of Meharry Medical Center in Nashville, Tennessee, one of the oldest hospitals to cater to African American patients, spoke for the group when he advocated child spacing, instead of birth control, as a way to improve the health of women and children. Ultimately, the attendees collectively concluded that "family planning" was not a priority in the worldwide black community.[64] Therefore, far from being subject to Western feminist ideas about birth control, these women (including delegates from the United States) rejected the oversimplified notion that birth control was a positive tool for women of African descent.

Although birth control was not a priority for this group, delegates did embrace some of the initiatives of feminists in the developed world. After years of rejecting the Equal Rights Amendment, the NCNW conference voted to support passage of the Equal Rights Amendment in the United States, claiming that this would not only offer American women "equality ... before the law" but also "set an example for other nations in the world where such rights have not been legislated for women."[65] In addition, although many of the delegates of African descent were elite, they advocated for consciousness-raising about the differences of class and region among black delegates. They spoke of the importance of creating a network of women from all classes who would help one another. Not only would this network provide solidarity, but it would help the women learn more about and combat the discrimination within their lives.[66] This awakening certainly invoked gender but also included race and class as categories affecting the attendees' lives.

After their weeklong IWY conference, the group of twenty-three international delegates traveled to Mississippi on July 3 to visit council-sponsored self-help projects in Jackson, Ruleville, and Okolona, Mississippi.[67] Upon arrival in Jackson, the delegation was honored at the Mississippi governor's mansion, suggesting the tremendous change that had occurred since WIMS first entered in 1964, thanks largely to the political influence of NCNW state chairman Jessie Mosley, who helped set up the meeting. The delegation then visited Tougaloo College and had a community picnic.[68] Delegation members also met with activists in Jackson, such as Patt Derian, who had first worked with WIMS and later with the council more broadly. They then spoke with Dr. Aaron Shirley, who had worked with the NCNW since the time of WIMS in 1964, to discuss the tremendous health-care problem facing the black poor in Mississippi.[69]

The delegation then visited the Delta, stopping first in Cleveland, Mississippi, to see the Eastgate Turnkey III project (see figure 9). Although by this time the housing project was no longer officially affiliated with the council, the community center was named for Height out of respect for her initiating role in the homeownership project.[70] From there, they traveled to view Fannie Lou Hamer's pig bank and attended a Fourth of July cookout, where one of the pigs was being roasted. The delegates later commented that, considering all the things they saw on their trip, they were most impressed by the pig bank. They later visited the Fannie Lou Hamer day-care center in Ruleville. Finally, the team traveled to Okolona, where they viewed the NCNW-sponsored child-care center and discussed how they might implement feeding or childcare programs in their home countries. When they returned to Jackson, the participants traveled to Liberty House, an NCNW-sponsored marketing and purchasing cooperative, owned by thirteen handicraft-producing cooperatives from four counties in Mississippi. As Liberty House struggled to survive in the early 1970s, the NCNW paid the Liberty House manager's salary and remained proud to be associated with the cooperative project.[71]

The group ended their visit at Bethune-Cookman College for the 100th anniversary of the birth of Mary McLeod Bethune. This celebration focused on Bethune's enterprising spirit in opening a school for young black girls in Florida in 1904, a time when few educational opportunities existed for black youth. In addition, the event gave the women a final opportunity to discuss what they had seen over the past month. Joining them were 114 NCNW members, who had traveled to the college for the birthday celebration and to meet the international delegates.[72] Much like with Wednesdays and Workshops in Mississippi and Project Womanpower, the council provided a safe and empowered space for black women to discuss solutions to the challenges of poverty and political disenfranchisement.[73] Again, the NCNW highlighted the message of self-help at the Bethune celebration. While half of the delegates returned home from Florida, twelve traveled to Howard University for an additional tour and farewell luncheon.[74]

While the IWY satellite conference was largely a success, the celebratory mood was tainted when one of the delegates, Madame Siga Sene, the vice president of the Economic and Social Council of Senegal, was accused of shoplifting a can of lotion and arrested in Florida. The police held her in custody for three hours. Meanwhile, Madame Sene's translator and Madame Salimatou Diallo, an official representative of the Organization of African Unity from Sierra Leone, tried to explain that Madame Sene was not shoplifting but was reading the product's label. The police would not listen to the translator, arguing that the black interpreter could not possibly know French. Finally, after the protest put up by Madame Diallo, the police let Madame Sene go, but she was "badly shaken." The NCNW called the store, the local city council, the State Department, and the Senegalese embassy to alert them to the incident and insist that the store manager and staff issue an apology. The following day, the clerk, who had first accused Madame Sene of shoplifting; the manager; supervisor; and owner of the store came to Bethune-Cookman College to apologize in front of the whole delegation of women. Madame Sene accepted the apology of the manager but insisted that "he might also do well . . . to bear in mind that money had no color."[75]

By having the participants visit Mississippi and Florida, the council exposed the parallels between the Deep South and African nations just emerging from colonialism, showing the international women that extreme poverty, hunger, high infant mortality rates, shortened life spans, and discrimination existed in the United States as well. The NCNW made a direct ideological connection between the activities of Workshops in Mississippi and its international programs. WIMS staff member Kate Wilkinson spoke before a NCNW group leaving for Africa in 1974—"the goal, again, [with poverty work in Mississippi] was to know what the people who had the problem wanted done about the problem[,] to . . . help all of us learn the skill of letting the people develop the program." Wilkinson continued, "And it's marvelous to think that Mississippi, who has been the taillight, can now be the headlight showing another place which way to go."[76] The time spent at Bethune-Cookman College reinforced that it was the network of women, brought together first by Mary McLeod Bethune, who made this possible.

Building an International Division

During the IWY conference, the council received word that it had received $825,000 more in funding from USAID to establish a permanent International Division over the course of three years.[77] USAID became more interested in the council's work as it "began to de-emphasize the trickle-down theory of assistance and developed a more direct people-to-people program. The trend now [was] to work with rural and poor populations[,] with special emphasis on participatory planning."[78] The council's international work reflected the principles that were present in Workshops in Mississippi and Project Womanpower (and the larger War on Poverty), with their emphases on creating "participatory planning" and self-help projects to aid women with housing, job creation, and day care, and USAID liked this. The NCNW also wanted to include local women in the planning of the projects. "Women don't just want to receive the benefits," Height stated in 1975, "they want to have a hand in development."[79] Thus, while the NCNW's international work was sponsored by USAID, the women of the countries who participated in it sought to use the council to further their own goals of economic and political freedom.

The council chose to work in countries that were feasible sites for both skills training and self-help economic projects. In early winter 1975, the council sent a delegation of Height; Margaret Hickey, chair of the Advisory Committee on Voluntary Foreign Aid; and the new director of the NCNW's International Division to investigate possible locations and seek out networks of communication in potential countries.[80] By February 1976, the council had decided on Botswana, Lesotho, and Swaziland (BLS) as the first three countries to work in. These countries were all chosen because of their proximity to (in the case of Lesotho, location within) South Africa, with its system of apartheid. Although recently politically independent (Botswana and Lesotho in 1966, and Swaziland in 1968), they remained economically dependent on South Africa: Botswana and Lesotho still used the South African rand, the countries' young men went to work in South African mines, and South Africa was a major importer of these nations' raw materials. Women in these countries remained home to head households, while their husbands were away working. These women sought economic liberation from the more developed South Africa, pointing out that the more South Africa industrialized, the harder it was for their local economies to compete. Thus, the council sought ways to help these women, who had been affected by grinding poverty and dislocation fueled by South Africa's apartheid government.[81]

As it designed its projects, the council wanted to hear from African women and men themselves as to what they believed might be most helpful. Far from simply toeing the line of economic modernization and expansion of American capitalism or dominating the meeting along the lines of a Western feminist agenda, the council listened to the concerns of African women. In December 1976, the council sponsored a meeting of eighty delegates from the United States and the BLS countries to meet at Wingspread—the Johnson Foundation conference center in Racine, Wisconsin. At this meeting, women and men called for the NCNW and its affiliated units to provide consultants and facilitators in setting up development projects. Height stressed the importance of working "as true partners" with the women abroad. Speakers at the conference stressed the importance of supporting not only the end of apartheid but also movements that returned the political and economic power of southern African countries back to black majorities. Other speakers talked about the racist and classist oppression that remained in postcolonial states due to the economic investment of the United States and European businesses in these areas. Ivy Matsepe, then a student at Rutgers University, who would become South Africa's minister of communications after the fall of apartheid, pointed out the tremendous toll that the industrialization of South Africa had taken on the lives of black African women. In the "'traditional'" economy of the countries in southern Africa, women had at least had some economic independence, but now women were dependent on the agricultural technology of the modern economy of South Africa. She also likened the situation for blacks in South Africa to those in the urban United States by pointing out that malnutrition and neglect for black well-being was on the rise in South Africa despite it being a modern nation.[82]

The USAID grant to help the NCNW create an International Division sought to make the council more effective at providing support for women's organizations in countries around the world. At the Wingspread conference, representatives from all three of the BLS countries asked specifically for trained personnel to help establish self-help projects in rural areas. Botswana called for trained personnel who could help rural communities better organize to make clearer demands of their government in development projects. A Lesotho representative called for trained personnel who could help establish health clinics, nutritional programs, and day cares in rural areas. And finally Swaziland asked for further technical support for a national project for women in development already funded by the UN. The council's grant to create an International Division fit nicely with these requests. First, the grant sought to identify and bring together the international activities of the NCNW and its affiliated organizations. The council would then create a skills bank registry of African American women who could serve as trained resource personnel in Africa on an as-needed basis to help boost the power of national women's groups in each of the BLS countries. The council was careful to "[e]nsure that [it was] not competitive" with the local women's groups. Undergirding the council's efforts was the desire to work in a respectful partnership with, not to dominate, the women's groups that were already in existence in these countries. Finally, the council sought to use its knowledge to help create agricultural cooperatives and leadership development projects in the region.[83]

In addition to helping boost the economic independence of women in these countries, African women called for the NCNW to use its power to push the U.S. government to support the black majority in South Africa and remove its ties to the apartheid South African government. According to the final report from the Wingspread conference, the top priority of southern African women was for the NCNW to "use its voice to sensitize the United States foreign policy to the need to deal in positive ways with liberation goals of Black South Africa."[84] The council had actually worked a long time in direct aid and lobbying efforts to end apartheid through its participation in the African Children's Feeding Scheme in the 1950s and ANLCA in the 1960s, but the call from African women first at the IWY conference and later in their work in the BLS countries strengthened their conviction to speak out more firmly against apartheid. In September 1976, Height represented the council at a gathering led by the Congressional Black Caucus to bring together 120 civil rights and governmental leaders to create the Black Leadership Conference on Southern Africa. The group produced a manifesto that outlined eleven demands for the U.S. government, essentially calling for complete support of efforts to create full independence for the black peoples of Namibia, Tanzania, and South Africa. This group also created the lobbying group Trans-Africa.[85] Height served on the board of TransAfrica, which continued to pressure the U.S. government under both Carter and Reagan to end its relationship with the oppressive white-supremacist administrations of Rhodesia and South Africa.[86] Despite pleadings from U.S. government officials, who tried to convince African Americans to stop economic boycotts in South Africa, the council continued to pressure the U.S. government and businesses to divest. The council also insisted on keeping a focus on the conditions of women and children who had been imprisoned for their activism in the region, calling on both Amnesty International and the UN Commission on Human Rights to investigate the abuse of these vulnerable political prisoners.[87] Though the NCNW did not make protesting apartheid the sole goal of its International Division, it did play a major role in its work.

The council's initial grant was to create an International Division and investigate the possibility of setting up programming abroad, but it ultimately reached a dead end with its economic development projects in the BLS countries. After two years, it had been unable to fully fund-raise the private money needed to support the International Division (a requirement of the USAID grant) and had several staff changes in the division, including that of director. It had also run up against major roadblocks in establishing its most promising development projects in each country. The NCNW was blocked from providing consultants for a six-week-long leadership training program for women agricultural extension workers in Swaziland after local officials decided to only use Swazi teaching assistants. The NCNW leadership decided to end plans for a chicken farm in Botswana after the proposed program town of Pelegano was deemed too remote by USAID. Finally, USAID rejected plans for a childcare program in Lesotho because childcare centers do not typically help the very poorest women. This led the International Division advisory board to declare in 1977 that "after so much expenditure of time, money and effort, NCNW can do nothing more at this point than to try to salvage the BLS operation, mainly through the preparation of a proposal that AID will accept for funding, a process already underway."[88] However, this effort was unsuccessful; by 1979, the council had closed down its checking accounts in all three countries and limited its work in Swaziland to establishing a pig farm with the help of the king.[89]

One of the most challenging factors in the NCNW's efforts to establish permanent projects was its relationship with USAID. The International Division was mainly funded by USAID. However, USAID placed restrictions on what the council could and could not do. The council was angered that it could not set up childcare centers in Lesotho, even though the local women had specifically asked for them. The NCNW recognized that it needed USAID for the continuation of its division but believed "we must also have our own definition and criteria of success."[90] USAID also required that the council fund-raise for its international work, but although the International Division formed a fund-raising committee, it was not successful. A USAID report from 1985 complained about the inability of the council, from its earliest efforts in 1975, to raise private matching funds.[91] The NCNW insisted that although it needed the funding from USAID, it also needed to ensure that its own goals were being met. The International Division board members agreed that ultimately, "NCNW must be satisfied that we are responding to the expressed needs of women in the countries and that we will utilize our own brand of expertise," not that of USAID. Thus, the council was determined to follow its "own definition and criteria of success" to help women of African descent meet their own goals. The women continued to look for outside sources of funding to keep themselves as independent as possible.[92]

Having run into difficulties in the BLS countries, the council shifted its focus to French-speaking West African countries in the late 1970s and instituted a new strategy that fit nicely with its long-standing commitment to professional development for black women. In the spring of 1978, the council went on a fact-finding mission to create links with Senegal, Ivory Coast, and Togo. Leading the team was Mrs. Irene Petty, wife of black diplomat Wilbert Petty.[93] Likely influenced by the debacle with Madame Sene in Florida, the council insisted that, out of respect for local customs and needs, only French-speaking NCNW delegates make the trip. According to the press release, "The ability to speak, read, write, think, and[,] most importantly, to listen in French was the team's greatest asset." As part of that trip, the council visited the countries' rural countrysides to see what might be implemented there. The delegates remarked, somewhat patronizingly, that they were pleasantly surprised that all the women had a hearty sense of self-worth " 'as integral human resources for the progress and development of their countries,' " and as it had with its earlier efforts in the BLS countries, the NCNW hoped to help "enable the women of Africa to participate more effectively and directly in the development of their countries." Its next step was to formalize the growing partnership between its organization and the women's organizations of West Africa.[94] On August 6, 1979, the International Communication Agency of the United States awarded the council a $89,266 grant to help make this partnership with French West African women a reality. The council established a "twinning" program to link itself to the national organizations of women in Senegal and Togo. At the heart of the process, the council claimed that it wanted to "develop an instrument for involving women in projects directed toward upgrading the quality of life for women and their families" and link its members to women of color around the world. In 1979, the council brought eight women from Togo and Senegal to the United States to tour council projects and to attend its national convention. A few months later, a team of NCNW women visited the two countries in return.[95]

Despite the council's limited effectiveness in the BLS countries and its inability to find private matching funds, USAID awarded another grant to the

NCNW in September 1979 to establish the LaKara Skills Development Training Center in the Lakara region in northern Togo, one of the poorest areas of the country and the world. Annual per capita income in the region was less than $58 in contrast with the GNP of the country at $260 per year; adult literacy was only 12 percent; and malnutrition was a severe problem. The purpose of the proposed training center was to help rural women in Togo upgrade their skills in farming, gardening, and handicraft production. The NCNW hoped that this would not only enrich the women but also provide them with better nutrition. The program was run as a collaboration between the council, the National Union of Togolese Women, the government of Togo, and USAID. While the project certainly expanded the NCNW's network of influence around West Africa, it also ran into difficulties, running six months behind schedule.[96] And although the project was ultimately limited in its effectiveness, it had established ties across the continent. By 1985, the NCNW had established regional representatives in Dakar, Senegal; Mbabne, Swaziland; and Nairobi, Kenya. It had also established a health and family planning program in Senegal that provided information not only about reproductive health and contraception but also about child spacing and prenatal health, concerns raised at the 1975 NCNW-sponsored IWY conference for women of African descent. Women from Kenya, Rwanda, Guinea, and Botswana all requested help from the NCNW's International Division for local projects in the 1980s.[97]

The most successful self-help project to come out of NCNW efforts in Africa in the 1970s and 1980s was a pig farm set up in the rural Lundzi-Mpuluzi area of western Swaziland with the help of King Sobhuza II after he learned about the pig bank at Hamer's Freedom Farm. The council sent John Davis, an extension worker from Mississippi, to Swaziland, where he taught rural women how to care for the pigs and how to market them as well.[98] The council, King Sobhuza, and USAID—through a grant to the council of $310,000 for this specific project—created a three-year pilot pig project.[99] The council was trying to address malnutrition as well as the lack of jobs for Swazi women. Women were the ones to feel the burden of poverty when their husbands were away at work in South Africa. They needed jobs close to where they lived. The Swazi king provided land for growing feed, as well as for a storage building, a manager's home, and an office. In the first year, the cooperative planted fifteen hectares of maize and produced four tons to help feed the pigs. Three years later, fourteen hectares produced seventy tons of maize. The government also created a water system for the piggery, which was expanded for the local population's use.[100] USAID funds helped build several buildings for the project, purchase a pickup truck and another small truck, a maize sheller, a tractor, and a feed mixer. They also helped provide for training pig owners in how to breed and care for the pigs and how to operate the cooperative. Pig owners provided pens for the pigs from local materials.[101] While the cooperative was mainly intended to provide wealth to the pig farmers, Sabenta, a Swazi literacy organization, worked with the program as well, to keep the literacy rate in this rural area above 50 percent.[102]

Like the previous NCNW international projects, the piggery faced some setbacks. It took a long time for the Swazi government to create the water system and over two years to create the cooperative organization and the piggery.[103] The council received more money to help continue the project, but by 1987, funding had run out, and the project had to be transferred to a truly cooperative structure, without outside help. The council warned that the management salaries of the enterprise would not be sustainable after the end of NCNW support and the transition to a cooperative format would likely fail. The council also had planned to deliver pigs to 75 families but only reached 28. Still, those families who did receive pigs did quite well and some even increased their income by more than the expected $475 through the program.[104]

While the council was not as successful as it had hoped to be in these African nations, there were still gains made. The people of the BLS countries, Togo, and Senegal felt a sense of solidarity with the council. In their initial trips to southern Africa, locals commented on the impact of having Height, an African American, come as the leader of an aid organization. "You have to bear in mind that these are countries that have been under colonial control so that they are more accustomed to seeing whites in our capacity than of seeing blacks," Height said. Madame Dombi, the wife of the ambassador to Botswana, said that she was glad to work with the council because it was the first black group that she or her husband had ever worked with.[105] While traveling to set up new programs in Togo and South Africa, Height and the other council members were welcomed with special treatment, such as a banner proclaiming "Welcome Home Sisters" and gifts of elephant tusks presented to the council by President Gnassingbé Eyadéma of Togo himself.[106] During the first fact-finding mission to Senegal, Dr. Tyson, a member of the 1978 fact-finding group, found that the women there were " 'excited about the possibility of collaborating with NCNW because we are a Black women's group.' "[107]

The council members were also excited about working with African women and expanding their network internationally. A report from the International Division at the 1983 annual convention pointed to the NCNW's uniqueness as "the only PVO [private volunteer organization] of women of color actively involved in working with women in the developing world by sharing technical assistance." They distributed an occasional publication called *ID Update* to highlight to women around the world, but especially stateside NCNW women, what the council was doing in the international realm. "All of us in the organization—members, board, advisory committees and staff—are working to sustain our interest and commitment to our sisters around the world."[108] By 1985, the council was asking its local sections to help sponsor specific projects in different countries of Africa.[109] The council was also an active participant in the Nairobi conference of 1985, hosting a daylong conference featuring distinguished women from Botswana, the Gambia, Guinea, Senegal, Swaziland, and Togo. Seven, including Height, came from the United States.[110] The council continued to be active throughout Africa over the next twenty-five years. Although the NCNW International Division closed down in 2009, it brought economic, health, and educational programs to individuals and communities in twenty-six African countries during its thirty-four years of existence.[111]

WHILE THE COUNCIL's earliest international postwar work focused on human rights policy, in the late 1960s and 1970s its activities also focused on uniting women's organizations around the world to help with development. Using its Mississippi hunger, housing, and childcare work as models, the NCNW sought to implement aid projects developed by local women across southern, western, and later eastern Africa. Although the International Division promoted itself as a nongovernmental voluntary organization, it was also funded by the U.S. government and thus somewhat circumscribed in the political demands it could make. Despite its testimony against apartheid, the council's moderate reputation led to its winning nearly $2 million dollars in USAID funding, which it could then transfer to African women in the 1970s and 1980s. Promoting its expertise as an organization that had both formal training and respectability but also the ability to speak to women of color around the world, the council's strategizing helped bring resources to and leverage political power on behalf of thousands of African women.

Conclusion

In July 1983, President Ronald Reagan became the first president to honor the National Council of Negro Women as an organization at the White House. Within a few months of Reagan taking office in 1981, he had "proceeded to perform radical surgery on the American economy and welfare system," working with Congress to cut $25 billion from welfare programs. He placed officials who were hostile to civil rights on the Civil Rights and Equal Employment Opportunity commissions and ordered his attorney general to combat affirmative action. He cut money from programs that the council had held so dear—food stamps, job creation, and welfare—and he supported strengthening the United States' relationship with the apartheid government in South Africa.[1] In fact, Merble Reagon recalls that on the eve of Reagan's election, the council had around $8 million in grants. Within a few days of Reagan's inauguration, he had cut funding to the council by $7 million, leaving the organization with hundreds of staff members, several dependent programs, and only one-eighth of its budget.[2]

Yet with all the damage Reagan had already wreaked on black Americans, including the NCNW members themselves, the council decided to accept his invitation. Why? Height claimed to have accepted the offer to visit the White House "with expectations of the good inherent in such an occasion" and hoped that they might be able to influence the president through their presence. At the White House reception, Height delivered a speech that highlighted the NCNW's many accomplishments as a private volunteer organization of black women while underscoring the large and growing disparity in the standards of living between the rich and the poor. She stressed that the federal government must play a larger role in reducing black poverty.[3] Unfortunately, the council's visit accomplished little, as the proportion of blacks who were poor increased over the next six years, and Reagan began his devastating War on Drugs, continued to support apartheid South Africa, and continued to roll back civil rights gains from the previous two decades.[4]

Although the NCNW's domestic and international development programs created in the late 1960s and 1970s were innovative and helped a large number of women, most could not survive the Reagan era. Membership dues, fundraising schemes, and financial investments never yielded the funds necessary to maintain the NCNW's poverty programming. Therefore, as it had done before, the council sought out new sources of funding, especially from 1980s corporate America. Since 1935, the council had fostered, both directly and indirectly, the development of young black women and men, and now it called on those same black professionals in the private sector to keep the organization afloat.

After struggling to find programming as meaningful and important as its poverty work in Mississippi in the late 1960s, the council found its stride with the creation and subsequent annual sponsorship of the Black Family Reunion. In her autobiography, Height identified Bill Moyers's January 1986 PBS documentary *The Vanishing Black Family*, which highlighted the explosive growth of teen pregnancy within black America, as a turning point. The council had long lamented the growing number of teen pregnancies around the country, but as seen with the creation of its Okolona day care and Operation Cope, Height insisted that it must be the black women themselves who controlled a more productive and positive dialogue about black families. In order to counter Moyers's negative portrayal of the state of the black family, Height joined forces with prominent NCNW member Camille Cosby and her famous husband, Bill, to organize a new NCNW event that would bring together and celebrate contemporary black families.[5] Height recruited former Project Womanpower southern regional coordinator Doris Dozier Crenshaw to be the organizer for the new event.[6] The Black Family Reunion continues to the present, outlasting the Million Man March and other family-oriented marches of the mid-1990s. For Height, this event provided an opportunity to showcase the variety and health of the black family, including black welfare mothers who had been so maligned by Reagan.[7] Height was proud to recall, "Our celebrations have been lauded for creating new community energy and fostering self-help approaches to many contemporary concerns."[8] As Crenshaw recalls, the NCNW welcomed all types of families, including those headed by single mothers, and they tried to provide them with as many resources as they could to help them stretch their budgets.[9]

The Black Family Reunion has consistently enjoyed strong support from the private sector. NCNW member Dr. Vanessa Weaver, a psychologist on the management staff of Procter and Gamble (P&G), helped foster a strong relationship between the NCNW and P&G when it became the first major corporate sponsor of the event. P&G lent Weaver to the council for three years to work on developing the annual event while still paying her salary.[10] The council was able to fund-raise to completely cover the costs of the event. The first Black Family Reunion, attended by 200,000 people, was held in Washington,

D.C., near the Washington monument. Meanwhile, additional reunions were planned in Atlanta, Philadelphia, and Los Angeles for the following year. In total, Height estimates that over 700,000 people attended Black Family Reunions by the end of their second year.[11]

Height continued to show her support for black families by speaking at the Million Man March in October 1995. She faced much criticism, especially from black and white feminist allies of the council, for her willingness to speak at the Farrakhan-led "'day of atonement and reconciliation.'" One group of friends calling from Martha's Vineyard urged her not to get involved in the event, arguing that she had "'never been tainted'" by militants like Farrakhan and should not do so now. Black women intellectuals such as Angela Davis and bell hooks criticized the male exclusivity, patriarchy, and even pro-imperialism of the event, though others, such as Alice Walker and Howard University interim president Joyce Ladner, supported the event. Joining Rosa Parks and Coretta Scott King in her support of the event, Height saw the event as an opportunity to foster stronger family bonds that would help black men and families. She agreed to speak at the event, taking a potentially divisive stand in favor of Farrakhan.[12] As Height recalls, many of her former critics came to see the value of the event and later called to apologize.[13]

In the 1990s, Height focused largely on fund-raising to buy the massive NCNW headquarters at 633 Pennsylvania Avenue in Washington, D.C. Much like she had done with the Bethune statue, Height raised funds from various allies in order to have a permanent, influential, and prominent space that reflected the importance and power of black women. The Vermont Avenue headquarters had been destroyed by fire in early 1966, and the council had been renting a space in Dupont Circle for decades, but by 1991, Height began the search for a new headquarters in earnest.[14] The building she picked out was owned by the Sears Corporation. Sears had refurbished it in 1983 for its work with the government, but it no longer needed it. Height described it lovingly: "A pale pink citadel between the Capitol and the White House, it was grand in an elegant, womanly sort of way, spacious and beautifully furnished." It was perfect, but it was also $20 million. Although the price tag was far outside the council's budget, Height began to network. She turned to prominent black women who might help put in a good word for the council with Sears. She called Paula Banks, president of the Sears Foundation; Reatha Clarke King of General Mills Foundation; and Elynor Williams of Sara Lee Corporation. NCNW board member Toni Fay, a high-ranking employee of Time Warner, then helped Height draft an inquiry to Sears. A few months later, the price on the building dropped. By the end of 1993, the price had dropped to $11 million. At this point, Height reached out to former NCNW honorees and Sears board members—Nancy Reynolds and Sybil Mobley—who then pushed Sears to give the NCNW first priority for purchasing the building. Sears called with an offer, but the council had to act fast.[15]

Like Bethune, who had $1.50 in her pocket when she began her girls' school in Florida, Height had very little money when she agreed to purchase the Pennsylvania Avenue "citadel." However, she did not want to lose the offer to purchase the building, and she did have friends in high places. Joining in the fund-raising for the building was Camille Cosby, Maya Angelou, Susan Taylor, Deloris Jordan (Michael Jordan's mother), and Norman Lear, who backed the council's campaign to raise money.[16] Money and support also poured in from corporate sponsors, including P&G, Anheuser-Busch, Time Warner, John Hancock, General Motors, the Ford Motor Company, and Chrysler. Thanks to the efforts of a wide variety of allies, the Sears board agreed to further re-duce the price of the building to $8 million and to set up a series of loans. As a result of all this help and its own fund-raising efforts, the council was finally able to buy the building in 1995.[17]

Since the acquisition of the building, the council has continued to attract and maintain support from high-profile black and white Americans, includ-ing Coretta Scott King, Oprah Winfrey, and Hillary Rodham Clinton.[18] In the final year of her life, at the age of ninety-eight, Dorothy Height visited President Barack Obama twenty-one times during his first year in office.[19] The council continues to support leadership and job training, lobbying, and activism to improve black women's economic and political power. However, the council has not returned to the innovative poverty projects that it imple-mented from the middle of the 1960s through the 1970s. Instead, out of a need for survival in a neoliberal era, its projects have moved back to advocat-ing personal and private strategies for black women's advancement. Still, the council has created a permanent and significant place for itself in both the geog-raphy and the programming of our nation's capital. NCNW women have done this not by marching in visible protest but through the "quiet, dogged, dignified persistence" of women like Height, who remain in positions of prominence in the United States and in the world.[20]

While the council has received much acclaim for the Black Family Re-union and its continued presence in Washington, D.C., its acceptance of cor-porate funding over the last thirty years has at times proved problematic. In 1990, the NCNW partnered with Quaker Oats Company, the maker of the racist Aunt Jemima pancake brand, to launch a yearlong program, A Tribute to Black Women Community Leaders, to honor black women's leadership,

community service, church activism, and career development in seven different cities. Quaker Oats tried to alter the Aunt Jemima brand in 1989 by re-
moving her head wrap, changing her hair, and giving her softer makeup to
make her look more modern. Journalist Lauren Adama DeLeon even labeled
her a black Betty Crocker, but consumers continued to criticize the logo.
Quaker Oats thus tried to tackle this bad publicity head on by funding the
NCNW. The company helped pay for leadership contests and fund-raising
breakfasts for local sections of the council in Charleston, Chicago, Cleveland,
Detroit, Houston, New Orleans, and Philadelphia.[21] Each city nominated a
finalist for the national winner, selected by a panel of NCNW judges. While
Height was at first skeptical of the proposition from Quaker Oats, once she
saw that both black and white women were included in company advertise-
ments and that, as she stated, there were "no more bandanas," she was willing
to take the company's money.[22] While the acceptance of this money did fuel
more programming for the NCNW, it did not fuel the types of antipoverty,
hunger, or black pride programs seen a little over a decade before. Instead, the
money helped sponsor more banquets honoring the community service of
mostly elite black women.

The council's work in the 1960s and 1970s with the poor and grassroots in
America and abroad was innovative and inspiring, but it was also a product of
the times. NCNW programs created to aid not only the organization but also
the wider black community were funded by philanthropic organizations and
federal programs seeking to eliminate poverty through social welfare programs. As austerity measures swept black communities across the world in
the 1980s, the NCNW could no longer secure grants and turned more toward
self-preservation, with a focus on broadening opportunities for its elite con-
stituents. The NCNW's current priorities include programs that offer career
planning to college students, estate planning, "acquiring and growing assets
within the Black community," and initiatives to push black children into STEM
(science, technology, engineering, and mathematics) careers. All these programs seek to boost the earning power of black women and men, yet they are
targeting African Americans who already enjoy a higher quality of life than
the black poor. The NCNW's continued focus on health education, especially around HIV and obesity, targets all types of women, but these initiatives
do not include the poor as leaders as its earlier work did. On the NCNW's
current home page, there is no mention of the tremendous problem of black
mass incarceration or public support for the Black Lives Matter movement,
the two most prominent social justice concerns today. Some local sections of
the NCNW likely engage in these issues, but the current national organization

has returned to its elite focus from the 1950s and early 1960s.[23] Still, as the council's story shows, its members are always working behind the scenes in creative, flexible ways to create change on behalf of black communities. Perhaps the story of the council's work in the late 1960s and 1970s can reignite interest in the poverty programming and social justice activism of a previous era.

RECENT SCHOLARSHIP HAS rightfully focused on the efforts of grassroots, radical, and poor women who fought for change in the civil rights and Black Power movements; however, the implicit dismissal and outright omission of contributions of moderates and middle- and upper-class black women has been glaring. For over eighty years, the National Council of Negro Women has played a significant role in fighting for racial and gender equity and self-determination in both formal spaces, such as international, national, state, and local committees, and informal spaces, such as within workshops and in women's homes. Since its founding in 1935 by the formidable Mary McLeod Bethune, the council has always insisted, unapologetically, that black women be central to American policymaking on employment, education, civil rights, human rights, hunger, housing, and healthcare. While painfully aware of the discrimination that they have faced daily, council members have been undaunted in insisting on their rightful place at the boardroom table. Through a network representing up to four million at its peak, the NCNW women have relied on their intellect, courage, elegance, and collective voice to push America towards change.

Beyond their efforts behind the scenes for change, women of the NCNW rank among the most visible leaders in twentieth century activism. Bethune carved a space for herself in government and refused to leave until black women's voices were heard. She insisted that black women be included in the military, defense industry, and diplomatic roles in the postwar world. Dorothy Ferebee and Vivian Mason continued to build the visibility and power of the NCNW, and Dorothy Height transformed the NCNW from a lobbying organization of affiliated clubs to an entity representing black women of all classes, complexions, and creeds. Height was also willing to forge alliances with men and white women who worked on the NCNW's behalf. When the NCNW won tax-exempt status in 1966 (retroactively to 1965), the organization was able to generate development projects in Mississippi and throughout the rest of the country.

Using its respectable reputation as a black moderate organization, the council secured money and resources from private foundations, corporations, and the federal government. With this money, it brought tangible resources to black communities in need. The NCNW won thousands of dollars in grants from the Ford Foundation, Rockefeller Brothers Fund, the Office of Economic Opportunity, the Department of Justice, and USAID, among many others. With this money, it then supported cooperative farms in Sunflower and Bolivar Counties in Mississippi; Macon County, Alabama; and the Lundzi-Mpuluzi region of Swaziland. It helped make homeownership a reality for low-income families across the U.S. It opened up educational and employment programs for women at home and abroad. It was these development projects that drew Mississippi civil rights legends Fannie Lou Hamer, Unita Blackwell, and Amzie Moore to work for the council.

Young activists in the late 1960s were also drawn to council work. Women like Frances Beal, Doris Dozier, and Gwendolyn R. Simmons were drawn to the possibilities inherent in working for an established well-respected black women's organization. The council provided these young women with employment, but in return these young women challenged the organization to grow ideologically and programmatically. While the council was initially distrustful of calls for Black Power, it would later embrace the concept, arguing that the organization was prepared to fight loudly and even militantly to protect black youth and communities.

The council's story in the 1960s and 1970s makes clear the importance of middle-class and moderate organizations in the civil rights and Black Power movements. The NCNW's careful strategizing enabled it to maintain its presence as an important policymaking body, while also bringing crucial resources to communities in need. Although certainly not radical in the sense that the women of the organization have not openly undermined American structures of economic and political power, the council has brought meaningful change to the people whose activism it touched. It has provided a means for more radical activists and organizations to receive financial support when they could not secure it on their own. And it has continued to thrive, to this day.

Acknowledgments

No book can ever be written alone. I am greatly indebted to a wide variety of sponsors, scholars, community activists, friends, and family members.

First, a thank-you to all the women and men whose words and stories fill this book. Thank you to Dorothy Irene Height, Merble Reagon, Doris Dozier Crenshaw, Gwendolyn Zoharah Simmons, Bettye Collier-Thomas, Unita Blackwell, Owen Brooks, John Doar, Patt Derian, Charles McLaurin, Gabrielle Beard, Susie Goodwillie Stedman, Doris Wilson, Edith Savage Jennings, Winifred Green, Wilma Clopton-Mosley, Margaret Boyer, Janet K. Shands, Mary F. Hendrick, Janet Purvis, Barbara Barber, Rims and Judy Barber, A. M. E. Logan, Helen Raebeck Rachlin, Holly Shulman, Earl Pfeiffer, Mary Spinks-Thigpen, Kewanna Riley, Nellie Adams, Ruby Ella Kirk, Louise Floyd Cole, and Sammie Lee Keyes Gray-Wiseman for letting me interview you. Thank you to Frances Beal and to her interviewer, Ula Taylor, for sharing your recollections about your time with the National Council of Negro Women. Thank you to Jacqueline Hamer for speaking with me about your mother and her childcare center. Thank you to the women of the NCNW, especially Victoria Sharpe and the women of the Gulfport Section, as well as the organizers and participants of the 2016 Mississippi State Convention for inviting me to your council gatherings. Thank you especially to Dorothy Height and the multitude of other NCNW women represented in this book. I am in awe of you and what you accomplished in your lifetimes. This book is dedicated to you.

Thank you also to institutions that have provided me with financial support as I have prepared this manuscript. Thank you to the National Endowment for the Humanities for my Summer Stipend Fellowship, the Woodrow Wilson Foundation for the Charlotte Newcombe Fellowship, the Moody Foundation at the LBJ Presidential Library, the University of Southern Mississippi Office of Research Administration, USM's Center for the Study of the Gulf South, the Smith College Archives for a traveling research fellowship, the Institute for Research on Women, the Rutgers Center for Historical Analysis, and the Rutgers University–Newark Teacher-Scholar Program.

Thank you to my wonderful editor Brandon Proia and the team at UNC Press, including Catherine Hodorowicz, Jad Adkins, Susan Raines Garrett, Dino Battista, and Stephanie Wenzel. Thank you also to Michelle Witkowski and the team at Westchester Publishing Services.

Thank you to the indispensable archivists, librarians, and researchers who have aided me in my work. Thank you especially to Kenneth Chandler at the National Archives for Black Women's History for his tireless efforts to help me with this project. Thanks also to Bethany Antos and the team at the Rockefeller Archive Center, Allen

Fischer at the Lyndon Baines Johnson Presidential Library, Jennifer Brannock at the McCain Archives, and Nadine Phillips and David Robinson in Interlibrary Loan at Cook Library at the University of Southern Mississippi.

Thanks also to the additional staff, past and present, at the National Archives for Black Women's History, including Joy Kinard, Robert Parker, Margaret Coleman Miles, and their many helpful assistants. Thanks also to Robby Luckett and Alfredteen Harrison at the Margaret Walker Center, Jackson State University, Jackson, Mississippi. Thank you also to the archivists and staff members at the University of Virginia, Charlottesville, Virginia; the Mississippi Department of Archives and History, Jackson, Mississippi; the Amistad Research Center, Tulane University, New Orleans, Louisiana; the University of Mississippi, Oxford, Mississippi; Millsaps College, Jackson, Mississippi; the Mississippi State Archives, Starkville, Mississippi; the University of Southern Mississippi, Hattiesburg, Mississippi; Smith College, Northampton, Massachusetts; the Moorland-Spingarn Research Center, Howard University, Washington, D.C.; the University of North Carolina, Chapel Hill; and the Library of Congress, Washington, D.C.

Thank you also to Marlene McCurtis and the rest of the team at the Wednesdays in Mississippi Film Project. I have enjoyed working with you on your valuable project. Thank you to Debbie Harwell for your encouragement, suggestions, and kindness at events over the past several years where we presented together on the history of WIMS. I offer great thanks to Holly Shulman, the talented historian and daughter of Polly Cowan, who has shared with me her time, reflections, and personal collection of WIMS material.

Thank you to the University of Southern Mississippi Department of History faculty, especially Jill Abney, Allison Abra, Douglas Bristol, Matt Casey, Kevin Greene, Andrew Haley, Joshua Haynes, Courtney Luckhardt, Deanne Nuwer, Andrew Ross, Heather Stur, Ken Swope, Pam Tyler, Susannah Ural, and Kyle Zelner, who have all read and commented on my work; Center for Black Studies affiliated faculty Loren Coleman, Marcus Coleman, Cheryl Jenkins, Sherita Johnson, and Marek Steedman; USM administrators Steven Moser, Gordon Cannon, Maureen Ryan, Julie Reid, Eric Tribunella, and Ellen Weinauer; USM library faculty Jennifer Brannock, Nadine Phillips, David Robinson, and Tisha Zelner; and USM staff Danielle Sypher-Haley, Ashlea Maddox, Rosalind Philips, and Cindy Warren. Thank you also to the members of the Fleshed Out research group. You all have been so supportive by commenting on my work, offering moral support, or both. Thank you also to the Department of History at Tulane, especially Rosanne Adderley, Emily Clark, Brian Demare, Karissa Haugeberg, Jana Lipman, Elizabeth McMahon, and Randy Sparks.

Thank you to the circle of scholars from Rutgers, Rice, and beyond who have helped me along the way, including Nancy Hewitt, Deborah Gray White, Steven F. Lawson, John Dittmer, Bettye Collier-Thomas, Ula Taylor, Sherie Randolph, Danielle McGuire, Gail Murray, Christina Greene, Michelle Mitchell, Emilye Crosby, Dorie Ladner, Meagan Parker Brooks, Maurice Hobson, Akinyele Umoja, Ann Gordon, Temma Kaplan, Ted Crackel, Mary-Jo Kline, Allison Schneider, Joel Wolfe, and John Boles.

Thank you so much to the fantastic women of the Delta Women's Writers Group. Your beautiful prose and great company have kept me inspired to keep going, even in the most difficult of times. Your work and your moral support have been invaluable. Thanks also to a network of friends who have sustained my family and me while I worked on this book—Bernadette Collins, Deborah Wheat, Samantha Wheat, Madalene Daniell, Allison Miller, Vanessa Holden, Sara Rzeszutek, Robin Chapdelaine, Rosemarie and Mark Strawn, Leslie Reardon, Jim Marsalis, Casey Greene, Amy and Craig Carey, Stephanie Casey, Debra and Chris Brown, Jill Wiest, Lori Gibbs, and countless others in Hattiesburg, New Orleans, New Jersey, and beyond.

Finally, thank you to my wonderful family members, who have been there for me for well over a decade of work on this project—Stephen Tuuri, Georgianna Tuuri, Rachel Tuuri, Sarah Coleman, Brandon Coleman, Melissa Parham, and Cody Parham.

Thank you most of all to my wonderful husband, Steven Kingsbury. You have been incredibly supportive during the late nights, early mornings, and lonely weekends while I've worked on this book. Thank you also to my daughter, Madeline, and son, Luke, who have waited patiently while I've worked on this book. I love you all very much.

Appendix 1

1964 Wednesdays in Mississippi Participants

Team #1—New York to Hattiesburg

Jean Benjamin: white; non-practicing Protestant; member of League of Women Voters, National Council of Women, Red Cross; wife of chairman of United Artists Corporation

Polly Cowan: white; Jewish; WIMS chairperson, NCNW Executive Board member, WMCA Call for Action chairperson; wife of former president of CBS and director of Brandeis University communications research center

Dorothy Height: black; Protestant; NCNW national president

Marian Logan: black; Protestant; president of Women's Auxiliary to the Manhattan Central Medical Society; NYC special projects coordinator for the SCLC; wife of surgeon and chairman of Haryou-ACT, active in the SCLC and the National Urban League

Ann McGlinchy: white; Catholic; retired history teacher; member of Catholic Interracial Council

Team #2—Boston area to Canton

Ruth Batson: black; Protestant; education commissioner for Massachusetts Commission Against Discrimination; education chairman of Massachusetts NAACP; Massachusetts Delegate to 1964 Democratic National Convention

Sister Catherine John Flynn: white; Catholic; Holy Sisters of Mary order; teacher at Immaculate Heart College in Los Angeles

Geraldine Kohlenberg: white; Jewish; teacher and tutor; wife of founder of Codex Corporation

Beryl Morris: black; Protestant; lieutenant, State Department of Correction, Bedford Prison for women

Alice Ryerson: white; Protestant; psychologist, Shady Hill School, Cambridge, Massachusetts; Cambridge YWCA member

Laya Wiesner: white; Jewish; president of Watertown League of Women Voters; wife of dean of science (and later president) at MIT

Pearl Willen: white; Jewish; president of the National Council of Jewish Women

Ilza Williams: black; Protestant; assistant principal, Clara Barton School; member of AKA, the NAACP, and the Urban League

Team #3—Washington, D.C., area to Meridian

Flossie Dedmond: black; Protestant; associate professor of English, Coppin State College; public relations director for AKA; former program coordinator for League of

Women's Clubs; NAACP member; CORE member; YWCA member; wife of head of Foreign Languages department at Morgan State

Wilhelmina Hetzel: white; Protestant; wife of director of United States Employment Service

Mary Cushing Niles: white; Protestant; former worker for U.S. government, 1941–57

Flaxie Pinkett: black; Protestant; president of John R. Pinkett, Inc., Real Estate and Insurance Firm; member of Delta Sigma Theta; executive committee for D.C. NAACP

Justine Randers-Pehrson: white; no religion listed; medical historian and technical translator

Margaret "Peggy" Roach: white; Catholic; executive assistant, National Council of Catholic Women

Geraldine P. Woods: black; Protestant; Delta Sigma Theta national president; NCNW National Board member

Team #4—Minneapolis area to Vicksburg

Virginia Bourne: white; no religion listed; national board member of the YWCA

Barbara Cunningham: white; Protestant; chairman of Brooklyn Center Human Relations Committee

Josie Johnson: black; Protestant; secretary of Mayor's Commission on Human Rights; Minneapolis NAACP

Mary Kyle: black; Catholic; reporter for *Twin City Observer*; member of Minnesota Commission for Civil Rights and Minnesota Urban League

Maxine Nathanson: white; Jewish; national board member of National Council of Jewish Women; National and State Women's Civil Rights Commission

Team #5—New York to Ruleville

Marie Barksdale: black; Protestant; executive director of Delta Sigma Theta Sorority; member of the NCNW

Lilace Reid Barnes: white; Protestant; former president and current member of the YWCA national board

Marjorie Dammann: white; Jewish; public relations assistant to Victor Weingarten; president of Jewish Family Service of New York; advisory board of Urban League of Westchester

Frances Haight: white; Protestant; president of International Social Service, Geneva, Switzerland; vice president of Citizens Committee for Children

Ethel Haserodt: white; Protestant; executive director of Passaic YWCA

Claudia Heckscher: white; Protestant; wife of director of Twentieth Century Fund, Inc.

Florynce Kennedy: black; no religion listed; attorney; chairman of Women's Division of the Federal Bar Association of New York, New Jersey, and Connecticut

Trude Lash: white; no religion listed; executive director of Citizens Committee for Children of New York, Inc.

Team #6—Chicago area to Canton

Etta Moten Barnett: black; Protestant; former Broadway actress; life member of the NCNW; life member of AKA; member of Church Women United; wife of founder of Associated Negro Press

Jean Davis: white; Protestant; president of Area Girl Scout Council; member of Chicago YWCA; member of League of Women Voters

Miriam Davis: white; Protestant; member of League of Women Voters; member of Girl Scouts

Narcissa Swift King: white; no religion listed; chairwoman of Women's Board of Chicago Urban League; life member of the NAACP

Lucy Montgomery: white; Protestant; women's board member of University of Chicago

Henrietta Moore: white; Protestant; secretary of Human Relations Committee

Arnetta Wallace: black; Protestant; former grand basileus of AKA; NCNW national board member

Sylvia Weinberg: white; Jewish; member of National Council of Jewish Women; Chicago YWCA

Team #7—New Jersey to Hattiesburg

Jane Gardner: white; Protestant; wife of an attorney active in political affairs

Priscilla Hunt: white; Protestant; vice president of Cambridge League of Women Voters; Public Affairs Commission of Cambridge (Mass.) YWCA

Hannah Levin: white; Jewish; assistant professor of psychology, Rutgers University–Newark

Helen Meyner: white; Protestant; columnist for *Newark Star-Ledger*; member of National Council of Women; served in Red Cross in Korea; wife of former governor of New Jersey

Ruth Hurd Minor: black; Protestant; member of LWV; member of the American Association of University Women; Women's Auxiliary Urban League; Special Consultant in Guidance and Curriculum for Roselle Public Schools

Olive Noble: white; Protestant; member of AAUW; member of CWU; lecturer on archaeology and art

Edith Savage: black; Protestant; supervisor at Mercer County Youth House; member of City of Trenton Planning Board

Sources: 1964 team application sheets, Series 19, Folders 12–18; debriefings found in Series 15, Subseries 5; and Final Report, Series 19, Folder 276, NCNW Papers, NABWH; as well as obituaries

Appendix 2

1965 Wednesdays in Mississippi Participants

Special Team of Art Teachers from Cambridge, Mass.

Mary Austin: white; Catholic; artist; teacher; director of PROJECT, Inc.

Laura Avery: white; Protestant; teacher at PROJECT, Inc.; director of local Family Planning Center

Rita DeLisi: white; Catholic; artist; teacher; director of PROJECT, Inc.

Merla Higgins: white; Protestant; art teacher

Team #1—New York City

Polly Cowan: white; Jewish; chairman of WIMS; life member of the NCNW; member of the LWV; member of the NAACP; board member of Citizen's Committee for Children

Ellen Dammond: black; Protestant; training supervisor for B. Altman & Company; national board YWCA; member of State Commission on Human Rights

Carol Guyer: white; Protestant; chairman of Contemporary Arts Committee, Asia Society; trustee in Experiment in International Living; daughter of Mr. J. C. Penney

Molly Harrower: white; Protestant; professor of research in clinical psychology at Temple University Medical Center; American Psychological Association; chairman of Advisory Council in Psychology for State of New York Education Department

Ellen Tarry: black; Catholic; intergroup relations specialist with Federal Housing and Home Finance Agency; member of LaFarge Committee of Catholic Interracial Council; member of Urban League Housing Committee

Gladys Zales: white; Jewish; chairman of Purchasing Department of Hadassah; board member of Hadassah; board member of Family and Children's Service of Stamford (Conn.)

Team #2—Philadelphia

Jean Dillinger: white; Protestant; chairman of Christian World Missions; member of Church Women United; member of the AAUW

Margery Gross: white; Jewish; assistant director of WIMS; member of the LWV; member of the NCJW; member of Hadassah

Anne Keller: white; Protestant; associate professor of pediatrics, University of Pennsylvania; member of the YWCA

Marjorie Penney: white; Protestant; director of Fellowship House and Fellowship Farm; honorary member of Delta Sigma Theta; member of American Baptist Woman's Home and Foreign Mission Society

Henrietta Smith: black; Protestant; social worker; board member of Columbia Branch YWCA; member of Philadelphia Health and Welfare Council; member of Philadelphia Chapter of National Association of Social Workers; member of Philadelphia Urban League

Helen Stanford: black; no religion listed; psychiatric social worker for Planned Parenthood; board member of Columbia Branch YWCA; member of WACS from 1944 to 1946; member of Academy of Certified Social Workers; member of Philadelphia Chapter of National Association of Social Workers

Team #3—New Jersey

Esther Higgs Cooke: black; Protestant; elementary school teacher for Special Service School in New York; executive board of the NAACP; member of Phi Delta Kappa; member of the YWCA

Blanche Goldstein: black; Protestant; beautician; teacher; board of directors, Ewing Community Club

Josie Harbison: white; Protestant; member of the LWV; member of the YWCA; coordinator for Gray Ladies of Red Cross in New Jersey Neuro-Psychiatric Institute; wife of professor of economics and director of Industrial Relations Section at Princeton

Hannah Levin: white; Jewish; assistant professor of psychology at Rutgers University–Newark; member of PTA; member of American Psychiatric Association

Sue Miller: white; Jewish; remedial reading teacher and tutor to children with learning disabilities; member of PTA; chairman of Community Fund of Great Neck (N.Y.)

Lorna Scheide: white; Protestant; member of the YWCA; member of the LWV; member of Women's International League for Peace and Freedom (WILPF); wife of director of Bach Aria Group

Team #4—Chicago

Marguerite Cassell: white; Protestant; board member of YWCA of Chicago; Women's Board of Urban League of Chicago; member of the LWV; wife of executive at Inland Steel Company

Dorothy Dawson: black; Catholic; teacher; president of Girls Athletic Association; member of Girl Scouts

Diana Guyer: white; Protestant; former member of Junior League of Pasadena (Calif.); member of the Urban League; wife of assistant to the president of Pacific Coast Stock Exchange

Elizabeth Haselden: white; Protestant; teacher; national chairperson, Christian Social Relations of United Church Women; member of the AAUW; member of Evanston (Ill.) Community Relations Commission

Buddy Mayer: white; Jewish; board of governors, International House at University of Chicago; Woman's Board, Michael Reese Hospital, Chicago; wife of president of Rothschild Enterprises

Dorothy Jones Singleton: black; Protestant; preschool director at Firman House

Selma Taub: white; Jewish; preschool teacher, Center for Disadvantaged Children; member of Evanston–Niles Township Chapter of National Council of Jewish Women

Team #5—Washington area

Virginia Bushrod: black; Protestant; household worker; member of the NAACP; member of the LWV

Bee Foster: white; Episcopalian; chairperson of Christian Education Episcopal Church-women, Diocese of Virginia; former president of the LWV of Virginia

Jean Frey: white; Protestant; chairperson of Resolutions Committee of National Assembly of Church Women United; member of the LWV; member of the YWCA; member of WILPF; member of the NAACP; member of the Urban League; wife of chairman and founder of Illinois Citizens for Freedom of Residence

Jane McClary: white; Protestant; author; member of the LWV; member of the Community Study Group of the Human Relations Council

Flaxie Pinkett: black; Protestant; president of John R. Pinkett, Inc., Real Estate and Insurance Firm; member of Delta Sigma Theta; executive committee for D.C. NAACP

Mildred Pitt: black; Protestant; equal employment officer at Agency for International Development; secretary of D.C. NAACP

Team #6—Philadelphia

Ruth Bacon: white; Protestant; nursery school teacher in Extension Division of Philadelphia Public Schools; member of the YWCA; member of the Citizens Committee on Public Education

Gertrude Barnes: black; Protestant; teacher of retarded educable children; president of Philadelphia Alumnae Chapter of Delta Sigma Theta; life member of the NCNW; former president, American Council on Human Rights; member, executive committee of Philadelphia branch of the NAACP; chairperson of Philadelphia Committee of National Women's Committee on Civil Rights

Rae Cohn: white; Jewish; national board member, Women's International League for Peace and Freedom; member of Executive Steering Committee of Northeast Philadelphia Community Relations Committee

Marjorie Duckrey: black; Protestant; social worker; president of Citizens Committee on Public Education; former executive director of YWCA in Philadelphia; member of NCNW; member of AAUW; member of NASW; member of Urban League Board of Directors

Shirley Lipsey: white; Jewish; teacher; member of National Council of Jewish Women; member of Hadassah; volunteer with Omaha Project AID

Team #7—Boston

Betty Barnes: white; Protestant; freelance researcher and editor; former member YWCA national board; former member Citizens Committee for Children; wife of editor at Simon and Schuster

Mary Cannady: black; Protestant; social worker; director of District Office of Family Service of Philadelphia; member of Alpha Kappa Alpha

Rae Dudley: black; Protestant; administrator of All-Day Neighborhood Schools for Board of Education of New York; member of Phi Delta Kappa; secretary of Women's Africa Committee; wife of judge of Supreme Court of New York and former ambassador to Liberia

Faith Griefen: white; Protestant; board and Public Affairs Committee for Cambridge (Mass.) YWCA; board of Vassar Club of Greater Boston; member of Belmont LWV; wife of senior vice president of Cabot, Cabot, and Forbes

Frances Perkins: black; Protestant; lecturer on preschool education at Tufts University and Brandeis University; member of Delta Sigma Theta; member of American Association of University Women; associate of Freedom House, Inc.; member of Urban League

Guest Perry: white; Protestant; librarian; former director of LWV; elected member of Watertown (Mass.) Democratic Town Committee

Frances Tillson: white; Protestant; member of Episcopal Church Women of Christ Church in Cambridge (Mass.); wife of treasurer of Episcopal Diocese of Massachusetts

Sources: 1965 team application sheets, Series 19, Folders 10 and 11; debriefings found in Series 15, Subseries 5; and Final Report, Series 19, Folder 276, NCNW Papers, NABWH; as well as obituaries

Appendix 3

Project Womanpower Staff

Name	*Position*
Janet Douglass	Director
Prathia L. Hall	Assistant Director
Merble H. Reagon	Research Assistant
Frances Y. Beal	Administrative Assistant
Andrea E. Hill	North Eastern Field Representative
Doris Dozier	Southern Field Representative
Gwendolyn R. Simmons	Midwestern Field Representative
Jeannette Tucker	Western Field Representative
Charlene White	Secretary
Edna Moore	Secretary
Aaron Rosenblatt	Research Consultant
William Tedder	Accountant

Source: NCNW, "Project Womanpower: Final Report to the Ford Foundation," front matter, Series 10, Folder 586, NCNWP

Appendix 4

NCNW International Seminar

Roster of Delegates

NCNW STAFF

Dorothy Height, president
Maida Springer Kemp, vice president
Ruth Hurd Minor, vice president
Dorothy Ferebee, past president
Ruth Sykes, special assistant to executive office
Ermon Kamara, director of 1975 IWY Seminar

INTERNATIONAL DELEGATES

Anna Margaret Abdallah, district party secretary and district commissioner, Tanzania
Emma Agyepong, Ashanti regional secretary for YWCA of Ghana
Janet Florence Asare, National Council of Women in Development, Ghana
Anna K. H. Bagenda, chairperson of the National Committee for IWY, Uganda
Joyce Bailey, professor and former coordinator for Caribbean Church Women, representing Jamaica
Desiree Bernard, president of the Law Society and member of the Council of Legal Education in the Caribbean; former secretary of Caribbean Women's Association, representing Guyana
Martha Bulengo, executive director of the Community Development Trust Fund of Tanzania; former chairperson of National Council of Social Services of Tanzania
Guillermina de Jorge, president of the Central de Capacitación, Dominican Republic
Salimatu Diallo, officer of the Organization of African Unity, representing Sierra Leone
Valetta Dlamini, home economics senior inspector of schools, Swaziland
Doris Johnson, president of the Senate in the Bahamas; founder and director of the National Women's Movement of the Bahamas; Caribbean regional director for International Alliance of Women
Catherine Mboya, past vice president of Associated Country Women of the World; treasurer of B'hai Assembly of Nairobi; former treasurer of Maendeleo Ya Wahawake Women's Organization in Kenya
Nancy Moatlhodi, small business owner; former school matron, Botswana
Victoria Mojekwu, chief nursing officer, Nigerian Ministry of Health; member of National Council of Women's Society in Nigeria; member of YWCA of Nigeria

Jane Anne Nakabiri, superintendent of Women Police; member of National Committee for IWY, Uganda

Elizabeth Mulenje Nkomeshya, member of Parliament; chieftainess of district, Zambia

Nellie Akwiri Okello, researcher and writer for African Training Center, Ethiopia; representing Kenya

Diana Opondo, educational and training program officer for women, representing Kenya

Nesta Patrick, president of the Caribbean Women's Association; government director for Services for Mentally Handicapped; former president of League of Women Voters; president of Child Welfare League; president of Union of Women's Citizens, representing Trinidad and Tobago

Dorenda Sampath, chairperson for Women's Advisory Committee of the Caribbean Conference of Churches; senior lecturer in education at Government Teacher's College in Trinidad, representing Trinidad and Tobago

Julianna Sendi, agricultural economist, affiliate of Economic Commission for Africa, representing Uganda

Siga Sene, vice president of Economic and Social Council in Senegal, social activities secretary for National Women's Movement in Senegal

Christabel Jabu Zondo, home economics officer in Ministry of Agriculture, Swaziland

Sources: "Preliminary Roster of Delegates" and corrected roster, Series 36, Folder 47; and Ermon Kamara, "International Women United for Equality, Development, Peace," Series 13, Folder 148, NCNWP.

Notes

Abbreviations

CCHP   Clarie Collins Harvey Papers, Amistad Research Center, Tulane University
COHCH   Center for Oral History and Cultural Heritage
FFR   Ford Foundation Records
FLHP-UM Fannie Lou Hamer Papers, University of Mississippi
LBJ   Lyndon Baines Johnson Presidential Library
MDAH   Mississippi Department of Archives and History
NABWH   National Archives for Black Women's History
NCNWP   National Council of Negro Women Papers
PCP   Polly Cowan Papers, National Archives for Black Women's History
RAC   Rockefeller Archive Center
RBFR   Rockefeller Brothers Fund Records
RFR   Rockefeller Foundation Records
SGS   Papers of Susan Goodwillie Stedman
TFR   Taconic Foundation Records

Introduction

1. Gray-Wiseman, interview by Tuuri, January 22, 2016.

2. Brooks, interview by Tuuri, April 16, 2008; and McLaurin, interview by Tuuri, April 23, 2008.

3. Brooks, interview by Tuuri, April 16, 2008.

4. For some examples of recent and classic acclaimed works on radical women, see Spencer, *The Revolution Has Come*; Gore, *Radicalism at the Crossroads*; Gore, Theoharis, and Woodard, *Want to Start a Revolution?*; Randolph, *Florynce "Flo" Kennedy*; McDuffie, *Sojourning for Freedom*; Ransby, *Eslanda* and *Ella Baker and the Black Freedom Movement*; and Springer, *Living for the Revolution*. For more on working-class and poor women's efforts, see Levenstein, *Movement without Marches*; Orleck, *Storming Caesars Palace*; and Williams, *Politics of Public Housing*. While certainly some individuals in the NCNW could be classified as working class, the council retained an organizational reputation as being elite and middle class, due largely to the dominance of the sororities in its leadership, its push for professional opportunities for black women, and its social activities. Likewise, while some individuals in the council were considered radical for their activism, the council's overall reputation was that of a moderate group working to integrate black women and communities into established American structures of economic

and political power. The black middle class is a complex group, defined not by income but by profession, church membership, secular club membership, family status, and lifestyle. However, as scholars are careful to point out, the space between the black middle class and the black working class can be very thin and is often dependent on whether these Americans lived in cities, small towns, or rural settings. See Collier-Thomas, *Jesus, Jobs, and Justice*, xxiii–xxv, 281. Theoharis also points out that while Rosa Parks's job as a seamstress, her husband's job as a barber, and her lack of higher education placed her in the working class, her demeanor, church membership, and community activism marked her as a "lady" and thus part of the middle class. See Theoharis, *Rebellious Life*, 72–73, chap. 3. For more explanations of how behavior affected class and status in the community, see Chappell, Hutchinson, and Ward, "Dress Modestly, Neatly . . . as If You Were Going to Church"; McGuire, *At the Dark End of the Street*, 91–98; and Greene, *Our Separate Ways*, 9.

5. NCNW was founded to unite the various black women's clubs formed between 1896 and 1935. Although this gave the council a large and influential voice on behalf of black women, few women joined the council directly. Collier-Thomas has argued that the council has maintained an "illusion of power" as it has claimed the potential membership of its affiliated organizations, though most of the women from those groups did not join the NCNW directly. According to Collier-Thomas, Bethune claimed that the NCNW spoke on behalf of 500,000 women in the 1930s and one million in the 1940s, and Height claimed four million in the 1970s. Collier-Thomas argues that this meant that the broader American public viewed the council, and its leadership, as more powerful than it actually was. See Collier-Thomas, "National Council of Negro Women," 861. However, while the council's direct membership has not been as large as the membership at some of its affiliated organizations, the network of black women's groups that it has represented makes it the largest black women's organization in America and a powerful lobbying force on behalf of black women. In 2001, the NCNW had 34 affiliate organizations, 257 community-based sections, and 45,000 direct members, but—through its affiliate organizations—continued to represent nearly 4 million women. See K. Anderson, "National Council of Negro Women," 446. Today, the NCNW claims to include 38 affiliate organizations, 200 community-based sections, and a total outreach of 3 million women. See NCNW home page, accessed August 7, 2017, http://www.ncnw.org.

6. Julie Gallagher raises this point as well with regard to the NCNW's postwar international work. See Gallagher, "National Council of Negro Women," 81. Although their focus is on telling the stories of individual radical women, Gore, Theoharis, and Woodard also emphasize the importance of complicating "the simplistic binary between reformist and radical." Gore, Theoharis, and Woodard, *Want to Start a Revolution*, 11.

7. I borrow this title of torchbearer from Crawford, Rouse, and Woods, *Trailblazers and Torchbearers*. For a classic work depicting women as the backbone of the movement, see Payne, "Men Led, but Women Organized." For more recent work, see Morris, *Womanpower Unlimited*, and "Local Women and the Civil Rights Movement in Mississippi"; and Sanders, *A Chance for Change*, 4, chap. 3.

8. Payne, "Sexism Is a Helluva Thing," 325–26. Jennifer Scanlon has pointed out that women made "careful choices about when to raise objections" to male civil rights movement leaders' choices and sexism, and that women leaders "found ways to exercise leadership that went unnoticed by the men," who "viewed them only as 'ladies.'" This oversight of male leaders has been transmitted to historians as well, who have been slow to recognize the leadership of women in the movement. See Scanlon, *Until There Is Justice*, 170–71. Theoharis has also pointed out the ways in which an incorrect memory of the civil rights movement has removed the militancy, courageous actions, and longevity of activism of Rosa Parks and Coretta King. Theoharis, "Matriarchs and Helpmates."

9. Despite the release of groundbreaking works such as Gerda Lerner's *Black Women in White America* in 1972, Paula Giddings's *When and Where I Enter* in 1984, Vicki Crawford, Jacqueline Rouse, and Barbara Woods's *Women in the Civil Rights Movement* in 1990, Belinda Robnett's *How Long? How Long?* in 1997, Bettye Collier-Thomas and V. P. Franklin's *Sisters in the Struggle* in 2001, Barbara Ransby's biography of Ella Baker in 2003, and many excellent studies on women in the movement since, there has been no full-scale monograph focusing solely on the NCNW. For classic monographs that include significant sections on the council, see Giddings, *When and Where I Enter*; D. G. White, *Too Heavy a Load*; Collier-Thomas, *Jesus, Jobs, and Justice*, Hanson, *Mary McLeod Bethune*, and Harwell, *Wednesdays in Mississippi*. In 1985, Tracey Fitzgerald published a brief book on the NCNW from 1935 to 1975; see Fitzgerald, *National Council of Negro Women*.

10. See Executive Board List, revised February 2, 2009, NCNWP; and Collier-Thomas, *N.C.N.W., 1935–1980*, xiii.

11. While Belinda Robnett's pathbreaking work *How Long? How Long?* points out that most formal leadership was male, the council provided formal women's leadership and often had access to top officials. See Robnett, *How Long? How Long?*, 84. See also the critique of bridge leadership in Gore, Theoharis, and Woodard, *Want to Start a Revolution?*, 9, 13–14.

12. "Dorothy I. Height," introduction, interview by Cowan, 1974–1976, v. Please note that these interviews from the *Black Women Oral History Project* are available publicly online at https://iiif.lib.harvard.edu/manifests/view/drs:45169917$1i (accessed August 1, 2016), as well as in the edited volume series *Black Women Oral History Project* (1991), edited by Ruth Edmonds Hill. The page numbers are slightly different for each set of interviews, but the content is mostly the same. I have chosen to use the online transcripts (and their pagination) in this book. Please note that though the *Black Women Oral History Project* title claims to include interviews dating 1976–1981, Cowan's interviews of Height were conducted from February 11, 1974, through November 6, 1976. See also "JFK Commission Notes Needs of Negro Women," *New York Amsterdam News*, August 17, 1963, 12.

13. Classic works include Chafe, *Civilities and Civil Rights*; Dittmer, *Local People*; Payne, *I've Got the Light of Freedom*; Jeffries, *Bloody Lowndes*; Crosby, *Little Taste of Freedom*; and Moye, *Let the People Decide*. More recent works that have deftly captured

the struggles of local people are Crosby, *Civil Rights History from the Ground Up*; and Hamlin, *Crossroads at Clarksdale.*

14. Christina Greene points out that a network of black women activists existed before direct action and was pivotal to maintaining the black freedom struggle. Greene, *Our Separate Ways*, 31.

15. Sacks, *Caring by the Hour*, 120–21, 132–33; Robnett, *How Long? How Long?* 8, 19–23; and Gilmore, *Gender and Jim Crow*, xxi, chaps. 6–8.

16. For instance, NCNW-sponsored Wednesdays in Mississippi (later Workshops in Mississippi) used this language. I draw on Chafe's concept of the authentic conversation that transgressed the paternalistic and deferential stances of progressive whites and blacks, respectively, in the South. Progressive whites were often interested in preserving "civility" over honest dialogue. See Chafe, *Civilities and Civil Rights*, 8–9.

17. Morris, *Womanpower Unlimited*, 172–73.

18. For more on racial uplift of black clubwomen in the late nineteenth and twentieth centuries, see Higginbotham, *Righteous Discontent*, 14–15, chap. 7; Shaw, *What a Woman Ought to Be*; and Wolcott, *Remaking Respectability*. For a class-based critique of the "politics of respectability," see A. Butler, "Only a Woman Would Do." For a more general discussion of uplift, see Gaines, *Uplifting the Race.*

19. Germany, *New Orleans After the Promises*, 8.

20. D. G. White, *Too Heavy a Load*, 157–60.

21. For more on this practice, see Gallagher, *Black Women and Politics*, 3–4. Black activists more often than not had to accommodate paternalist structures until the civil rights movement. See Chafe, *Civilities and Civil Rights*, 8–10, 40; and Greene, *Our Separate Ways*, 46–48.

22. Anna Arnold Hedgeman was the only woman on the initial committee to organize the March on Washington. Despite her efforts to include representatives from black women's organizations on the march's administrative committee, none were invited. See Scanlon, *Until There Is Justice*, 157, 163–70; Hedgeman, *Trumpet Sounds*, 172–73, 179–80; and Hedgeman, *Gift of Chaos*, 69, 86.

23. Height, interview by Cowan, March 28, 1975, 135; Height, *Open Wide the Freedom Gates*, 145–46; and Height, "We Wanted the Voice of Women."

24. Height, interview by Cowan, March 28, 1975, 135. See also D. G. White, *Too Heavy a Load*, 178.

25. See T. M. Morris, *Womanpower Unlimited*, 6–7; Hamlin, *Crossroads at Clarksdale*, 60–62; and Sanders, *Chance for Change*, 80–81. For activist mothering, see Naples, *Grassroots Warriors*, esp. 11; for "othermothering," see Collins, *Black Feminist Thought*, chap. 8, esp. 178–83. Nicholas Grant has pointed out that this othermothering extended to the NCNW's international work as well. See Grant, "National Council of Negro Women," 77.

26. Postwar liberals embraced Gunnar Myrdal's idea that racism was a problem of the heart, and so moral suasion was often seen as an appropriate tactic for combating racism. For more on American liberals' moral conviction regarding integration, see Jackson, *Gunnar Myrdal and America's Conscience*, 187–89; Gerstle, *American Crucible*, 193; and Murakawa, *First Civil Right*, 49.

27. "Mary McLeod Bethune Awards Presented," *Call and Post*, December 24, 1966, 6B.

28. T. M. Morris, *Womanpower Unlimited*, 172.

29. Height, interview by Cowan, May 25, 1975, 175.

30. Doris Dozier Crenshaw, who worked for Project Womanpower, recalls that the wage was about five times what teachers were making in Alabama. Crenshaw, interview by Tuuri, May 24, 2017.

31. NCNW, *Women and Housing*, 149-a.

32. See note 4 of this chapter.

33. Crenshaw, interview by Tuuri, May 24, 2017.

34. "Capahosic, VA, July 8 1966 Evening Session and July 9 A.M.," internal transcription provided to author by archivist Kenneth Chandler in 2015, Series 15, Subseries 5, Folder 13, Side 1, NCNWP. Hereafter, all files from Series 15, Subseries 5 and Subseries 6 are audio recording transcripts provided by Chandler in 2015, unless otherwise noted. The 2015 transcripts do not have internal page numbers.

35. Although many activists often worried about being co-opted by government funding (especially after the established Democratic party blocked the MFDP challenge), others were more concerned about creating change than who or what organization funded the change. Crenshaw has commented that Height helped support young activist women and that working for the council and using liberal Ford Foundation money for Project Womanpower was not a problem for her. "We didn't run around talking about who funded us. . . . Nobody ever asked." Crenshaw, interview by Tuuri, May 24, 2017. Sanders has pointed out that most local people did not worry that using federal funds for poverty projects would co-opt their efforts to improve conditions for local black communities. Thus, many locals broke ranks with SNCC in 1965 and worked in Head Start. See Sanders, *A Chance for Change*, 3–4, 7–9.

36. Reagon, interview by Tuuri, July 26, 2017.

37. Beal, "Double Jeopardy"; and Beal, interview by Taylor, June 21, 2017.

38. Cathy Aldridge, "Dump 'Black Power' Line, Women Urged," *New York Amsterdam News*, December 24, 1966, 1.

39. Collier-Thomas, *Jesus, Jobs, and Justice*, 455n.

40. "Vow Militant Action," *New York Amsterdam News*, July 26, 1969, 5; and Dorothy Height, Statement on "Launching Black Women's Movement and Against Administration Action on School Desegregation," Series 10, Folder 109, NCNWP.

41. Malcolm X, "Speech at the Founding Rally," accessed October 2, 2016, http://www.blackpast.org/1964-malcolm-x-s-speech-founding-rally-organization-afro-american-unity#stharsh.sbToYQrt.dpuf. White has argued that the council only moved in this direction after white backlash in 1968, but the NCNW's earlier efforts in 1966 and 1967 suggest otherwise. See more information in chapters 5–7 of this book and D. G. White, *Too Heavy a Load*, 205–6.

42. Height, *Open Wide the Freedom Gates*, 152.

43. NCNW alternated between calling their homeownership program Turnkey III, Homeownership Opportunities Program, and Project Homes. See for instance, George Schermer Associates, "Turnkey III—How It Began," Series 13, Folder 141, NCNWP; and

NCNW, *Women and Housing*, 149-c. I will use Turnkey III hereafter to refer both to the NCNW project and to the larger federal program.

44. See Orleck, *Storming Caesar's Palace*, 113–14; and D. G. White, *Too Heavy a Load*, 235.

45. Dorothy Height to Section Presidents, National Officers, and Affiliated Organizations, memo about the Poor People's Campaign, April 30, 1968, 1, Series 10, Folder 108, NCNWP. See also Simmons, interview by Tuuri, May 24, 2017.

46. "Tape of Press Conference of Nat. Council of Negro Women, Nov. 26, 1969," Series 15, Subseries 5, Folder 85, Side 1, NCNWP.

47. D. G. White, *Too Heavy a Load*, 253–54. I calculate size of the organization by the strength of its affiliate membership in addition to its direct membership. See note 5 of this chapter.

Chapter One

1. NCNW, "Silver Anniversary Convention Workbook," November 1960, Series 2, Folder 152, NCNWP.

2. "The Silver Anniversary National Convention," 7, Series 2, Folder 153, NCNWP.

3. Ibid., 1.

4. For more, see Bonastia, *Southern Stalemate*.

5. NCNW, "Silver Anniversary Convention Workbook."

6. "Recommendations Evolving from Task Group Discussions at 26th Annual Convention N-C-N-W," November 16–17, 1961, Series 2, Folder 159, NCNWP.

7. Collier-Thomas, *N.C.N.W., 1935–1980*, 2. For a listing of the leaders and organizations represented, see Hanson, *Mary McLeod Bethune*, 168–69. This YWCA branch, led by Cecelia Cabaniss Saunders, was fiercely independent and had a long proud history of fostering smart, strong black women. See Ransby, *Ella Baker*, 70–73; Scanlon, *Until There Is Justice*, 56–60; and Weisenfeld, *African American Women*, 188–90.

8. NCNW, "Women United: Souvenir Book Sixteenth Anniversary," 1951, 14, Series 13, Folder 1, NCNWP.

9. "The Power in Four Million Women," 1973, 2013 final edited transcript, 12, Series 15, Subseries 3, Folder 20, Side 1, NCNWP.

10. D. G. White, *Too Heavy a Load*, 155. See also 148–49.

11. For more on the structure of the early council, see NCNW, "Tentative By-Laws of the National Council of Negro Women," April 9, 1936, Series 1, Folder 1, NCNWP; Collier-Thomas, *N.C.N.W., 1935–1980*, 4; and Collier-Thomas, "National Council of Negro Women," 856. For more on the transition to a state model under Height, see chapter 7 of this book.

12. Hanson, *Mary McLeod Bethune*, 36–44.

13. This was the motto of the National Association of Colored Women, which saw the role of an educated black woman to be that of a race leader, who would educate those black men and women who were less fortunate than herself. For more on black women race leaders and the concept of racial uplift within black women's clubs, see Giddings,

When and Where I Enter, chap. 6; Cooper, *Beyond Respectability;* Higginbotham, *Righteous Discontent;* Shaw, *What a Woman Ought to Be and Do;* and D. G. White, *Too Heavy a Load.* For more on the concept of racial uplift in general, see Gaines, *Uplifting the Race.*

14. In 1923, the school merged with the Cookman Institute of Jacksonville, Florida, and in that same year, the United Methodist Church took over the site, and it became a junior college in 1931. In 1941, the school became a four-year baccalaureate program. In 2007, the school received university status. "History," Bethune-Cookman University, accessed July 7, 2011, http://www.cookman.edu/about_BCU/history/index .html.

15. A. Robertson, *Mary McLeod Bethune in Florida,* 18; and McCluskey, "Multiple Consciousness in the Leadership of Mary McLeod Bethune," 75.

16. A. Robertson, *Mary McLeod Bethune in Florida,* 18–19.

17. Hanson, *Mary McLeod Bethune,* 96, 106, 108; and Giddings, *When and Where I Enter,* 200.

18. Hanson, *Mary McLeod Bethune,* 121; Giddings, *When and Where I Enter,* 202.

19. Hanson, *Mary McLeod Bethune,* 120–21, 137; Giddings, *When and Where I Enter,* 201–2; and Collier-Thomas, *N.C.N.W., 1935–1980,* 4.

20. Collier-Thomas, *N.C.N.W., 1935–1980,* 4.

21. D. G. White, *Too Heavy a Load,* 155.

22. McCluskey, "Multiple Consciousness in the Leadership of Mary McLeod Bethune," 71; Height, *Open Wide the Freedom Gates,* 260.

23. See Hanson, *Mary McLeod Bethune,* 138–41, 155.

24. Collier-Thomas, *N.C.N.W., 1935–1980,* 13; and Kiesel, *She Can Bring Us Home,* 155.

25. Height, *Open Wide the Freedom Gates,* 260. For more on Lampkin, see Sullivan, *Lift Every Voice,* 137–40.

26. Height, *Open Wide the Freedom Gates,* 260–61. For more on the racism facing African diplomats in need of housing, see Krenn, "The Unwelcome Mat."

27. Scanlon, *Until There Is Justice,* 91.

28. Grant, "National Council of Negro Women," 64–65.

29. "Women United: Souvenir Book Sixteenth Anniversary," 10–15.

30. McCluskey and Smith, *Mary McLeod Bethune,* 6–7.

31. McCluskey, "Multiple Consciousness in the Leadership of Mary McLeod Bethune," 71.

32. Ibid., 74.

33. Collier-Thomas, *N.C.N.W., 1935–1980,* 5.

34. As quoted in Higginbotham, *Righteous Discontent,* 193.

35. Ibid., 222.

36. Contrary to Higginbotham, Anthea Butler has argued that impoverished black women implemented their own version of a politics of respectability, with lessons on temperance, thrift, and racial uplift found in biblical scripture. She argues that these women's version of respectability did not try to imitate the black middle class's or seek acceptance from whites. See Butler, "Only a Woman Would Do," 157; and Collier-Thomas, *Jesus, Jobs, and Justice,* 161n.

37. D. G. White, *Too Heavy a Load*, 150–52.

38. gloria-yvonne, "Mary McLeod Bethune," 23–24.

39. Hanson, *Mary McLeod Bethune*, 4, 185–86; Collier-Thomas, *N.C.N.W., 1935–1980*, 5; and Collier-Thomas, "National Council of Negro Women," 856.

40. Bates, *Pullman Porters*, 159–60; Hanson, *Mary McLeod Bethune*, 148; gloria-yvonne, "Mary McLeod Bethune," 25, 28–30; Collier-Thomas and Franklin, "For the Race in General," 35; and Collier-Thomas, "National Council of Negro Women," 856.

41. Meyer, "Sadie Alexander." See also Mack, "Social History of Everyday Practice."

42. Hine, "Mabel K. Staupers and the Integration of Black Nurses into the Armed Forces during World War II," 184–86, 198–99.

43. Hine, "Black Professionals and Race Consciousness," 1292.

44. Ibid., 1280.

45. Hanson, *Mary McLeod Bethune*, 177–78.

46. Collier-Thomas and Franklin, "For the Race in General," 35–38.

47. Delta Sigma Theta protested lynching and segregation, and established libraries and jobs projects throughout the South. Alpha Kappa Alpha (AKA) immunized over 2,000 and offered health care to 2,600 other black Mississippians between 1935 and 1942 through a traveling immunization program. See D. G. White, *Too Heavy a Load*, 158–59.

48. Ibid., 162, 168.

49. Collier-Thomas, *N.C.N.W., 1935–1980*, 9.

50. Kiesel, *She Can Bring Us Home*, 158–60.

51. Giddings, *When and Where I Enter*, 249.

52. Kiesel, *She Can Bring Us Home*, 167–72.

53. Ibid., 157–58.

54. Hanson, *Mary McLeod Bethune*, 187–88; Quigley, *Just Another Southern Town*, 130; and Plummer, *Rising Wind*, 196, 198. Quigley points out that in Spring 1952, Bethune had a speaking engagement scheduled in Englewood, New Jersey, that was withdrawn after protests that the House Un-American Activities Committee had once linked her to subversive organizations. See *Just Another Southern Town*, 187; Walter White, "False Red Charge Is Hard to Refute," *Akron Beacon Journal*, May 12, 1952, 6; and Englewood, NJ School Board Controversy Records, Collection NABWH_002, NABWH.

55. Kiesel, *She Can Bring Us Home*, 188–90; Height, interview by Cowan, October 6, 1974, 65–70; and Plummer, *Rising Wind*, 213.

56. Kiesel, *She Can Bring Us Home*, 196–97.

57. Collier-Thomas, *N.C.N.W., 1935–1980*, 15.

58. NCNW, "Project in Local Communities to Foster the Implementation of the Supreme Court Decision Outlawing Segregation in Local Schools," March 1955, 1–2, Office of the Messrs., Rockefeller Records, Welfare Interests—General, Series P, Welfare area: Negro Organizations, Box 37, Folder 400, RAC.

59. Collier-Thomas, *N.C.N.W., 1935–1980*, 15.

60. D. G. White, *Too Heavy a Load*, 186–87.

61. Dana S. Creel to Nelson A. Rockefeller, Memorandum, February 28, 1957, Dana S. Creel to Nelson A. Rockefeller, Memorandum, June 19, 1956, and Dana S. Creel to Nelson A. Rockefeller, Memorandum, September 14, 1954, Office of the Messrs., Rockefeller Records, Welfare Interests—General, Series P, Welfare area: Negro Organizations, Box 37, Folder 400, RAC.

62. Height, interview by Cowan, February 11, 1974, 3.

63. Height, *Open Wide the Freedom Gates*, 30–32.

64. Height, interview by Cowan, February 11, 1974, 4.

65. Ibid., 15.

66. Ibid., 9.

67. Ibid., 11, 14.

68. Ibid., 14–15; and Height, interview by Cowan, April 10, 1974, 17–24. For more on women in the Popular Front, see McDuffie, *Sojourning for Freedom*, chap. 3.

69. Height, interview by Cowan, February 11, 1974, 12; and *Open Wide the Freedom Gates*, 69.

70. Height, interview by Cowan, February 11, 1974, 14.

71. Height, interview by Cowan, April 10, 1974, 20–21. Height's quote is in the context of explaining her work in the 1930s with the Popular Front and the respect that she developed for communists and other radicals at that time. Although it is difficult to pin down a singular definition, I define militancy in this book as a total commitment to black advancement, often expressed through participation in black separatist or communist groups, and a willingness to use or endorse violence to achieve that end. Recently, scholars have added nuance to the idea of militancy. Charles Payne has questioned the context in which we understand militancy, arguing that equating militancy with masculinity has led us to view the community-building activities of radical women as less militant than their use of violence. See Payne, "Sexism Is a Helluva Thing," 325. Jeanne Theoharis has also pointed out that Rosa Parks has been overlooked as a militant due to her respectable demeanor and dress and this has led to an inaccurate political memory of who she really was. See "Matriarchs and Helpmates," 397, 408–9.

72. Height, interview by Cowan, February 11, 1974, 5.

73. Ibid., 11.

74. Height, interview by Shulman, January 24, 2003, 30.

75. Ibid., 38.

76. For more on Saunders, see Weisenfeld, *African American Women*, 115–20.

77. Height, interview by Cowan, February 11, 1974, 17; Scanlon, *Until There Is Justice*, 56–58; and Height, *Open Wide the Freedom Gates*, 78–80.

78. "Introduction," interview with Dorothy Height, *Black Women Oral History Project*, interview by Cowan, 1974–1976, iv. https://iiif.lib.harvard.edu/manifests/view/drs: 45169917$10i. Nancy Marie Robertson's careful study also points to the important ways in which white and black women disagreed as they moved toward integration. See N. M. Robertson, *Christian Sisterhood*, esp. chap. 3.

79. For more on the YWCA's integration programs, see Lynn, *Progressive Women in Conservative Times*; Helen Laville, "'If the Time Is Not Ripe, Then It Is Your Job to

Ripen the Time!' The Transformation of the YWCA from Segregated Association to Interracial Organization, 1930–1965," *Women's History Review* 15, no. 3 (July 2006): 359–83; C. Greene, *Our Separate Ways*; A. Lewis, "'Barrier Breaking Love of God'"; and N. M. Robertson, *Christian Sisterhood*.

80. A. Lewis, "'Barrier Breaking Love of God,'" 116.

81. Ibid., 117.

82. Laville, "'Women of Conscience' or 'Women of Conviction'?," 280.

83. Crenshaw, interview by Tuuri, May 24, 2017.

84. For more on the Harlem branch YWCA, see Weisenfeld, *African American Women*, chaps. 4, 6.

85. Height, interview by Cowan, February 11, 1974, 13.

86. Scanlon, *Until There Is Justice*, 59. For more on Burroughs, see Collier-Thomas, *Jesus, Jobs, and Justice*, 128–38.

87. Ransby, *Ella Baker*, 69–71. The other pillar was the 135th Street Library. See also Scanlon, *Until There Is Justice*, 56–60.

88. Ransby, *Ella Baker*, 71–72.

89. Height, interview by Cowan, April 10, 1974, 21–24.

90. Ibid., 27–28.

91. Height, interview by Cowan, October 6, 1974, 62; and Height, *Open Wide the Freedom Gates*, 155.

92. Height, interview by Cowan, May 25, 1975, 188–89.

93. "Delta Sigma Theta Mourns Beloved 10th National President and Civil Rights Matriarch, Dr. Dorothy Irene Height," April 10, 2010, http://www.deltasigmatheta.org /downloads/10th_National_President_Dr_Dorothy_Irene_Height.pdf.

94. D. G. White, *Too Heavy a Load*, 192.

95. Ibid., 193; Giddings, *In Search of Sisterhood*, 225–26, 233–38. While at the council, she continued this trend of serving as long as possible. She served as NCNW president from 1957 until 1998, and then informally continued to serve as president emerita until her death in 2010.

96. Talbert, interview by Bolton, 1997.

97. Height, interview by Polly Cowan, March 28, 1975, 128–30.

98. Height, *Open Wide the Freedom Gates*, 156.

99. NCNW, "Progress Report for the Mary McLeod Bethune Memorial as Presented to the Secretary of the Interior," May 25, 1965, 11, Folder 877, Box 87, TFR; Bethune Memorial Progress Report, "The Education Foundation," October 1963, 2, Series 8, Folder 209, NCNWP; and "Montclair, Williamsburg Pledge Funds for Memorial," *Pittsburgh Courier*, June 2, 1962, 9.

100. Minutes of 27th National Convention, December 29, 1962–January 1, 1963, 5, Series 2, Folder 164, NCNWP. For more on Bethune House, see "'Bethune House' Dedication Caps NCNW Meet: Low-Cost Apartment Building Memorial to Beloved Founder," *Pittsburgh Courier*, December 5, 1964, 9.

101. Carmichael, *Ready for Revolution*, 248.

102. "Jimmy Hill Plugs for Scholarships," *Pittsburgh Courier*, October 17, 1964, 7.

103. A. Robertson, "Backbone of the Civil Rights Movement," 67–69.

104. NCNW Progress Report, Fall 1966, 5, Series 13, Folder 50, NCNWP.

105. White has argued that under Height, the council experienced a shift from the principle that the race could rise no higher than its women to the idea that women could rise no higher than the race. See D. G. White, *Too Heavy a Load*, 179–81. Certainly this may have occurred in the public spaces of the movement, but Height and the council continued to promote the activism and policy-making power of black women within the NCNW. See especially chaps. 4–8 of this book.

106. Michael Barker, "Elite Philanthropy, SNCC, and the Civil Rights Movement," *Swans Commentary*, November 15, 2010, http://www.swans.com/library/art16/barker69 .html. For more on Kennedy's attempt to shift civil rights activism, see Dickerson, *Militant Mediator*, 244.

107. Height, *Open Wide the Freedom Gates*, 141.

108. Height, interview by Cowan, March 28, 1975, 131.

109. Height, *Open Wide the Freedom Gates*, 142.

110. Deborah White has stated that the civil rights movement subsumed gender and class issues beneath race and that the 1960s was a "masculine decade." See D. G. White, *Too Heavy a Load*, 179.

111. Crenshaw, interview by Tuuri, May 24, 2017.

112. Murray, "November 14, 1963," 233. See also Height, *Open Wide the Freedom Gates*, 145. Although Dorothy Height incorrectly states that "Mahalia Jackson, who sang the national anthem, was the only female voice" heard that day, the spirit of her comment is correct. Houck and Dixon tracked down the audio recording of the event provided by Alan Ribback, who later became Moses Moon. Daisy Bates actually gave an address on behalf of women. See Houck and Dixon, *Women and the Civil Rights Movement*, x. See also Hedgeman, *Trumpet Sounds*, 172–73, 179–80; Hedgeman, *Gift of Chaos*, 69, 86; and Scanlon, *Until There Is Justice*, 163–70.

113. Murray, "November 14, 1963," 233 and Scanlon, *Until There Is Justice*, 170.

114. Introduction, *Women and the Civil Rights Movement*, x. For more on sexism in the movement see Crenshaw, interview by Tuuri, May 24, 2017.

115. Height, *Open Wide the Freedom Gates*, 144.

116. Feldstein, *Motherhood in Black and White*, 2.

117. Frazier, *Black Bourgeoisie*, 221.

118. Ibid. For the pressures facing ambitious middle-class black women and sensitivity over the plight of the black male, see Giddings, *When and Where I Enter*, 250–56.

119. Moynihan, *Negro Family*, 29.

120. Hylan Lewis, " 'Recent Changes and the Negro Family—Lights and Shadows': (Excerpts from a paper presented to the National Council of Negro Women)," in NCNW, "Silver Anniversary Convention Workbook."

121. D. G. White, *Too Heavy a Load*, 180–81.

122. For more on the consultation's work, see Gallagher, *Black Women and Politics*, 127–32.

123. D. Harris, *Black Feminist Politics*, 65–69.

124. President's Commission on the Status of Women, *Four Consultations*, 30.

125. Ibid., 35.

126. Ibid.; "Problems of Women Discussed at Commission-Sponsored Meet," *Baltimore Afro American*, May 4, 1963, 6; and "JFK Commission Notes Needs of Negro Women," *New York Amsterdam News*, August 17, 1963, 12.

127. Moynihan, *Negro Family*, 33–34.

128. For more information on the controversy surrounding the Moynihan Report, see Rainwater and Yancy, *Moynihan Report and the Politics of Controversy*; and Patterson, *Freedom Is Not Enough*; D. G. White, *Too Heavy a Load*, 201; and Giddings, *When and Where I Enter*, 325–32.

129. Geary, *Beyond Civil Rights*, 142–43.

130. See Scanlon, *Until There Is Justice*, 171.

131. Height, interview by Cowan, May 29, 1974, 51–54.

132. See footnote 105.

133. Height, *Open Wide the Freedom Gates*, 145–46.

134. Christina Greene points out that while interviewing black female civil rights leaders, she also encountered "shifting attitudes toward sexism within the movement," but that this "seem[s] to indicate an evolving consciousness about gender divisions" as well as the fact that women's contributions "were overlooked and undervalued." C. Greene, *Our Separate Ways*, 97–98.

135. "Freedom Fighters Sexually Abused: Sex abuses in Jackson jail told," *Afro-American*, June 15, 1963, 1.

136. McGuire, *At the Dark End of the Street*, 195.

137. James Booker, "Women Tell Of Sex Abuses In Dixie," *New York Amsterdam News*, June 15, 1963, 1.

138. Height, *Open Wide the Freedom Gates*, 140.

139. Lee, *For Freedom's Sake*, 47–52.

140. McGuire, *At the Dark End of the Street*, 196–98.

141. Height, interview by Cowan, March 28, 1975, 134–35; Height, *Open Wide the Freedom Gates*, 146.

142. Height, *Open Wide the Freedom Gates*, 146.

143. Height, interview by Polly Cowan, March 28, 1975, 136; and Educational Foundation of National Council of Negro Women, "Wednesdays in Mississippi 1964," February 1965, Folder 876, Box 87, Series 1: Grants, Taconic Foundation Records (FA 407), RAC.

144. Height, interview by Polly Cowan, March 28, 1975, 136.

145. Lawson, *Running for Freedom*, 104–5.

146. Ibid. See also Robnett, *How Long? How Long?*, 141–42.

147. As quoted in Carson, *In Struggle*, 88. Also confirmed in Doar, interview by Tuuri, October 23, 2007.

148. For more information about this assumption within the black community, see Houck and Dixon, *Women and the Civil Rights Movement*, xv–xvii. Charles Payne argues that while there was a certain plausibility to the notion that black women would

face less severe repercussions, most black women were subject to violent reprisals, and that their participation in larger numbers than men was in large part due to religious convictions and preexisting social networks between women, which made such participation possible. See Payne, *I've Got the Light of Freedom*, 274–78. Jenny Irons also found in her study of black and white women's participation in the civil rights movement that black women participated in "high risk" activist activities and were exposed to beatings from police, being followed by police, and having personal memorabilia destroyed. See Irons, "Shaping of Activist Recruitment and Participation," 696.

149. For the "culture of dissemblance," see Hine, "Rape and the Inner Lives of Black Women." For more on the "tradition of testimony" surrounding the sexual exploitation of black women, see McGuire, "It Was Like All of Us Had Been Raped," 914; and McGuire, *At the Dark End of the Street*, esp. xix–xx. For more on Ida B. Well's and other black clubwomen's tradition of testimony in both speaking out against lynching and calling for the protection of black women against sexual violence, see Feimster, *Southern Horrors*, chaps. 4, 8.

150. Merble Reagon has reflected that the council's reputation was one of women who hosted teas and wore hats and white gloves. See Reagon, interview by Tuuri, July 26, 2017.

Chapter Two

1. Height, *Open Wide the Freedom Gates*, 142–43.

2. Ibid., 151. At Cowan's funeral in 1976, Height spoke of their deep friendship. See Height, untitled funeral oration, [1976], Series 1, "Biographical Information, 1973," PCP.

3. Lawson, *Running for Freedom*, 103–4.

4. Polly Cowan, "Aint Nothin Goin to Change Around Heah: Selma Alabama, October 1963," [ca. 1975], 8, Series 1, Box 1, PCP.

5. Polly Cowan, "The Freedom to Vote, October 4–5, 1963," 1, Box 1, Series 1, PCP.

6. Riehm, "Dorothy Tilly," 26–29; and Irons, "Shaping of Activist Recruitment," 703–5.

7. Riehm, "Dorothy Tilly," 28–30. For more on the CIC, see Collier-Thomas, *Jesus, Jobs, and Justice*, 316–17, 321–23, 325–28. For more on the limitations of white moderate churchwomen's work, see C. Greene, *Our Separate Ways*, 45.

8. Riehm, "Dorothy Tilly," 28.

9. See Hall, *Revolt Against Chivalry*; and Collier-Thomas, *Jesus, Jobs, and Justice*, 327–28. For more on the Commission on Interracial Cooperation and the Southern Regional Council, see McDonough, "Men and Women of Good Will."

10. Riehm, "Dorothy Tilly," 24, 31; and Collier-Thomas, *Jesus, Jobs, and Justice*, 371, 404–6.

11. Riehm, "Dorothy Tilly," 28, 32–39; and Collier-Thomas, *Jesus, Jobs, and Justice*, 405–6.

12. Height, interview by Cowan, February 2, 1975, 125. By adhering to gendered expectations of the southern lady, these white women maintained their "civility." See Chafe, *Civilities and Civil Rights*; and C. Greene, *Our Separate Ways*, 45, 57–59.

13. Riehm, "Dorothy Tilly," 24.

14. Ibid.

15. Wilkerson-Freeman, "Stealth in the Political Arsenal of Southern Women," 45; and Laville, "Women of Conscience," 286. For another contemporary example of middle-class white women being shielded from violence by embracing traditional roles, see Swerdlow, *Women Strike for Peace*. Swerdlow examines how the women of the Women Strike for Peace (WSP) movement used their role as concerned mothers to call for an end to the nuclear arms race in 1962. The House Un-American Activities Committee (HUAC) called the women before a hearing because it suspected WSP of supporting communism, but they made a mockery of the hearing. As "traditional" mothers, these women claimed that their authority in developing WSP came from their domestic, private role. Embracing women's traditional roles helped them call for radical political change in the Cold War without being labeled communist.

16. See Fosl, *Subversive Southerner*; and Sullivan, *Freedom Writer*.

17. See PCSW, *American Women*, 78–80, 83, 85; "JFK Commission Notes Needs of Negro Women," *New York Amsterdam News*, August 17, 1963, 12; and Gallagher, *Black Women and Politics*, 124–27.

18. D. Harris, *Black Feminist Politics*, 60–61, 64.

19. Gallagher, *Black Women and Politics*, 132.

20. For both external and internal pressures and limits of postwar activist work in these mainstream white organizations, see C. Greene, *Our Separate Ways*, 57–60.

21. Pamphlet produced by the National Women's Committee on Civil Rights, August 15, 1963, American Association of University Women Archives, 1881–1976, reel 146. As quoted in Laville, " 'Women of Conscience,' " 285.

22. Smith was the chairperson of the organization, and Polly Cowan a special consultant, due in part to her generous financial donations to the group. See Laville, " 'Women of Conscience,' " 289–93, 289n42.

23. Laville, " 'Women of Conscience,' " 293.

24. Ibid., 289–93.

25. See Shirley Smith, "My Southern Journey," October 10, 1963, 1, Series 1, Box 1, PCP; and Height, "We Wanted the Voice of a Woman," 88.

26. Cowan, "Aint Nothin Goin to Change," 5–6.

27. Height, *Open Wide the Freedom Gates*, 158.

28. Cowan, "Aint Nothin Goin to Change," 8; Height, *Open Wide the Freedom Gates*, 158–59; and Height, interview by Cowan, March 28, 1975, 137–38.

29. Height, *Open Wide the Freedom Gates*, 158.

30. Height, interview by Cowan, March 28, 1975, 140.

31. For more on the courage of young activists during the movement, see de Schweinitz, *If We Could Change the World*; and A. Harris, *Ain't Gonna Let Nobody Turn Me 'Round*.

32. Height, *Open Wide the Freedom Gates*, 157.

33. "Dorothy Height," speech in Houck and Davis, *Women and the Civil Rights Movement*, 223.

34. Height, interview by Cowan, March 28, 1975, 141; and Height, *Open Wide the Freedom Gates*, 160.

35. Cowan, "Aint Nothin Goin to Change," 15–16.

36. Cowan, "Freedom to Vote," 2.

37. Height, interview by Cowan, March 28, 1975, 138; Cowan, "Aint Nothin Goin to Change," 8–9; and Height, *Open Wide the Freedom Gates*, 158–59.

38. Cowan, "Ain't Nothin Goin to Change," 19–20. Crenshaw also recalls being at a rally in Montgomery's First Baptist Church, surrounded by hostile whites, who forced the activists to spend the night in the church. Crenshaw, interview by Tuuri, May 24, 2017.

39. Cowan, "Aint Nothin Goin to Change," 20. See also Wynn quote in Robnett, *How Long? How Long?*, 111.

40. Cowan, "Freedom to Vote," 3. These women had been contacted beforehand by Dorothy Tilly and Shirley Smith. See also Shirley Smith, "My Southern Journey," October 10, 1963, 4, Box 1, Series 1, PCP. "Kathrine Cothran," obituary, *Selma Times-Journal*, March 16, 2010, http://www.selmatimesjournal.com/2010/03/16/kathrine-cothran/.

41. Cowan, "Freedom to Vote," 4. For more on the conflation of civil rights activism and communism in the minds of southerners, see Woods, *Black Struggle, Red Scare*; Fosl, "Anne Braden and the 'Protective Custody' of White Southern Womanhood"; Lawson, "Race, Rock and Roll, and the Rigged Society"; and Lewis, *White South and the Red Menace*.

42. Cowan, "Freedom to Vote," 4.

43. Ibid.

44. Christina Greene emphasizes that it was black women, including Height, who pushed liberal white women toward racial inclusivity. See C. Greene, *Our Separate Ways*, 60–61.

45. Cowan, "Freedom to Vote," 6. Most southern white women who became involved in the movement did so behind the scenes, as there was less to lose that way. See Irons, "Shaping of Activist Recruitment," 698–99, 705.

46. Cowan, "Freedom to Vote," 6.

47. Ibid., 9.

48. Irons, "Shaping of Activist Recruitment," 698–99.

49. "Additional Report on Selma, Alabama," October 13 [1963], 1, Series 19, Folder 32, NCNWP.

50. Lawson, *Running for Freedom*, 106.

51. Schutt, interview by Dittmer, February 22, 1981, 36–39.

52. Anne Karro, "What Can We Do?" Testimony of Jail Abuse, November 6, 1963, Series 1, Box 1, PCP.

53. In a letter dated January 10, 1964, Paul H. Douglas told Anne Karro that he had submitted Karro's *Washington Post* article about her abuse in Danville, Virginia, to the Congressional Record. Douglas goes on to say that letters written to the *Saturday Review* inspired by reprints of Karro's account caused members of the American Medical Association in Massachusetts and Philadelphia to write the Medical Association in Danville. See Senator Paul H. Douglas to Mrs. Jacob I. Karro, January 10, 1964, Series 1, Box 1, PCP.

54. For a reference to this sequence of events for the November 14 letter that mentions the " 'Cadillac Caravan' (after Mrs. Peabody's venture)," see Polly Cowan, "Report

for Wednesdays in Mississipp" [*sic*], 1, Series 19, Folder 119, NCNWP. See also Height, interview by Cowan, March 28, 1975, 146–47.

55. "Women in the Civil Rights Movement: Variations on a Theme," November 1963, Series 19, Folder 32, NCNWP. Cowan states in an interview in 1968 that she wrote the letter about "Conversation Caravans" while in England in November 1963. See Cowan, interview by John Britton, 11. See also Polly Cowan, "Report for Wednesdays in Mississipp" [*sic*], 1.

56. See "Women in the Civil Rights Movement." Confirmation of this letter as her first development of the project can be found in Cowan, "Outline," 3; and Cowan, "Synopsis," Series 1, Folder "Book Material I—Synopsis, Outline, Table of Contents, N.D.," PCP.

57. Cowan, *Orphan in History*, 5; and Shulman, "Polly Spiegel Cowan."

58. Cowan, *Orphan in History*, 6. Debra Schultz has argued that although many Jewish civil rights workers were secular, a sense of their spiritual tradition played a role in their political, antiracist consciousness. See Schultz, *Going South*, 4. These activist Jewish women also tried to avoid prioritizing their own ethnic or religious heritage, and were willing to support the largely Christian-based civil rights movement in the South. See Schultz, *Going South*, 22.

59. "Women in the Civil Rights Movement."

60. Ibid.

61. Ibid.

62. Polly Cowan, "Freedom to Vote," 9.

63. "Draft of NCNW Convention notes, Saturday, November 16—morning," 3, Series 2, Folder 167, NCNWP.

64. For a reference to this sequence of events for Height's presentation of the Selma report to the YWCA, see Polly Cowan, "Report for Wednesdays in Mississipp" [*sic*], "Background."

65. Elizabeth Barnes and Frances Tennenbaum, "Women [*sic*] in Mississippi (WIMS) Preliminary Report," 1964, 3, Series 19, Folder 280, NCNWP.

66. Polly Cowan and Susan Goodwillie, " 'He Who Would Free Himself Must Strike the Blow . . .' Report of Inter-Organization Committee, March 15–16, 1964," [1964] Series 19, Folder 191, NCNWP.

67. Many white progressives viewed "civil rights" as too controversial to support. See Chafe, *Civilities and Civil Rights*, 138–40.

68. Cowan, "Outline," 5.

69. For more on Freedom Summer, see McAdam, *Freedom Summer*; Schultz, *Going South*; Rothschild, *Case of Black and White*; and Adickes, *Legacy of a Freedom School*.

70. Carson, *In Struggle*, 78; and Dittmer, *Local People*, 118–20.

71. Polly Cowan, "Editorial Comment: Consultation Program: Inter-Organization Women's Committee," Series 19, Folder 191, NCNWP.

72. See, for example, Dittmer, *Local People*, chaps. 1–4; and Payne, *I've Got the Light of Freedom*, introduction and chaps. 1–3.

73. See Sinsheimer, "Freedom Vote of 1963," 235–36.

74. Cowan, "Editorial Comment," 5.

75. For more on Church Women United's activism, see C. Jones, "How Shall I Sing the Lord's Song?"; Collier-Thomas, *Jesus, Jobs, and Justice*, 367, 371, 398–404, 440–42; Denomme, "To End This Day of Strife"; and Tuuri, "Building Bridges of Understanding," 109–12. United Church Women became Church Women United in 1964. I will refer to the organization as Church Women United throughout the book.

76. Height, *Open Wide the Freedom Gates*, 165; Cowan and Goodwillie, "He who would free himself"; "Recording Date: Unknown, Mississippi," Side 2, Series 15, Subseries 6, Folder 3, NCNWP; and Womanpower Unlimited Newsletter, undated excerpt, Series 1, Box 19, Folder 15, CCHP.

77. T. M. Morris, "Local Women and the Civil Rights Movement," 194. For more on WU's early activism with the Freedom Riders, see *Womanpower Unlimited*, 21–24. For more about the challenges and possibilities of black women using motherhood as a justification for their activism, see Feldstein, *Motherhood in Black and White*.

78. T. M. Morris, *Womanpower Unlimited*, 35–36, 43–44. For more on flexible alliances, see Hamlin, "Collision and Collusion"; Hamlin, *Crossroads at Clarksdale*, 4–5, 53; Carson, *In Struggle*, 163–64; and Tuuri, "By Any Means Necessary."

79. T. M. Morris, *Womanpower Unlimited*, 47–50.

80. Cowan, "Outline," 6–7; and "Report for Wednesdays in Mississipp" [sic].

81. For more on this issue, see Laville, "Women of Conscience."

82. For a reference to this sequence of events for Cowan and Smith's May trip to Jackson, see Cowan, "Report for Wednesdays in Mississipp" [sic].

83. Polly Cowan, "Preface," May 28, 1964, Series 19, Folder 277, NCNWP.

84. For more on the concerns of black and white YWCA leaders about the influx of Wednesdays women, see Tuuri, "Building Bridges of Understanding," 83–86.

85. "Wednesdays in Mississipp" [sic], 1; Cowan, interview by Britton, March 8, 1968, 16–17; Tuuri, "Building Bridges of Understanding," 89–90; and Harwell, *Wednesdays in Mississippi*, 60–61.

Chapter Three

1. "WIMS Team #2 1964 Conference," Series 15, Subscries 5, Folder 20, Side 1, NCNWP.

2. Ruth Batson Registration Form, [1964], Series 19, Folder 13, NCNWP. For more on Batson's activism, see Theoharis, " 'They Told Us Our Kids Were Stupid,' " 18–25; Theoharis, "We Saved the City"; and "WIMS Team #2 1964," Side 1.

3. "WIMS Team #2 1964," Side 1.

4. Ibid.

5. T. M. Morris, *Womanpower Unlimited*, 113–14.

6. Harwell, *Wednesdays in Mississippi*, 181.

7. T. M. Morris, *Womanpower Unlimited*, 121.

8. Height, interview by Shulman, January 24, 2003, draft of transcript, 42. For more on Wilson, see T. M. Morris, *Womanpower Unlimited*, 122–23.

9. Finding aid to the Papers of Claire Harvey Collins, CCHP.

10. Ibid.

11. T. M. Morris, *Womanpower Unlimited*, 123–25; and see WIMS schedules in Series 19, Folders 302–308, NCNWP.

12. For more on MPE, see Bolton, *Hardest Deal of All*, 113–15.

13. Green, interview by Tuuri, September 17, 2007.

14. Kay Pittman, "Mothers Fight Private Schools—and Win," *Memphis Press-Scimitar*, October 21, 1964, clipping found in Series 19, Folder 198, NCNWP. Other white-only women's organizations formed to save the public schools erupted all over the South, including New Orleans, Atlanta, and Little Rock. For more on Thomas and Esther Ethridge, see "Thomas R. Ethridge," obituary, *Clarion-Ledger*, August 31, 2010, http://www.legacy.com/obituaries/clarionledger/obituary.aspx?n=thomas-r-ethridge &pid=145011517.

15. Pittman, "Mothers Fight Private Schools—and Win."

16. Green, interview by Tuuri, September 17, 2007.

17. Polly Cowan, Commission on Civil Rights Report, 11, Series 19, Folder 48, NCNWP.

18. Pittman, "Mothers Fight Private Schools—and Win."

19. T. M. Morris, *Womanpower Unlimited*, 113.

20. Justine Randers-Pehrson, "Report of a Team Member," July 20, 1964, 3, Series 19, Folder 304, NCNWP; Tuuri, "Building Bridges," 118; Harwell, *Wednesdays in Mississippi*, 89; and Polly Cowan, "Report for Wednesdays in Mississipp" [*sic*], 3, Series 19, Folder 119, NCNWP.

21. Schutt, interview by Dittmer, February 22, 1981, 6.

22. "WIMS Team #1 1964—Conference, 7-13-64," Series 15, Subseries 5, Folder 17, Side 2, NCNWP.

23. Schutt, interview by unnamed, July 16, 1965, 1–2.

24. Ibid., 3. White southern women who became involved in the civil rights movement often attributed this to their faith. See C. Greene, *Our Separate Ways*, 45.

25. Schutt, interview by unnamed, July 16, 1965, 3–6.

26. Ibid., 15–16.

27. For more on Schutt, see "WIMS Team #1 1964—Conference, 7-13-64," Side 2; "WIMS Team #2 1964," Side 1; and Morris, *Womanpower Unlimited*, 80–83.

28. Height, interview by Shulman, January 24, 2003, draft of transcript, 43.

29. A. Lewis, "'Barrier Breaking Love of God,'" 127–29.

30. Hewitt, interview by Younger, May 15, 1997, 9.

31. Ibid., 2. Other white Mississippians who aided WIMS were Florence Gooch, Patt Derian, Willie Hume Bryant, Winifred Green, Eleanor Fontaine, Jeanette King, Joan Moore, Jay Shands, Patt Terry, Janet Purvis, Mary Ann Henderson, and Mary F. Hendrick.

32. Susie Goodwillie Diary, June 27–30, SGS.

33. Harwell, *Wednesdays in Mississippi*, 53.

34. McAdam, *Freedom Summer*, 41.

35. For more on the women who had children participating in Freedom Summer and the ways in which they used their roles as mothers as a part of their activism, see Harwell, "Wednesdays in Mississippi," *Journal of Southern History*, 628–29; and T. M. Morris, *Womanpower Unlimited*, 125.

36. Shirley Smith to David Hunter, July 27, 1964, Series 19, Folder 164, NCNWP.

37. Ibid.

38. For more on the politics of SNCC women's clothing, see Ford, "SNCC Women, Denim, and the Politics of Dress"; and Ford, *Liberated Threads*, chap. 3.

39. Shirley Smith to David Hunter, July 27, 1964.

40. "Wednesdays in Mississippi Appendix #1," appendix to letter from Shirley Smith to David Hunter, July 27, 1964, Series 19, Folder 164, NCNWP. For more on the Stern Fund, see Institute for Media Analysis, *Stern Fund*.

41. Institute for Media Analysis, *Stern Fund*, 31, 33, 156.

42. Polly Cowan to Max Stern, June 19, 1964; and David Hunter to Dorothy Height, July 2, 1964, Series 19, Folder 164, NCNWP.

43. Marian Logan Registration Form [May 1964], Series 19, Folder 12, NCNWP.

44. Richard D. Lyons, "Marian Logan, 73, a Civil Rights Aide and Cabaret Singer," *New York Times*, November 28, 1993.

45. "Profiles of Members of First Wednesday in Mississippi Team," Series 19, Folder 302, NCNWP. Height, interview by Shulman, January 24, 2003, draft of transcript, 35.

46. Brandeis University Office of Planned Giving, "A Lifetime of Commitment," *Brandeis Today and Tomorrow*, accessed September 2, 2016, http://giving.brandeis .giftplans.org/index.php?cID=174.

47. Jean Benjamin Registration Form [May 1964], Series 19, Folder 12, NCNWP; and "Jean K. Benjamin," obituary notice, *New York Times*, October 6, 2007, http:// query.nytimes.com/gst/fullpage.html?res=9B07E6DF163AF935A35753C1A9619 C8B63.

48. "Profiles of Members of First Wednesday in Mississippi Team."

49. For more on Catholic women's interracial activism, see O'Halloran, "Organized Catholic Laywomen," chap. 4 and 5.

50. For more on the challenges to the domestic homemakers ideal, see Hartmann, "Women's Employment and the Domestic Ideal in the Early Cold War Years"; and Lynn, "Gender and Progressive Politics"; and for more on the cultural influence of the homemaker ideal, see May, *Homeward Bound*.

51. "List of Team Members, cont'd." Series 19, Folder 301, NCNWP.

52. For more information on the history of black women working in contrast to white, see J. Jones, *Labor of Love, Labor of Sorrow*; and Glenn, *Unequal Freedom*.

53. For more on middle-class black women's professions, see Shaw, *What a Woman Ought to Be*. Also, Susan Lynn points out that black women in the postwar years pursued college degrees at higher rates than either black men or white women. See Lynn, *Progressive Women in Conservative Times*, 12.

54. "Colleges and Universities Attended by Wednesdays Ladies" and "Out of 45," handwritten note on 1964 participants, Series 19, Folder 51, NCNWP. See also 1964

team application sheets, Series 19, Folders 12–18, NCNWP; and debriefings found in Series 15, Subseries 5; and Final Report, Series 19, Folder 276, NCNWP.

55. In some cases, as in the case of Dorothy Height and the YWCA, these voluntary organizations paid these women a salary.

56. For more on the liberal belief that American democracy was based on a creed of racial equality, see Gerstle, *American Crucible*, 193. For the role of consumer capitalism in postwar liberal America, see Cohen, *Consumer's Republic*.

57. Woods, *Black Struggle*, 2.

58. Hewitt, interview by Younger, May 15, 1997, 10.

59. See Shirley Smith to David Hunter, July 27, 1964, 1–2 and appendix 2, Series 19, Folder 164, NCNWP. For more on the importance of book donations to Hattiesburg Freedom Schools, see Adickes, *Legacy of a Freedom School*, 56–59.

60. Shirley Smith to David Hunter, July 27, 1964, 1.

61. For more on this liberal white mind-set, see Gerstle, *American Crucible*, 193; and Tuuri, "Building Bridges of Understanding," 111–12.

62. See T. M. Morris, *Womanpower Unlimited*, 127.

63. The Chicago Team, the sixth team to go to Mississippi in 1964, was the first to have white women stay in private homes.

64. "WIMS Team #1 1964," Side 2.

65. Cowan, Commission on Civil Rights Report, 8; and "WIMS Team #1 1964 Conference, 7-13-64," Series 15, Subseries 5, Folder 17, Side 1, NCNWP.

66. When the women of Team 3 who visited Meridian, Mississippi, expressed their concern over the fact that it was so close to Philadelphia, where the bodies of Schwerner, Chaney, and Goodman were discovered, Cowan told the women that she was sorry that they were fearful, but that she chose all the locations for the WIMS women to visit because she believed them to be safe. "WIMS Team #3 1964 Conference Mississippi Review, Team #3 Washington—Maryland," Series 15, Subseries 5, Folder 42, Side 2, NCNWP.

67. Cowan, Commission on Civil Rights Report, 7; and Height, *Open Wide the Freedom Gates*, 173–74.

68. Cowan, Commission on Civil Rights Report, 7.

69. "WIMS Team #1 1964," Side 2.

70. "WIMS Team #1 1964," Side 1.

71. "WIMS Team #3 1964 Conference Mississippi Review, Team #3 Washington—Maryland," Series 15, Subseries 5, Folder 42, Side 1, NCNWP.

72. "WIMS Team #5 1964 Conference," Series 15, Subseries 5, Folder 18, Side 2, NCNWP.

73. Ibid., and Bolton, *Hardest Deal of All*, 31–32, 64–66, 83–86. For more on teachers losing jobs for activism, see 46–47. See also Dittmer, *Local People*, 43–45, 73–75.

74. Ruth Hurd Minor Reflection Report, Series 19, Folder 308, NCNWP.

75. Cowan, Commission on Civil Rights Report, 5.

76. "WIMS Team #1 1964," Side 1.

77. "WIMS Team #5 1964," Side 2.

78. Cowan, Commission on Civil Rights Report, 5; and Harwell, *Wednesdays in Mississippi*, 76.

79. Harwell, *Wednesdays in Mississippi*, 110–13, 129.

80. Cowan, Commission on Civil Rights Report, 5.

81. "WIMS Team # 2 1964," Side 1; and "WIMS Team #5 1964," Side 2.

82. Randolph, *Florynce "Flo" Kennedy*, 94.

83. "WIMS Team # 2 1964," Side 1; Geraldine Kohlenberg, "Comments on the July 15th Wednesdays in Mississippi," 5, and Ruth Hughes, "Wednesdays in Mississippi Project," July 14–16, 1964, 7–8, Series 19, Folder 303, NCNWP.

84. "WIMS Team #1 1965 Conference," Series 15, Subseries 5, Folder 22, Side 2, NCNWP.

85. Goudsouzian, *Down to the Crossroads*, 204.

86. Ibid., 197–201, 204, 218.

87. "WIMS Team #1 1964," Side 1.

88. "WIMS Team #2 1964," Side 1.

89. Ethel Haserodt to Dorothy Height, February 5, 1965, Series 19, Folder 60, NCNWP.

90. "WIMS Team #5 1964," Side 2.

91. Ethel Haserodt to Dorothy Height, February 5, 1965.

92. Polly Cowan, "PSC Speech, Paterson, New Jersey, September 17, 1966, Panel 'Building Bridges . . . ,'" Series 19, Folder 95, NCNWP; and "Laya Wiesner, Widow of Late MIT President, Dies at 79; Championed Women on Campus," *MIT News*, September 28, 1998, http://newsoffice.mit.edu/1998/layawiesner. For more on METCO, see Kaufman, "Building a Constituency for School Desegregation"; Eaton, *Other Boston Busing Story*; and Formisano, *Boston Against Busing*, 38, 230–31. For more on the personal effect on northern participants, see Harwell, 133–38.

93. "WIMS Team #5 1964," Side 2.

94. Cowan, Commission on Civil Rights Report, 4–5.

95. "WIMS Team #1 1964," Side 2.

96. "WIMS Team #5 1964 Conference," Series 15, Subseries 5, Folder 18, Side 1, NCNWP.

97. Ibid.

98. Ibid.

99. Jean Benjamin, "Mississippi–July 1964," Reflection Report, 3, Series 19, Folder 302, NCNWP.

100. Harwell, *Wednesdays in Mississippi*, 115; and Randolph, *Florynce "Flo" Kennedy*, 93.

101. "WIMS Team #5 1964," Side 1 and "WIMS Team #5 1964," Side 2. See also Randolph, *Florynce "Flo" Kennedy*, 91–94.

102. Randolph, *Florynce "Flo" Kennedy*, 91.

103. "WIMS Team #5 1964," Side 2.

104. "WIMS Team #5 1964," Side 1.

105. "WIMS Team #2 1964," Side 1. Ellen Tarry also reflected on this same question in 1965. See Tarry, *Third Door*, 311–12.

106. "WIMS Team #2 1964," Side 1.

107. Ibid.

108. Green, interview by Tuuri, September 17, 2007.

Chapter Four

1. Dittmer, *Local People*, 285–302.

2. Ransby, *Ella Baker*, 331–32.

3. Ruth Hughes, "Wednesdays in Mississippi Project," July 14–16, 1964, 3, Series 19, Folder 303, NCNWP; Harwell, *Wednesdays in Mississippi*, 81–82; and "WIMS Team #2 1964 Conference," Series 15, Subseries 5, Folder 20, Side 1, NCNWP.

4. The debriefing of the final WIMS team, which likely occurred after Fannie Lou Hamer's Atlantic City speech before the Credentials Committee, says nothing about her testimony. See WIMS Team #7 1964, Series 15, Subseries 5, Folder 38, Sides 1 and 2, NCNWP. See also the 1965 Boston Team debriefing for more on the tension between WIMS and the approach of the FDP. "Team #07 Boston 1965," September 9, 1965, Series 15, Subseries 5, Folder 24, Side 1, NCNWP.

5. Edith Savage to Polly Cowan, September 13, 1964, Series 19, Folder 308, NCNWP.

6. Dittmer, *Local People*, 315.

7. Ibid.

8. As quoted in ibid., 316.

9. Ibid., 318.

10. See NCNW, "1964 Convention Registrations," 2, Series 2, Folder 176, NCNWP.

11. Height and Cowan, "'Wednesdays in Mississippi' 1964 Report," February 1965, Series 19, Folder 270, NCNWP. For more, see Tuuri, "Building Bridges of Understanding," 151–52; and Harwell, *Wednesdays in Mississippi*, 140.

12. Vinovskis, *Birth of Head Start*, 6–7.

13. Schulman, *Lyndon B. Johnson*, 84.

14. "Elizabeth Wickenden Dies," NASW News, June 2001, http://www.socialworkers .org/pubs/news/2001/06/wickenden.htm; and 29th Annual NCNW Convention Handbook, Series 2, Folder 174, NCNWP.

15. 29th Annual Convention Report, Nov. 11–15, 1964, Series 2, Folder 173, NCNWP.

16. See letters in Series 19, Folders 60 and 113, NCNWP. For more on Green's civil rights work, see Rosen, *World Split Open*, 71; and Cobble, "More Than Sex Equality," 57–58. For Green's support of the FDP, see Dittmer, *Local People*, 293, 298, and on Edward's, see 267. On Neuberger, see Wolfgang Saxon, "Maurine Neuberger Dies at 93; Consumer Advocate in Senate," *New York Times*, February 24, 2000, http://www .nytimes.com/2000/02/24/us/maurine-neuberger-dies-at-93-consumer-advocate-in -senate.html.

17. Height and Cowan, "'Wednesdays in Mississippi' 1964 Report," February 1965.

18. Polly Cowan to Robert C. Weaver, October 28, 1964, Series 19, Folder 60, NCNWP.

19. Vinovskis, *Birth of Head Start,* 92–93.

20. Ibid., 89.

21. Ibid., 89–93.

22. Dittmer, *Local People,* 368–72; and Vinovskis, *Birth of Head Start,* 97–99.

23. Polly Cowan to Dudley Morris, February 24, 1965, Series 19, Folder 183, NCNWP. See also Tuuri, "Building Bridges of Understanding," 157–58.

24. Polly Cowan to Gwendolyn Wallace, February 24 1965, Series 19, Folder 183; and Polly Cowan to David Hunter, March 11, 1965, Series 19, Folder 164, NCNWP.

25. Susie Goodwillie to Jane Holden, March 31, 1965, Series 19, Folder 23, NCNWP.

26. Remarks of William L. Taylor, Staff Director-Designate, U.S. Commission on Civil Rights at the 17th Annual Conference of the National Civil Liberties Clearing House, Washington, D.C., April 2, 1965, 11, Series 19, Folder 119, NCNWP.

27. Susie Goodwillie to Tiny Hoffman, June 16, 1965, Series 19, Folder 20, NCNWP.

28. For more on this assumed feminine skill of bridge building, see Lynn, *Progressive Women in Conservative Times,* 3–4; and Tuuri, "Most Meaningful Thing," 91.

29. Susie Goodwillie to Team Member, June 1, 1965, Series 19, Folder 184, NCNWP.

30. Susie Goodwillie to Sister Claire Marie, May 31, 1965, Series 19, Folder 22, NCNWP.

31. Susie Goodwillie to Jane Holden, March 31, 1965.

32. WIMS staff to Caroline Smith, June 16, 1965, Series 19, Folder 73, NCNWP.

33. Citizens Crusade Against Poverty, "Memorandum on Meeting of CCAP Task Force on Head Start Project of Office of Economic Opportunity," June 9, 1965, Series 19, Folder 183, NCNWP. On Reuther's political maneuvering to diminish the FDP challenge, see Dittmer, *Local People,* 291, 294–97.

34. Citizens Crusade Against Poverty, "Memorandum on Meeting of CCAP Task Force."

35. Ibid.; and Dittmer, *Local People,* 379–80.

36. Margery Gross and Frances Tenenbaum, "Wednesdays in Mississippi—Final Report," 1965, 6–7, Series 19, Folder 276, NCNWP.

37. "Suggestions for Supplies and Wardrobe to Take to Mississippi," Series 19, Folder 198, NCNWP.

38. Draft letter to 1965 participants, June 10, 1965, Series 19, Folder 60, NCNWP.

39. Gross and Tenenbaum, "Wednesdays in Mississippi—Final Report," 20–22. For more on the MCHR, see Dittmer, *Good Doctors.*

40. Harwell, *Wednesdays in Mississippi,* 149–50; T. M. Morris, *Womanpower Unlimited,* 137; and Tarry, *Third Door,* 309.

41. Gross and Tenenbaum, "Wednesdays in Mississippi—Final Report," 8–9.

42. "WIMS Team #1 1965 Conference," Series 15, Subseries 5, Folder 22, Side 1, NCNWP.

43. Ibid.

44. Ibid.

45. For more on the desperation for white resource teachers to help with integration requirements from the federal government, see Harwell, *Wednesdays in Mississippi,* 152. For more on "resource teachers," see Sanders, *Chance for Change,* 55.

46. Sanders, *Chance for Change*, 52; For more on salary increases and educational opportunities for parent teachers, see Thelma Barnes, interview by Owen Brooks and Jerry Ward, July 23, 1996, 83, 88, Delta Oral History Project, Tougaloo College, https:// www2.dickinson.edu/departments/commstud/Delta%20website/narrations%20in%20 PDF%20format/Barnes,%20Thelma(pic).pdf.

47. Sanders, *Chance for Change*, 94–95; and Barnes, interview by Brooks and Ward, 90–91.

48. Gross and Tenenbaum, "Wednesdays in Mississippi—Final Report," 8.

49. Rae Cohn to Susie Goodwillie, August 26, 1965, Series 19, Folder 10, NCNWP.

50. Gross and Tenenbaum, "Wednesdays in Mississippi—Final Report," 10.

51. "Second WIMS Conference Report," November 11–12, 1965, 5, Series 2, Folder 187, NCNWP.

52. Ibid.

53. Ibid., 4–5. For more on Mississippi Action for Progress, see Dittmer, *Local People*, 377–82.

54. "Team #07 Boston 1965," Side 1.

55. Sanders, *Chance for Change*, 4.

56. Ibid., 50.

57. Ibid., 6.

58. Ibid., 58.

59. Ibid., 4.

60. Ibid., 80–81.

61. Greenberg, *Devil Has Slippery Shoes*, 99.

62. Ibid., 99–100.

63. Polly Cowan to Susie Buffett, June 1–2, 1965, Series 19, Folder 27, NCNWP.

64. Gross and Tenenbaum, "Wednesdays in Mississippi—Final Report," 11–12.

65. Tarry, *Third Door*, 311. According to Tiyi Morris, there were 8 black women but 120 white women at these desegregation institutes. T. M. Morris, *Womanpower Unlimited*, 138.

66. Gross and Tenenbaum, "Wednesdays in Mississippi—Final Report," 12.

67. Ibid.; and Gabrielle Beard, interview by Tuuri, May 1, 2008.

68. See Tarry, *Third Door*, 314; and C. Bolton, *Hardest Deal of All*, 160–61, 206–7.

69. "WIMS Team #1 1965," Side 1.

70. Ibid.

71. Ibid.

72. A. Lewis, " 'Barrier Breaking Love of God,' " 229–30.

73. "WIMS Team #1 1965," Side 1.

74. Ibid.

75. Ibid.

76. Ibid.

77. Webb, *Fight Against Fear*, 192.

78. T. M. Morris, *Womanpower Unlimited*, 143.

79. "WIMS Team #1 1965," Side 1.

80. For more on Father Nathaniel Machesky and Kate Foote Jordan, see P. T. Murray, "Father Nathaniel."

81. Gross and Tenenbaum, "Wednesdays in Mississippi—Final Report," 15; and Harwell, *Wednesdays in Mississippi*, 158–60.

82. Jean Dillinger, 1965 WIMS Reflection Report, July 13–15, 1965, 2, Series 19, Folder 311, NCNWP.

83. "WIMS Team #1 1965," Side 1.

84. Hubert Humphrey to Susie Goodwillie, September 21, 1965, Series 19, Folder 60, NCNWP; and Polly Cowan to Edith Savage, June 30, 1965, and Polly Cowan to Mrs. Jones, October 15, 1965, Series 19, Folder 34, NCNWP.

85. Polly Cowan, to team member, October 9, 1965, Series 19, Folder 54, NCNWP.

86. "Second WIMS Conference Report, November 11–12, 1965," Series 19, Folder 56, NCNWP.

87. See Sugrue, *Origins of the Urban Crisis*.

88. Chafe, *Unfinished Journey*, 305; and Horne, *Fire This Time*, 3.

89. A proposed budget for WIMS in 1967 included a potential trip to Los Angeles to conduct workshops there. This project never materialized. See "Projected Budget, 1967," Series 19, Folder 42, NCNWP.

90. Polly Cowan to Modie Spiegel, [late 1965/early 1966], Series 19, Folder 163, NCNWP.

91. See the Future of WIMS, Winter 1966 Questionnaires of Ethel Hasserodt, Jean Davis, Anne Keller, and Marjorie Dammann, Series 19, Folder 267, NCNWP.

92. See the Future of WIMS, Winter 1966 Questionnaires of Florynce Kennedy, Edith Savage, and other WIMS members in Series 19, Folder 267, NCNWP.

93. "Confidential Draft, Wednesdays in Mississippi—Boston Project, Winter 1966," 1–2, Series 19, Folder 41, NCNWP.

94. Ibid. For more information about the history of the problematic assumption that poor nonwhite women who require government assistance lack initiative and responsibility, see Quadagno, *Color of Welfare*; Roberts, *Killing the Black Body*; Smith, *Welfare Reform and Sexual Regulation*; Abramovitz, *Regulating the Lives of Women*; and Gordon, *Pitied but Not Entitled*.

95. "WIMS Boston Project—Meeting at Ruth Batson's—Thursday Evening, February 10, 1966," 1, Series 19, Folder 41, NCNWP.

96. Ibid., 3.

97. Ibid., 2. For more on Snowden, see Theoharis, "We Saved the City," 67, 79.

98. "WIMS Boston Project, February 10, 1966," 2.

99. Ibid.

100. "WIMS—Boston Project, Meeting at Packard Manse," March 22, 1966, 3, and "WIMS-Boston Project, Progress Report, February 18, 1966," Series 19, Folder 41; and "Wednesdays in Mississippi," attached materials in letter Polly Cowan to Modie Spiegel, [late 1965/early 1966], NCNWP. For more on Hicks, see Hartmann, *From Margin to Mainstream*, 44–45; and Formisano, *Boston Against Busing*. For more on Operation Exodus, see Teele, *Evaluating School Busing*. For more on Ruth Batson

and African American efforts at school desegregation, see Theoharis, "We Saved the City."

101. "Paterson Report, November, 1965–September 1966," Appendix 2, Series 19, Folder 261, NCNWP.

102. Ibid., 1; Grace Smith, "Interracial Conference: Women Build Bridge of Understanding," clipping from *Morning Call*, Paterson, NJ, September 19, 1966; and "Progress Report" October, 1966, Series 19, Folder 262, NCNWP.

103. Press Release, [ca. September 1966], Series 19, Folder 262, NCNWP.

104. "Paterson Report, November, 1965–September 1966," 3, Series 19, Folder 261, NCNWP.

105. WIMS, "Observations—Community Organization—Paterson, NJ, October 1966," 2, Series 19, Folder 262, NCNWP.

106. Ibid., 2–3. For more on the discomfort felt by white and black middle-class women as poor black women became more assertive, see C. Greene, *Our Separate Ways*, 181–82, 197, 202.

107. WIMS, "Observations—Community Organization—Paterson, NJ," 6.

108. See Gross and Tenenbaum, "Wednesdays in Mississippi—Final Report," 13. For more on the limitations of the personal approach, see C. Greene, *Our Separate Ways*, chap. 7, esp. 216.

Chapter Five

1. For the number of attendees, see Pauline Cowan, interview by Britton, March 8, 1968, 39.

2. Blackwell, interview by Wright, August 10, 1968, 28. See also Giddings, *When and Where I Enter*, 287.

3. Ibid; and Gabe Beard to Dorothy Height, October 15, 1966, Series 19, Folder 221, NCNWP.

4. Blackwell, interview by Britton, August 10, 1968, 29; and Giddings, *When and Where I Enter*, 287. Doris Dozier Crenshaw also confirmed that she helped recruit Blackwell, though in her interview, Crenshaw says that she began working for the council in 1967; this date conflicts with Blackwell's 1968 interview and contemporary NCNW records. See Crenshaw, interview by Tuuri, May 24, 2017; "Minutes of Meeting," November 3, 1966, and "Mississippi Women's Planning Session," Schedule of Staff Meetings and Interviews, November 16–22, 1966, Series 19, Folder 221, NCNWP.

5. D. G. White, *Too Heavy a Load*, 183–86, 203; and Height, *Open Wide the Freedom Gates*, 151–52.

6. National Council of Negro Women, *Women and Housing*, 149-c. Unita Blackwell writes that the number was 8,761 in *Barefootin'*, 185, but all other records suggest the higher number. For information on her appointment, see "CAPAHOSIC—Tape 5—Aug. 5, 1967, Sat. Morning (middle) Unita Blackwell," Series 15, Subseries 5, Folder 97, Side 1, NCNWP.

7. Blackwell, *Barefootin'*, 178. See also Blackwell, interview by Britton, August 10, 1968, 31.

8. Carson, *In Struggle*, 75, as cited originally from Forman, *Making of Black Revolutionaries*, 276.

9. Blackwell, interview by Tuuri, January 16, 2008.

10. For more on the controversies surrounding "maximum feasible participation of the poor," see Dittmer, *Local People*, chap. 16; and Sanders, *Chance for Change*, 2–3.

11. For more on Duke, see Pfeiffer, interview by Tuuri, April 10, 2014; and "Mrs. Duke appointed to Secty. Romney staff," *Pittsburgh Courier*, August 21, 1971, 12.

12. Blackwell, *Barefootin'*, 181, 207, 210, 214, 248. Crenshaw also credits the council with helping her make future contacts. See Crenshaw, interview by Tuuri, May 24, 2017.

13. "CAPAHOSIC—Tape 5—Aug. 5, 1967, Unita Blackwell," Side 1. This was a problem that other civil rights activists also faced when local whites began to reluctantly work with blacks. See Eagles, *Price of Defiance*, 257–58.

14. "Representative Projects of the National Council of Negro Women," 1965, Series 2, Folder 187, NCNWP.

15. Carson, *In Struggle*, 203.

16. Ibid., 208–11.

17. "Capahosic, VA, July 8, 1966, Evening Session and July 9 A.M.," Series 15, Subseries 5, Folder 13, Side 1, NCNWP.

18. Ibid.

19. Ibid; and Series 15, Subseries 5, Folders 13 and 14, NCNWP.

20. "Capahosic, VA, July 8, 1966, Evening Session and July 9 A.M.," Side l.

21. Ibid.

22. Ibid.

23. Ibid.

24. "Okolona Center: Family Development through Education," NCNW Application Report to Title X—Rural Housing, Section 1002, August 1968, 4–5, Series 13, Folder 130, NCNWP.

25. Dorothy Height referred to the changing Articles of Incorporation in her letter to prospective WIMS participants. See Dorothy Height to Friend, November 7, 1966, Series 19, Folder 221, NCNWP.

26. Dorothy Height, "Dear Friend," November 7, 1966.

27. Mrs. Aaron Henry to Miss Height, November 12, 1966, Series 19, Folder 221, NCNWP.

28. Mississippi Women's Planning Session Report, ii–iii, Series 19, Folder 221, NCNWP.

29. Ibid., 2.

30. Ibid., 4. While much has been written about Unita Blackwell and Annie Devine, Hattiesburg activist Jeanette Smith remains relatively unknown. For more on Jeanette Smith, see Shankar and Turner, "'People Who Stood Up.'"

31. Mississippi Women's Planning Session Report, iii.

32. "Workshop in Mississippi on Program Grant Writing," January 27–29, 1967, 1, Series 19, Folder 227, NCNWP.

33. Ibid., 1–2; and Polly Cowan to "Dear," June 1967, draft of letter, Series 19, Folder 227, NCNWP.

34. See "A Community Follow Up Report on Women's Workshop," for Oxford, Laurel, Madison County, Okolona, Biloxi, and Greenwood, Series 19, Folder 227, NCNWP.

35. Polly Cowan to Ruth Batson, February 2, 1967, Series 19, Folder 62, NCNWP; and "Synopsis," 4, Series 1, PCP. See also Blackwell, interview by Wright, August 10, 1968.

36. For examples of how WIMS subsumed its identity within the NCNW, see National Council of Negro Women, Inc. and Workshops in Mississippi, "Closing the Communication Gap: The Problem Solving Approach, Report of a Demonstration Rural Training Workshop, June 27–28, 1967, Sunflower County, Mississippi," October 1967, 2, 3, and 5, and *Rural Opportunities*, August 1967, vol. 2, no. 8, reprint from War on Poverty bulletin, Rural Services Division, Community Action Program, Office of Economic Opportunity, Series 19, Folder 50, NCNWP.

37. National Council of Negro Women and Workshops in Mississippi, "Closing the Communication Gap," 1.

38. Ibid., 3.

39. *Rural Opportunities*, August 1967. For more on the Sunflower County Progress, Inc., coalition, see Brooks and Houck, *Speeches of Fannie Lou Hamer*, 70.

40. *Rural Opportunities*, August 1967.

41. For more on the process of children learning their place in segregated society, see Ritterhouse, *Growing Up Jim Crow*. For more on Sunflower County, see Moye, *Let the People Decide*; and Asch, *Senator and the Sharecropper*.

42. National Council of Negro Women and Workshops in Mississippi, "Closing the Communication Gap," 4.

43. Helen Rachlin, interview by Tuuri, March 11, 2009.

44. National Council of Negro Women and Workshops in Mississippi, "Closing the Communication Gap," 5.

45. Height, *Open Wide the Freedom Gates*, 191.

46. National Council of Negro Women and Workshops in Mississippi, "Closing the Communication Gap," 3; and Rachlin, interview by Tuuri, March 11, 2009.

47. For more on sterilizing poor black women in Mississippi, see Roberts, *Killing the Black Body*, 89–98; and McGuire, *At the Dark End of the Street*, 192.

48. Height, *Open Wide the Freedom Gates*, 190–93.

49. See Polly Cowan to Dorothy Steffens, June 24, 1967, Series 19, Folder 75, NCNWP.

50. See Polly Cowan to Julian Tatum, July 22, 1967, Series 19, Folder 31, NCNWP.

51. Draft of "Closing the Communications Gap, June 28–9, 1967," Series 19, Folder 50, NCNWP.

52. Darlene Clark Hine, Patricia Hill Collins, Tiyi Morris, William Chafe, and Tiffany Gill have written about the importance of all-black women's spaces, such as beauty parlors or black women's organizations, in creating a "safe space." The council invited white men and women into this space but maintained its control of the space. Thus, it provided an opportunity for black women to air their grievances in an "authentic" way in front of white officials. See Hine, "Rape and the Inner Lives of Black Women"; Collins, *Black Feminist Thought*, 100–102; T. M. Morris, *Womanpower Unlimited*, 47; Chafe, *Civilities and Civil Rights*, 9; and Gill, *Beauty Shop Politics*.

53. "CAPAHOSIC—Tape 5—Aug. 5, 1967 Unita Blackwell," Side 1.

54. Ibid.

55. J, Secretary, to Dorothy Height, July 6, 1966, FA732E Reel 1816, 066003640000, FFP.

56. Recommendation Report of Public Affairs, Ford Foundation, 7, attached to letter from Paul Ylvisaker to McGeorge Bundy, May 12, 1966, FA732E Reel 1816, 066003640000, FFP.

57. It seems that Polly Cowan provided a key personal connection that helped the NCNW acquire tax-exempt status. See Polly Cowan to Ruth Sykes, December 4, 1967, Series 19, Folder 115, NCNWP. For more on Project Womanpower staff, see Jeanne Noble, "An Evaluation of the National Council of Negro Women's Proposal," December 13, 1965, 17-18, FA732E Reel 1816, 066003640001, FFP; Doris Dozier Crenshaw has stated that Project Womanpower gave Dorothy Height her first professional staff. See Crenshaw, interview by Tuuri, May 24, 2107.

58. "Project Womanpower Final Report," August 31, 1968, 132–3, Series 10, Folder 587, NCNWP. See also Blackwell, interview by Wright, August 10, 1968, 32.

59. Beal and Ross, "Interview with Frances Beal," 151.

60. Crenshaw, interview by Tuuri, May 24, 2017.

61. Ibid.; and Height, *Open Wide the Freedom Gates*, 149–50, 152.

62. Reagon, interview by Tuuri, July 26, 2017.

63. Recommendation Report of Public Affairs, Ford Foundation, 5, attached to letter from Paul Ylvisaker to McGeorge Bundy, May 12, 1966. See also Crenshaw, interview by Tuuri, May 24, 2017.

64. See Springer, *Living for the Revolution*, 84, 148; and Tuuri, "By Any Means Necessary," 39–40.

65. Simmons, interview by Tuuri, May 24, 2017.

66. Reagon, interview by author, July 26, 2017.

67. Crenshaw, interview by author, May 24, 2017; and Simmons, interview by Tuuri, May 24, 2017.

68. Prathia Hall, interview by Belinda Robnett, August 8, 1992, as quoted in Robnett, *How Long? How Long?*, 180. See also Giddings, *When and Where I Enter*, 314–24; and E. F. White, *Dark Continent*, 25–28. For patriarchy in the shift to black nationalism in Los Angeles, see Horne, *Fire This Time*, 11–12, 198–99.

69. Simmons, interview by Tuuri, May 24, 2017. Simmons uses "bad" to mean heroic or tough here. Nell Painter points out that during the era of Black Power, "whatever or whoever gained white approval became suspect. White disapproval earned Black Power points. For instance, the word 'bad' spread as an index of the good or admirable when applied to African Americans." See Painter, *Creating Black Americans*, 333.

70. "Minutes of Meeting," November 3, 1966; and "Mississippi Women's Planning Session," Schedule of Staff Meetings and Interviews, November 16–22, 1966.

71. Arneda J. Hazell, "Evaluation of Progress of National Council of Negro Women," November 13, 1967, 4, Series 10, Folder 576, NCNWP.

72. "Project Womanpower: Current Situation," July 1967, 1–2, Series 10, Folder 584, NCNWP; and Blackwell, interview by Wright, August 10, 1968, 30.

73. Simmons, interview by Tuuri, May 24, 2017.

74. Reagon, interview by Tuuri, July 26, 2017.

75. Ibid.

76. "Project Womanpower: Current Situation," July 1967, 3; and Crenshaw, interview by Tuuri, May 24, 2017.

77. "Project Womanpower: Current Situation," July 1967, 4; and "Report to Affiliate Meeting," January 20, 1968, 4, Series 10, Folder 584, NCNWP; and Simmons, interview by Tuuri, May 24, 2017.

78. See progress reports for July 1967; September 1967; and January 20, 1968, Series 10, Folder 584, NCNWP.

79. Simmons, interview by Tuuri, May 24, 2017.

80. "Project Womanpower Final Report," 125.

81. Laurie Green cites Emilye Crosby's and Christina Greene's local studies, which showed that while women would do dangerous work for the freedom movement, they "considered it a given that men would lead both their organizations and their households." See Green, "Challenging the Civil Rights Narrative," 58; Crosby, *Little Taste of Freedom*, 137–38; and C. Greene, *Our Separate Ways*, 97.

82. Simmons, interview by Tuuri, May 24, 2017; and Reagon, interview by Tuuri, July 26, 2017.

83. "Project Womanpower Final Report," 131.

84. Simmons, interview by Tuuri, May 24, 2017.

85. Height, interview by Cowan, May 25, 1975, 179.

86. Ruth A. Sykes to Christopher Edley, May 10, 1966, FA732E, Reel 1816, 066003640000, FFP.

87. Beal and Ross, "Interview with Frances Beal," 150; and NCNW website, accessed September 17, 2016, http://ncnw.org/. In her interview, Beal recalls the motto's words in a different order. The logo was used as the main logo of the national organization until 2016 (though it is still used in many local and national council materials, including their Twitter feed), and the motto continues to be used. See NCNW website; and NCNW Headquarters Twitter feed, https://twitter.com/NCNWHQ/media, accessed November 12, 2017.

88. "Project Womanpower Final Report," 137.

89. Reagon, interview by Tuuri, July 26, 2017.

90. Cowan, interview by Britton, March 8, 1968, 41–42.

91. Finding aid to the Papers of Polly Cowan, PCP.

92. See Tibaldo-Bongiorno and Bongiorno, *Revolution '67*; and Woodard, *Nation within a Nation*, 78–80.

93. Woodward, "It's Nation Time in NewArk," 295; and *Nation within a Nation*, 80.

94. Kerner Commission, *Report of the National Advisory Commission*, 30–38; Tibaldo-Bongiorno and Bongiorno, *Revolution '67*; and Woodard, *Nation within a Nation*, 82–83.

95. Woodard, *Nation within a Nation*, 74, 84–90.

96. Kerner Commission, *Report of the National Advisory Commission*, 1.

97. Kerner Commission, *Report of the National Advisory Commission*, 1. See also Woodard, *Nation within a Nation*, 75–78.

98. This workshop series was also called the Community Service Institutes. From now on, I will refer to "What's Happening to My World" without the use of quotation marks.

99. The dates for the Newark workshops were November 14–December 19, 1967; May 7–June 11, 1968; and April 19–June 18, 1969. The dates of the Paterson workshops were March 5–April 10, 1968, and October 16–November 20, 1968.

100. Commission on Community Cooperation, "Description of Commission," 2, Series 10, Folder 119, NCNWP.

101. Commission on Community Cooperation, "Program for Housewives," 2, Series 10, Folder 119, NCNWP.

102. "Draft—Community Service Institute—Tape—October, 24, 1967," internal transcription, 3, Series 10, Folder 119, NCNWP.

103. See Naples, *Community Activism and Feminist Politics*, 4.

104. Historian William Chafe describes "middle Americans," including white ethnic men and women, as "blue-collar workers, lower-echelon bureaucrats, school teachers, and white collar employees. Although not poor, they suffered many of the tensions of marginal prosperity, including inflation, indebtedness, and fear of losing what they had worked so hard to attain." But middle Americans were also threatened by the recent turn in African American communities toward black power, believing that the black community was arguing for immediate compensation for jobs, goods, and education that middle Americans had received through hard work and patience. Chafe suggests that "to many [whites], it seemed that blacks were seeking an unfair advantage." See *Unfinished Journey*, 323.

105. "What's Happening to My World? Report of 3 Workshops for Urban Women," 8, Series 10, Folder 120, NCNWP.

106. Commission on Community Cooperation, "The Workshop in Action," 1, Series 10, Folder 127, NCNWP.

107. Ibid., 22.

108. Ibid.

109. Ibid.

110. "What's Happening to My World? Report of 3 Workshops for Urban Women," 13.

111. Emily Schneider, "Report of a Study of the Participants in Paterson Women's Workshop," 6–7, Series 10, Folder 147, NCNWP.

112. Ibid.; and "What's Happening to My World?," 12–13, 15.

113. "Paterson Report" 7, Series 10, Folder 147, NCNWP.

114. This debunking of racial stereotypes of the black mother mirrors black Boston mother Ruth Batson's activism of the late 1950s and 1960s. In "They Told Us Our Kids Were Stupid," Theoharis writes about how Ruth Batson helped push for local change in schools by stressing her role as a responsible, conscientious mother. As a black woman, this action not only helped her child but was also a challenge to racial stereotypes of the time, which claimed that the black family was dysfunctional and that

ultimately it did not, or could not, care about a child's education. See also Feldstein, *Motherhood in Black and White*.

115. "What's Happening to My World?," 18.

116. Carson, *In Struggle*, 142.

Chapter Six

1. Height, *Open Wide the Freedom Gates*, 187–88. See also Nembhard, *Collective Courage*, 180–81. While Height says that Barnes ran in 1967, it was actually June 1968. See Newman, *Divine Agitators*, 167; and "Kick-Off Rally for Mrs. Thelma Barnes," 1968, Box 9, Folder 5, FLHP, https://digitallibrary.tulane.edu/islandora/object/tulane%3A21228. See also "No Unfairness Found in County Vote Result," *Delta Democrat Times*, Monday, June 10, 1968, 1. NCNW records also show that the pigs arrived in October 1968. See NCNW Workshops in Mississippi, "Operation Daily Bread, October 1968," National Council of Negro Women, 1968, 2–4, Series 13, Folder 132, NCNWP.

2. Newman, *Divine Agitators*, 167.

3. Biography of Peggy Jean Connor, Peggy Jean Connor Papers, University of Southern Mississippi, Hattiesburg, Mississippi.

4. NCNW, Inc., "Progress Report: Self-Help Campaign Against Hunger," [1969], 1, Series 26, Folder 89, NCNWP.

5. NCNW, Inc., "Progress Report: Self-Help Campaign Against Hunger," [1969], 2.

6. For more on the public-private cooperation within the War on Poverty, see Fergus, *Liberalism, Black Power*; Clark, *War on Poverty*; and U.S. Department of Housing and Urban Development, *Evolution of HUD's Public-Private Partnerships*.

7. For more on stereotypes of dependency and dysfunctionality, see Orleck, *Storming Caesars Palace*, 82–87.

8. Workshops in Mississippi, "Operation Daily Bread, October 1968," 4.

9. McAlpin worked with the Heifer Project, in cooperation with the Prentiss Institute, in 1968. For more information on the relationship between the Prentiss Institute and the Heifer Project, see Jayman Matthews, "Remembrance of Days Past: The Prentiss Institute at 100," *World Ark*, March/April 2007, 26; and Robert A. Hall, "National Council of Negro Women, Inc. Pig Program," March 17, 1969, Series 26, Folder 85, NCNWP.

10. Lee, *For Freedom's Sake*, 147–48; "Interviews with Fannie Lou Hamer about the Pig Bank," 1973, Series 15, Subseries 6, Folder 1, Side 2, and Dorothy Height, "Dear Friend," September 1973, Series 26, Folder 85, NCNWP.

11. "Interviews with Fannie Lou Hamer and Others about the Pig Bank," Side 2.

12. Ibid.

13. NCNW, Inc., "Progress Report: Self-Help Campaign Against Hunger," [1969], 8–9.

14. "Operation Daily Bread," 20–21.

15. For 1969 materials, see NCNW, Inc., "Progress Report: Self-Help Campaign Against Hunger," [1969], 9; and for 1973 materials, see "Interviews with Fannie Lou Hamer and Others about the Pig Bank," Side 2. See also McLaurin, interview by author, 2008; and Lee, *For Freedom's Sake*, 148.

16. NCNW, Inc., "Progress Report: Self-Help Campaign Against Hunger," [1969], 10.

17. Diane Ward to Dorothy Height, [1969], Series 26, Folder 73, NCNWP.

18. McLaurin, interview by Tuuri, April 23, 2008.

19. See Brooks, *Voice That Could Stir an Army*, 199,

20. As quoted in ibid., 211.

21. Ibid.

22. McLaurin, interview by Tuuri, April 23, 2008.

23. Nembhard, *Collective Courage*, 186.

24. Ibid., 184, 186; and D. G. White, *Too Heavy a Load*, 196.

25. NCNW and WIMS, "Closing the Communication Gap: The Problem-Solving Approach, Report of a Demonstration Rural Training Workshop, June 27–28, 1967, Sunflower County, Mississippi," 3–4, Series 19, Folder 50, NCNWP.

26. Burstein, "New Techniques in Public Housing," 538–39.

27. For Forest Heights, the minimum family income was $3,000, and the maximum family income was $5,000 (depending on the number of children the family had). See Thiokol, *Forest Heights*, 3.

28. Gray-Wiseman, interview by Tuuri, January 22, 2016.

29. Clifford Goldman and Peter Abeles, "The Merits and Limits of Dynamism," 2–3, Reports I-3254, Catalogued Reports, FA 739A, Box 93, Report 002263; and Jack Wiersma to Christopher Edley, February 21, 1968, FA732E, Reel 1816, 066003640000, FFR. Burstein and Duke together met with Mr. Jack Weirsma in Jackson, Mississippi, in May 1967 to discuss plans for the project. See also "Get Homes for Less: Gulfport Family among First in Housing Plan," *Delta Democrat Times*, March 23, 1969. See also Pfeiffer, interview by Tuuri, April 10, 2014.

30. Goldman and Abeles, "Merits and Limits of Dynamism," 3–6; and Burstein, "New Techniques in Public Housing."

31. Thiokol, *Forest Heights*, 25.

32. Wiersma to Edley, February 21, 1968.

33. Goldman and Abeles, "Merits and Limits of Dynamism," 66.

34. Ibid., 3.

35. Blackwell, interview by Tuuri, January 16, 2008.

36. Goldman and Abeles, "Merits and Limits of Dynamism," 1.

37. Ibid., 17–18, 70; and NCNW, Treasurer's Report, for year ending September 30, 1973, Record Group 3, Series 1, Box 646, Folder 3868, RBFR.

38. Height, *Open Wide the Freedom Gates*, 195.

39. Goldman and Abeles, "Merits and Limits of Dynamism," 11–12.

40. Robert C. Weaver, Secretary of Housing and Urban Development to President Lyndon B. Johnson, February 7, 1968, White House Central Files, Subject Files, EX HS 2, Box 3, LBJ.

41. Goldman and Abeles, "Merits and Limits of Dynamism," 12; Robert C. Weaver, "Charting a Pathway to the Future," Address to the National Council of Negro Women Annual Convention, November 9, 1967, 8 and 12, Series 20, Folder 101, NCNWP; and "New Housing Program Offers Hope for Low-Income Families," *Los Angeles Sentinel*, November 30, 1967.

42. OEO, "OEO Extends Contract with the National Council of Negro Women," February 7, 1968, FA732E, Reel 1816, 066003640000, FFR; and Goldman and Abeles, "Merits and Limits of Dynamism," 12.

43. Thiokol was contracted by HUD, OEO, and the local housing authority in July 1968 to screen and train occupants and evaluate the effectiveness of the program. See Thiokol, *Forest Heights*, title page and 3.

44. John Simley and David Salamie, "Thiokol Corporation," International Directory of Company Histories, 1998, http://www.encyclopedia.com/doc/1G2-2842600144.html.

45. Goldman and Abeles, "Merits and Limits of Dynamism," 13.

46. Ibid., 13–14.

47. Ibid., 14.

48. Ibid., 19–20.

49. Ibid., 21–24, 58.

50. Ibid., 27.

51. Ibid., 24–25. In 1962, the Mississippi legislature passed a law that banned public housing in Mississippi without a citywide referendum. See "Progress to Date on Housing in Mississippi, 5/25," Series 19, Folder 187, NCNWP.

52. Goldman and Abeles, "Merits and Limits of Dynamism," 26.

53. Ibid., 51. See also Louise Rogers, "Joint Meeting: Homebuyers Here," *Delta Democrat-Times*, September 10, 1972, 10.

54. McLaurin, interview by Tuuri, April 23, 2008.

55. Brooks, interview by Tuuri, April 16, 2008.

56. McLaurin, interview by Tuuri, April 23, 2008; and Riley, interview by Tuuri, January 22, 2016.

57. Goldman and Abeles, "Merits and Limits of Dynamism," 19.

58. Ibid., 44.

59. Ibid., 45–46.

60. Ibid., 51.

61. Ibid., 46–49.

62. Comptroller General of the United States, "Problems in the Homeownership Opportunities Program for Low-Income Families," 2–3, 25–28, 41.

63. George Schermer Associates, "Turnkey III—How It Began," 48, Series 13, Folder 141, NCNWP.

64. Ibid., 48–49, 52.

65. Ibid., 58.

66. Office of the Federal Register, *Title 24 Housing and Urban Development*, 269; and NCNW, *Women and Housing*, 149–c.

67. [Dorothy Duke], "National Council of Negro Women," undated report on Housing Project, 13, Series 19, Folder 187, NCNWP.

68. Gray-Wiseman, interview by Tuuri, January 22, 2016.

69. Goldman and Abeles, "Merits and Limits of Dynamism," 40.

70. Ibid., 38.

71. Ibid., 37.

72. Ibid., 39–40.

73. Ibid., 41.

74. Comptroller General of the United States, *Problems in the Homeownership Opportunities Program for Low-Income Families*, 10, 21, 34.

75. Gray-Wiseman, interview by Tuuri, January 22, 2016; and "Interviews with Fannie Lou Hamer and Others about the Pig Bank," 1973, Side 2, 31.

76. Height, *Open Wide the Freedom Gates*, 197.

77. Spinks-Thigpen, interview by Tuuri, November 19, 2015.

78. Riley, interview by Tuuri, January 22, 2016.

79. Ibid.

80. Ibid.; and Spinks-Thigpen, interview by Tuuri, November 19, 2015.

81. Gray-Wiseman, telephone conversation with Tuuri, September 24, 2016.

82. Thiokol, *Forest Heights*, 16–19.

83. Ibid., 19

84. Ibid., 20.

85. Aten and Boan, *Disaster Ministry Handbook*, 30.

86. Spinks-Thigpen, interview by Tuuri, November 19, 2015.

87. Riley, interview by Tuuri, January 22, 2016.

88. NCNW, announcement of Katrina Fund grant, accessed July 1, 2016, http://ncnw .org/images/katrina_fund.pdf. See also "New Bush-Clinton Katrina Fund Grants Highlight Recovery Effort," September 15, 2006, https://www.clintonfoundation.org/main/ news-and-media/press-releases-and-statements/press-release-new-bush-clinton -katrina-fund-grants-highlight-recovery-effort.html. Although Forest Heights is not mentioned in her memoir, Natasha Trethewey's *Beyond Katrina* is a moving memoir of the impact of Hurricanes Camille and Katrina on black families in Gulfport.

89. Gail Gibson, "Residents Still Wait for Help in Mississippi: Life in FEMA Trailers Frustrates Community," *Baltimore Sun*, August 27, 2006.

90. "Everybody Should Do Their Best," Habitat for Humanity website, accessed October 2, 2016, http://www.habitat.org/disaster/programs/details/ms_mary_thigpen.aspx.

91. Comptroller General of the United States, *Problems in the Homeownership Opportunities Program for Low-Income Families*, 1.

92. Lena Mitchell, "History of Okolona College Added to Mississippi Historical Trail," July 27, 2014, http://djournal.com/news/history-okolona-college-added-mississippi -historical-trail/.

93. "Recording Date Unknown, Mississippi," Series 15, Subseries 6, Folder 3, Side 2, NCNWP.

94. "Okolona Center: Family Development through Education," NCNW Application Report to Title X—Rural Housing, Section 1002, April 1968, 4, Series 13, Folder 130, NCNWP.

95. "Recording Date Unknown, Mississippi," Subseries 6, Folder 3, Side 2.

96. "Okolona Center: Family Development through Education," April 1968, i–ii.

97. Ibid., ii.

98. Ibid.

99. "Recording Date: Unknown, Mississippi," Subseries 6, Folder 3, Side 2; and Height, *Open Wide the Freedom Gates*, 198.

100. Elizabeth Anne Payne et al., "The Unknown Grandmother," 313–18; for more on the impact of Rosenwald schools on black education in Mississippi, see C. Bolton, *Hardest Deal of All*, 25–28.

101. "Okolona—Southgate," Series 15, Subseries 6, Folder 27, Side 2, NCNWP; Elizabeth Anne Payne et al., "The Unknown Grandmother," 317–18, 325–26.

102. "Interviews with Fannie Lou Hamer and Day Care Center Workers Recording Date: 1973," Series 15, Subseries 6, Folder 1, Side 1, NCNWP. See also "Fannie Lou Hamer Child Care and Family Service Center," 1979, Series 32, Folder 17, NCNWP; and "Fannie Lou Hamer Daycare Center," *Black Woman's Voice* 4, no. 1 (January 1976): 6.

103. NCNW, Inc., "Sunflower County Garment Manufacturing Plant and Day Care/Family Service Center," [1971], 2–3, Series 35, Folder 4, NCNWP.

104. McLaurin, interview by Tuuri, April 23, 2008.

105. David Rushing, "Fannie Lou Hamer died 25 years ago," *Enterprise-Tocsin*, March 21, 2002, B1; and telephone conversation with Mrs. Jacqueline Hamer, November 21, 2017.

106. "The National Council of Negro Women and Rural Poverty," Folder 3, Box 1, FLHP-UM, Miss., 4.

107. Ibid., 5.

108. "Delegate Agency Basic Information," Folder 3, Box 1, FLHP-UM.

109. See Barbara Mueth, "Author Fights for Black Heritage," *Clarion-Ledger*, April 8, 1975; Sherry Lucas, "Jessie Mosley," *Clarion-Ledger*, June 30, 1991; and Jackson Section National Council of Negro Women, Inc., "Black Women: New Directions: Hand in Hand with Black Men," 2nd Annual Benefit Banquet, May 1, 1982, Jackson, Miss., MDAH. See also Clopton-Mosley, interview by McCurtis, January 23, 2008.

110. Height, interview by Cowan, May 25, 1975, 164–65.

111. "Notice of Public Auction Sale," *Clarion-Ledger*, September 20, 1989, 28.

112. Brooks, interview by Tuuri, April 16, 2008.

113. McLaurin, interview by Tuuri, April 23, 2008.

114. "Recording Date: Unknown, Mississippi," Subseries 6, Folder 3, Side 2.

115. Blackwell, *Barefootin'*, 166; and Blackwell, interview by Tuuri, January 16, 2008.

Chapter Seven

1. By 1974, there were monuments to Joan of Arc, Queen Isabella of Spain, and Olive Risely Seward in Washington, D.C., but Bethune was the only American female leader and the only African American to have a statue.

2. Minutes, Thirty-Seventh Convention, November 10–16, 1975, 2, Series 2, Folder 244, NCNWP.

3. "Be Part of the First Memorial to a Black American," *Black Woman's Voice* 2, no. 1 (Nov/Dec 1972): 2.

4. For more on the misogyny of black nationalism, see, for example, D. G. White, *Too Heavy a Load*, 217–18; Giddings, *When and Where I Enter*, 314–24; and Kelley, *Freedom Dreams*, 142–43.

5. "Mary McLeod Bethune—Dedication—Lincoln Park," July 10, 1974, Series 15, Subseries 5, Folder 86, Side 1, NCNWP.

6. "A Monument to a Monument," accessed May 19, 2015, http://www.nps.gov/mamc /learn/kidsyouth/upload/Bethune-Student-Packet.pdf. Jenny Woodley points out that NCNW's choice of Berks as the sculptor, insistence that the statue be large and made out of bronze, and placement in such a prominent location in Washington, D.C., helped to establish Bethune and black women's history as important to American history. See Woodley, " 'Ma Is in the Park,' " 4–7, 13–15, 21–22, 29.

7. Savage, *Monument Wars*, 264–65.

8. NCNW, "Mary McLeod Bethune Memorial Fund Drive Progress Report," July 8, 1970, Series 8, Folder 212, NCNWP; "Mary McLeod Bethune Memorial—the Story of a Living Tribute to Black Americans," *Black Woman's Voice* 1, no. 1 (August 1971): 7.

9. "Task Force Bethune Committee Meeting," January 18, 1974, Series 15, Subseries 6, Folder 24, Side 1, NCNWP. See also Woodley, " 'Ma Is in the Park,' " 7.

10. "Task Force Bethune Committee Meeting," January 18, 1974, Side 1.

11. "Task Force Bethune Committee Meeting," January 18, 1974, Series 15, Subseries 6, Folder 24, Side 2, NCNWP. Woodley has pointed out that the NCNW initially wanted the statue to be a living memorial as a "place for cultural and intellectual exchange, and a community meeting place." The council also wanted to help the neighboring community and campaigned against a proposed eight-lane freeway that would have cut through the area. See " 'Ma Is in the Park, ' " 15–17. See also Height, *Open Wide the Freedom Gates*, 213.

12. Keith Butler, "Drums, Flutes Spark Welcome," *Washington Post*, July 11, 1974, B1.

13. Height, *Open Wide the Freedom Gates*, 214; National Park Service, Capitol Hill Parks, "Lincoln Park," accessed May 19, 2015, http://www.nps.gov/cahi/learn /historyculture/cahi_lincoln.htm; and "Mary McLeod Bethune—Dedication," Side 1.

14. "Mary McLeod Bethune—Dedication," Side 1.

15. Ibid.; and Savage, *Standing Soldiers, Kneeling Slaves*, 114.

16. Height, *Open Wide the Freedom Gates*, 212; and F. P. Bolton, "Extension of Remarks."

17. Height, *Open Wide the Freedom Gates*, 212.

18. Ibid., 212–14.

19. "Jackie Backs Drive to Build Memorial to Negro Woman," *Oakland Tribune*, November 18, 1961, 8.

20. Height, *Open Wide the Freedom Gates*, 213.

21. D. G. White, *Too Heavy a Load*, 198.

22. National Council of Negro Women, Inc., "It Is Two Minutes to Midnight," inside cover, Series 13, Folder 127, NCNWP.

23. Ibid., 2.

24. Ibid., 3.

25. Ibid., 4–5.

26. Ibid., 19.

27. "Project Womanpower Final Report," August 31, 1968, 120, Series 10, Folder 587, NCNWP.

28. Ibid., 120–22, 134.

29. Ibid., 122–23, 130–31.

30. For more on the Poor People's Campaign, see Mantler, *Power to the Poor*, chaps. 4, 5.

31. Dorothy Height to Section Presidents, National Officers, and Affiliated Organizations, memo about the Poor People's Campaign, April 30, 1968, 1, Series 10, Folder 108, NCNWP.

32. Height to Section Presidents, Poor People's Campaign, April 30, 1968, 2.

33. Lillian Wiggins, "'Woman Power' Major Factor in Solidarity Day Activities," *Afro-American*, June 22, 1968, 16.

34. Frances M. Flippen, "Report of National Convention of the National Council of Negro Women, Inc., November 6–11, 1968," Series 2, Folder 208, NCNWP. See also White, *Too Heavy a Load*, 209.

35. "Workbook 33rd Annual Convention," November 6–10, 1968, 1, 4–5, Series 2, Folder 210, NCNWP.

36. "An Assessment of the Leadership Development Training of the National Council of Negro Women," 23, 35, Reports 3255–6261: Catalogued Reports; Box 266, Report 005976, FFR; Jeanne Noble, "An Evaluation of the National Council of Negro Women's Proposal," December 13, 1965, 7, FA732E Reel 1816, 066003640001, FFP; and "Negro Women Organize," *Call and Post*, July 26, 1969, 8B; National Council of Negro Women constitutions, as found in Series 1, Folders 1–3, NCNWP; White, *Too Heavy a Load*, 208–9; and Collier-Thomas, *N.C.N.W., 1935–1980*, 18.

37. "Negro Women Organize." See also White, *Too Heavy a Load*, 206.

38. "Vow Militant Action," *New York Amsterdam News*, July 26, 1969, 5.

39. "Proposed Constitutional Revisions to Be Voted On at the 1969 Convention," Series 2, Folder 218, NCNWP.

40. "President's Report on Implementation of the New State Mechanism of NCNW," Series 2, Folder 225, NCNWP; and "Discussion Paper—Some Functions and Relationships of National Council to a State Organization System," [ca. 1973], 4, Series 2, Folder 237, NCNWP.

41. "Resolutions Adopted by 1969 Convention of the National Council of Negro Women, Inc.," Series 2, Folder 219, NCNWP.

42. 35th National Convention National Council of Negro Women, "Working Paper for Organizational Growth and Development 'For Reaching and Greater Involvement of the 4 Million!,'" [ca. 1971], 1, Series 2, Folder 226, NCNWP.

43. Letter from Dorothy Height to Delta Sigma Theta, February 7, 1970, Record Group 3, Series 1, Box 645, Folder 3863, RBFR; Bernice White, "It's NOT a Man's World," *Afro-American*, October 24, 1970, 5; "'Black Women Unite!' Ruby Dee Chairs National Council Drive," *Pittsburgh Courier*, December 19, 1970, 23; and "Black Women's Unity Drive," *Black Woman's Voice* 1, no. 1 (August 1971): 4–5.

44. See, for instance, Height, "An Open Letter to Black Women," *Black Woman's Voice* 1, no. 1 (August 1971): 3; and Height, "On Unity," *Black Woman's Voice* 2, no. 1 (November/December 1972): 9.

45. Bernice White, "It's NOT a Man's World," *Afro-American*, April 10, 1971, 5.

46. 35th National Convention National Council of Negro Women, "Working Paper for Organizational Growth and Development," 2.

47. "Proposed Constitutional Revisions to be Voted On at the 1969 National Convention," 5–6, Series 2, Folder 218, NCNWP.

48. Ibid., 3–4; and "Constitutional Changes," "The 1969 NCNW Convention," Series 2, Folder 219, NCNWP.

49. "Assessment of Leadership Development Training," 1, 17–18.

50. Collier-Thomas, *N.C.N.W., 1935–1980*, 4, 25.

51. "Chicago Meet Sets Action," *Black Woman's Voice*, Fall 1973, 5.

52. Reagon, interview by Tuuri, July 26, 2017.

53. Beal, interview by Taylor, June 21, 2017.

54. "Assessment of Leadership Development Training," 4, 8–9.

55. Ibid., 7–8. Beal, Crenshaw, and Simmons all agree that Height encouraged them to help direct the council in a way that they believed would benefit black communities. See Beal, interview by Taylor; Crenshaw, interview by Tuuri; and Simmons, interview by Tuuri.

56. "Assessment of Leadership Development Training," 7.

57. Ibid., 34. Crenshaw also recalls that some council women disliked the initiatives of Project Womanpower and the more activist staff, but they were in the minority. See Crenshaw, interview by Tuuri, May 24, 2017.

58. "Assessment of Leadership Development Training," 9–12.

59. Ibid., 12–13.

60. Ibid., 16.

61. Excerpted quote from 1973 council report to the Ford Foundation and found in ibid., 17.

62. Ibid., 5, 18, 36.

63. "Chicago Meet Sets Action."

64. "Assessment of Leadership Development Training," 22, 36.

65. Ibid., 36.

66. Ibid., 31.

67. NCNW, "A Proposal: The Black Women's Institute for Research and Education," May 20, 1981, 2, Subgroup 1.10: Projects (A84), Series 200, Box R2176, FA 479, RFR.

68. T. M. Morris, *Womanpower Unlimited*, 38–39, 181–82.

69. Minutes of Jackson Metropolitan Council, March 16, 1948, Series 17, Folder 219, NCNWP.

70. T. M. Morris, *Womanpower Unlimited*, 172.

71. Ibid.

72. Ibid., 174.

73. "Assessment of Leadership Development Training," 24–25.

74. NCNW, "1960–1961 Register," Series 13, Folder 65; NCNW, "Official Roster 1962–63," Series 13, Folder 68; NCNW, "Official Roster 1963–1964," Series 13, Folder 69; and NCNW, "Tentative Roster," 1966–1967, Series 13, Folder 70, NCNWP.

75. NCNW, "1973–1974 Roster," Series 13, Folder 76; and NCNW, "Directorate," 1978, Series 13, Folder 79, NCNWP.

76. "National Council of Negro Women's 40th National Convention," *Black Women's Voice* 9, no. 1 (April 1982): 8, as found in Subgroup 1.13, Series 200, Box R2378, "National Council of Negro Women, 1982–83," RFR.

77. For more on black founders and early members of NOW, see Giddings, *When and Where I Enter*, 303–4; and Randolph, " 'Women's Liberation or . . . Black Liberation.' "

78. Charlayne Hunter, "Many Blacks Wary of 'Women's Liberation' Movement in U.S.," *New York Times*, November 17, 1970, 47, 60; and "Goals Set by Women's Political Caucus," *New York Times*, July 13, 1971, 37.

79. Crenshaw, interview by Tuuri, May 24, 2017. Here, Crenshaw articulates a womanist position that was concerned with the well-being of not only black women but also black communities, especially the poor. Scholar Layli Phillips has identified womanism as being anti-oppressionist, vernacular, nonideological, communitarian, and spiritualized. See Phillips, "Introduction," xxiv–xxvi.

80. Beal, interview by Taylor, June 21, 2017. Again, as seen above, Beal articulated a vision beyond black women's personal advancement, and was concerned with eradicating all people's oppression.

81. NCNW, Minutes of Advisory Board Meeting, International Division, December 17–18, 1977, 8, Series 37, Folder 1, NCNWP.

82. See, for instance, Giddings, *When and Where I Enter*, chap. 17; D. G. White, *Too Heavy a Load*; Springer, *Living for the Revolution*, 19–44; and Roth, *Separate Roads to Feminism*, 11–14, and chap. 3. The council's concern with the total well-being of the race, including eradicating poverty and oppression, suggests a womanist consciousness, though Alice Walker would not coin the term until 1979. See Phillips, "Introduction," xix.

83. Beal, interview by Taylor, June 21, 2017.

84. Ibid.

85. "National Council of Negro Women, 1971 National Convention Washington, D.C., *Commitments for Action*," Series 2, Folder 225, NCNWP. For more on black women's history in reproductive rights, see Nelson, *Women of Color and the Reproductive Rights Movement*; and Roberts, *Killing the Black Body*.

86. "NCNW protests sterilization," *Black Woman's Voice*, Fall 1973, 9.

87. National Council of Negro Women in National Convention Assembled, "Resolution on the case of Professor Angela Davis," copy of draft, November 6, 1971, 1–2, 5, Series 2, Folder 226, NCNWP; and "Report on the 35th National Convention of the National Council of Negro Women," 2, Series 2, Folder 225, NCNWP.

88. Earl Caldwell, "Angela Davis Acquitted on All Charges," *New York Times*, 1, 21, June 5, 1972; and National Council of Negro Women in National Convention Assembled, "Resolution on the case of Professor Angela Davis," 4.

89. National Council of Negro Women in National Convention Assembled, "Resolution on the case of Professor Angela Davis," 2, 4.

90. Becky Thompson points out that black feminist and WIMS participant Florynce Kennedy identified the feminist movement with the prisoners of Attica, who were striking against inhumane conditions in the prison. Black liberation was a goal for many black and multiracial feminists in the 1970s. See Thompson, "Multiracial Feminism," 343–44.

91. Douglas Wells, "WICS Banquet Cites Dedicated Workers," *Atlanta Daily World*, May 14, 1972, 3; and Laura K. Fox, "The Status of WICS: Report to National Convention," November 9, 1967, S2 F199, NCNWP.

92. Reagon, interview by Tuuri, July 26, 2017. Seven Sisters schools were all-women's colleges in the Northeast formed in the 1800s, sometimes in affiliation with male Ivy League schools. Original Seven Sisters schools were Mount Holyoke, Vassar, Wellesley, Smith, Radcliffe, Bryn Mawr, and Barnard.

93. Reagon, interview by Tuuri, July 26, 2017.

94. "Miss Height speaker on careers program," *Afro-American*, January 30, 1971, 15; "NCNW Career Center Enters 3rd Year," *Black Woman's Voice* 2, no. 1 (November/December 1972): 6; and "National Council of Negro Women," Grants Database, Andrew W. Mellon Foundation, accessed August 22, 2016, https://mellon.org/grants/grants-database/grants/national-council-of-negro-women-inc/27400038/.

95. NCNW, Center for Career Advancement brochure, Record Group 3, Series 1, Box 645, Folder 3863, RBFR; and "NCNW Career Center Enters 3rd Year."

96. "NCNW Career Center Enters 3rd Year."

97. Reagon, interview by Tuuri, July 26, 2017; and "Mission and History," Women's Center for Education and Career Advancement, accessed November 27, 2017, https://wceca.org/about/us.

98. Reagon, interview by Tuuri, July 26, 2017; and "Mission and History," Women's Center for Education and Career Advancement, accessed November 27, 2017, https://wceca.org/about/us.

99. Reagon, interview by Tuuri, July 26, 2017.

100. "Second Draft, Year-End Report from NCNW, as Revised March 20, 1975," 5–6, Series 26, Folder 94, NCNWP.

101. 36th National Convention of the National Council of Negro Women, Inc., "Resolutions," December 3–9, 1973, Series 2, Folder 236, NCNWP.

102. "NCNW Endorses Full Employment Coalitions," *Black Woman's Voice* 3, no. 1 (March 1974), 3.

103. NCNW, Inc., "Sunflower County, Mississippi, Garment Manufacturing Plant, and Day Care/Family Service Center," [1971], Series 35, Folder 4; and "Attachment 2 for *Final Evaluation*: Experiment and Demonstration Project, Career Development Entrepreneurship, Women's Opportunity Program," Series 35, Folder 17, NCNWP.

104. Charles McLaurin to Dianne P. Ford, March 17, 1980, Series 35, Folder 2, NCNWP; McLaurin, interview by author, April 23, 2008; "Program to Help Women," *Delta-Democrat Times*, April 6, 1980, 2A, clipping found in Series 35, Folder 15; and

Reports from Charles McLaurin to Alma Brown, National Program Director, April 23, 1979, to May 25, 1979, and June 1 to June 30, Series 35, Folder 39, NCNWP.

105. See "NCNW and Welfare Reform," *Black Woman's Voice* 1, no. 1 (August 1971): 9; and National Council of Negro Women, "Plan of Action," Report at 38th National Convention, November 6–13, 1977, 14, Series 2, Folder 251, NCNWP.

106. Beal, interview by Taylor, June 21, 2017.

107. See Hinton, *From the War on Poverty*, 3, 16, 20–21, and chap. 1; Hinton, "War within Our Own Boundaries," 107; Hinton, "Creating Crime"; and Murakawa, *First Civil Right*, 75. See also Felker-Kantor, "Kid Thugs Are Spreading Terror."

108. Noble, "An Evaluation of the National Council of Negro Women's Proposal," 4; Poinsett, *Walking with Presidents*, 63, 107–8; and "Belford V. Lawson and Marjorie M. Lawson Residence, African American Heritage Trail," Cultural Tourism DC site, accessed September 18, 2016, https://www.culturaltourismdc.org/portal/belford -v.-lawson-and-marjorie-m.-lawson-residence-african-american-heritage-trail.

109. Rhetta M. Arter, Independent Evaluator's Report for Operation Sisters United, 8, Series 13, Folder 146, NCNWP.

110. Murakawa, *First Civil Right*, 17; and Richie, *Arrested Justice*, 77–97. Hinton also points out that during the 1960s and 1970s, many black activists "imagined involved community control, oversight, and inclusion in the development and implementation of urban law enforcement programs." But this version of crime control was different from what local, state, and federal agencies implemented. See Hinton, *From the War on Poverty*, 9.

111. "National Council Negro Women [*sic*] Awarded $654,193 in Grants," *New York Amsterdam News*, August 27, 1966, 4. Volunteers Unlimited first received $154,000 for one year, but then was granted an extension of six months and $68,000 more for a total of $222,000. See "Volunteers Unlimited," [1967], 1–3, Series 10, Folder 704, NCNWP.

112. "Volunteers Unlimited Training Materials," September 1968, appendix C, p. 1, Series 13, Folder 102, NCNWP.

113. Rhetta M. Artec, Volunteers Unlimited Final Report, September 1968, B2, G7–8.

114. "Volunteers Unlimited," [1967], 1–3.

115. Hinton, "Creating Crime," 809–11.

116. Hinton, "War within Our Boundaries," 103, 109; and Murakawa, *First Civil Right*, 71, 79–80, 89.

117. Thompson, "Why Incarceration Matters," 727–32; Murakawa, *First Civil Right*, 9, 13; Hinton, "War within Our Own Boundaries"; and Hinton, *From the War on Poverty*, 49–133.

118. Murakawa, *First Civil Right*, 73; and Hinton, *From the War on Poverty*, 2. Hinton says that the vast majority of LEAA funding went to police operations; thus, NCNW's program was in the minority of the programs funded.

119. Murakawa, *First Civil Right*, 73.

120. National Council of Negro Women, Inc., "Policies and Procedures Operation Sisters United," 1–2, Series 13, Folder 113.

121. Collier-Thomas, *N.C.N.W., 1935–1980*, 21.

122. NCNW, "'Fulfilling the Promise,' 1979 NCNW Annual Report," 4, Series 2, Folder 257, NCNWP; and Collier-Thomas, *N.C.N.W., 1935–1980*, 21.

123. NCNW, "Black Women: New Directions," Fortieth National Convention program, 1981, Series 2, Folder 263, NCNWP; and Hinton, *From the War on Poverty*, 2.

124. Office of Juvenile Justice and Delinquency Prevention, *Programs for Young Women in Trouble*, 24.

125. D. G. White, *Too Heavy a Load*, 254–55.

126. See Thompson, "Why Incarceration Matters"; and Alexander, *New Jim Crow*.

127. National Council of Negro Women, Inc., National Convocation on Hunger in the U.S.A. Statement of Purpose, May 27, 1969, Series 26, Folder 10, NCNWP.

128. National Council of Negro Women, Inc., "National Convocation on Hunger in the U.S.A." [pre-Convocation Report], 1969, 5, Series 26, Folder 77, NCNWP.

129. Ibid., 6.

130. "Co-sponsoring Organizations with Names of Presidents and Executive Directors," [1969] Series 26, Folder 10, NCNWP.

131. Art Carter, "Hunger in the U.S. Called 'National Disgrace': 'Don't Let Them Louse Up the Moon, Too'—Mrs. Hamer," *Afro-American*, June 7, 1969, 6; and "Convocation On Hunger To move Private Sector," *New York Amsterdam News*, May 24, 1969, 10.

132. NCNW, Inc., in Cooperation with Other National Co-Sponsoring Organizations, "Reports on Hunger Workshops in Twenty Cities," Series 26, Folder 95, NCNWP.

133. "White House Highlights: Dr. Holloman, Miss Height give Nixon minority report," *Afro-American*, December 13, 1969, 6.

134. "Resolution to Support the Moratorium," Resolution at 34th Annual Convention, 1969, Series 26, Folder 10, NCNWP.

135. National Convocation on Hunger in the U.S.A. Statement of Purpose, May 27, 1969, Series 26, Folder 10, NCNWP.

136. Ibid.

137. National Council Negro Women, Inc., "Progress Report: Self-Help Campaign Against Hunger," [1969], 12–19, Series 26, Folder 89, NCNWP. See also "Action on Food Stamps," *Black Woman's Voice*, Special Convention Edition, Summer 1976, 2.

138. "Proceedings," transcript of 1972 Black Women's Institute: National Hunger Convocation, 3, 5, Series 26, Folder 24; and "Women Pledge to Fight Hunger with N. Council," *Pittsburgh Courier*, May 13, 1972, 13.

139. "Second Draft, Year End Report from National Council of Negro Women, as Revised March 20, 1975," 3; and "Back of Letter for November House Mailing," [1974], Series 26, Folder 94, NCNWP.

140. NCNW, *Women and Housing*, 149-c.

141. Ibid., 142.

142. Ibid., 148.

143. Ibid., 143–44.

Chapter Eight

1. Height, *Open Wide the Freedom Gates*, 246.

2. Agency for International Development, *Women in Development*, 96, http://files .eric.ed.gov/fulltext/ED212893.pdf.

3. Ghodsee, "Revisiting the United Nations," 6–7; Height, *Open Wide the Freedom Gates*, 246–47; and Sheila Rule, "At Nairobi Women's Parley, Old Wounds Still Fester," July 15, 1985, http://www.nytimes.com/1985/07/15/style/at-nairobi-women-s-parley-old-wounds-still-fester.html.

4. Height, *Open Wide the Freedom Gates*, 247.

5. Assistant Inspector General for Audit, *Memorandum Audit Report*, 1, http://pdf.usaid.gov/pdf_docs/PDAAR460.pdf; and Gertrude Martin, "Southern African Women in Development: How Shall the National Council of Negro Women Respond?," October 1977 draft of final report, 4, Series 37, Folder 37, NCNWP.

6. For instance, Patt Derian, who worked with WIMS and NCNW in the 1960s, became the first assistant secretary of state for human rights under President Jimmy Carter.

7. For a careful review of the different types of criticism of NGOs as imperialist, see Funk, "Women's NGOs," 265–74. For critical takes on the role of NGOs, see Petras, "NGOs," 1991; and Petras and Veltmeyer, *Globalization Unmasked*. Most criticisms focus on the 1980s and 1990s as a period in which NGOs worked alongside the structural reorganization efforts of the World Bank and the IMF. NCNW's work was certainly not enforcing economic austerity, but in promoting NGO projects that would help individual women, it may have laid the groundwork for a more personal approach to aid and moved women away from participating in class-based political movements (see Petras and Veltmeyer's criticism). However, the NCNW did work with African governments and was a vocal opponent of colonialism. More than anything, its programs were trying to create a worldwide network of women of African descent and helping to fuel self-help programs for women when their governments were not providing these services. Other critics argue that NGOs promote only Western interests, but the NCNW was attempting to take seriously the concerns of international women.

8. "National Council of Negro Women on Assisting Black Africans," *New York Amsterdam News*, November 20, 1976, B8; Ethel Payne, "From Where I Sit: Turning Screws in South Africa," *Pittsburgh Courier*, December 3, 1977, 6; and Kenneth B. Noble, "Lobby Views Success as Being Out of Favor," *New York Times*, November 29, 1983; and Erhagbe, "African Americans' Ideas and Contributions," 385–87.

9. Gallagher, "National Council of Negro Women," 84; and Plummer, *Rising Wind*, 125, 132–33.

10. Plummer, *Rising Wind*, 135–36.

11. The NCNW faced challenges to gain this status as well. See Gallagher, "National Council of Negro Women," 85.

12. Lauren, "Seen from the Outside," 25; and NCNW, "Women United," 22, 60. Note that Gallagher says that it was Ferebee and Sampson who attended the San Francisco meeting, but the 1951 NCNW yearbook, "Women United," says that Eunice Hunton Carter went with Bethune and Ferebee (see citation above). See Gallagher, "National Council of Negro Women," 98. It's likely that all three attended along with Bethune.

13. Gallagher, "National Council of Negro Women," 83.

14. See Laville, *Cold War Women*, 31; and Gallagher, "National Council of Negro Women," 83, 86–87; and Collier-Thomas, *N.C.N.W., 1935–1980*, 6.

15. "Women United," 22; and Plummer, *Rising Wind*, 92, 95–96.

16. "Women United," 86; Rosen, *World Split Open*, 28–29; Swerdlow, "Congress of American Women"; Plummer, *Rising Wind*, 144; and Grant, "National Council of Negro Women," 62.

17. Gallagher, "National Council of Negro Women," 89.

18. Plummer, *Rising Wind*, 213; Gallagher, "National Council of Negro Women," 89–93; and Grant, "National Council of Negro Women," 62.

19. Height, interview by Cowan, October 6, 1974, 66–70.

20. Grant, "National Council of Negro Women," 60.

21. Ibid., 65–68.

22. "Women United," 54; and Laville and Lucas, "American Way," 569–72.

23. "Women United," 54. Laville and Lucas argued in 1996 that Sampson's history has been either ignored or vilified, and that both understandings of her are incorrect. See Laville and Lucas, "American Way," 566–68.

24. Joan Cook, "Edith Sampson, 1st Black Woman Elected to Bench in Illinois, Is Dead," *New York Times*, October 11, 1979, D19; and Laville and Lucas, "American Way," 572–73.

25. Krenn, *Black Diplomacy*, 40–41.

26. Laville, *Cold War Women*, 53. See also Dudziak, *Cold War Civil Rights*, 59–60.

27. Anderson, "Bleached Souls and Red Negroes," 103–4; Laville and Lucas, "American Way," 576; and Dudziak, *Cold War Civil Rights*, 63–66.

28. Height, interview by Cowan, November 10, 1974, 94.

29. Ibid., 94–95; and Height, *Open Wide the Freedom Gates*, 223–24.

30. Height, interview by Cowan, November 10, 1974, 98–99. Laville points out that "the distinction between a State Department employee and a representative of an organization such as the LWV or the NAACP became increasingly difficult to make, both being funded by their government to travel the world as advocates for the USA." See Laville, *Cold War Women*, 5.

31. Height, interview by Cowan, November 10, 1974, 97–98, 100; and Height, *Open Wide the Freedom Gates*, 226.

32. Height, interview by Cowan, November 10, 1974, 99.

33. Ibid., 100.

34. Height, *Open Wide the Freedom Gates*, 227.

35. Laville, *Cold War Women*, 171–77.

36. Ibid., 179–80.

37. Height, interview by Cowan, November 10, 1974, 101.

38. Ibid., 102.

39. Ibid.

40. Erhagbe, "African-Americans' Ideas and Contributions," 287–88.

41. Ibid., 290; and Height, *Open Wide the Freedom Gates*, 230–31.

42. Height, *Open Wide the Freedom Gates*, 231; Height, interview by Cowan, November 10, 1974, 104–5; and Wolfgang Saxon, "S.O. Adebo, 80, a U.N. Envoy, Pioneered Nigeria Civil Service," obituary, *New York Times*, November 11, 1994, B6.

43. Dudziak, *Cold War Civil Rights*, 230.

44. Height, *Open Wide the Freedom Gates*, 232; and American Negro Leadership Conference on Africa, November 23, 24, 25, 1962: Resolutions, 1, NAACP Administrative Files, A199, cited in Erhagbe, "African-Americans' Ideas and Contributions," 294.

45. Erhagbe, "African-Americans' Ideas and Contributions," 310–14.

46. Height, *Open Wide the Freedom Gates*, 232–33.

47. The council was a regular observer of the CSW; see "Women United," 60.

48. Tinker, "Empowerment Just Happened," 272.

49. Ibid., 275–76; Jaquette and Staudt, "Women, Gender, and Development," 20–23.

50. Clark, *Victory Deferred*, 57–58.

51. Ibid., 56–58; Jaquette and Staudt, "Women, Gender, and Development," 50n4; and Tinker, "Empowerment Just Happened," 276.

52. Clark, *Victory Deferred*, 57. See also Peet and Hartwick, *Theories of Development*, 88.

53. Clark, *Victory Deferred*, 58–59. While perhaps this shift to funding individuals and communities directly may have been borne of good intentions, as neoliberalism began to take shape in the United States in the late 1970s and throughout the world in the 1980s and 1990s, austerity programs put in place by the World Bank and International Monetary Fund strangled national economies abroad. These two organizations insisted that countries privatize government services and eliminate social welfare programs in order to receive loans to help with economic development and maintenance. These changes drastically increased the gap between rich and poor nations and people around the world. Voluntary nongovernmental organizations were left to pick up the pieces of social welfare programs that were cut under these new requirements. These NGOs could only help small numbers of people and often functioned as pawns of their financial backers. However, the neoliberal revolution in global aid had not yet been realized when the NCNW first created its international division under USAID. See Peet and Hartwick, *Theories of Development*, 84–91, for more on the shift to neoliberalism in aid in the 1980s, and 98–102 for an excellent critique of neoliberalism in development.

54. NCNW, "International Training Program," A Grant Proposal to USAID, n.d., [ca. 1976], 4–5, Series 37, Folder 46, NCNWP.

55. For more on the Sahel drought from 1968 to 1974, see M. Greene, "Impact of the Sahelian Drought in Mauritania," 1094.

56. NCNW, "Proposal for the Establishment of a Women's International Development Program," [1975], Series 37, Folder 29, NCNWP.

57. Ibid.

58. L. E. Stanfield to Dorothy Height, May 12, 1975, Series 36, Folder 84, NCNWP.

59. Height, interview by Cowan, November 10, 1974, 199–202.

60. Ermon O. Kamara, "International Women United for Equality, Development, Peace," National Council of Negro Women, Inc., 1975, iii, Series 13, Folder 148, NCNWP; and Tinker, "Empowerment Just Happened," 270.

61. Height, interview by Cowan, November 10, 1974, 192–93.

62. Kamara, "International Women United," 23. See Orleck, *Storming Caesars Palace*.

63. Kamara, "International Women United," 28, 33.

64. Ibid., 24.

65. Ibid., v.

66. Ibid., iv.

67. Ibid., 101–2.

68. Height, interview by Cowan, October 5, 1975, 203.

69. Ibid., 202–3.

70. Dorothy I. Height to Amzie Moore, August 19, 1975, Series 36, Folder 14, NCNWP; Height, interview by Cowan, October 5, 1975, 204, and Clifford Goldman and Peter Abeles, "The Merits and Limits of Dynamism," 51, Reports I-3254, Catalogued Reports, FA 739A, Box 93, Report 002263, FFR.

71. Height, interview by Cowan, October 5, 1975, 205; and "NCNW Programs," *Black Woman's Voice*, Fall 1973, 8.

72. Height, interview by Cowan, October 5, 1975, 211.

73. Again, they were creating safe spaces for conversations important to black women, but this time, they were doing so globally. See Collins, *Black Feminist Thought*, 100–102.

74. Height, interview by Cowan, October 5, 1975, 206–7.

75. Height, *Open Wide the Freedom Gates*, 238–39; Height, interview by Cowan, October 5, 1975, 207–9; "Women Accused of Stealing $2 Hand Lotion," *Jet*, August 7, 1975, 14.

76. "Recording Date: Unknown, Mississippi," audio recording, Series 15, Subseries 6, Folder 3, Side 2, NCNWP. Based on information in the recording as well as information found in "Continuation of Grant Proposal," enclosure of Willie T. Raspberry to Dorothy Height, March 19, 1974, 3, Series 31, Folder 30, the date of this recording is likely 1974, Although the transcript of the recording does not list this quote's speaker, based on the context of what this speaker says and her voice in the audio recording, she is likely Kate Wilkinson. See also Height, *Open Wide the Freedom Gates*, 198. Height also makes this comparison between projects in Mississippi and Africa in her speech at Polly Cowan's funeral. See also Height, Speech at funeral of Polly Cowan, [November, 1976], 5, Series 1, PCP.

77. USAID press release, July 22, 1975, Series 36, Folder 84, NCNWP.

78. Martin, "Southern African Women in Development." Note that the draft of this report written in October 1977, incorrectly lists the year of the conference as 1977, but the conference took place in December 1976 in Racine, Wisconsin; see materials in Series 37, Folders 50 and 51, NCNWP, for more on the December 14–15, 1976, conference.

79. Height, interview by Cowan, October 5, 1975, 211.

80. Ibid., 212.

81. NCNW, "International Division Newsletter," vol. 1, no. 1 (Spring 1977): 5; and Height, interview by Cowan, February 1, 1976, 213–15.

82. Martin, "Southern African Women in Development," 5, 7–10.

83. Ibid., 12, 14–23.

84. Ibid., 1.

85. Culverson, "Cold War to Global Interdependence," 231; and "Speaking Out: The African-American Manifesto," *Ebony* 32, no. 2 (December 1976): 88–90.

86. "Speaking Out"; Culverson, "Cold War to Global Interdependence," 231–33; and Noble, "Lobby Views Success."

87. Payne, "Turning screws in South Africa," *Pittsburgh Courier*, November 26, 1977, 5.

88. Minutes of Advisory Board Meeting, Dec. 17–18, 1977, 1–2, Series 37, Folder 1, NCNWP.

89. Virginia Caye, "Trip Report: Swaziland, Lesotho, and Botswana," March 1– May 28, 1979, 1 and 7–8, Series 37, Folder 39, NCNWP.

90. Minutes of Advisory Board Meeting, Dec. 17–18, 1977, 4.

91. Assistant Inspector General for Audit, *Memorandum Audit Report, No. 85-19*, http://pdf.usaid.gov/pdf_docs/PDAAR460.pdf.

92. Minutes of Advisory Board Meeting, Dec. 17–18, 1977, 4–5.

93. NCNW, "Press Release," May 1978, 1, Series 37, Folder 28, NCNWP. For more on Wilbert Petty, see "Diplomat Assures in Africans or Us," *Afro-American*, October 22, 1983, 7.

94. NCNW, "Press Release," May 1978, 2–3; and "NCNW Furthers Outreach to Women of Africa," *Philadelphia Tribune*, July 7, 1978, 5.

95. NCNW, "'Fulfilling the Promise,' 1979 NCNW Annual Report," 8–9, Series 2, Folder 257, NCNWP; and Memo from Ruth A. Sykes to Bessie Chukuocha, Barbara Smith, and Donald Brannon, August 22, 1979, Series 37, Folder 40, NCNWP.

96. NCNW, Status Report on Grant No. AID/afr-G-1601 Lakara Skills Training Center Project, August 10, 1981, 2–5, http://pdf.usaid.gov/pdf_docs/xdaan268a.pdf.

97. "International Division Offers Help to Third World Women," *Black Woman's Voice* 10, no. 1 (1985), 3, as found in Subgroup 1.13 (A87), Series 200, Box R2378, RFR.

98. Height, *Open Wide the Freedom Gates*, 188–89.

99. "National Council Receives $310,000 Grant from AID," *Afro-American*, April 26, 1980, 13; and USAID, "Evaluation Executive Summary," Lundzi-Mpuluzi Pig Production, June 16, 1982, 171, http://pdf.usaid.gov/pdf_docs/PDAAR957.pdf.

100. NCNW, "Final Report: The Lundzi-Mpuluzi Pig Production Project," USAID Report, April 14, 1987, [7], http://pdf.usaid.gov/pdf_docs/PDBBJ789.pdf.

101. Ibid., [3–4].

102. Ibid., [8].

103. USAID, "Evaluation Executive Summary," Lundzi-Mpuluzi Pig Production, June 16, 1982, 172, http://pdf.usaid.gov/pdf_docs/PDAAR957.pdf.

104. Ibid., 170; and NCNW, "Final Report: The Lundzi-Mpuluzi Pig Production Project," USAID Report, April 14, 1987, [4–5].

105. Height, interview by Cowan, February 1, 1976, 226.

106. Height, *Open Wide the Freedom Gates*, 245.

107. "NCNW Furthers Outreach to Women of Africa."

108. Vivian Lowery Derryck, "International Divison," Forty-First National Convention Program, November 2–6, 1983, Series 2, Folder 265, NCNWP.

109. "International Division Offers Help to Third World Women," 3.

110. Rockefeller Foundation Internal Memo, August 1, 1985; and NCNW, "Third International Leaders' Seminar: Dialogue between African and American Women on Developments during the Decade," projects RG 1.9–RG 1.15, Subgroup 1.13: Rockefeller Foundation Records Project (A87), S200: United States, R2378, RFR.

111. See "Frequently Asked Questions," NCNW website, accessed May 1, 2017, http://www.ncnw.org/faq/. According to Height, the NCNW was the only private voluntary African American women's organization registered with USAID at the time of her autobiography's publication in 2003. Height, *Open Wide the Freedom Gates*, 244.

Conclusion

1. Chafe, *Unfinished Journey*, 451–53; and Culverson, 232–33.

2. Reagon, interview by Tuuri, July 26, 2017.

3. Dorothy Height, "Statement Made by Dorothy I. Height," July 28, 1983, as found in NCNW, Inc., Forty-First National Convention Program, 1983, Series 2, Folder 265, NCNWP.

4. Chafe, *Unfinished Journey*, 465–66.

5. Height, *Open Wide the Freedom Gates*, 214–16. In the Reagan era, Bill Cosby, as onscreen patriarch of the *Cosby Show*, helped redefine what black families looked like for many Americans. Height befriended both Cosby and his wife, and they have been important donors to the council from the 1980s to the present. However, his role as a champion of black family values has been undermined by his conservative criticism of poor black communities, especially young men (see Dyson, *Is Cosby Right?*), and the multiple rape allegations that have come to light since 2014. See Lorne Manly and Graham Bowley, "Cosby Team's Strategy: Hush Accusers, Insult Them, Blame the Media," *New York Times*, December 28, 2014, https://www.nytimes.com/2014/12/29/arts/cosby-teams-strategy-hush-accusers-insult-them-blame-the-media.html. Women had accused Cosby of assault while Dorothy Height was still alive, but Height was silent on these accusations. In fact, in her 2003 autobiography, Height called Cosby a proponent of "family values." Perhaps Height's silence was due to the fact that Camille Cosby herself has been a vocal defender of her husband amid these allegations. Serge F. Kovaleski, "Wife of Bill Cosby Places Fault with News Media," *New York Times*, December 15, 2014, https://www.nytimes.com/2014/12/16/us/bill-cosbys-wife-comes-to-his-defense.html.

6. After her time with Project Womanpower, Dozier Crenshaw went to work for Joe Reed, the first black city councilman in Montgomery; Ben Brown, one of the first black legislators in Georgia; Jimmy Carter; Jesse Jackson; and Walter Mondale. After all that political organizing, she was asked by Coretta Scott King to help with mobilization for the first celebration of Martin Luther King Day. See Crenshaw, interview by Tuuri, May 24, 2017; and Sewell, "Doris Dozier Crenshaw," *Congressional Record* 161: E1773.

7. Kornbluh, *Battle for Welfare Rights*, 159; Levenstein, *Movement without Marches*, 190; Nadasen, *Welfare Warriors*, 196; and Orleck, *Storming Caesars Palace*, 5, 86.

8. National Council of Negro Women, Inc., *Black Family Reunion Cookbook*, iii.

9. Crenshaw, interview by Tuuri, May 24, 2017.

10. Height, *Open Wide the Freedom Gates*, 216.

11. Ibid., 216–17.

12. Ibid., 278–79; Estes, *I Am a Man*, 181–82; Harris-Lacewell, *Barbershops, Bibles, and BET*, 210–18; D. G. White, *Lost in the USA*, 112–14; and Michel Marriott, "Black Women Are Split over All-Male March on Washington," *New York Times*, October 14, 1995, http://www.nytimes.com/1995/10/14/us/black-women-are-split-over-all-male-march-on-washington.html.

13. Height, *Open Wide the Freedom Gates*, 279–80.

14. Ibid., 262–63, 273.

15. Ibid., 273–75.

16. Ibid., 275–77.

17. Ibid., 258, 277, 280–83.

18. Ibid., 284–86.

19. "Obama's Remarks at Dorothy Height's Funeral Service," *New York Times*, April 29, 2010, http://www.nytimes.com/2010/04/30/us/politics/30height-text.html.

20. Ibid.

21. Kern-Foxworth, *Aunt Jemima, Uncle Ben, and Rastus*, 99, 104–105.

22. "Strange Bedfellows," *Philadelphia Inquirer*, October 30, 1991, 2E.

23. Quote is from NCNW, "Economic and Entrepreneurial Development," accessed July 18, 2017, http://www.ncnw.org/economic-and-entrepreneurial-development-center/. Other programs can be found at http://www.ncnw.org/programs/power-of-property-ownership/, http://www.ncnw.org/programs/career-centermentoring/, http://www.ncnw.org/programs/stem-education/, and http://www.ncnw.org/programs/health/ (all accessed July 18, 2017).

Bibliography

Primary Sources

MANUSCRIPT COLLECTIONS

California
  Berkeley
    Personal Collection of Dr. Ula Taylor
      Beal, Frances. Interview by Ula Taylor. June 21, 2017
  Los Angeles
    Interview Collection of the Wednesdays in Mississippi Film Project
      Clopton-Mosley, Wilma. Interview by Marlene McCurtis, Jackson, Mississippi, January 23, 2008
      Hendrick, Mary F. Interview by Marlene McCurtis, Jackson, Mississippi, January 21, 2008
      Purvis, Janet. Interview by Marlene McCurtis, Jackson, Mississippi, January 22, 2008
      Shands, Janet K. Interview by Marlene McCurtis, Jackson, Mississippi, January 24, 2008
      Shirley, Ollye Brown. Interview by Marlene McCurtis, Jackson, Mississippi, January 23, 2008
Louisiana
  New Orleans
    Amistad Research Center, Tulane University
      Papers of Clarie Collins Harvey
      Papers of Fannie Lou Hamer
Massachusetts
  Cambridge
    Black Women Oral History Project, Arthur and Elizabeth Schlesinger Library, Radcliffe College
      Height, Dorothy. Interview by Polly Cowan, February 11, April 10, May 29, October 6, November 10, 1974; February 2, March 28, May 25, October 5, 1975; February 1, May 31, November 6, 1976
  Northampton
    Sophia Smith Collection, Smith College
      YWCA Papers
Mississippi
  Hattiesburg

McCain Library and Archives, University of SouthernMississippi
    Blackwell, Unita. Interview by Michael Garvey, April 21 and May 12, 1977
    Talbert, Ernestine Denham. Interview by Charles Bolton, 1997
    Peggy Jean Connor Papers
Jackson
    Margaret Walker Center, Jackson State University
        Harvey, Clarie Collins. Interview by Alfredteen Harrison, September 17,
            1994
        Harvey, Clarie Collins. Interview by Alfredteen Harrison, October 8, 1994
        Womanpower Unlimited Papers
    Millsaps College
        Schutt, Jane. Interview by unnamed, July 16, 1965
    Mississippi Department of Archives and History
        Clarie Collins Harvey Subject File
        Harvey, Clarie Collins. Interview by John Dittmer, April 21, 1981
        Jessie Mosley Subject File
        Mississippi State Sovereignty Commission Papers
        Schutt, Jane. Interview by John Dittmer, February 22, 1981
        Unita Blackwell Subject File
Oxford
    Archives and Special Collections, University of Mississippi
        The Papers of Fannie Lou Hamer
Starkville
    Mississippi State Archives
        Papers of Patt Derian
New York
    Sleepy Hollow
        Rockefeller Archive Center
            Ford Foundation Records
            Rockefeller Brothers Fund Records
            Rockefeller Foundation Records
            Taconic Foundation Records
North Carolina
    Chapel Hill
        Southern Oral History Program Collection, Oral Histories of the American South,
            University of North Carolina
            Derian, Patt. Interview by Jack Bass and Walter DeVries, March 25, 1974
            Fairfax, Jean. Interview by Dallas A. Blanchard, October 15, 1983
Texas
    Austin
        Lyndon B. Johnson Presidential Library
            White House Central Files
            White House Name File—Dorothy Height

Virginia
  Charlottesville
    Personal Collection of Holly Shulman
      Davis, Jean. Interview by Holly Cowan Shulman, June 27, 2002
      Davis, Miriam. Interview by Holly Cowan Shulman, Washington, D.C., November 16, 2002
      Grieffen, Faith. Interview by Christy Jones, Lexington, Massachusetts, July 25, 2003
      Hayes, Alice Ryerson. Interview by Christy Jones, Wake Forest, Illinois, July 27, 2003
      Height, Dorothy I. Interview by Holly Cowan Shulman, October 16, 2002
      Height, Dorothy I. Interview by Holly Cowan Shulman, January 24, 2003
      Mayer, Buddy. Interview by Holly Cowan Shulman, Chicago, Illinois, June 25, 2002
      Radov, Sylvia Weinberg. Interview by Amy Merle, Chicago, Illinois, June 25, 2002
      Stedman, Susie Goodwillie. Interview by Holly Cowan Shulman, Westport Island, Maine, October 20, 2002
      Wednesdays in Mississippi Memorabilia
    University of Virginia
      Wednesdays in Mississippi Papers
      Papers of Jean S. Davis, 1965–2001
      Papers of Marguerite Cassell, 1965–2001
      Papers of Susan Goodwillie Stedman, 1964
      Papers of Sylvia Weinberg Radov, 1965–66
      Wednesdays in Mississippi General Background Material, 1965
Washington, D.C.
  Library of Congress
    National Council of Jewish Women Papers
    USAID Electronic Files
  Moorland-Spingarn Research Center, Howard University
    The Civil Rights Documentation Project
      Batson, Ruth. Interview by Katherine M. Shannon, December 27, 1967
      Blackwell, Unita. Interview by Robert Wright, Mayersville, Mississippi, August 10, 1968
      Cowan, Polly. Interview by John Britton, New York City, March 8, 1968
      Devine, Annie. Interview by Robert Wright, Canton, Mississippi, September 29, 1968
      Hamer, Fannie Lou. Interview by Robert Wright, August 9, 1968
      Height, Dorothy. Interview by James Mosby, New York City, February 13, 1970
      Murray, Pauli. Interview by Robert Martin, August 15 and 17, 1968

National Archives of Black Women's History, Mary McLeod Bethune Council
    House
National Council of Negro Women Papers
Papers of Polly Cowan

INTERVIEWS BY TUURI

Adams, Nellie, Ruby Ella Kirk, and Louise Cole, group interview, February 8, 2016
Barber, Barbara. Jackson, Mississippi, June 13, 2008
Barber, Rims. Jackson, Mississippi, April 18, 2008
Beard, Gabrielle. Greensboro, North Carolina, May 1, 2008
Blackwell, Unita. Mayersville, Mississippi, January 16, 2008
Boyer, Margaret. Oxford, Mississippi, April 24, 2008
Brooks, Owen. Jackson, Mississippi, April 16, 2008
Collier-Thomas, Bettye. Cherry Hill, New Jersey, January 12, 2017
Crenshaw, Doris Dozier. Telephone interview, May 24, 2017
Derian, Patt. Chapel Hill, North Carolina, April 30, 2008
Doar, John. New York City, October 23, 2007
Gray-Wiseman, Sammie Lee Keyes. Gulfport, Mississippi, January 22, 2016, and
    telephone conversation, September 24, 2016
Green, Winifred. New Orleans, Louisiana, September 17, 2007
Jennings, Edith Savage. Trenton, New Jersey, July 9, 2009
Logan, A. M. E. Jackson, Mississippi, December 19, 2007
McLaurin, Charles. Ruleville, Mississippi, April 23, 2008
Pfeiffer, Earl. Telephone interview. April 10, 2014
Rachlin, Helen Raebeck. New York City, March 11, 2009
Reagan, Merble. Telephone interview, July 26, 2017
Riley, Kewanna. Gulfport, Mississippi, January 22, 2016
Shulman, Holly Cowan. Washington, D.C., December 13, 2007
Simmons, Gwendolyn Zoharah. Telephone interview, May 24, 2017
Spinks-Thigpen, Mary. Gulfport, Mississippi, November 19, 2015
Stedman, Susie Goodwillie. Westport Island, Maine, June 2009
Wilson, Doris. Pittsburgh, Pennsylvania, May 17, 2008

NEWSPAPERS AND PERIODICALS

Aframerican Woman's Journal (NCNW)
Akron Beacon Journal (Akron, Ohio)
Atlanta Daily World
Baltimore Sun
Black Woman's Voice (NCNW)
Call and Post (Cleveland, Ohio)
Chicago Defender
Clarion-Ledger
Delta Democrat-Times
Ebony
Enterprise-Tocsin (Indianola, Mississippi)
International Division Newsletter
(NCNW)
Jet
Los Angeles Sentinel
New York Amsterdam News
New York Times
Oakland Tribune

Philadelphia Inquirer   *Sisters* (NCNW)
Philadelphia Tribune   *Telefact* (NCNW)
Pittsburgh Courier   *Washington Post*
Selma Times-Journal   *World Ark*

GOVERNMENT DOCUMENTS

Agency for International Development. *Women in Development: 1980 Report to
    the Committee on Foreign Relations, United States Senate, and the Committee on
    Foreign Affairs, United States House of Representatives.* Washington, D.C.: Office
    of Women in Development, 1980. http://files.eric.ed.gov/fulltext/ED212893.pdf.
Bolton, Frances P., Hon. "Extension of Remarks." 86th Congress, First Session.
    Congressional Record, August 17, 1959.
Comptroller General of the United States. *Problems in the Homeownership
    Opportunities Program for Low-Income Families.* Washington, D.C.: U.S. General
    Accounting Office. March 27, 1974. http://gao.gov/assets/210/201113.pdf.
Daniel P. Moynihan and the Office of Policy Planning and Research. United States
    Department of Labor. *The Negro Family: The Case for National Action.* Washington,
    D.C.: Government Printing Office, 1965.
National Advisory Commission on Civil Disorders. *Report of the National Advisory
    Commission on Civil Disorders.* Washington, D.C.: Government Printing Office,
    1968.
National Council of Negro Women and the U.S. Department of Housing and Urban
    Development. *Women and Housing: A Report on Sex Discrimination in Five
    American Cities.* Washington, D.C.: Government Printing Office, June 1975.
Office of the Assistant Inspector General for Audit. *Memorandum Audit Report on
    National Council of Negro Women Audit Report No. 85-19*, August 26, 1985. http://pdf
    .usaid.gov/pdf_docs/PDAAR460.pdf.
Office of the Federal Register Government Printing Office. *Title 24 Housing and
    Urban Development: Parts 700 to 1699.* Washington, D.C.: 2013.
President's Commission on the Status of Women. *American Women: Report of
    the President's Commission on the Status of Women.* Washington, D.C.: Government
    Printing Office, 1963.
————. *Four Consultations: Private Employment Opportunities, New Patterns in
    Volunteer Work, Portrayal of Women by the Mass Media, Problems of Negro Women.*
    Washington, D.C.: Government Printing Office, 1963.
Sewell, Terri A. "Tribute to Doris Doris Dozier Crenshaw." *Congressional Record* 161.
    114th Cong., 1st sess., December 11, 2015. Washington, D.C.: Government Printing
    Office, 2015.
U.S. Agency for International Development, Africa Bureau. "Evaluation Executive
    Summary." Lundzi-Mpuluzi Pig Production. June 16, 1982. *Evaluation Review Project* III,
    169–72. http://pdf.usaid.gov/pdf_docs/PDAAR957.pdf.
U.S. Congress. *Congressional Record.* 86th Cong., 1st sess., 1959. Washington, D.C.:
    Government Printing Office, 1959.

U.S. Department of Housing and Urban Development. *The Evolution of HUD's Public-Private Partnerships.* Washington, D.C.: Office of Policy Development and Research, October 2015, https://www.huduser.gov/hud50th/HUD2-048-Public -Private_Partnership_508.pdf.

U.S. Department of Justice, Office of Juvenile Justice and Delinquency Prevention. *Programs for Young Women in Trouble.* Washington, D.C.: National Criminal Justice Reference Service, July 1981, microfilm, #79977.

Secondary Sources

Abramovitz, Mimi. *Regulating the Lives of Women: Social Welfare Policy from Colonial Times to the Present.* Boston: South End Press, 1992.

Adickes, Sandra. *The Legacy of a Freedom School.* New York: Palgrave Macmillan, 2005.

Alexander, Michelle. *The New Jim Crow: Mass Incarceration in the Age of Colorblindness.* New York: New Press, 2010.

Anderson, Carol. "Bleached Souls and Red Negroes: The NAACP and Black Communists in the Early Cold War, 1948–1952." In *Window on Freedom: Race, Civil Rights, and Foreign Affairs 1945–1988,* edited by Brenda Gayle Plummer, 93–113. Chapel Hill: University of North Carolina Press, 2003.

———. *Bourgeois Radicals: The NAACP and the Struggle for Colonial Liberation, 1941–1960.* New York: Cambridge, 2015.

———. *Eyes off the Prize: The United Nations and the African American Struggle for Human Rights, 1944–1955.* New York: Cambridge, 2003.

Anderson, Karen. "National Council of Negro Women." In *Organizing Black America: An Encyclopedia of African American Organizations,* edited by Nina Mjagkij, 446–51. New York: Garland, 2001.

Asch, Chris Myers. *The Senator and the Sharecropper: The Freedom Struggle of James O. Eastland and Fannie Lou Hamer.* Chapel Hill: University of North Carolina Press, 2008.

Aten, Jamie D., and David M. Boan. *Disaster Ministry Handbook.* Downers Grove, Ill.: Intervarsity Press, 2016.

Barker, Michael. "Elite Philanthropy, SNCC, and the Civil Rights Movement." *Swans Commentary,* November 15, 2010, http://www.swans.com/library/art16/barker69 .html.

Bates, Beth Tompkins. *Pullman Porters and the Rise of Protest Politics in Black America, 1925–1945.* Chapel Hill: University of North Carolina Press, 2001.

Beal, Frances M. "Double Jeopardy: To Be Black and Female." In *Sisterhood Is Powerful: An Anthology of Writings from the Women's Liberation Movement,* edited by Robin Morgan. New York: Random House, 1970.

Beal, Frances M., and Loretta J. Ross. "Excerpts from the *Voices of Feminism Oral History Project*: Interview with Frances Beal." *Meridians: Feminism, Race, Transnationalism* 8, no. 2 (2008): 126–65.

Belfrage, Sally. *Freedom Summer.* New York: Viking, 1965.

Blackwell, Unita. *Barefootin': Life Lessons from the Road to Freedom*. New York: Crown, 2006.

Bloom, Jack M. *Class, Race, and the Civil Rights Movement*. Bloomington: Indiana University Press, 1987.

Bolton, Charles. *The Hardest Deal of All: The Battle over School Integration in Mississippi, 1870–1980*. Jackson: University Press of Mississippi, 2005.

Bonastia, Christopher. *Southern Stalemate: Five Years without Public Education in Prince Edward County, Virginia*. Chicago: University of Chicago Press, 2011.

Brooks, Maegan Parker. *A Voice That Could Stir an Army: Fannie Lou Hamer and the Rhetoric of the Black Freedom Movement*. Jackson: University Press of Mississippi, 2014.

Brooks, Maegan Parker, and Davis W. Houck, eds. *The Speeches of Fannie Lou Hamer: "To Tell It Like It Is."* Jackson: University Press of Mississippi, 2011.

Burstein, Joseph. "New Techniques in Public Housing." *Law and Contemporary Problems* 32, no. 3 (Summer 1967): 528–49.

Butler, Anthea. "'Only a Woman Would Do': Bible Reading and African American Women's Organizing Work." In *Women and Religion in the African Diaspora: Knowledge, Power, and Performance*, edited by R. Marie Griffith and Barbara Dianne Savage, 155–178. Baltimore: Johns Hopkins University Press, 2006.

Butler, Judith. *Gender Trouble: Feminism and the Subversion of Identity*. New York: Routledge, 1990.

Carmichael, Stokely. *Ready for Revolution: The Life and Struggle of Stokely Carmichael*. New York: Scribner, 2005.

Carmichael, Stokely, and Charles V. Hamilton. *Black Power: The Politics of Liberation in America*. London: Cape, 1968.

Carson, Clayborne. *In Struggle: SNCC and the Black Awakening of the 1960s*. 1981. Reprint, Cambridge, Mass.: Harvard University Press, 1995.

Chafe, William H., ed. *The Achievement of American Liberalism*. New York: Columbia, 2003.

———. *Civilities and Civil Rights: Greensboro, North Carolina and the Black Struggle for Freedom*. New York: Oxford University Press, 1981.

———. *The Unfinished Journey: America since World War II*. 7th ed. New York: Oxford University Press, 2011.

Cha-Jua, Sundiata Keita, and Clarence Lang. "The 'Long Movement' as Vampire: Temporal and Spatial Fallacies in Recent Black Freedom Studies." *Journal of African American History* 92 (Spring 2007): 265–88.

Chappell, Marissa, Jenny Hutchinson, and Brian Ward, "'Dress Modestly, Neatly ... as If You Were Going to Church': Respectability, Class and Gender in the Montgomery Bus Boycott and the Early Civil Rights Movement." In *Gender and the Civil Rights Movement*, edited by Peter J. Ling and Sharon Monteith, 69–100. New Brunswick, N.J.: Rutgers University Press, 2004.

Clark, Robert F. *Victory Deferred: The War on Global Poverty (1945–2003)*. Lanham, Md.: University Press of America, 2005.

———. *The War on Poverty: History, Selected Programs, and Ongoing Impact*. Lanham, Md.: University Press of America, 2002.

Cobble, Dorothy Sue. "More Than Sex Equality: Feminism after Suffrage." In *Feminism Unfinished: A Short, Surprising History of American Women's Movements*, edited by Dorothy Sue Cobble, Linda Gordon, and Astrid Henry, 1–67. New York: W. W. Norton, 2014.

Cohen, Lizabeth. *A Consumer's Republic: The Politics of Mass Consumption in Postwar America*. New York: Vintage, 2004.

Collier-Thomas, Bettye. *Jesus, Jobs, and Justice: African American Women and Religion*. Philadelphia: Temple University Press, 2014.

———. "National Council of Negro Women." In *Black Women in America: An Historical Encyclopedia*. Vol. 2, edited by Darlene Clark Hine, Rosalind Terborg Penn, and Elsa Barkely Brown, 853–64. Brooklyn: Carlson, 1993.

———. *N.C.N.W., 1935–1980*. Washington, D.C.: National Council of Negro Women, 1981.

Collier-Thomas, Bettye, and V. P. Franklin. "For the Race in General and Black Women in Particular." In *Sisters in the Struggle: African American Women in the Civil Rights-Black Power Movement*, edited by Franklin and Collier-Thomas, 21–41. New York: New York University Press, 2001.

Collins, Patricia Hill. *Black Feminist Thought: Knowledge, Consciousness, and the Politics of Empowerment*. New York: Routledge, 2000.

Cooper, Brittney C. *Beyond Respectability: The Intellectual Thought of Race Women*. Urbana: University of Illinois, 2017.

Cowan, Paul. *An Orphan in History: One Man's Triumphant Search for His Jewish Roots*. Woodstock, Vt.: Jewish Lights, 2002.

Crawford, Vicki L., Jacqueline Rouse, and Barbara Woods, eds. *Women in the Civil Rights Movement: Trailblazers and Torchbearers*. 1990. Reprint, Bloomington: Indiana University Press, 1993.

Crenshaw, Kimberle. "Mapping the Margins: Intersectionality, Identity Politics, and Violence against Women of Color." *Stanford Law Review* 43, no. 6 (July 1991): 1241–99.

Crosby, Emilye. *A Little Taste of Freedom: The Black Freedom Struggle in Claiborne County, Mississippi*. Chapel Hill: University of North Carolina Press, 2005.

———, ed. *Civil Rights History from the Ground Up: Local Struggles, a National Movement*. Athens: University of Georgia Press, 2011.

Culverson, Donald R. "From Cold War to Global Interdependence: The Political Economy of African American Antiapartheid Activism, 1968–1988." In *Window on Freedom: Race, Civil Rights, and Foreign Affairs, 1945–1988*, edited by Brenda Gayle Plummer, 221–38. Chapel Hill: University of North Carolina Press, 2003.

Curry, Constance, ed. *Deep in Our Hearts: Nine White Women in the Freedom Movement*. Athens, Ga.: University of Georgia Press, 2000.

———. *Silver Rights*. Chapel Hill, N.C.: Algonquin Books, 1995.

Davis, Angela. *Women, Race, and Class*. New York: Random House, 1983.

De Schweinitz, Rebecca. *If We Could Change the World: Young People and America's Long Struggle for Racial Equality*. Chapel Hill: University of North Carolina Press, 2009.

Dickerson, Dennis C. *Militant Mediator—Whitney M. Young, Jr.* Lexington: University Press of Kentucky, 1998.

Dittmer, John. *The Good Doctors: The Medical Committee for Human Rights and the Struggle for Social Justice in Health Care*. New York: Bloomsbury Press, 2009.

———. *Local People: The Struggle for Civil Rights in Mississippi*. Urbana: University of Illinois Press, 1995.

Dollinger, Marc. *The Quest for Inclusion: Jews and Liberalism in Modern America*. Princeton, N.J.: Princeton University Press, 2000.

Dudziak, Mary. *Cold War Civil Rights: Race and the Image of American Democracy*. Princeton, N.J.: Princeton University Press, 2000.

Dyson, Michael Eric. *Is Cosby Right? Or Has the Black Middle Class Lost Its Mind?* New York: Basic Civitas Books, 2005.

Eagles, Charles W. *The Price of Defiance: James Meredith and the Integration of Ole Miss*. Chapel Hill: University of North Carolina Press, 2009.

Eaton, Susan. *The Other Boston Busing Story: What's Won and Lost across the Boundary Line*. New Haven, Conn.: Yale University Press, 2001.

Estepa, Andrea. "Taking the White Gloves Off: Women Strike for Peace and 'the Movement,' 1967–73." In *Feminist Coalitions: Historical Perspectives on Second-Wave Feminism in the United States*, edited by Stephanie Gilmore, 84–112. Urbana: University of Illinois Press, 2008.

Estes, Steve. *I Am a Man: Race, Manhood, and the Civil Rights Movement*. Chapel Hill: University of North Carolina Press, 2005.

Evans, Sara. *Personal Politics: The Roots of Women's Liberation in the Civil Rights Movement and the New Left*. New York: Knopf, 1979.

Feimster, Crystal N. *Southern Horrors: Women and the Politics of Rape and Lynching*. Cambridge: Harvard University Press, 2011.

Feldstein, Ruth. *Motherhood in Black and White: Race and Sex in American Liberalism, 1930–1965*. Ithaca, N.Y.: Cornell University Press, 2000.

Felker-Kantor, Max. "'Kid Thugs Are Spreading Terror through the Streets': Youth, Crime, and the Expansion of the Juvenile Justice System in Los Angeles, 1973–1980." *Journal of Urban History*, January 22, 2016. doi:10.1177/0096144215623260.

Fergus, Devin. *Liberalism, Black Power, and the Making of American Politics, 1965–1980*. Athens: University of Georgia Press, 2009.

Ferguson, Karen. *Top Down: The Ford Foundation, Black Power, and the Reinvention of Racial Liberalism*. Philadelphia: University of Pennsylvania Press, 2013.

Findlay, James F. *Church People in the Struggle: The National Council of Churches and the Black Freedom Movement, 1950–1970*. New York: Oxford University Press, 1993.

Fitzgerald, Tracey. *The National Council of Negro Women and the Feminist Movement, 1935–1975*. Washington, D.C.: Georgetown University Press, 1985.

Ford, Tanisha C. *Liberated Threads: Black Women, Style, and the Global Politics of Soul*. Chapel Hill: University of North Carolina Press, 2015.

———. "SNCC Women, Denim, and the Politics of Dress." *Journal of Southern History*, August 2013, 625–58.

Forman, James. *The Making of Black Revolutionaries 1972.* Reprint, Seattle: University of Washington Press, 1997.

Formisano, Ronald P. *Boston Against Busing: Race, Class, and Ethnicity in the 1960s and 1970s.* Chapel Hill: University of North Carolina Press, 1991.

Fosl, Catherine. "Anne Braden and the 'Protective Custody' of White Southern Womanhood." In *Throwing Off the Cloak of Privilege*, edited by Gail S. Murray, 101–130. Gainesville: University Press of Florida, 2004.

———. *Subversive Southerner: Anne Braden and the Struggle for Racial Justice in the Cold War South.* New York City: Palgrave, 2002.

Frazier, E. Franklin. *Black Bourgeoisie.* 1957. Reprint, New York: Free Press, 1997.

———. *The Negro Family in the United States.* Chicago: University of Chicago Press, 1939.

Funk, Nanette. "Women's NGOs in Central and Eastern Europe and the Former Soviet Union: The Imperialist Criticism." In *Women and Citizenship in Central and Eastern Europe*, edited by Jasmina Lukić, Joanna Regulska, and Darja Zaviršek, 265–86. Aldershot, U.K.: Ashgate, 2006.

Gaines, Kevin. *African Americans in Ghana: Black Expatriates and the Civil Rights Era.* Chapel Hill: University of North Carolina Press, 2006.

———. *Uplifting the Race: Black Leadership, Politics, and Culture in the Twentieth Century.* Chapel Hill: University of North Carolina, 1996.

Gallagher, Julie A. *Black Women and Politics in New York City.* Urbana: University of Illinois Press, 2012.

———. "The National Council of Negro Women, Human Rights, and the Cold War." In *Breaking the Wave: Women, Their Organizations, and Feminism, 1945–1985*, edited by Kathleen A. Laughlin and Jacqueline L. Castledine, 80–98. New York: Routledge, 2011.

Geary, Daniel. *Beyond Civil Rights: The Moynihan Report and Its Legacy.* Philadelphia: University of Pennsylvania Press, 2015.

Germany, Kent. *New Orleans after the Promises: Poverty, Citizenship, and the Search for the Great Society.* Athens: University of Georgia, 2007.

Gerstle, Gary. *American Crucible: Race and Nation in the Twentieth Century.* Princeton, N.J.: Princeton University Press, 2002.

Ghodsee, Kristen. "Revisiting the United Nations Decade for Women: Brief Reflections on Feminism, Capitalism and Cold War Politics in the Early Years of the International Women's Movement." *Women's Studies International Forum* 33 (2010): 3–12. doi:10.1016/j.wsif.2009.11.008.

Giddings, Paula. *In Search of Sisterhood: Delta Sigma Theta and the Challenge of the Black Sorority Movement.* 1988. Reprint, New York: Armistad, 2006.

———. *When and Where I Enter: The Impact of Black Women on Race and Sex in America.* 1984. Reprint, New York: Armistad, 2006.

Gill, Tiffany. *Beauty Shop Politics: African American Women's Activism in the Beauty Industry.* Urbana-Champaign: University of Illinois Press, 2010.

Gilmore, Glenda. *Gender and Jim Crow: Women and the Politics of White Supremacy in North Carolina, 1896–1920.* Chapel Hill: University of North Carolina, 1996.

Gilmore, Stephanie, ed. *Feminist Coalitions: Historical Perspectives on Second-Wave Feminism in the United States.* Urbana: University of Illinois Press, 2008.

Glenn, Evelyn Nakano. *Unequal Freedom: How Race and Gender Shaped American Citizenship and Labor.* Boston: Harvard University, 2004.

gloria-yvonne. "Mary McLeod Bethune, the National Council of Negro Women, and the Prewar Push for Equal Opportunity in Defense Projects." In *The Economic Civil Rights Movement: African Americans and the Struggle for Economic Power,* 22–34. New York: Routledge, 2013.

Gordon, Linda. *Pitied But Not Entitled: Single Mothers and the History of Welfare.* New York: Free Press, 1994.

Gore, Dayo F. *Radicalism at the Crossroads: African American Women Activists in the Cold War.* New York: New York University Press, 2011.

Gore, Dayo F., Jeanne Theoharis, and Komozi Woodard, eds. *Want to Start a Revolution? Radical Women in the Black Freedom Struggle.* New York: New York University Press, 2009.

Goudsouzian, Aram. *Down to the Crossroads: Civil Rights, Black Power, and the Meredith March Against Fear.* New York: Farrar, Straus, and Giroux, 2014.

Grant, Nicholas. "The National Council of Negro Women and South Africa: Black Internationalism, Motherhood, and the Cold War." *Palimpsest* 5, no. 1 (2016): 59–87.

Green, Laurie. "Challenging the Civil Rights Narrative: Women, Gender, and the Politics of Protection." In *Civil Rights from the Ground Up: Local Struggles, A National Movement,* edited by Emilye Crosby, 52–80. Athens: University of Georgia Press, 2011.

Greenberg, Polly. *The Devil Has Slippery Shoes: A Biased Biography of the Child Development Group of Mississippi (CDGM), a Story of Maximum Feasible Poor Parent Participation.* 1969. Reprint, Washington D.C.: Youth Policy Institute, 1990.

Greene, Christina. *Our Separate Ways: Women and the Black Freedom Movement in Durham, North Carolina.* Chapel Hill: University of North Carolina Press, 2005.

Greene, Mark. "Impact of the Sahelian Drought in Mauritania, West Africa." *Lancet* 303, no. 7866 (June 1974): 1093–97.

Guy-Sheftall, Beverly, ed. *Words of Fire: An Anthology of African-American Feminist Thought.* New York: New Press, 1995.

Hall, Jacquelyn Dowd. "The Long Civil Rights Movement and the Political Uses of the Past." *Journal of American History* 91 (March 2005): 1233–63.

———. *Revolt against Chivalry: Jessie Daniel Ames and the Women's Campaign against Lynching.* New York City: Columbia University Press, 1979.

Hamlin, Françoise N. "Collision and Collusion: Local Activism, Local Agency, and Flexible Alliances." In *The Civil Rights Movement,* edited by Ted Ownby, 35–58. Jackson: University of Mississippi Press, 2013.

———. *Crossroads at Clarksdale: The Black Freedom Struggle in the Mississippi Delta after World War II.* Chapel Hill: University of North Carolina Press, 2012.

Hanson, Joyce A. *Mary McLeod Bethune and Black Women's Political Activism*. Columbia: University of Missouri Press, 2003.

Harley, Sharon. "'Chronicle of a Death Foretold': Gloria Richardson, the Cambridge Movement, and the Radical Black Activist Tradition." In *Sisters in the Struggle: African American Women in the Civil Rights-Black Power Movement*, edited by Bettye Collier-Thomas and V. P. Franklin. New York: New York University Press, 2001.

Harris, Anthony. *Ain't Gonna Let Nobody Turn Me 'Round: A Coming-of-Age Story and Personal Account of the Civil Rights Movement in Hattiesburg, Mississippi*. Self-published, CreateSpace, 2013.

Harris, Duchess. *Black Feminist Politics from Kennedy to Obama*. New York: Palgrave Macmillan, 2011.

Harris-Lacewell, Melissa Victoria. *Barbershops, Bibles, and BET: Everyday Talk and Black Political Thought*. Princeton, N.J.: Princeton University Press, 2004.

Hartmann, Susan. *From Margin to Mainstream: American Women and Politics since 1960*. New York: McGraw-Hill, 1996.

———. *The Other Feminists: Activists in the Liberal Establishment*. New Haven, Conn.: Yale University Press, 1998.

———. "Women's Employment and the Domestic Ideal in the Early Cold War Years." In *Not June Cleaver: Women and Gender in Postwar America, 1945–1960*, edited by Joanne Meyerowitz, 84–100. Philadelphia: Temple University Press, 1994.

Harwell, Debbie. *Wednesdays in Mississippi: Proper Women Working for Radical Change*. Jackson: University Press of Mississippi, 2014.

———. "Wednesdays in Mississippi: Uniting Women across Regional and Racial Lines, Summer 1964." *Journal of Southern History* 76, no. 3 (August 2010): 617–54.

Hedgeman, Anna Arnold. *The Gift of Chaos: Decades of American Discontent*. New York: Oxford University Press, 1977.

———. *The Trumpet Sounds: A Memoir of Negro Leadership*. New York: Holt, Rinehart, and Winston, 1964.

Height, Dorothy I. *Living with Purpose: An Activist's Guide to Listening, Learning, and Leading*. Washington, DC: Dorothy Height Education Foundation, 2010.

———. *Open Wide the Freedom Gates: A Memoir*. New York: PublicAffairs, 2003.

———. "We Wanted the Voice of a Woman to Be Heard." In *Sisters in the Struggle: African American Women in the Civil Rights-Black Power Movement*, edited by Bettye Collier-Thomas and V. P. Franklin, 83–92. New York: New York University Press, 2001.

Higginbotham, Evelyn Brooks. "African-American Women's History and the Metalanguage of Race." *Signs* 17, no. 2 (1992): 251–74.

———. *Righteous Discontent: The Women's Movement in the Black Baptist Church, 1880–1920*. Cambridge, Mass.: Harvard University Press, 1994.

Hine, Darlene Clark. "Black Professionals and Race Consciousness: Origins of the Civil Rights Movement, 1890–1950." *Journal of American History* 89, no. 4 (March 2003): 1279–94.

———. "Mabel K. Staupers and the Integration of Black Nurses into the Armed Forces during World War II." In *Hine Sight: Black Women and the Re-Construction of American History*, 183–201. Bloomington: Indiana University Press, 1997.

———. "Rape and the Inner Lives of Black Women: Thoughts on the Culture of Dissemblance." In *Hine Sight: Black Women and the Re-Construction of American History*, 37–47. Bloomington: Indiana University Press, 1997.

Hine, Darlene Clark, Wilma King, and Linda Reed. *We Specialize in the Wholly Impossible: A Reader in Black Women's History*. Brooklyn: Carlson, 1995.

Hine, Darlene Clark, and Kathleen Thompson. *A Shining Thread of Hope: The History of Black Women in America*. New York: Broadway Books, 1998.

Hinton, Elizabeth. "Creating Crime: The Rise and Impact of National Juvenile Delinquency Programs in Black Urban Neighborhoods. *Journal of Urban History* 41 no. 5 (2015): 808–24.

———. *From the War on Poverty to the War on Crime: The Making of Mass Incarceration in America*. Cambridge, Mass.: Harvard University Press, 2016.

———. "'A War within Our Own Boundaries': Lyndon Johnson's Great Society and the Rise of the Carceral State." *Journal of American History* 102, no. 1 (June 2015): 100–112.

Holsaert, Faith S., and Martha Prescod Norman Noonan, Judy Richardson, Betty Garman Robinson, Jean Smith Young, and Dorothy M. Zellner, eds. *Hands on the Freedom Plow: Personal Accounts by Women in SNCC*. Urbana: University of Illinois Press, 2012.

hooks, bell. *Feminist Theory: From Margin to Center*. Boston: South End Press, 1984.

Horne, Gerald. *Fire This Time: The Watts Uprising and the 1960s*. New York: Da Capo Press, 1997.

Houck, Davis W., and David E. Dixon, eds. *Rhetoric, Religion and the Civil Rights Movement, 1954–1965*. Waco, Tex.: Baylor University Press, 2006.

———. *Women and the Civil Rights Movement, 1954–1965*. Jackson: University Press of Mississippi, 2009.

Institute for Media Analysis. *The Stern Fund: The Story of a Progressive Family Foundation*. New York: Institute for Media Analysis, 1992.

Irons, Jenny. "The Shaping of Activist Recruitment and Participation: A Study of Women in the Mississippi Civil Rights Movement." *Gender and Society* 12 (1998): 692–709.

Jackson, Walter A. *Gunnar Myrdal and America's Social Conscience: Social Engineering and Racial Liberalism*. Chapel Hill: University of North Carolina Press, 1990.

Jaquette, Jane S., and Kathleen Staudt. "Women, Gender, and Development." In *Women and Gender Equity in Development Theory and Practice: Institutions, Resources, and Mobilization*, edited by Jane S. Jaquette and Gale Summerfield, 17–52. Durham, N.C.: Duke University Press, 2006.

Jeffries, Hasan. *Bloody Lowndes: Civil Rights and Black Power in Alabama's Black Belt*. New York: New York University Press, 2009.

Jones, Cherisse R. " 'How Shall I Sing the Lord's Song?' United Church Women Confront Racial Issues in South Carolina, 1940s–1960s." In *Throwing Off the Cloak of Privilege: White Southern Woman Activists in the Civil Rights Era*, edited by Gail S. Murray, 131–52. Gainesville, Fla.: University of Florida, 2004.

Jones, Jacqueline. *Labor of Love, Labor of Sorrow: Black Women, Work, and the Family, from Slavery to the Present*. New York: Basic Books, 2010.

Joseph, Peniel E., ed. *The Black Power Movement: Rethinking the Civil Rights–Black Power Era*. New York City: Routledge, 2006.

———, ed. *Neighborhood Rebels: Black Power at the Local Level*. New York: Palgrave Macmillan, 2010.

———. *Waiting 'til the Midnight Hour: A Narrative History of Black Power in America*. New York: Holt, 2006.

Kaufman, Polly Welts. "Building a Constituency for School Desegregation: African-American Women in Boston, 1962–1972." *Teachers College Record* 92, no. 4 (1991): 619–31.

Kelley, Robin. *Freedom Dreams: The Black Radical Imagination*. Boston: Beacon Press, 2002.

Kern-Foxworth. *Aunt Jemima, Uncle Ben, and Rastus: Blacks in Advertising, Yesterday, Today, and Tomorrow*. Westport, Conn.: Greenwood Press, 1994.

Kiesel, Diane. *She Can Bring Us Home: Dr. Dorothy Boulding Ferebee, Civil Rights Pioneer*. Lincoln: University of Nebraska Press, 2015.

Kornbluh, Felicia. *The Battle for Welfare Rights: Politics and Poverty in Modern America*. Philadelphia: University of Pennsylvania Press, 2007.

———. "Welfare Rights, Consumerism, Northern Protest." In *Freedom North: Black Freedom Struggles outside the South, 1940–1980*, edited by Jeanne Theoharis and Komozi Woodard, 199–222. New York City: Palgrave, 2003.

Krenn, Michael. *Black Diplomacy: African Americans and the State Department, 1945–69*. 1999. London: Routledge, 2015.

———. "The Unwelcome Mat: African Diplomats in Washington, D.C., during the Kennedy Years." In *Window on Freedom: Race, Civil Rights, and Foreign Affairs, 1945–1988*, edited by Brenda Gayle Plummer, 163–80. Chapel Hill: University of North Carolina Press, 2003.

Lauren, Paul Gordon. "Seen from the Outside: The International Perspective on America's Dilemma." In *Window on Freedom: Race, Civil Rights, and Foreign Affairs, 1945–1988*, edited by Brenda Gayle Plummer, 21–43. Chapel Hill: University of North Carolina Press, 2003.

Laville, Helen. *Cold War Women: The International Activities of American Women's Organizations*. Manchester, U.K.: Manchester University Press, 2002.

———. " 'If the Time Is Not Ripe, Then It Is Your Job to Ripen the Time!' The Transformation of the YWCA in the USA from Segregated Association to Interracial Organization, 1930–1965." *Women's History Review* 15, no. 3 (2006): 359–83.

———. " 'Women of Conscience' or 'Women of Conviction'? The National Women's Committee on Civil Rights." *Journal of American Studies* 43, no. 2 (2009): 277–95.

Laville, Helen, and Scott Lucas. "The American Way: Edith Sampson, the NAACP, and African American Identity in the Cold War." *Diplomatic History* 20, no. 4 (Fall 1996): 565–90.

Lawson, Steven F. *Black Ballots: Voting Rights in the South, 1944–1969*. New York: Columbia University Press, 1976.

———. "Freedom Then, Freedom Now: The Historiography of the Civil Rights Movement." *American Historical Review* 96 (1991): 456–71.

———. "Race, Rock and Roll, and the Rigged Society: The Payola Scandal and the Political Culture of the 1950s." In *The Achievement of American Liberalism*, edited by William H. Chafe, 205–42. New York: Columbia University Press, 2003.

———. *Running for Freedom: Civil Rights and Black Politics in America since 1941*. Second Edition. New York: McGraw-Hill, 1997.

Lawson, Steven F., and Charles Payne. *Debating the Civil Rights Movement, 1954–1968*. New York: Rowman and Littlefield, 1998.

Lee, Chana Kai. *For Freedom's Sake: The Life of Fannie Lou Hamer*. Urbana: University of Illinois Press, 2000.

Lerner, Gerda, ed. *Black Women in White America: A Documentary History*. 1972. Reprint, New York: Vintage, 1992.

Levenstein, Lisa. *A Movement without Marches: African American Women and the Politics of Poverty in Postwar Philadelphia*. Chapel Hill: University of North Carolina Press, 2009.

Lewis, George. *The White South and the Red Menace: Segregationists, Anticommunism, and Massive Resistance, 1945–1965*. Gainesville: University Press of Florida, 2004.

Ling, Peter, and Sharon Monteith, eds. *Gender and the Civil Rights Movement*. New Brunswick, N.J.: Rutgers University Press, 2004.

Lynn, Susan. "Gender and Progressive Politics: A Bridge to Social Activism of the 1960s." In *Not June Cleaver: Women and Gender in Postwar America, 1945–1960*, edited by Joanne Meyerowitz, 103–127. Philadelphia: Temple University Press, 1994.

———. *Progressive Women in Conservative Times: Racial Justice, Peace, and Feminism, 1945 to the 1960s*. New Brunswick, N.J.: Rutgers University Press, 1992.

Mack, Kenneth Walter. "A Social History of Everyday Practice: Sadie Alexander and the Incorporation of Black Women into the American Legal Profession." *Cornell Law Review* 87, no. 6 (2002): article 3, http://scholarship.law.cornell.edu/clr/vol87/iss6/3.

Mantler, Gordon K. *Power to the Poor: Black-Brown Coalition and the Fight for Economic Justice, 1960–1974*. Chapel Hill: University of North Carolina Press, 2013.

Massey, Douglas S., and Nancy A. Denton. *American Apartheid: Segregation and the Making of the Underclass*. Cambridge, Mass.: Harvard University Press, 1993.

May, Elaine Tyler. *Homeward Bound: American Families in the Cold War Era*. New York: Basic Books, 1988.

McAdam, Doug. *Freedom Summer*. New York: Oxford University Press, 1988.

McCluskey, Audrey Thomas. "Multiple Consciousness in the Leadership of Mary McLeod Bethune." *NWSA Journal* 6, no. 1 (Spring 1994): 69–81.

McCluskey, Audrey Thomas, and Elaine M. Smith, eds. *Mary McLeod Bethune: Building a Better World, Essays and Selected Documents*. Bloomington: Indiana University Press, 1999.

McDuffie, Erik S. *Sojourning for Freedom: Black Women, American Communism, and the Making of Black Left Feminism*. Durham, N.C.: Duke University Press, 2011.

McGirr, Lisa. *Suburban Warriors: The Origins of the New American Right*. Princeton, N.J.: Princeton University Press, 2001.

McGuire, Danielle. *At the Dark End of the Street: Black Women, Rape, and Resistance—a New History of the Civil Rights Movement from Rosa Parks to the Rise of Black Power*. New York: Vintage, 2010.

———. " 'It Was Like All of Us Had Been Raped': Sexual Violence, Community Mobilization, and the African American Freedom Struggle." *Journal of American History* 91, no. 3 (2004): 906–31.

McMillen, Neil. *The Citizen's Council: Organized Resistance to the Second Reconstruction, 1954–1964*. 1971. Reprint, Urbana: University of Illinois Press, 1994.

Mills, Kay. *This Little Light of Mine: The Life of Fannie Lou Hamer*. New York: Dutton, 1993.

Moraga, Cherríe, and Gloria Anzaldúa, eds. *This Bridge Called My Back: Writings by Radical Women of Color*. Watertown, Mass.: Persephone Press, 1981.

Morris, Aldon D. *The Origins of the Civil Rights Movement: Black Communities Organizing for Change*. New York: Free Press, 1984.

Morris, Tiyi M. "Local Women and the Civil Rights Movement in Mississippi: Revisioning Womanpower Unlimited." In *Groundwork: Local Black Freedom Movements in America*, edited by Jeanne Theoharis and Komozi Woodard, 193–214. New York: New York University Press, 2005.

———. *Womanpower Unlimited and the Black Freedom Struggle in Mississippi*. Athens: University of Georgia Press, 2015.

Moye, J. Todd. *Let the People Decide: Black Freedom and White Resistance Movements in Sunflower County, Mississippi, 1945–1986*. Chapel Hill: University of North Carolina Press, 2004.

Mueller, Carol. "Ella Baker and the Origins of 'Participatory Democracy.' " In *Women in the Civil Rights Movement: Trailblazers and Torchbearers, 1941–1965*, edited by Vicki L. Crawford, Jacqueline Anne Rouse, and Barbara Woods, 51–70. Bloomington: Indiana University Press, 1993.

Murakawa, Naomi. *The First Civil Right: How Liberals Built Prison America*. New York: Oxford, 2014.

Murray, Gail. "White Privilege, Racial Justice: Women Activists in Memphis." In *Throwing Off the Cloak of Privilege*, edited by Gail S. Murray, 204–29. Gainesville: University Press of Florida, 2004.

Murray, Paul T. "Father Nathaniel and the Greenwood Movement." *Journal of Mississippi History* 72, no. 3 (2010): 277–311.

Murray, Pauli. "November 14, 1963, National Council of Negro Women, Leadership Conference, Washington, D.C." In *Women and the Civil Rights Movement, 1954–1965*, edited by Davis W. Houck and David E. Dixon, 228–40. Jackson, Miss.: University Press of Mississippi, 2009.

———. *Pauli Murray: The Autobiography of a Black Activist, Feminist, Lawyer, Priest and Poet*. Knoxville: University of Tennessee Press, 1989.

Nadasen, Premilla. *Welfare Warriors: The Welfare Rights Movement in the United States*. New York: Routledge, 2005.

Naples, Nancy. *Community Activism and Feminist Politics*. New York: Routledge, 1997.

———. *Grassroots Warriors: Activist Mothering, Community Work, and the War on Poverty*. New York: Routledge, 1998.

National Council of Negro Women. *The Black Family Reunion Cookbook: Recipes and Food Memories™ from the National Council of Negro Women*. Memphis: Wimmer Companies, 1991.

Nelson, Jennifer. *Women of Color and the Reproductive Rights Movement*. New York: New York University Press, 2003.

Nembhard, Jessica Gordon. *Collective Courage: A History of African American Cooperative Economic Thought and Practice*. State College, Penn.: The Pennsylvania State Press, 2014.

Newman, Mark. *Divine Agitators: The Delta Ministry and Civil Rights in Mississippi*. Athens: University of Georgia Press, 2004.

Olson, Lynne. *Freedom's Daughters: The Unsung Heroines of the Civil Rights Movement from 1830 to 1970*. New York: Scribner, 2001.

Orleck, Annelise. *Storming Caesars Palace: How Black Mothers Fought Their Own War on Poverty*. Boston: Beacon, 2005.

Painter, Nell Irvin. *Creating Black Americans: African-American History and Its Meanings, 1619 to the Present*. New York: Oxford University Press, 2007.

Patterson, James T. *Freedom Is Not Enough: The Moynihan Report and America's Struggle over Black Family Life: From LBJ to Obama*. New York: Basic Books, 2010.

Pattillo-McCoy, Mary. *Black Picket Fences: Privilege and Peril among the Black Middle Class*. Chicago: University of Chicago, 1999.

Payne, Charles M. *I've Got the Light of Freedom: The Organizing Tradition and the Mississippi Freedom Struggle*. Berkeley: University of California Press, 1995.

———. "Men Led, but Women Organized: Movement Participation of Women in the Mississippi Delta." In *Women in the Civil Rights Movement: Trailblazers and Torchbearers*, edited by Vicki L. Crawford, Jacqueline Anne Rouse, and Barbara Woods, 1–12. 1990. Reprint, Bloomington: Indiana, 1993.

———. "'Sexism Is a Helluva Thing': Rethinking Our Questions and Assumptions." In *Civil Rights History from the Ground Up: Local Struggles, a National Movement*, edited by Emily Crosby, 319–29. Athens: University of Georgia Press, 2011.

Payne, Elizabeth Anne, Hattye Raspberry-Hall, Michael de L. Landon, and Jennifer Nardone. "The Unknown Grandmother, African American Memory, and Lives of Service in Northern Mississippi." In *Mississippi Women: Their Histories, Their Lives—Volume 2*, edited by Elizabeth Anne Payne, Martha H. Swain, and Marjorie Julian Spruill, 313–32. Athens: University of Georgia Press, 2010.

Peet, Richard, and Elaine Hartwick. *Theories of Development: Contentions, Arguments, Alternatives.* New York: Guilford Press, 2009.

Petras, James. "NGOs: In the Service of Imperialism." *Journal of Contemporary Asia* 29, no. 4 (1999): 429–440.

Petras, James, and Henry Veltmeyer. *Globalization Unmasked: Imperialism in the 21st Century.* London: Fernwood Publishing, 2001.

Phillips, Layli. "Introduction to *The Womanist Reader,*" edited by Layli Phillips, xix–lv. New York: Routledge, 2006.

Piven, Frances Fox, and Richard Cloward. *Regulating the Poor: The Functions of Public Welfare.* 1971. Reprint, New York: Vintage Books, 1993.

Plummer, Brenda Gayle. *In Search of Power: African Americans in the Era of Decolonization, 1956–1974.* New York: Cambridge, 2013.

———. *Rising Wind: Black American and U.S. Foreign Affairs, 1935–1960.* Chapel Hill: University of North Carolina Press, 1996.

———, ed. *Window on Freedom: Race, Civil Rights, and Foreign Affairs, 1945–1988.* Chapel Hill: University of North Carolina Press, 2003.

Poinsett, Alex. *Walking with Presidents: Louis Martin and the Rise of Black Political Power* 1997. Lanham, Md.: Rowman & Littlefield, 2000.

Quadagno, Jill. *The Color of Welfare: How Racism Undermined the War on Poverty.* New York: Oxford University Press, 1996.

Quigley, Joan. *Just Another Southern Town: Mary Church Terrell and the Struggle for Racial Justice in the Nation's Capital.* New York: Oxford University Press, 2016.

Rainwater, Lee, and William L. Yancy. *The Moynihan Report and the Politics of Controversy: A Trans-Action Social Science and Public Policy Report.* Cambridge, Mass.: MIT Press, 1967.

Randolph, Sherie M. *Florynce "Flo" Kennedy: The Life of a Black Feminist Radical.* Chapel Hill: University of North Carolina Press, 2015.

———. "'Women's Liberation or . . . Black Liberation, You're Fighting the Same Enemies': Florynce Kennedy, Black Power, and Feminism." In *Want to Start a Revolution? Radical Women in the Black Freedom Struggle,* edited by Dayo F. Gore, Jeanne Theoharis, and Komozi Woodard, 223–47. New York: New York University Press, 2009.

Ransby, Barbara. *Ella Baker and the Black Freedom Movement: A Radical Democratic Vision.* Chapel Hill: University of North Carolina, 2003.

———. *Eslanda: The Large and Unconventional Life of Mrs. Paul Robeson.* New Haven, Conn.: Yale University Press, 2014.

Richie, Beth E. *Arrested Justice: Black Women, Violence, and America's Prison Nation.* New York: New York University Press, 2012.

Riehm, Edith Holbrook. "Dorothy Tilly and the Fellowship of the Concerned." In *Throwing off the Cloak of Privilege: White Southern Women Activists in the Civil Rights Era,* edited by Gail S. Murray, 23–48. Gainesville: University Press of Florida, 2004.

Ritterhouse, Jennifer. *Growing Up Jim Crow: How Black and White Southern Children Learned Race.* Chapel Hill: University of North Carolina Press, 2006.

Roberts, Dorothy. *Killing the Black Body: Race, Reproduction, and the Meaning of Liberty*. New York City: Vintage, 1999.

Robertson, Ashley. "The Backbone of the Civil Rights Movement: The National Council of Negro Women's Role in the Struggle." In *In Spite of the Double Drawbacks: African American Women in History and Culture*, edited by Lopez D. Matthews, Kenvi Phillips, Ida Jones, and Marshanda Smith, 65–73. Association of Black Women Historians, CreateSpace, 2012.

———. *Mary McLeod Bethune in Florida: Bringing Social Justice to the Sunshine State*. Charleston, S.C.: History Press, 2015.

Robertson, Nancy Marie. *Christian Sisterhood, Race Relations, and the YWCA, 1906–46*. Urbana: University of Illinois Press, 2007.

Robinson, Jo Ann Gibson, and David J. Garrow. *The Montgomery Bus Boycott and the Women Who Started It: The Memoir of Jo Ann Gibson Robinson*. Knoxville: University of Tennessee Press, 1987.

Robnett, Belinda. *How Long? How Long? African American Women in the Struggle for Civil Rights*. New York: Oxford University Press, 1997.

Rosen, Ruth. *The World Split Open: How the Modern Women's Movement Changed America*. New York: Penguin Books, 2006.

Rossinow, Doug. *The Politics of Authenticity: Liberalism, Christianity, and the New Left in America*. New York: Columbia University Press, 1998.

Roth, Benita. *Separate Roads to Feminism: Black, Chicana, and White Feminist Movements in America's Second Wave*. Cambridge: Cambridge University Press, 2004.

Rothschild, Mary Aickin. *A Case of Black and White: Northern Volunteers and the Southern Freedom Summers*. Westport, Conn.: Greenwood Press, 1982.

Sacks, Karen Brodkin. *Caring by the Hour: Women, Work, and Organizing at Duke Medical Center*. Urbana: University of Illinois Press, 1988.

Sanders, Crystal R. *A Chance for Change: Head Start and Mississippi's Black Freedom Struggle*. Chapel Hill: University of North Carolina Press, 2016.

Savage, Kirk. *Monument Wars: Washington, D.C., the National Mall, and the Transformation of the Memorial Landscape*. Berkeley: University of California Press, 2009.

———. *Standing Soldiers, Kneeling Slaves: Race, War, and Monument in Nineteenth-Century America*. Princeton, N.J.: Princeton University Press, 1997.

Scanlon, Jennifer. *Until There Is Justice: The Life of Anna Arnold Hedgeman*. New York: Oxford, 2016.

Schulman, Bruce J. *Lyndon B. Johnson and American Liberalism: A Brief Biography with Documents*. Boston: Bedford/St. Martins, 1995.

Schulman, Bruce J., and Julian E. Zelizer. *Rightward Bound: Making America Conservative in the 1970s*. Cambridge, Mass.: Harvard University Press, 2008.

Schultz, Deborah. *Going South: Jewish Women in the Civil Rights Movement*. New York: New York University Press, 2001.

Sellers, Cleveland. *The River of No Return: The Autobiography of a Black Militant and the Life and Death of SNCC*. 1973. Reprint, Jackson: University Press of Mississippi, 1990.

Shankar, Guha, and Catherine Turner. " 'People Who Stood Up': Mississippi Women in the Civil Rights Movement." Folklife Today: American Folklife and Veterans History Project, Library of Congress. June 4, 2017, https://blogs.loc.gov/folklife/2017/06 /standing-up-and-speaking-out-mississippi-women-in-the-civil-rights-movement.

Shaw, Stephanie. *What a Woman Ought to Be and Do: Black Professional Women Workers during the Jim Crow Era*. Chicago: University of Chicago, 1996.

Shulman, Holly C. "Polly Spiegel Cowan, Civil Rights Activist, 1913–1976." *Jewish Women's Archive, Sharing Stories, Inspiring Change*, December 4, 2017, https://jwa .org/weremember/cowan-polly.

Silver, James. *Mississippi: The Closed Society*. New York: Harcourt, 1964.

Sinsheimer, Joseph. "The Freedom Vote of 1963: New Strategies of Racial Protest in Mississippi." *The Journal of Southern History* 55, no. 2 (May 1989): 217–44.

Sitkoff, Harvard. *The Struggle for Black Equality, 1954–1980*. New York: Hill and Wang, 1981.

Smith, Anna Marie. *Welfare Reform and Sexual Regulation*. Cambridge: Cambridge University Press, 2007.

Spencer, Robyn. *The Revolution Has Come: Black Power, Gender, and the Black Panther Party in Oakland*. Durham, N.C.: Duke University Press, 2016.

Springer, Kimberly. *Living for the Revolution: Black Feminist Organizations, 1968–1980*. Durham, N.C.: Duke University Press, 2005.

Staudt, Kathleen. *Women, Foreign Assistance, and Advocacy Administration*. New York: Praeger, 1985.

Sugrue, Thomas J. *The Origins of the Urban Crisis: Race and Inequality in Postwar Detroit*. Princeton, N.J.: Princeton University Press, 1996.

Sullivan, Patricia. *Freedom Writer: Virginia Foster Durr, Letters from the Civil Rights Years*. Athens: University of Georgia Press, 2006.

———. *Lift Every Voice: The NAACP and the Making of the Civil Rights Movement*. New York: New Press, 2010.

Swerdlow, Amy. "The Congress of American Women: Left-Feminist Peace Politics in the Cold War." In *U.S. History as Women's History*, edited by Linda K. Kerber, Alice Kessler-Harris, and Kathryn K. Sklar, 296–312. Chapel Hill: University of North Carolina Press, 1995.

———. *Women Strike for Peace: Traditional Motherhood and Radical Politics in the 1960s*. Chicago: University of Chicago Press, 1993.

Tarry, Ellen. *The Third Door: The Autobiography of an American Negro Woman*. 1966. Reprint, Tuscaloosa: University of Alabama Press, 1992.

Teele, James E. *Evaluating School Busing: Case Study of Boston's Operation Exodus*. New York: Praeger, 1973.

Theoharis, Jeanne. "Accidental Matriarchs and Beautiful Helpmates: Rosa Parks, Coretta Scott King, and the Memorialization of the Civil Rights Movement." In *Civil Rights History from the Ground Up: Local Struggles, a National Movement*, edited by Emilye Crosby, 385–418. Athens: University of Georgia Press, 2011.

————. " 'I'd Rather Go to School in the South': How Boston's School Desegregation Complicates the Civil Rights Paradigm." In *Freedom North: Black Freedom Struggles outside the South, 1940–1980*, edited by Jeanne Theoharis and Komozi Woodard, 125–51. New York: Palgrave, 2003.

————. " 'A Life History of Being Rebellious': The Radicalism of Rosa Parks." In *Want to Start a Revolution? Radical Women in the Black Freedom Struggle*, edited by Dayo Gore, Jeanne Theoharis, and Komozi Woodard, 115–37. New York: New York University Press, 2009.

————. *The Rebellious Life of Mrs. Rosa Parks*. Boston: Beacon Press, 2013.

————. " 'They Told Us Our Kids Were Stupid': Ruth Batson and the Educational Movement in Boston." In *Groundwork: Local Freedom Movements in America*, edited by Jeanne Theoharis and Komozi Woodward, 17–44. New York: New York University Press, 2005.

————. " 'We Saved the City': Black Struggles for Educational Equality in Boston, 1960–1972." *Radical History Review* 81 (Fall 2001): 61–93.

Theoharis, Jeanne, and Komozi Woodard, eds. *Freedom North: Black Freedom Struggles outside the South, 1940–1980*. New York: Palgrave, 2003.

————, eds. *Groundwork: Local Black Freedom Movements in America*. New York: New York University Press, 2005.

Thiokol Chemical Corporation. *Forest Heights Low Income Home Ownership Program: Research and Final Report, Submitted to Office of Research and Technology, U.S. Department of Housing and Urban Development*. Ogden, Utah: Thiokol Chemical, 1970.

Thompson, Becky. "Multiracial Feminism: Recasting the Chronology of Second Wave Feminism." In *Feminist Studies* 28, no. 2 (Summer 2002): 336–60.

Thompson, Heather. "Why Incarceration Matters: Rethinking Crisis, Decline, and Transformation in Postwar American History." *Journal of American History* 97, no. 3 (December 2010): 703–34.

Tibaldo-Bongiorno, Marylou, and Jerome Bongiorno. *Revolution '67*. DVD. San Francisco, Calif.: California Newsreel, 2007.

Tinker, Irene. "Empowerment Just Happened: The Unexpected Expansion of Women's Organizations." In *Women and Gender Equity in Development Theory and Practice*, edited by Jane S. Jaquette and Gale Summerfield, 268–301. Durham, N.C.: Duke University Press, 2006.

Trethewey, Natasha. *Beyond Katrina: A Meditation on the Mississippi Gulf Coast*. Athens: University of Georgia Press, 2010.

Tuuri, Rebecca. " 'By Any Means Necessary': The National Council of Negro Women's Flexible Loyalties in the Black Power Era." In *Untangling the Threads of Sisterhood*, edited by Leslie Brown, Jacqueline Castledine, and Anne Valk, 32–48. New Brunswick, N.J.: Rutgers University Press, 2017.

————. " 'This Was the Most Meaningful Thing That I've Ever Done': The Personal Civil Rights Approach of Wednesdays in Mississippi." *Journal of Women's History* 28, no. 4 (2016): 91–112.

Umoja, Akinyele K. *We Will Shoot Back: Armed Resistance in the Mississippi Freedom Movement.* New York: New York University Press, 2013.

Valk, Anne M. *Radical Sisters: Second-Wave Feminism and Black Liberation in Washington, D.C.* Urbana: University of Illinois Press, 2008.

Vinovskis, Maris A. *The Birth of Head Start: Preschool Education Policies in the Kennedy and Johnson Administrations.* Chicago: University of Chicago Press, 2005.

Von Eschen, Penny M. *Race against Empire: Black Americans and Anticolonialism, 1937–1957.* Ithaca, N.Y.: Cornell University Press, 1997.

Wall, Wendy. *Inventing the "American Way": The Politics of Consensus from the New Deal to the Civil Rights Movement.* Oxford: Oxford University Press, 2008.

Webb, Clive. *Fight against Fear: Southern Jews and Black Civil Rights.* Athens: University of Georgia, 2003.

Weiner, Josephine. *The Story of WICS.* Washington, D.C.: Women in Community Service, 1979.

Weisenfeld, Judith. *African American Women and Christian Activism: New York's Black YWCA, 1905–1945.* Cambridge, Mass.: Harvard University Press, 1997.

White, Deborah G. *Lost in the USA: American Identity from the Promise Keepers to the Million Mom March.* Urbana: University of Illinois Press, 2017.

———. *Too Heavy a Load: Black Women in Defense of Themselves, 1894–1994.* New York: W. W. Norton, 1999.

White, E. Frances. *Dark Continent of Our Bodies: Black Feminism and the Politics of Respectability.* Philadelphia: Temple University Press, 2001.

Wilkerson-Freeman, Sarah. "Stealth in the Political Arsenal of Southern Women: A Retrospective for the Millennium." In *Southern Women at the Millennium: A Historical Perspective,* edited by Melissa Walker, Jeanette R. Dunn, and Joe P. Dunn, 42–82. Columbia: University of Missouri, 2003.

Williams, Rhonda. *Concrete Demands: The Search for Black Power in the 20th Century.* New York: Routledge, 2015.

———. *The Politics of Public Housing: Black Women's Struggles against Urban Inequality.* Oxford: Oxford University Press, 2004.

———. "The Pursuit of Audacious Power: Rebel Reformers and Neighborhood Politics in Baltimore, 1966–1968." In *Neighborhood Rebels: Black Power at the Local Level,* edited by Peniel E. Joseph, 215–42. New York: Palgrave Macmillan, 2010.

Wolcott, Victoria. *Remaking Respectability: African American Women in Interwar Detroit.* Chapel Hill: University of North Carolina, 2001.

Woodard, Komozi. "It's Nation Time in NewArk: Amiri Baraka and the Black Power Experiment in Newark, New Jersey." In *Freedom North: Black Freedom Struggles outside the South, 1940–1980,* edited by Jeanne Theoharis and Komozi Woodard, 287–312. New York: Palgrave, 2003.

———. *A Nation within a Nation: Amiri Baraka (LeRoi Jones) and Black Power Politics.* Chapel Hill: University of North Carolina Press, 1999.

Woodley, Jenny. "'Ma Is in the Park': Memory, Identity, and the Bethune Memorial." *Journal of American Studies* (May 17, 2017): 1–29. doi:10.1017/S0021875817000536.

Woods, Jeff. *Black Struggle, Red Scare: Segregation and Anti-Communism in the South, 1948–1968*. Baton Rouge: Louisiana State University, 2004.

X, Malcolm. "Speech at the Founding Rally of the Organization of Afro-American Unity." In *By Any Means Necessary: Speeches, Interviews, and a Letter by Malcolm X*. New York: Pathfinder Press, 1970, http://www.blackpast.org/1964-malcolm-x-s -speech-founding-rally-organization-afro-american-unity#stharsh.sbToYQrt.dpuf.

UNPUBLISHED WORKS

Denomme, Janine Marie. "'To End This Day of Strife': Churchwomen and the Campaign for Integration, 1920–1970." PhD diss., University of Pennsylvania, 2001.

Erhagbe, Edward. "African-Americans' Ideas and Contributions to Africa, 1900–1985: From 'Idealistic Rhetoric' to 'Realistic Pragmatism'?" PhD diss., Boston University, 1992.

Lewis, Abigail. "'The Barrier Breaking Love of God': The Multiracial Activism of the Young Women's Christian Association, 1940s to 1970s." PhD diss., Rutgers University, 2008.

McDonough, Julia Anne. "Men and Women of Good Will: A History of the Commission on Interracial Cooperation and the Southern Regional Council, 1919–1954." PhD diss., University of Virginia, 1993.

Meyer, Lauren. "Sadie Alexander, Black Women's Work and Economic Citizenship in the New Deal Era." Paper presented at the 2017 Berkshire Conference on the History of Women, Genders, and Sexualities, Hofstra University, Hempstead, N.Y., June 3, 2017 (in possession of author).

O'Halloran, Ruth. "Organized Catholic Laywomen: The National Council of Catholic Women, 1920–1995." PhD diss., Catholic University of America, 1996.

Poff, Erica. "Wednesdays in Mississippi: 1964/1965." Master's thesis, Sarah Lawrence College, 2002.

Tuuri, Rebecca. "Building Bridges of Understanding: The Activism of Wednesdays in Mississippi." PhD diss., Rutgers University, 2012.

Wilkinson, Kate. "A Sociological Analysis of an Action Group: 'Wednesdays in Mississippi.'" Master's thesis, University of Mississippi, 1966.

Index

AAUW. *See* American Association of University Women (AAUW)

Abernethy, Thomas, 9–10, 128, 146

Abortion, 165–66

Abzug, Bella, 164

ACMHR. *See* Alabama Christian Movement for Human Rights (ACMHR)

Action Fellowships, 28–29

Activist Mothering, 5

Adams, Victoria Gray, 80

Adebo, Chief Simeon O., 186

Adult Education Act, 170

Africa, 10, 16, 116, 180–81, 184–87, 189, 195–202, 270n7, 272n53

African Children's Feeding Scheme, 181, 197

Agyepong, Emma, 189, *gallery fig. 10*

Alabama Christian Movement for Human Rights (ACMHR), 29

Albert, Carl, 152

Alexander, Sadie, 2, 19

Alford, Helene, 63

Allen, Alexander J., 13

Alpha Kappa Alpha, 13, 68, 71, 234n47

American Academy of Pediatrics, 174

American Association of University Women (AAUW), 41, 182

American Home Economics Association, 174

American Negro Leadership Conference on Africa (ANLCA), 185–87

American Nurses' Association, 174

Americans for Democratic Action, 82

America's Town Meeting of the Air, 182–84

Ames, Jessie Daniel, 39

Anderson, Marian, 175

Angelou, Maya, 206

ANLCA. *See* American Negro Leadership Conference on Africa (ANLCA)

ASNLH. *See* Association for the Study of Negro Life and History (ASNLH)

Association for the Study of Negro Life and History (ASNLH), 16–17

Association of Southern Women for the Prevention of Lynching (ASWPL), 39

ASWPL. *See* Association of Southern Women for the Prevention of Lynching (ASWPL)

Attica Prison uprising and massacre, 166, 267n90

AT&T, 7, 168

Aunt Jemima, 206–7

Bailey, Herman Kofi, 120

Baird, T. C., 118–19

Baker, Ella, 12, 26, 49

Ball, Thomas, 149, 151

Banks, Paula, 205

Barksdale, Marie, 83, 108

Barnes, Barbara, 93

Barnes, Thelma, 128, 140

Barnett, Claude, 6, 67

Barnett, Etta Moten, 6, 67

Barry, Marion, 29

Bates, Daisy, 30, 49, 237n112

Batson, Ruth, 6, 56–58, 68, 74, 76–77, 81, 99–100, 108–9, 257n114

Battle, Wallace, 145

BBB. *See* Better Business Bureau (BBB)

Beal, Frances, 8, 114–15, 120, 150, 158–59, 164–66, 171, 256n87, 266n80

Beard, Gabe, 93, 108

Beck, Burt, 74

Beech, Bob, 70

Benjamin, Jean, 6, 61, 66, 69, 76, 245n47, 247n99

Berks, Robert, 150, 263n6

Bethune-Cookman College, 151, 193–95. *See also* Daytona Educational and Industrial Training School for Negro Girls

Bethune, Mary McLeod, 2, 13–17, 48, 228n5, *gallery figs. 1, 2;* and broker politics, 14–16; and Council of African Affairs, 180; investigation of, 21, 234n54; legacy of, 208; Mason and, 22; and racial uplift, 15, 16–17; respect for, 115; statute of, 84, 149–54, 262n1; steps down from presidency, 20; Tilly and, 39; Vermont Ave headquarters and, 21; in World War II, 179–80

Bethune House apartment building, 28

Better Business Bureau (BBB), 182

Birth control, 165, 192

Black Family Reunion, 204–6

Black Freedom Movement, 5, 11, 58, 78

Black Leadership Conference on Southern Africa, 179

Black Lives Matter, 120, 207

Black Panthers, 165–66, 173, 190–91

Black Power, 2, 8, 25, 73, 106–7, 116, 129, 208–9, 255n69, 257n104

"Black slave markets," 26–27

Blackwell, Unita, 1–2, 10, 34, 103–6, 108–9, 113, 120, 133–34, 148, 158, 209

Black Women's Liberation Caucus, 115

Black Women's Unity Drive, 162, 164

Boddie, Jeanette, 65

Bolton, Frances, 152, 263n16

Boserup, Ester, 187

Boston New Era Club, 20

Botswana, 10, 195–99, 200–2

Boyer, Roscoe, 108

Boynton, Amelia P., 35, 38, 42, 46

Boy Scouts, 174

Braden, Anne, 40

Brawley, Lucinda, 29

Brooks, Owen, 1, 3, 137, 148

Brown, Ben, 275n6

Brown, Ed, 28–29,

Browne, Roscoe Lee, 151

Brown v. Board of Education, 22, 28, 74, 152

Bryant, Willie Hume, 244n31

Burroughs, Nannie Helen, 26

Burstein, Joseph, 133, 135, 136, 138

Butler, Anthea, 233n36

"Cadillac Crowd," 47–50

Campbell, James, 118–19

Caribbean Women's Association, 189

Carmichael, Stokely, 28–29, 73, 106, 115

Carnation Company, 174, 175

Carter, Eunice Hunton, 179–80, 185, 270n12

Carter, James, 192

Carter, Jimmy, 105, 177, 197, 270n6, 275n6

Carther, Sally Mae, 147

Cassell, Marguerite, 93–94

Catholic Interracial Council, 99

CAW. *See* Congress of American Women (CAW)

CCAP. *See* Citizens' Crusade Against Poverty (CCAP)

CCC. *See* Commission on Community Cooperation (CCC)

CDGM. *See* Child Development Group of Mississippi (CDGM)

Central Intelligence Agency (CIA), 184–85

Chafe, William, 230n16, 254n52, 257n104

Chain of Friendship, 57–58

Chaney, James, 59, 246n66

Childcare, 9–10, 35, 103, 106, 109, 110, 113, 116, 110, 118, 145–48, 156, 193

Child Development Group of Mississippi (CDGM), 86–87, 90–91, 105

Child spacing, 192

China, 183

Chisholm, Shirley, 151, 153, 175

Christian World Missions, 89

Church Women United (CWU), 52–54, 59, 61–63, 68, 81, 89–90, 97

CIA. *See* Central Intelligence Agency (CIA)

CIC. *See* Commission on Interracial Cooperation (CIC)

Citizens' Council, 60–63, 69, 116

Citizens' Crusade Against Poverty (CCAP), 87–88

Civil Rights Act, 70, 82, 84–85, 103, 112, 128, 152

Civil Rights Congress (CRC), 182–83

Clark, Jim, 35, 37, 46

Clark, Kenneth, 24

Clark, Mark, 166

Clark, Robert, 188

Clarke, John Henrik, 118–19

Clinton, Hillary, 206

Clubs, women's, 17–18, 50–51

COFO. *See* Council of Federated Organizations (COFO)

Cohn, Rae, 90

Cold War, 55, 68, 181–82, 240n15

Collier–Thomas, Bettye, 16, 228n5

Collins, Francis, 134, 140–41

Collins, Patricia Hill, 230n25, 254n52, 273n73

Commission on Community Coopera- tion (CCC), 121–27

Commission on Interracial Cooperation (CIC), 39

Commission on the Status of Women (CSW), 31, 40, 180, 187

Committee of Correspondence, 184–86

Communism, 21, 24–25, 27, 40, 45, 68, 181–86, 235n71, 240n15, 241n41

Community gardens, 130–31

Congress of American Women (CAW), 180

Congress of Racial Equality (CORE), 8, 12, 36, 51, 71, 82, 114, 148

Connor, Eugene "Bull," 29

Connor, Peggy Jean, 128, 258n3

Consultation on the Problems of Negro Women, 31–32

Cookman Institute, 15

Coolidge, Calvin, 15

CORE. *See* Congress of Racial Equality (CORE)

Cosby, Bill, 204, 275n5

Cosby, Camille, 204, 206, 275n5

Cothran, Kathrine, 44–47

Council for United Civil Rights Leadership (CUCRL), 29–30, 59

Council on African Affairs (CAA), 180–81, 185, 187

Council of Federated Organizations (COFO), 6, 51–52, 71–72, 74, 77, 82–83, 138, 148

Cowan, Louis, 48, 63

Cowan, Paul, 48–49

Cowan, Polly, 6, 37–38, 41–50, 58, 61, 65, 70, 74–75, *gallery fig. 5*; Civil Rights Act and, 84–85; Hamer and, 109–10; Head Start and, 86; Wednesdays in Mississippi and, 51, 54, 81, 98–100; Women's Center for Education and Career Advancement and, 167; Workshops in Mississippi and, 113

Cox, Courtland, 28–29

CRC. *See* Civil Rights Congress (CRC)

Crenshaw, Doris Dozier, 8, 26, 30, 103, 109, 115–17, 119, 159, 164, 204, 209, 252n4, 255n57, 265n55, 266n79, 275n6

Crissman, Mary, 14

Crystal, Elaine, 94

CSW. *See* Commission on the Status of Women (CSW)

CUCRL. *See* Council for United Civil Rights Leadership (CUCRL)

Currier, Stephen, 29, 76

Curry, Constance, 78

CWU. *See* Church Women United (CWU)

Dakar, 200

Dammann, Marjorie, 67, 74–76, 97

Dammond, Ellen, 93–94

Dandridge, Gloria Richardson, 159, 162

David, Ruby, 147

Davis, Angela, 166–67, 205

Davis, Dovey, *gallery fig. 10*

Davis, Jean, 72, 97

Day care, 145–48. *See also* Childcare.

Daytona Educational and Industrial
 Training School for Negro Girls, 15,
 17, 20

Dearborn Foundation, 185

Dedmond, Flossie, 67, 71, *gallery fig. 4*

Dee, Ruby, 9, 154, 157–58, 162

Delta Ministry, 1, 138, 140, 148

Delta Opportunities Corporation, 147,
 170

Delta Sigma Theta, 3, 13, 26, 64, 68, 136,
 183, 234n47

Democratic National Convention
 (1964), 56, 80

Democratic Party, 231n35. *See also*
 Mississippi Freedom Democratic
 Party (MFDP)

Denny, George, 182–83

Department of Housing and Urban
 Development, 132–36, 138–39, 141–42,
 150, 176

Derian, Patt, 78, 84, 86–87, 89–90, 193,
 244n31, 270n6

Desegregation, 2, 18–19, 28–30, 38, 41, 49,
 70, 92–95, 100, 108

Devil Has Slippery Shoes, The (Greenberg),
 91–92

Devine, Annie, 6, 10, 72–73, 78, 80–81, 85,
 109–10, 253n30

"Dial for Truth," 61

Diallo, Salimatu, 194, *gallery fig. 10*

Dillinger, Jean, 89–90, 95

Dissemblance, 36.

Dittmer, John, 82

Doar, John, 35

Dorsey, L. C., 131

Douglas, Paul H., 241n53

Douglass, Janet, 8

Dozier, Doris. *See* Crenshaw, Doris
 Dozier

Dream Defenders, 120

Du Bois, W. E. B., 24, 179

Duke, Dorothy, 1, 104–5, 133–34, 136, 140,
 176

Duncan, Ruby, 190

Dunnigan, Alice, 32–33

Durr, Virginia, 40

Economic and Social Council
 (ECOSOC), 180

ECOSOC. *See* Economic and Social
 Council (ECOSOC)

Educational Foundation, 84

Elitism, 20–21

Emancipation Group (statue), 149–50,
 152

Employment, 167–71

Equal Rights Amendment, 40, 165, 192

Erhagbe, Edward, 186–87

Ethridge, Esther, 60

Ethridge, Thomas, 60

Evers, Medgar, 34, 63

Eyadéma, Gnassingbé, 211

Fairfax, Jean, 13

Fair Share, 28

Farmer, James, 24, 185

Farrakhan, Louis, 205

Fauntroy, Walter, *gallery fig. 6*

Fay, Toni, 205

Fellowship of the Concerned, 39–40, 61

Feminism, 166, 197; black, 8, 14–15, 115;
 involvement in women's development,
 187; limitations of 164–65, 167, 177, 192;
 Western nongovernmental organizations as promoting, 270n7

Ferebee, Dorothy B., 20–22, 37, 41–43,
 44, 179, 181, 208, 270n12, *gallery fig. 1*

Field, Marshall, 16, 49
Fitts, Kay, *gallery fig. 9*
Fleeson, Doris, 49
Flynn, John, 67
Fontaine, Eleanor, 244n31
Ford, Gerald, 152
Ford Foundation, 114, 135, 141, 160
Forest Heights, 140–44, 261n88. *See also*
   Turnkey III
Forman, Jim, 42, 43
Foster, Miles, 147
Frazier, E. Franklin, 30–31, 33, 92
Freedom Day (Selma, 1963), 37, 42–44
Freedom Farm of Fannie Lou Hamer, 9,
   128, 130
Freedom Rides, 51, 53
Freedom Schools, 69–70
Freedom Summer, 5, 38, 51, 53–57, 64,
   72–75, 78, 82, 115, 119

Gallagher, Julie, 180, 228n6
Gamble, James N., 15
Gantt, Harvey, 29
Gardens, community, 130–31
Gardner, Louise, 12
Genocide, 182–83
Germany, Kent, 4
Ghana, 16, 177, 185, 188–89
Gill, Tiffany, 254n52
Giovanni, Nikki, 175
Girl Scouts, 66, 72, 97
Gooch, Florence, 84, 244n31
Goodman, Andrew, 59, 246n66
Goodwillie, Susie, 50, 58–59, 62–63, 69,
   86–88
Gray-Wiseman, Sammie Lee, 1, 9, 140,
   142
Great Society, 4, 84
Green, Winifred, 60–61, 78, 244n31
Greenberg, Polly, 85–86, 91–92
Greene, Christina, 230n14, 238n134,
   241n44, 256n81
Gregory, Dick, 42

Griffin, L. Francis, 13
Guinea, 16, 185, 200, 202
Gulfport, 140–44, 261n88
Guyer, Carol, 89–90

Habitat for Humanity, 144
Haight, Frances, 68, 72, 74, 77
Hall, Prathia, 8, 35, 38, 42, 55, 114, 116, 120,
   159–62
Hamer, Fannie Lou, 2, 6, 9–10, 34, 76, 78,
   80–81, 110–11, 128, 130–32, 147, 158, 164,
   170, 174, 193, 200, 209, *gallery fig. 5*
Hampton, Fred, 166
Harlem, 24–25
Harper, Consuello, 131
Harper, Jack, 113, 136
Harrington, Michael, 83
Harris, Duchess, 32
Harris, Joe, 137, 147,
Harris, Patricia, 2
Harvey, Clarie Collins, 52–53, 55, 57, 58,
   59–60, 63, 69–70, 162
Harvey, Juanita, 147
Harvey, Martin Luther, Jr., 59
Haserodt, Ethel, 73–74, 97
Hattiesburg, 69–70
Hattiesburg Freedom Schools, 69
Headquarters, Vermont Avenue, 16, 21,
   205; Pennsylvania Avenue, 205–6
Head Start, 85–92, 106, 109, 117, 131–32,
   147
Heckscher, Claudia, 72, 74, 76
Hedgeman, Anna Arnold, 2, 25, 26, 49,
   230n22
Heifer Project, 130, 258n9
Height, Dorothy, 1–3, 22–36, 231n35,
   235n71, *gallery figs. 1, 2, 4, 5, 6, 10*; Barnes
   and, 128; Beal and, 159; Bethune statute
   and, 149–51, 153; on black power, 8;
   Blackwell and, 104–6; clubwomen and,
   50–51; Cosby and, 275n5; on discrimination, 93; dues and, 156–57; Hall and,
   160; international delegations and,

Height, Dorothy (cont.)
    183–87; International Division and,
    177–78; March on Washington and, 5;
    at Million Man March, 205; presi-
    dency of, 27–30; in Selma, 37–47; and
    Sun–n–Sand Motel, 69–70; Turnkey
    III and, 139; Wednesdays in Missis-
    sippi and, 58, 62, 74–75, 81, 95–96;
    welfare and, 155–56; at YWCA,
    25–26
Henderson, Mary Ann, 244n31
Hendrick, Mary F., 244n31
Henry, Aaron, 109
Henry, Noelle, 109
Herman, Alexis, 177
Hetzel, Wilhelmina, *gallery fig. 4*
Hewitt, Ann, 62–63, 68, 84, 89, 90, 108,
    112, 167
Hewitt, Jack, 63
Hickey, Margaret, 195
Hicks, Louise Day, 76, 100
Higginbotham, Evelyn Brooks, 17–18
Hine, Darlene Clark, 19, 36, 254n52
Hines, Jewell, 65
Hinton, Elizabeth, 171, 268n110
H. J. Heinz Company, 174
Hobbs, Sam, 44
Holland, Endesha Ida Mae, 29
Holm, Jeanne M., 86, 152
Holsaert, Faith, 34
Hoover, Herbert, 15
Horne, Lena, 2, 6, 34
Horne, Madie, 100, 123
House Un–American Activities
    Committee, 21, 234n54, 240n15. *See
    also* Communism
Housing, work on, 132–45, 175–76, 189,
    192. *See also* Turnkey III
Housing Act of 1937, 139
HUD. *See* Department of Housing and
    Urban Development (HUD). *See also*
    Housing
Humphrey, Hubert, 80, 95, *gallery fig. 6*

Humphrey–Hawkins Full Employment
    Bill, 170
Hunger, work on, 130–33
Hunger, USA, 130
Hunter, David, 64
Hunter, Gertrude, 90–91
Hunton, Alphaeus, 180
Hurricane Katrina, 144, 261n88

IBM, 7, 146
Incarceration, 171–73
India, 180, 183
International Assembly of Women, 180
International Council of Women, 188
International Division (NCNW),
    177–78, 195, 198
International Women's Year (IWY), 178,
    187–95
Interracial Conference of Women, 22
Interracial Prayer Fellowship Committee
    (Jackson, Miss.), 53
Irwin Sweeney Miller Foundation, 146
Issaquena County, Miss., 118
Ivory Coast, 199
IWY. *See* International Women's Year
    (IWY)

Jack, Hulan, 24
Jackson, Ada, 21, 181
Jackson, Jesse, 275n6
Jackson, Jonathan, 166
Jamison, Bessie, 100
Javits, Jacob, 16
Jewish women, 71, 94, 252n58
Jim Crow, 12, 49
Job Corps, 84, 106, 167
Job creation in the 1970s, 167–71
Johnson, Campbell C., 28
Johnson, Doris, 189
Johnson Foundation, 196
Johnson, June, 34
Johnson, Lyndon, 80, 83–86, *gallery fig. 6*
Jones, Charles, 50

Jones, Lillie Belle, 60
Jordan, Barbara, 152–53
Jordan, Deloris, 206
Joyce, Rosa Miller, 44–47
Juvenile delinquency, work to combat, 20, 84, 171–73

Karro, Anne, 47, 241n53
Keller, Anne, 89, 97
Kemp, Maida Springer. *See* Springer, Maida.
Kennedy, Florynce, 6, 67, 72, 74, 76–77, 97–98, 164, 267n90
Kennedy, Jacqueline, 153
Kennedy, John F., 3, 29, 31, 34, 40–41, 65, 83, 171
Kenya, 116, 177, 200
Kerner Commission, 122
Kiesel, Diane, 21
King, Coretta Scott, 95, 151, 175, 205, 206, 275n6
King, Jeanette, 244n31
King, Mae, *gallery fig. 10*
King, Martin Luther, Jr., 29, 97, 106, 155, 185
King, Narcissa Swift, 68
King, Reatha Clarke, 205
Ku Klux Klan (KKK), 60, 94
Kyle, Mary, 67

Ladies' Auxiliary of the Brotherhood of Sleeping Car Porters, 20
Ladner, Joyce, 205
Lampkin, Daisy, 2, 16, 28
Lash, Trude, 71–72, 74–76, 100
Latin America, 183–84
Law, Bernard, 94–95
Law Enforcement Assistance Administration (LEAA), 173
Lawson, Marjorie, 2, 171
LEAA. *See* Law Enforcement Assistance Administration (LEAA)
League of United Latin American Citizens, 167

League of Women Voters (LWV), 69, 97, 136, 182, 271n30
Lear, Norman, 206
Lesotho, 10, 116, 177, 195–99
Levin, Hannah, 67
Levin, Tom, 91–92
Lewis, Abigail, 26
Lewis, Hylan Garnet, 31, 33
Lewis, John, 106
Liberia, 16, 151, 185
Liberty House, 193
Lindsay, Inabel, 32
Lindsay, Mary, 6
Lincoln Park, 149–53
Lions Clubs International, 182
Lipscomb, Ernestine, 63
Literacy, 191–92
Lodge, Henry Cabot, 16
Logan, Arthur, 66
Logan, Marian Bruce, 65–66, 69–70, 72–73, 75
Los Angeles, 96–97, 118, 156, 205
Louis and Pauline Cowan Foundation, 65
Ludlow, Louis, 18
Lyon, Danny, 44

Malcolm X, 8, 115, 157
Mallory, Arenia, 2
Malone, Annie Turnbo, 26
Malone, Elizabeth, 109
Mannes, Marya, 49
March on Washington, 5, 30, 34, 230n22, *gallery fig. 3*
Marcy, Mildred, 187
Marshall, Burke, 29
Marshall, Thurgood, 13, *gallery fig. 6*
Mason, Natalie, 108–9
Mason, Vivian, 21–22, 36, 164, 180–81, 208, *gallery figs. 1, 2*
Massachusetts Committee Against Discrimination, 56

Matriarchy, accusations of 30–31; black women lending credence to the idea of, 31–33; black women rejecting the idea of, 33, 91; discussions within Project Womanpower, 119; Head Start leaders lending credence to idea of, 91–92; Height's feelings towards, 32–34
Matsepe, Ivy, 196
Mauritania, 177, 188
Mayer, Jean, 175
Mbabne, 200
McAlpin, Willis, 130, 258n9
McCarthyism, 21, 234n54, 240n15. *See also* Communism
McCluskey, Audrey Thomas, 16–17
McCulloch, William, *gallery fig. 6*
McGlinchy, Anne, 66
McGrory, Mary, 49
McGuire, Danielle, 34
McLaurin, Charles, 1, 3, 131, 137, 148, 170
McNamara, Robert, 188
Merck Corporation, 146
Meredith March Against Fear, 73, 154
Metropolitan Council for Educational Opportunity (METCO), 74
Meyner, Helen, 67
MFDP. *See* Mississippi Freedom Democratic Party (MFDP)
Middle class, 1–2, 20, 27–28, 31, 38, 49, 51–54, 71, 98–99, 104, 227n4, 233n36, 240n15
Miller, Coleman, 103
Million Man March, 204–5
Minor, Ruth Hurd, 71–72, *gallery fig. 9*
Mississippians for Public Education (MPE), 60–61, 77
Mississippi Council for Human Relations, 62
Mississippi Freedom Democratic Party (MFDP), 1, 6, 57, 80–82, 84, 128, 133, 148, 231n35
Mitchell, Clarence, *gallery fig. 6*
Mitchell, Juanita, 24

Moatlhodi, Nancy, *gallery fig. 10*
Mobley, Sybil, 206
Mockabee, Gilbert, 147
Mojekwu, Victoria, *gallery fig. 9*
Mondale, Walter, 275n6
Moore, Amzie, 10, 137, 209,
Moore, Joan, 244n31
Moore, Richard V., 151
Moragne, Lenora, *gallery fig. 9*
Morris, Beryl, 67, 77
Morris, Tiyi, 7, 53, 57–58, 162–63, 254n52
Mosley, Jessie, 109, 147–48, 162–63, 193
Motley, Constance Baker, 24
Moyers, Bill, 204
Moynihan, Daniel Patrick, 31, 32, 91–92
Moynihan Report, 31–33, 96, 119,
MPE. *See* Mississippians for Public Education (MPE)
Murakawa, Naomi, 171–72
Murray, Pauli, 26, 30, 40, 164
Myrdal, Gunnar, 230n26

NAACP. *See* National Association for the Advancement of Colored People (NAACP)
NACW. *See* National Association of Colored Women (NACW)
National Advisory Commission on Civil Disorders, 122
National Association for the Advancement of Colored People (NAACP), 13, 24, 30, 51, 56, 65, 68, 72, 81–82, 107, 109, 128, 179, 182
National Association of Colored Graduate Nurses, 19
National Association of Colored Women (NACW), 14–16, 18, 20, 232n13
National Association of Home Builders, 134–35, 139
National Association of Social Workers, 74, 88
National Baptist Convention, 17
National Christian Youth, 25

National Council of Catholic Women, 50, 66, 68, 167

National Council of Churches, 62, 82

National Council of Jewish Women (NCJW), 50, 64, 68, 167

National Council of Women, 15, 66, 68, 188

National Emergency Civil Rights Mobilization, 20

National Negro Congress, 21

National Organization for Women, 164

National Tenants Organization, 139

National Welfare Rights Organization (NWRO), 10–11, 171, 174

National Women's Committee on Civil Rights (NWCCR), 37, 41, 43, 50, 53, 58, 64

National Women's Political Caucus, 164

National Youth Administration, 15

NCJW. *See* National Council of Jewish Women (NCJW)

Negro Family in the United States, The (Frazier), 30–31

Nehru, Jawaharlal, 180

Neuberger, Maurine, 84

Newark, New Jersey, 121–23

New York University (NYU), 23–24, 92

Nigeria, 16, 116, 185–86, 188

Niles, Mary Cushing, 65

Nixon, Pat, 105

Nixon, Richard, 8, 151, 157, 170, 174, 175, 183

Nkomeshya, Elizabeth, 189, *gallery fig. 9*

Nkrumah, Kwame, 16

Noble, Jeanne, 2, 34, 92, 161

Nonviolent Action Group, 28

Northern Student Movement, 115–16

Nussbaum, Perry, 94

NWCCR. *See* National Women's Committee on Civil Rights (NWCCR)

NWRO. *See* National Welfare Rights Organization (NWRO)

NYU. *See* New York University (NYU)

Obama, Barack, 206

OEO. *See* Office of Economic Opportunity (OEO)

Office of Economic Opportunity (OEO), 85, 106, 111–12, 134, 147, 175–76

Office of Juvenile Delinquency and Youth Development, 172

Okello, Nellie, *gallery fig. 10*

Operation Cope, 169–70, 204

Operation Sisters United, 173

Opondo, Diana, *gallery figs. 9, 10*

Organization of Afro-American Unity, 8

Other America, The: Poverty in the United States (Harrington), 83

Othermothering, 5

Packer, L. F., 147

Page, Melba Linda, 12

Palmer, Lillian, 110–11

Pandit, Vijaya Lakshmi, 180

Pan-Pacific and South-East Asia Women's Association, 188

Parker, Daniel, 190

Parks, Rosa, 22, 36, 49, 205, 238n148

Parsons, Rose, 185

Patrick, Nesta, 189

Payne, Charles, 2, 235n71

PCSW. *See* Commission on the Status of Women (CSW)

Percy, Charles, 187

Percy Amendment, 187–89

Petty, Irene, 199

Petty, Wilbert, 199

Pig bank, Mississippi, 9, 130–32; Swaziland, 10, 198, 200–201

Pig farm. *See* pig bank

Pinkett, Flaxie, 67, *gallery fig. 4*

Ponder Annelle, 34

Poor People's Campaign, 10, 155–56

Popular Front, 24, 235n71

Porter, William, 29

Powell, Adam Clayton, 24

Prentiss Institute, 258n9

Presbyterian Commission on Religion and Race, 65

President's Commission on the Status of Women (PCSW). *See* Commission on the Status of Women (CSW)

Price, Lucilla, 63

Prison, *See* Incarceration

Procter and Gamble (P&G), 204–5

Project Womanpower, 7–9, 114–21, 155, 160, 190, 231n35, 275n6

Quaker Oats Company, 206–7

Quinn, Dorothy C., 12

Rachlin, Helen, 112, 121–26, 167

Racial uplift, 4, 14–15, 17–18, 81–82, 98, 155, 170, 192, 232n13, 233n36

Radicalism, 1–2, 24–25, 106–7, 115, 120, 148, 157–60, 180–81, 208–9, 227n4, 235n71, 240n15

Ramses Club, 24

Randers–Pehrson, Justine, *gallery fig. 4*

Randolph, A. Philip, 18, 30, 185

Randolph, Sherie, 76–77

Raspberry, Willa Mae Tucker, 110, 146

Rauschenbach, Marion, 100

Raymond, George J., 73, 78

Reagan, Ronald, 169, 173, 197, 203, 204

Reagon, Merble, 8, 114–15, 117, 120, 121, 159, 167–69, 203, 239n150

Red Cross, 185

Red Scare, 21, 234n54, 240n15. *See also* Communism

Reese, Frederick, 35

Relf, Minnie Lee and Mary Alice, 166

Respectability, 10, 17–18, 124, 165, 180, 202; in the civil rights movement, 76, 83, 88; of motherhood, 53, 240n15

Reuther, Walter, 87

Reynolds, Nancy, 206

Richardson, Gloria. *See* Dandridge, Gloria Richardson

Riley, Kewanna, 143

Roach, Margaret "Peggy," 68, *gallery fig. 4*

Robb, Inez, 49

Robeson, Paul, 24, 182

Robinson, Gwendolyn. *See* Simmons, Gwendolyn R.

Robnett, Belinda, 229n11

Rockefeller, John D., 15

Rockefeller, Nelson A., 22

Rockefeller Brothers Fund, 7, 160, 209

Roe v. Wade, 165

Romney, George, 132, 142

Roosevelt, Eleanor, 15–16, 18, 27, 40, 180

Roosevelt, Franklin D., 15–16, 18

Roosevelt, Sara Delano, 15

Ruffin, Josephine St. Pierre, 20

Rural Housing Alliance, 139

Rushing, Albert, 134, 140–42

Rustin, Bayard, *gallery fig. 6*

Rwanda, 200

Safe spaces, 114, 117, 194, 254n52

Safe Streets Act, 173

San Quentin uprising, 166

St. Louis, 135–36

Sampson, Edith, 2, 21, 89–90, 180–84, 270n12, 271n23, *gallery fig. 2*

Sanders, I. S., 71–72

Sanders, Thelma, 59–60, 72, 77

Savage, Edith, 67, 80–81, 95

Scanlon, Jennifer, 229n8

Schaeffer, Ruth, 23

Schneider, Emily, 125–26

Scholarships, 28–29

Schultz, Debra, 242n58

Schutt, Jane, 47, 52, 61–62, 63, 69

Schwerner, Mickey, 50, 59, 246n66

SCLC. *See* Southern Christian Leadership Conference (SCLC)

Scotia Seminary, 14

SCPI. *See* Sunflower County Progress, Inc. (SCPI)

SDEDD. *See* South Delta Economic Development District (SDEDD)

SDS. *See* Students for a Democratic Society (SDS)

Selma, Alabama, 5, 35, 37–49, 52, 55, 160

Sene, Siga, 189, 194

Senegal, 177, 189, 199–201

Sexual abuse, 27, 34–37, 44, 46–47, 166

Sexism, 19; efforts of the council to combat, 164; relationship to racism, 177, 190; shifting attitudes towards, 34, 238n134; within the civil rights movement, 5, 34; within the historical profession, 2, 235n71

Shelter, 132–145. *See also* Turnkey III

Sherrod, Charles, 104, 105

Shirley, Aaron, 148, 193

Shriver, Sargent, 85–86, 88

Sierra Leone, 116, 177, 185

Simmons, Gwendolyn R., 8, 115–19, 209, 255n69, 265n55

16th Street Baptist Church, 37, 43

Smathers, George A., 152

Smith, Caroline, 88

Smith, Elaine M., 17

Smith, H. R., 147

Smith, Jeanette, 108–9

Smith, John, 121–22

Smith, Lillian, 40

Smith, Shirley, 37, 41–46, 54, 58, 64, 69

SNCC. *See* Student Nonviolent Coordinating Committee (SNCC)

South Africa, 10, 16, 195–98, 203

South America, 183–84

South Delta Economic Development District (SDEDD), 137

Southern Christian Leadership Conference (SCLC), 8, 36, 51, 65, 81–82, 106–7, 114. *See also* Poor People's Campaign

Southern Manifesto, 152

Southern Regional Council, 38–39, 59

Spinks, Elberta, 119

Spinks-Thigpen, Mary, 142–44,

Springer, Kimberly, 115

Springer, Maida, 2, 16, 180, *gallery fig. 10*

Staupers, Mabel Keaton, 2, 19, 152, 179

Steinem, Gloria, 164

Stennis, John, 86, 88

Sterilization, 52, 113, 165–66, 192

Stern Family Fund, 64–65

Student Nonviolent Coordinating Committee (SNCC), 1, 30, 36, 50–52, 56–57, 74, 81, 104–5, 107, 115

Students for a Democratic Society (SDS), 8, 114–16

Sugarman, Jules, 86

Sullivan, Leon, *gallery fig. 6*

Sunflower County Progress, Inc. (SCPI), 111

Sun-n-Sand Motel, 69–70

Swaziland, 10, 195–99, 200–201

Taconic Foundation, 29, 37, 76

Talbert, Ernestine Denham, 28

Tarry, Ellen, 92–95

Taylor, Recy, 36

Taylor, Susan, 206

Taylor, William, 86

Terry, Patt, 244n31

Thiokol Chemical Corporation, 135, 136, 143, 144,

Third World Women's Alliance (TWWA), 8, 115, 159, 171

Thompson, Becky, 267n90

Thompson, Dolphin, 152

Tilly, Dorothy, 38–40, 44, 46, 61

Togo, 177, 199–201

Touré, Hadja Andrée, 16

Touré, Ahmed Sékou, 185

Testimony against sexual violence, 34, 36, 166, 239n149.

TransAfrica, 197

Travancore, 183

Tribute to Black Women Community Leaders, 206–7

Trinidad and Tobago, 189

Truman, Harry, 16, 19–20, 31, 39, 182

Turner, Bessie, 34
Turnkey I, 133
Turnkey II, 133
Turnkey III, 9, 104, 132–45, 193
Turnkey IV, 136–37
Turpeau, Anne, *gallery fig. 10*
Tuskegee Institute, 117
TWWA. *See* Third World Women's
    Alliance
Tyson, Cicely, 151

UNCIO. *See* United Nations Conference
    on International Organization
    (UNCIO)
UNESCO, 188
UNICEF, 188
United Christian Youth Movement, 25
United Church Women, 50
United Nations Conference on Interna-
    tional Organization (UNCIO), 179
United Nations World Conference on
    Women, Copenhagen (1980), 177–78;
    Nairobi (1985), 202
United States Agency for International
    Development (USAID), 9–10, 177–79,
    189–90, 195, 198–201
United States Commission on Civil
    Rights, 47, 59, 62, 75, 79, 85–86,
Urban League, 13, 16, 66, 68, 71, 76, 98,
    124, 139
Uruguay, 184
USAID. *See* United States Agency
    for International Development
    (USAID)

Vivell, Diane, 59, 62–63, 69
Volunteers Unlimited, 172, 268n111
Voter registration, 19–20, 35
Voting Rights Act, 5, 128

Walden, Oceola, 88
Walker, Alice, 205, 266n82
Walker, Maggie Lena, 26

Wallace, Arnetta G., 68
Waller, William, 59
War on Poverty, 4, 7, 83–84, 105–6, 112,
    133, 175, 188
Washington, Walter, 151, *gallery fig. 6*
Washington Debutante Cotillion, 12
Watts rebellion, 96–97
WC. *See* Woman's Convention (WC)
WCECA. *See* Women's Center for
    Education and Career Advancement
    (WCECA)
Weaver, Robert, 85, 134–35, *gallery fig. 6*
Weaver, Vanessa, 204
Weddington, Sarah Ragle, 177
Wednesdays in Mississippi (WIMS), 49,
    56–89, 92–102, 108–9, 111–14. *See also*
    Workshops in Mississippi
Weingarten, Victor, 67, 76
Welfare, 74, 81, 111, 124–25, 155–56, 171,
    174, 203–4, 207
Wells, Ida B., 15, 36,
Westport Connecticut Society of
    Friends, 77
White, Deborah Gray, 14, 16, 153
White, Thomas, 15
White, Walter, 179
White House Conference on Food,
    Nutrition, and Health, 174
WICS. *See* Women in Community
    Service (WICS)
Wiesner, Jerome, 65
Wiesner, Laya, 6, 56, 65, 74
Wilkerson-Freeman, Sarah, 39–40
Wilkins, Roy, 185, *gallery fig. 6*
Wilkinson, Kate, 92, 108, 194–95, 273n76
Willen, Pearl, 64, 68
Williams, Elynor, 205
Williams, Ethel James, 24
Williams, Ilza, 68, 72, 77–78, 83, 100
Wilson, Doris, 56–58, 63, 69
Wilson, Emma J., 14
WIMS. *See* Wednesdays in Mississippi
    (WIMS)

Winfrey, Oprah, 206
WINS. *See* Women Integrating Neigh-
  borhood Services (WINS)
Wolfe, Deborah, 32
Womanism, 266n79
Womanpower Unlimited (WU), 3, 6–7,
  52–53, 57–58, 71
Woman's Convention (WC), 17–18
Women in Community Service (WICS),
  106, 167, 191
Women Integrating Neighborhood
  Services (WINS), 28
*Women and Housing: A Report on Sex
  Discrimination in Five American Cities*,
  150, 176
Women's Army Auxiliary Corps, 18
Women's Center for Education and
  Career Advancement (WCECA),
  167–69
Women's clubs, 17–18, 50–51, 232n13
Women's International Democratic
  Federation, 180, 185
Women's International League for Peace
  and Freedom, 90
Women's Inter-Organization
  Council, 50
Women's Liberation. *See* Feminism
Women's National Abortion Action
  Coalition, 166
Women's Opportunity Program, 170
Women Strike for Peace (WSP), 59,
  240n15
Woodard, Komozi, 122

Woodley, Jenny, 263nn6, 11
Woods, George, 188
Woods, Geraldine, 64, 68
Workshops in Mississippi, 108–14, 121,
  123, 133, 150, 154–55, 194, 230n16
World Bank, 188, 270n7
World War II, 16, 18–19, 48, 152, 179–80
WSP. *See* Women Strike for Peace
  (WSP)
WU. *See* Womanpower Unlimited (WU)
Wynn, Prathia. *See* Hall, Prathia

Yancy, Bobbi, 50
Young, Andrew, 13, 82, 151
Young, Aurelia, 60
Young, Jack, 60
Young, Whitney, 185, *gallery fig. 6*
Young Communist League, 27
Young Women's Christian Association
  (YWCA), 38–39, 50; Harvey and, 59;
  Height and, 3, 23–27, 183; white
  women and, 53; Wilson and, 57–58;
  WIMS and, 59, 62, 68, 71, 77, 93–94,
  97–98
Youth Emergency Fund, 34
Youth Service Corps, 172
YWCA. *See* Young Women's Christian
  Association (YWCA)

Zales, Gladys, 6, 94
Zambia, 189
Zigler, Edward, 86
Zondo, Christabel, *gallery fig. 9*